Charles Seale-Hayne Library

University of Plymouth

(01752) 588 588

LibraryandITenquiries@plymouth.ac.uk

X.media.publishing

Springer
Berlin
Heidelberg
New York
Hong Kong
London
Milan
Paris
Tokyo

Dick C. A. Bulterman Lloyd Rutledge

SMIL 2.0

Interactive Multimedia
for Web and Mobile Devices

With 105 Figures and 81 Tables

 Springer

Dick C. A. Bulterman
Lloyd Rutledge

CWI
P.O. Box 94079
1090 GB Amsterdam
The Netherlands

Dick.Bulterman@cwi.nl
Lloyd.Rutledge@cwi.nl

http://www.XmediaSMIL.net/

ISSN 1612-1449
ISBN 3-540-20234-X Springer-Verlag Berlin Heidelberg New York

Library of Congress Cataloging-in-Publication-Data
Bulterman, Dick C.A., 1951–
    SMIL 2.0: interactive multimedia for Web and mobile devices/Dick C.A. Bulterman,
    Lloyd Rutledge.
        p. cm. – (X.media.publishing)
        ISBN 3-540-20234-X (alk. paper)
        1. SMIL (Document markup language) I. Rutledge, Lloyd, 1966– II. Title. III. Series.
QA76.76.H94B858 2004
006.7'4–dc22   2004041320

Springer-Verlag is a part of Springer Science+Business Media
springeronline.com

© Springer-Verlag Berlin Heidelberg 2004
Printed in Germany

The use of general descriptive names, trademarks, etc. in this publication does not imply, even in the absence of a specific statement, that such names are exempt from the relevant protective laws and regulations and therefore free for general use.

Cover design: KünkelLopka, Heidelberg
Typesetting and data preparation by the authors
Printed on acid-free paper   33/3142 GF – 543210

Dedications

Dick C.A. Bulterman:

There are many people in my private life — old and young, near and far, and alive and dead — to whom I wish to dedicate this book, but singling any of them out would do a disservice to the rest. The choice in my professional life is much simpler: one person stands out as an influence that has changed the way I think and work. Andy van Dam is a gifted and insightful researcher and teacher. He has served as an inspiration (and occasionally a warning!) during the 30 years since I first showed up at Brown, and I am pleased to dedicate this book to him.

Lloyd Rutledge:

Writing a book is but one of life's milestones, splitting a cherished past from a future looked forward to. With this in mind, I have two dedications for this work. To the memory of my mother Helen, who passed on when work on this book began. And to Marie-Louise, with whom I married during this work's final stages.

Preface

SMIL 2.0: Multimedia for Web and Mobile Devices is a comprehensive introduction to — and resource guide for — the W3C SMIL 2.0 language. It covers all aspects of the SMIL specification and covers all of SMIL's implementation profiles, from the desktop through the new world of mobile SMIL devices.

Motivation for this Book

When the SMIL 2.0 recommendation was being developed, it was clear to us that the richness of the SMIL language could easily overwhelm many Web authors and designers. In the 500+ pages that the SYMM working group needed to describe the 32 SMIL elements and the 150 SMIL attributes, there was not much room for background information or extensive examples. The focus of the specification was on the components of the SMIL language, not on the rationale or the potential uses of SMIL's declarative power.

The existing literature on SMIL is not extensive. Other books published on aspects of the SMIL language are neither complete nor always correct in their handling of SMIL concepts or the various SMIL implementations. The documentation provided by major vendors of SMIL players is also not geared to the development of a complete picture of what SMIL can do — and what it can't do! The academic literature, while often containing thoughtful analysis of SMIL, is inaccessible to most of SMIL's users.

We wrote this book to bridge the gap between the theory and practice of creating SMIL presentations for multiple platforms and multiple profiles. In so doing, we hope that the use of SMIL's facilities and features moves beyond the trivial and enters the mainstream of Web multimedia.

Should You Read This Book?

We wrote this book for three communities:

- *Existing* SMIL *authors*: many existing SMIL users need and want more information on the language so that they can create better presentations, for more profiles, with less effort.
- *New* SMIL *authors*: SMIL is currently available on nearly a million desktop and mobile devices. It represents a media delivery platform that has unprecedented reach. Designers and authors who want to exploit the

potential of SMIL need to have a solid introduction to the language and to have a wealth of examples that can help them get started.

- *Developers and students of multimedia technology*: The SMIL standard is a complex document. For researchers, developers and students of internet media technology, it is easy to lose sight of the big picture when architecting delivery systems for SMIL technology. We have done our best to de-mystify SMIL and to make the basic concepts addressed by SMIL clear and accessible.

This book is intended to augment the documentation provided by individual SMIL player vendors. We have decided to focus our efforts on explaining SMIL technology; together with authoring guidelines and documentation provided and maintained by the W3C, RealNetworks, Microsoft, Oratrix, Apple and other player vendors, we are confident that you will be able to create, maintain, and debug a complete range of SMIL presentations, for a complete range of SMIL players.

Now that a number of open-source SMIL players are available, we also expect that this book — together with the SMIL 2.0 specification provided by W3C — will provide a comprehensive guide for designers and implementers of new or modified SMIL players.

Structure of the Book

This book is divided into four sections. *Part One* provides a general introduction to the SMIL language and a reader's guide to a (complex) SMIL example. It also contains background information on Web multimedia technology that, while not limited to SMIL, is useful for users who are new to networked multimedia. *Part Two* provides an overview of the basic elements and attributes used by all implementations of SMIL. It covers each of the functional groups of SMIL technology, from structure to transitions. *Part Three* contains a discussion of advanced SMIL features. These are elements and attributes that are either profile or player specific, or that make use of esoteric SMIL features. *Part Four* contains reference information on the composition of five of SMIL's profile implementations.

Each chapter is structured to meet the needs of the three target readership groups defined above. An XML-like structure of each chapter is:

```
<chapter>
  <BackgroundInformation />
  <ElementsAndAttributes>
    <ElementDefinitions />
    <AttributeDefintions />
    <SpecialValuesDefinitions />
  </ElementsAndAttributes>
  <Examples/>
</chapter>
```

We expect that many current SMIL authors will want to jump directly to the element and attribute definitions in each chapter; these provide detailed information that can answer questions quickly and (relatively!) painlessly about the structure of the language and the permissible attribute values. For new SMIL users, the example sub-section provides a host of easy-to-digest uses of the technology; often starting here will give a good idea of what SMIL can do in the functional group covered by that chapter. For readers interested in not only the *how* of SMIL but also the *why*, the background information in each chapter provides the motivations and limitations of SMIL technology. Note that for chapters that explain lots of elements and/or attributes, the examples are presented in the context of the definition of the constructs. For chapters covering many concepts, the chapter structure is sometimes repeated as a local sub-structure instance.[1]

Notational Conventions

In order to provide a predictable presentation of SMIL constructs, this book adopts the following simple notational conventions:

- *Element definitions*: SMIL's XML elements are displayed in a mono-space font, together with their angle brackets. Examples are: `<body>`, `<transition>`, `<switch>`. Unless used in the content of an example, a trailing '/' is not used.
- *Attribute definitions*: SMIL's XML attributes are displayed in a mono-space font, without other ornamentation. Examples are: `clipBegin`, `dur`, `begin`.
- *Attribute values*: SMIL's XML attribute value definitions are displayed in an separate italic font. Examples are: *indefinite, media, auto*.
- *Code examples*: The code examples in the book are set in separate areas and have a colored background. (See the XML-like code on the previous page for an example.) When code fragments are embedded in a sentence, the fragment is set in a single mono-space font. An example: `src="snarf.mpg"`.

While the integration of proportional and mono-spaced fonts on the same line sometimes yields strange spacing artifacts, we have done our best to minimize these in the text. Our goal has been to provide clarity without generating unnecessary white space. (The book is long enough as it is!)

In order to facilitate the search for constructs in the text, each first definition of an element, attribute or special value is highlighted with a separate heading. Examples are:

Element: <audio>
Attribute: clipEnd
Value: *auto*

These definitions are placed in the Index as the primary reference for the element, attribute or value construct.

---

1 If all of this talk of elements, attributes and structure has you confused, make sure you read the introduction to XML structure in Chapter 2: *Understanding SMIL 2.0 Code*!

Element and Attribute Tables

Most chapters in *Part Two* and *Part Three* of this book contain element and attribute tables. These tables define either an element structure or a set of values for complex SMIL attributes.

An example of an element table is given below.

		\<seq\>	\<par\>	Profiles				
attributes		*general timing*						
			endsync					
		media description		L	M	B	1	H
		region						
		test						
		core						
parents		\<body\>			M	B	1	
		\<priorityClass\>		L				H
parents & children		\<seq\>, \<par\>			M	B	1	
		\<excl\>		L				H
		\<switch\>			M	B	1	
		\<a\>						
children		*media object*			M	B	1	
		animation		L				H

The table gives the name of the element and defines the major attributes, parents and children for that construct. It also defines which SMIL profiles make use of the construct's components. Each profile is represented by a single letter and a background color. The decoding of the profile colors and letters is:

L	SMIL 2.0 Language profile
M	3GPP SMIL Mobile profile
B	SMIL 2.0 Basic profile
1	SMIL 1.0 Language
H	XHTML+SMIL

Those SMIL constructs used by the SVG language are indicated as:

S	SVG pseudo-profile

Note that for the 3GPP SMIL mobile profile, several versions of the 3GPP standards exist. We use 3GPP/PSS5 as a guide.

Each of the attributes contain a background color code that defines the functional group to which they belong. When appropriate, a distinction is made between basic and advanced attributes by giving basic attributes a lighter tint. The color coding is:

Functional Group		
Modules	Structure	Meta-Information
	Timing	Time Manipulation
	Linking	Content Control
	Media Objects	Layout
	Animation	Transitions

An example of an attribute table is shown below.

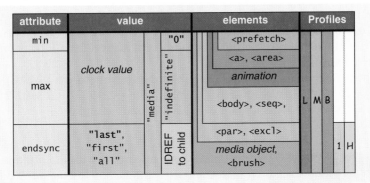

attribute	value			elements	Profiles
`min`	*clock value*	"media"	"0"	<prefetch>	L M B
max			"indefinite"	<a>, <area> *animation* <body>, <seq>,	
endsync	"last", "first", "all"		IDREF to child	<par>, <excl> *media object*, <brush>	1 H

In each attribute table, the default values for the attribute are shown in bold.

Quick Tips

In addition to being a reader's guide to the SMIL specification, our book is geared to helping you create SMIL presentations. Each section contains a number of *Quick Tips* that can be useful when you first work with SMIL. These tips, together with the examples, will get you started with multimedia on the Web in the shortest possible time.

> **Quick Tip**
>
> This is the format of a Quick Tip block.

On-Line Information

We maintain a Web site for this book at `http://www.XmediaSMIL.net/`. This site contains full versions of all of the examples used in our book plus links to various sites of interest. It will also contain a corrections and errata section that contains fixes for errors that inadvertently made their way into this publication.

About the Authors

Dick Bulterman is head of the research theme Convergent Media Interfaces at CWI, the Dutch national center for mathematics and computer science in Amsterdam. He joined CWI in 1988 as head of the Computer Systems and Telematics department. In 1991, he founded the Multimedia and Human-Computer Interaction research theme and directed the development of CWI's CMIF research from 1991-1998. From 1998-2001, he was managing director and CTO of Oratrix Development, a CWI spin-off company specializing in full-featured SMIL authoring systems and custom SMIL player engines.

Bulterman received a Ph.D. in computer science from Brown University in 1981. Before joining CWI, he was on the faculty of the division of Engineering at Brown, where he worked on computer architecture and high-speed signal processing networks. He holds an undergraduate degree in economics and mathematics from Hope College.

Dick Bulterman joined the W3C's Structured Multimedia (SYMM) working group in 1996. He was an active member of the SMIL 1.0 and SMIL 2.0 design teams. He lives in Amsterdam with his wife and two children.

Lloyd Rutledge is a researcher with the Multimedia and Human-Computer Interaction theme at CWI in the Netherlands. His research area is the semi-automatic generation of multimedia presentations. He received his Sc.D in computer science from the University of Massachusetts Lowell in 1996. He is CWI's advisory committee representative to W3C. Like his co-author, Lloyd Rutledge was part of the SYMM working group of the W3C, participating the development of SMIL 1.0 and 2.0. He lives with his wife in Amsterdam.

Table of Contents

Common Acronyms and Terms

The following list of acronyms and common names are used throughout the book. They are usually identified in the text by the use of a SMALL CAPS font.

ADSL	Asymmetric Digital Subscriber Line
Ambulant	The CWI open-source player for SMIL 2.0
CDATA	Character Data
CSS	Cascading Style Sheets
DOCTYPE	Document Type definition string identifier
DTD	Document Type Definition
GRiNS	The Oratrix GRiNS player for SMIL 2.0
HTML	HyperText Markup Language
HTML+TIME	Microsoft's XHTML+SMIL player in IE-6
HTTP	HyperText Transfer Protocol
IANA	Internet Assigned Numbers Authority
ID	Identifier string
IDREF	Reference to an ID
IE	The Microsoft Internet Explorer browser
IETF	Internet Engineering Task Force
IP	Internet Protocol
ISP	Internet Service Provider
MPEG-4	Multimedia standard developed by the Motion Picture Experts Group
NTSC	National Television Standards Committee *North-American and Asian Television Standard*
PAL	Phase Alternation Line *World-Wide Television Standard*
RealOne	The RealNetworks RealOne player for SMIL 2.0
RSVP	Resource Reservation Protocol
RTCP	Real-Time Control Protocol
RTP	Real-Time Transfer Protocol
RTSP	Real-Time Streaming Protocol
SMIL	Synchronized Multimedia Integration Language

SMPTE	Society of Motion Picture and Television Engineers
SVG	Scalable Vector Graphics language
TCP	Transmission Communications Protocol
UDP	User Datagram Protocol
URI	Uniform Resource Identifier
W3C	World Wide Web Consortium
XHTML	XML-Compliant Hypertext Markup Language
XHTML+SMIL	The XHTML+SMIL profile of SMIL 2.0
XML	Extensible Markup Language

Acknowledgements

During the production and review of this book, we received a great deal of assistance from many people. Along with our families, we would like to thank the following organizations and individuals for their support.

Reviews of early drafts and the final technical reviews were performed by:

- *Sjoerd Mullender* of Oratrix/CWI;
- *Jack Jansen, Kleanthis Kleanthous* and *Kees Blom* of the GRiNS and Ambulant player development teams at Oratrix and CWI;
- *Michael Minnema;* and
- *Luiz Fernando Gomes Soares* and *Rogerio Rodrigues* of PUC-Rio.

While we are grateful to all of these people, the technical reviews performed by Sjoerd stood out in this high-class crowd. Sjoerd was the design and implementation leader of the GRiNS SMIL 1 and SMIL 2 players (which were also implemented by Jack Jansen and Kleanthis Kleanthous), and his energy and willingness to share his knowledge of even the most minor details of SMIL was a tremendous help in completing this manuscript.

Additional technical information and assistance for various SMIL profiles came from:

- *Jeff Ayars, Rob Lanphier* and *Eric Hyche* of RealNetworks, Inc.
- *Philipp Hoschka, Thierry Michel, Ivan Herman* and *Steven Pemberton* of W3C;
- *Aaron Cohen* of Intel and the Oregon State Health University;
- *Patrick Schmitz*, Microsoft (now at ludicrum.org);
- *Debbie Newman* and *Pablo Fernicola* of Microsoft;
- *Nick Dyer* and *Phil Sheppard* of Three/Hutchison 3G UK Limited;
- *Nick Roberts* of Vodafone; and
- *Antti Koivisto* of Nokia.

Out of this group, we are especially indebted to Aaron Cohen for his skillful leadership of the SMIL 2.0 working group. Without him, there probably would have been no SMIL 2.0 — and thus, no SMIL 2.0 book!

Many people supported the production of this manuscript, including:

- *Alain Uginet, Jeroen Tak* and *Katelijn Arnold* of Oratrix;
- *Teus Hagen* and *Frances Brazier* of Stichting NLnet;

- *Jan Schipper* and *Tobias Baanders* of CWI;
- *Michael Strang* and *Simon Plumtree* of Pearson Education Ltd.; and
- *Jutta Maria Fleschutz* and *Gabriele Fischer* of Springer Verlag.

We are very grateful for the flexibility offered by Springer in providing us with the opportunity to produce a full-color book and to bring various versions of the book to market. The nice chapter and margin icons were designed by Tobias Baanders. The rest were done by Dick Bulterman and Lloyd Rutledge.

We would also like to thank those organizations and people who allowed us to use their content in illustrations in our book.

- Microsoft Corporation;
- *Geoff Freed* of NCAM/WGBH;
- *Jacoba Alida, Henri J. François* and *Johanna Wilhelmina* of Singel Media;
- *Henri "Peaches" Bulterman* of Marietta, Georgia; and
- RTV Slovenia.

Finally, we thank our co-members of the W3C/SYMM team.

Part One

Introduction

This part consists of introductory and background information on SMIL 2.0. This section contains enough information to get you familiar with SMIL, including the basic constructs in the language and the XML environment in which SMIL is specified. It also contains a complete SMIL example that illustrates many of SMIL's main features.

Topics Covered

Chapter 1 provides a general introduction to SMIL and its various implementations. It illustrates what SMIL can do by sketching six applications of SMIL technology. It also describes the background of SMIL and contrasts SMIL with other multimedia formats. It also contains a review of authoring tools and players for SMIL 2.0.

Chapter 2 looks at the structure of SMIL presentations. We start with a brief review of the XML language and discuss how XML elements and attributes form the core of SMIL's definition. We then look at how SMIL presentations can be encoded for each of the SMIL 2.0 profiles.

Chapter 3 provides general information on encoding and accessing multimedia information in Web and stand-alone environments. This section contains background context that explains the operational considerations that need to be addressed when designing presentations for the Web.

Goals

By the time you finish this part, you should be able to look at any SMIL file and understand its basic structure. This is true for not only the SMIL 2.0 Language profile, but also for SMIL presentations written for the XHTML+SMIL and SMIL Mobile profiles.

Prerequisites

In order to get the most out of this part, you should have some affinity with the Web and the Internet. While experience with creating and sharing digital media is not essential, a basic understanding of how media is encoded and how Web servers and clients are structured will be helpful in putting information in this section to immediate practical use.

1

An Overview of SMIL 2.0

In August 2001, the World Wide Web Consortium (W3C) released version 2.0 of Synchronized Multimedia Integration Language, or SMIL (pronounced "smile"). SMIL 2.0 was developed to bring presentation-level interactive multimedia to the Web. It is a text-based, non-proprietary, XML standardized format that is woven into the W3C's XML-based family of cooperative and interdependent languages. SMIL 2.0 is the only format for encoding multimedia presentations that is released and supported by the W3C.

SMIL 2.0 is not an animation language or a media format, but a way of combining animation and media objects into a single coherent presentation. SMIL lets you add sophisticated selection, linking and activation control to the media objects in your presentation; in this way, it is a bit like a multimedia version of HTML. Unlike HTML or XHTML, however, SMIL has a stricter separation between content and structure and it provides non-invasive control of presentation linking and layout.

1.1 Using SMIL 2.0: Six Examples

Before jumping into the details of what SMIL 2.0 can do, this section gives an overview of six presentation examples that illustrate SMIL behavior from the presentation of a single media item to the definition of a complete interactive newscast. We will return to some of these examples later in this book.

> **Quick Tip**
>
> Each of the presentations discussed in this book can be found on our Web site: http://www.xmediaSMIL.net, in the section on book demos. We suggest that you play these demos to better understand the example and discussion presented in each chapter.

1.1.1 Hi Mom!

The first presentation represents perhaps the most pervasive use of SMIL in current players: the presentation of a single piece of video content. Figure 1-1 shows how a single media object can be placed in a player window and then

Figure 1-1. *Hi Mom!*, a single media presentation.

presented to a wide audience. The movie content can range from home videos to commercial content. The video may also be accompanied by audio.

For this example to work in a streaming environment, you need to place the media content on a streaming server and then access it via the SMIL player.

1.1.2 Welcome to New York

The second SMIL example is a slideshow that gives a short tour of New York. It is typical of an entry-level use of multimedia SMIL. Figure 1-2 gives two views of the presentation: one on a desktop player (using RealOne) and the other on a PDA SMIL player (using GRiNS) that supports the 3GPP mobile implementation of SMIL. (Don't worry about what 3GPP means; we'll get back to the various implementations of SMIL later in this chapter.)

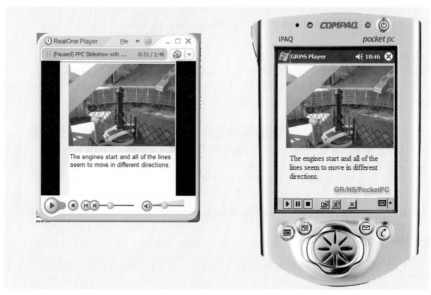

Figure 1-2. *Welcome to New York*, a simple SMIL slideshow presentation.

The *New York* presentation consists of a sequence of slide objects, each of which contains an image, a text caption and an audio caption. A single piece of background audio plays as a background tune while each of the slide objects is shown.

Although the structure of this presentation is pretty straightforward, it is too complex for the most simple implementations of SMIL. In the MMS standard for mobile SMIL, for example, each of the slide objects could be shown (containing text, audio and image), but the background audio music would not be supported.

The *New York* presentation uses functionality that is essentially similar to that of SMIL 1.0. The most striking 'new' feature is the support for transitions between images, which gives the entire presentation a smoother visual feeling. In many ways, the combination of images and transitions provides many of the advantages of video at only a fraction of the bandwidth cost!

1.1.3 Happy Birthday!

The *Welcome to New York* SMIL demo shows a linear presentation in which the order of the content is determined by the author. The *Happy Birthday!* presentation demonstrates a presentation in which the viewer can select the content to be viewed.

Figure 1-3 shows two implementations of *Birthday!*: the version at left is for the SMIL 2.0 Language profile (and is rendered in the RealNetworks RealOne player), while the version at right is for the XHTML+SMIL profile (and is rendered in Microsoft's Internet Explorer browser). Both versions provide identical functionality — the viewer can select one of the four images on the left side, at which point a video is shown in the main display area on the right— but as we will see in Chapter 2: *Understanding SMIL 2.0 Code*, the encodings of the native SMIL presentations are totally different.

Figure 1-3. *Happy Birthday!*, as shown in native SMIL and XHTML+SMIL players.

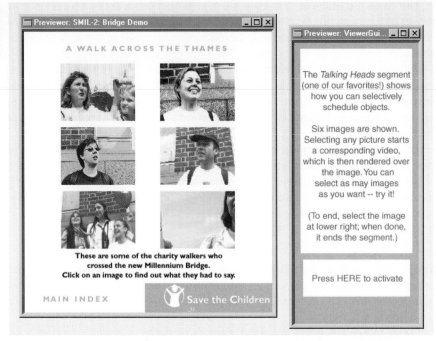

Figure 1-4. *Crossing the Bridge*, a multi-window, interactive presentation.

1.1.4 Crossing the Bridge

Although the SMIL 2.0 specification was approved by the W3C as a Recommendation in mid-August, 2001, the foundation for the specification was defined in
mid-2000. Based on the interim specification, the first full SMIL 2.0 presentation
was released in September 2000. *Crossing the Bridge*[1] was a collection of test
cases that allowed SMIL 2.0's timing, interaction, layout, transitions and animation constructs to be evaluated by candidate SMIL 2.0 players.

Figure 1-4 shows a view of the presentation as rendered by the Ambulant
desktop player. Two windows are shown: the main content window (shown at
left) and a second window containing help text and general presentation control (at right). The two windows are used to partition presentation navigation
and control. They are presented as two independent windows to the user, but
they are still logically connected: the content across the multiple windows
shares a common presentation timeline.

---

1 The *Bridge* presentation showcased the opening of the Millennium Bridge across the
  river Thames in London. As part of the ceremonies, several thousand people came to
  London as part of a drive organized by charitable organizations, one of which — Save
  the Children, UK — was highlighted in the presentation. A day later, the bridge was
  closed to the general public for safety reasons.

In the presentation fragment shown, a user is able to select one of six images; clicking on any of the images starts a corresponding video clip that is displayed on top of the image. The viewer determines which (if any) of the mini-presentations get activated, as well as the order in which they are shown. (This functionality is implemented using SMIL 2.0's *exclusive* construct.) Note that the user must first select the *Press HERE to activate* button in the right window before any of the images are activated at left. The user also can choose to go to another part of the presentation by clicking on the *Main Index* label at lower left, or to pause the presentation and surf to the *Save the Children* Web site by selecting the image at lower right. (Both types of navigation are implemented using SMIL's linking functionality.)

The functionality in this example could also be supported in SMIL 1.0, but with substantially more author effort.

1.1.5 The Evening News

The use of multiple profiles, as shown in the *Birthday!* example above, gives one dimension of adaptability of a SMIL 2.0 source document. Within a profile, many opportunities also exist to make content that adapts itself to the needs (and wishes) of the viewer. As an example of what you can do with SMIL 2.0, consider the evening news example in Figure 1-5.

Figure 1-5(a) shows a "desktop" version of the newscast. The user is presented with a number of picture icons, each representing a segment of the 35-minute news. A news story is started when the user clicks on the associated picture. The user may also view the entire newscast in a predetermined

Figure 1-5. *The Evening News*, an interactive newscast that can be tailored for various display sizes and user preferences.

sequence or use the general navigation buttons at bottom right to navigate across stories or within an item.

In this picture, English language titles and captions are shown, although the user could also have selected the original Slovenian titles. Each of the assets for all the available languages and resolutions are encoded in a single SMIL file, with the SMIL player selecting the appropriate media based on configuration files or user preference dialogues.

Note the three icons at the bottom portion of Figure 1-5(a). When selected, each will start a video that will interrupt the running item, and when the interrupting object is completed, the original item will pick up where it left off in the presentation. (This can be used for advertising inserts or other out-of-context messages.)

Figure 1-5(b) shows the same presentation, but this time visually packaged for a mobile device. The structure of the mobile version is the same as the desktop version, except that general 'story classes', such as *National*, *Local*, and *Weather*, are used instead of the individual story icons. (This is to conserve screen space.) The rocker panel of the device can also be used to select stories.

Perhaps the most important aspect of this example is that both the desktop and the mobile versions are encoded in the same SMIL file. This allows the document to be authored once and used in multiple configurations.

1.1.6 Flags

The final presentation in this section illustrates the use of SMIL timing to animate graphics encoded in the Web graphics format SVG. Figure 1-6 shows two views of a single presentation. If the base language selected within the player is American English, the flag at left is shown. If any European language is selected, then the European flag at right is shown. Although it is difficult to see in this printed version, each of the flags has stars that rotate during the presentation — this rotation is accomplished by applying SMIL 2.0's animation facilities in the GRiNS embedded SVG player.

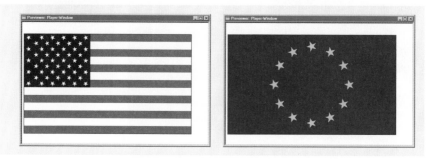

Figure 1-6. *Flags*, an example of SMIL-based animation in the SVG language.

1.2 SMIL 2.0 and SMIL 1.0

SMIL 2.0 is the successor to SMIL 1.0, which was the W3C's foundation for multimedia on the Web. During its three-year reign, SMIL 1.0 quickly gained widespread — if little-known! — use, primarily as the internal synchronization format for RealNetworks's RealPlayer. It was also supported in Apple's Quick-Time player. Through these two multimedia players alone, SMIL 1.0 was installed on more than 200 million desktops worldwide.

SMIL 2.0 extends SMIL 1.0 in many key areas. The primary changes it provides are:

- improved synchronization and interactive activation facilities,
- a profile-based specification structure,
- new support for animation and media transitions, and
- extended support for content control and layout.

SMIL 2.0's elements and attributes are spread across 50 modules that are managed in over 10 functional groups. The partitioning of constructs makes it easy for the designers of new XML languages to select timing and presentation control primitives for integration and reuse.

The new functionality and specification structure in SMIL comes at a cost: where SMIL 1.0 was described in a document that spanned 29 pages, SMIL 2.0 needs over 500 pages to cover all of its elements and attributes. As a result, understanding how all the pieces fit together is not always an easy task. That's why this book was written: to provide a readable overview of SMIL's features and facilities, and to help designers create SMIL presentations for devices as wide-ranging as mobile telephones to sophisticated media servers.

This chapter provides a broad introduction to SMIL 2.0. Rather than jumping right into a discussion of SMIL code, we start with important background information that will help you understand SMIL in its various forms. We begin with a background discussion on the design goals that guided the development of SMIL 2.0. We then provide five examples that each illustrate different facets of SMIL functionality. A description of SMIL modularization and profiles comes next, followed by a sampling of some of the tools that are available to build and manage SMIL presentations. We close the chapter with a short comparison of SMIL and other important multimedia formats.

1.3 SMIL 2.0's Design Goals

SMIL 2.0 is a collection of XML elements and attributes that can be used to describe the temporal and spatial coordination of one or more media objects. SMIL 2.0 allows a user to define how independent media objects are to be integrated into a media presentation and it provides rules that define when (and if) various media objects are actually rendered for the end-user. The media presentation created by SMIL may be delivered via a streaming server or it may be played from components stored locally (or on a CD-ROM).

SMIL aims to do for multimedia what HTML did for hypertext: bring it onto every presentation device (PCs, mobile/handheld systems, even TVs) with an easy-to-author descriptive format that can be displayed on a variety of readily available cross-platform players. With SMIL, simple multimedia can be created simply and more complex behavior can be added in increments.

SMIL's syntax is fully XML compliant, making it a member of the family of XML standards from the W3C such as SVG, XPointer, XSLT, namespaces and XHTML (the XML encoding of HTML). SMIL provides the Web with new features not found in these other languages, such as adaptivity to different market groups, user abilities, system configurations and run-time system delays.

The goals for SMIL 2.0's design can be partitioned across three categories:

- *Maintain a declarative, XML format*: while the integration of multimedia content is often the province of scripts or other programmed definition, SMIL 2.0 was developed to remain a fully declarative rather than procedural format. In this way, a SMIL description doesn't define *how* a presentation is implemented, but rather *what* it is that the author wants — the implementation of the specification left up to the SMIL player. Also, in keeping with the first version of SMIL, SMIL 2.0 is fully XML compliant.[2]

- *Extend the functionality of SMIL 1.0*: the design of SMIL 1.0 was kept simple and relatively frills-free. SMIL 2.0 provides some desirable additions, including: support for increased interaction, enhanced timing semantics, extended content control and layout facilities plus new animation and transitions primitives.

- *Introduce a module-based structure*: SMIL 2.0 is defined as a collection of over 50 modules that are partitioned into 10 functional groups. By using a module structure, key aspects of SMIL 2.0 can be integrated into other XML-based languages without requiring support for the entire SMIL 2.0 specification. Even before the release of the SMIL 2.0 Language specification, the modularization policy bore fruit: parts of SMIL were integrated into several other XML languages — such as SVG — and more examples of module reuse are expected.

In addition to these three classes of goals, SMIL 2.0 also removed some ambiguities that existed in SMIL 1.0 and SMIL 2.0 provided a more W3C-compliant approach to naming elements and attributes.

1.4 SMIL Modules and Profiles

As shown in Figure 1-7, SMIL 2.0 defines 10 major functional groupings of elements and attributes as the top-level sections of the specification. These are *Animation, Metainformation, Content Control, Structure, Layout, Timing and Synchronization, Linking, Time Manipulations, Media Objects,* and *Transition Effects.* Of

---

2 SMIL 1.0 was not simply an XML-compliant language, it was the *first* XML language released by the W3C when it was published in 1998.

these, *Timing and Synchronization* is the core of the SMIL specification. The number of modules per functional grouping varies from 2 to about 20. In general, the more modules per group, the finer the granularity of each module. The structure of this book corresponds to the functional grouping of SMIL. We will consider all of the elements and attributes of each functional group in detail in the relevant chapters.

For a designer using SMIL, the notions of modules and functional groups are not very important. What is important is the result of the grouping of modules into a number of SMIL *profiles*. Each profile provides a fixed collection of elements and attributes, drawn from one or more modules from various functional groups. The purpose of the profile model is to enable customizing the integration of SMIL's functionality into a wide variety of XML-based languages without requiring language authors to learn new timing semantics for each variant.

The major SMIL profiles are:

- SMIL *2.0 Language:* the host-language version of SMIL 2.0, containing the majority of SMIL's elements, attributes and features;
- SMIL *2.0 Basic*: SMIL 2.0 baseline subset for low-power devices with a minimal set of elements and attributes;
- *3GPP Mobile* SMIL: SMIL profile defined for mobile telephones that contains most of SMIL's features except animation and some interactivity;
- *XHTML+SMIL*: SMIL timing elements integrated into XHTML; and
- SMIL *1.0*: the original version of SMIL.

SMIL functionality is also integrated into a number of other languages. Although these languages are not SMIL profiles, they do form important examples of how SMIL can be integrated for use in other domains:

- SVG — graphics animated with SMIL timing
- *XMT* — SMIL subset for use with MPEG-4 multimedia streaming

The scope of each of these profiles and applications of SMIL are briefly discussed in the following sections.

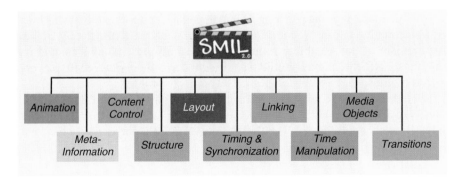

Figure 1-7. SMIL module architecture.

1.4.1 SMIL 2.0 Language Profile

The SMIL 2.0 Language profile includes essentially the entire set of elements and attributes defined in the SMIL 2.0 specification. Presentations encoded for this profile use SMIL as the document *host language*. (That is, the outer-most structure container is <smil>, not <html> or <svg>.) The SMIL Language profile exposes all of SMIL's functionality directly, using the element and attribute names defined in the specification. Many of the examples in this book are given using the SMIL 2.0 Language profile.

Oratrix's GRiNS/SMIL 2.0 player was the first player to support the SMIL 2.0 Language profile. RealNetworks began their support for SMIL 2.0 with the RealOne player. RealOne is the successor to the RealPlayer-6/7/8 series, and enjoys wide acceptance in the media publishing and media user communities.

Both the RealOne and GRiNS players required major engineering efforts to support the entire SMIL specification. This effort has proven to be a barrier for other groups hoping to implement SMIL. In order to stimulate the further acceptance of the SMIL 2.0 Language profile, both the RealOne player and the GRiNS player are being released in open-source versions. The open-source RealOne player is available as part of Real's Helix architecture; the code base and any extensions will become part of RealNetworks' intellectual property. The Ambulant player is an open-source implementation of SMIL 2.0 being developed (in part) by the team that built the GRiNS player. Ambulant is available under a GNU GPL open-source licensing agreement.

1.4.2 SMIL 2.0 Basic

The effort required to develop a complete SMIL 2.0 Language profile implementation is justified for desktop and server systems that need to support a wide range of media presentations, but the functionality of SMIL Profile is often considered to be beyond the needs of applications for low-power devices (such as PDAs and telephones). In order to manage the process of sub-setting SMIL functionality for these devices, the W3C developed the SMIL *2.0 Scalability Framework*. The SMIL 2.0 Basic profile defines the least complex subset of elements and attributes that still remains sufficiently SMIL-like to justify the use of a SMIL host language tag. As long as a SMIL subset supports at least this level of functionality, it can be considered to be part of the SMIL family. A key requirement of the scalability framework is that all presentations created for the sub-setted SMIL player should also present correctly in other SMIL players, including those that use the full SMIL 2.0 Language profile.

SMIL Basic is used in various SMIL players. X-Smiles (from the Helsinki University of Technology) is a Java implementation of parts of SMIL for integration into a browser environment. The INRIA PocketPC SMIL player is also based on SMIL Basic.

1.4.3 3GPP/PSS SMIL

The main standardization body for content on third-generation mobile telephones is 3GPP: the *Third Generation Partnership Project* consortium. This industry forum of device manufacturers selected SMIL as the basis for putting images, graphics, text and video on a wide range of mobile devices. The first versions of these specifications (which were called PSS for *Packet Switched Services*) were relatively bare-bones SMIL, but starting with version 5, a reasonable subset of the full SMIL 2.0 Language profile is offered that allow essentially all of the core functionality in Part 2 of this book to be supported

Various organizations, including CWI, InterObjects, Oratrix, PacketVideo and RealNetworks, have announced support for 3GPP SMIL players on various mobile telephone and PDA devices. Many other vendors hoping to cash-in on expected growth in the mobile market are also developing 3GPP SMIL players. This is an area in which significant growth can be expected.

In early 2001, the MMS-2.0 multimedia messaging service protocol was announced by a consortium of industry partners. MMS-2.0 is intended for mobile image slide shows. It is SMIL-like, but does not contain substantial SMIL functionality. Unlike SMIL Basic documents, MMS-2.0 presentations cannot play on general SMIL players.

Currently, the name MMS is used in the mobile telephone world to mean a particular standard for encoding messages (this is MMS-2.0), but also to mean the entire suite of future multimedia messaging (including the 3GPP/SMIL profile and its future extensions). To avoid confusion, we will use the term MMS to only mean the MMS-2.0 sub-SMIL language. 3GPP SMIL will be used for more generic multimedia messaging services for mobile devices.

1.4.4 XHTML+SMIL Profile

The XHTML+SMIL profile is an example of a profile that does not use SMIL as the host language. Instead, XHTML+SMIL integrates SMIL constructs directly with HTML constructs into a single XML format. XHTML+SMIL documents allow a high degree of local synchronization of text fragments and presentation components inside of an HTML base. Since, however, XHTML has no inherent notion of time, XHTML+SMIL documents usually have only limited temporal scope. The playing of XHTML+SMIL is best suited for multimedia presentations with heavy use of text within one predominantly textflow-based layout, and less dependence on other more time-intensive media. The XHTML+SMIL profile includes most of the timing, animation, media and content control facilities defined in the SMIL 2.0 specification. XHTML+SMIL does not use any SMIL layout constructs — it uses HTML and CSS constructs instead.

Even though XHTML+SMIL has not progressed to full W3C Recommendation status because only one implementation has been provided to W3C for testing, it enjoys very wide distribution: Microsoft's implementation of XHTML+SMIL is called HTML+TIME and has been available in *Internet Explorer* since version 5.5.

1.4.5 SMIL 1.0

SMIL 1.0 was the first version of SMIL. It is not technically a SMIL 2.0 profile, but since many SMIL 2.0 players can open and execute a SMIL 1.0 file, we include it in our discussion. SMIL 1.0 defines the core functionality supported in all of the functional groups of SMIL 2.0, but none of the SMIL 2.0 extensions. In nearly all functional groups, the "basic" module (such as the *BasicLinking* or *BasicLayout* module) has functionality that corresponds to the original behavior of SMIL 1.0. One of the major differences between SMIL 1.0 and SMIL 2.0 is that the names of many elements and attributes were changed from a hyphenated form (such as `background-color`) to a camel-case form (such as `backgroundColor`). Many current SMIL Language profile players support both forms, but mobile players usually do not.

SMIL 1.0 is supported by a wide range of media players. The first public implementation of SMIL 1.0 was in the CWI/Oratrix GR*i*NS/SMIL 1.0 player. By far the most important player (in terms of installed base) to support the profile was the RealNetworks RealPlayer (versions 6, 7 and 8). SMIL 1.0 is also supported by Apple's *QuickTime* (starting with version 4.1). There are also a variety of other SMIL 1.0 players, developed mostly by research labs and universities; these include *Soja (by Helio)*, *Schmunzel* (Salzburg Research and Sun Microsystems), *S2M2* (NIST: the U.S. National Institute of Standards and Technology) and *HPAS* (DEC/ Compaq/HP).

1.4.6 SVG

SMIL 2.0 constructs have also been integrated into *SVG (Scalable Vector Graphics)*, the W3C's Recommendation for vector graphics. These constructs from SMIL enable SVG constructs to be animated. This animation of XML-defined constructs by SMIL 2.0 is defined in the W3C Recommendation SMIL *Animation*.

Several players provide support for SMIL animation and SVG. Of these, the largest installed base belongs to Adobe's SVG *Viewer*. The Corel SVG player has limited support for SMIL animation.

1.4.7 XMT

The *eXtensible MPEG-4 Textual Format (XMT)* is the official XML encoding of MPEG-4 presentations. XMT represents higher-level author intent from which final-form (that is, adapted to a particular use and environment) MPEG-4 presentations can be generated. XMT can be parsed to SMIL for playback on SMIL browsers, or processed into the binary MPEG-4 final form format for playback on MPEG-4 browsers. IBM has made a converter from XMT to MPEG-4 as a research tool, but it is not yet publicly available.

1.5 Creating SMIL Presentations

This book is about the structure of SMIL 2.0 and SMIL's elements and attributes. There are several ways that you can use this information to create SMIL presentations. This section provides a brief sampling of editing alternatives in order of increasing functionality. It does not pretend to be complete.

> **Quick Tip**
>
> An up-to-date list of SMIL editors is at W3C's main SMIL page:
> `http://www.w3.org/AudioVideo/`.

1.5.1 Notepad (and Other Text Editors)

Clearly, the most popular SMIL editor to date has been a simple text editor. SMIL's XML format and its regular structure allow a text editor to be a convenient base for making simple presentations. The advantages of using a text editor include:

- *price*: a text editor is usually free;
- *ease of use*: if you can type, you can type SMIL; and
- *full SMIL 2.0 Language profile support*: you have access to all of SMIL elements and attributes when you use a text editor.

   The disadvantages of using a text editor for creating SMIL include:

- *you are on your own*: a text editor doesn't help spot language errors or simplify data entry;
- *you get no performance feedback*: typing a SMIL file that presents six videos in parallel on a mobile phone is easy — but what you really want is an editor that says: *you're crazy to try this!*; and
- *multiple versions of a document require multiple versions of the text*: if you want to create for multiple devices, make sure your RSI insurance is paid up!

   While full-feature SMIL editors are good for serious development, a text editor lets you get started with creating SMIL immediately.

1.5.2 SMIL Syntax Validator

CWI, the Dutch national center for mathematics and computer science in Amsterdam provides the SMIL *Syntax Validator*. For those that write their SMIL code directly with text editors, the validation of this code with the DTDs (Document Type Definitions) of SMIL family formats is essential. Tools like this help authors make sure the code they write conforms to SMIL. This validator checks code written for SMIL 1.0 and the SMIL 2.0 Language profile.

1.5.3 Perly SMIL

Another tool for the hand-coding inclined is the *Perly* SMIL Perl module. This is a module of functions in the programming language Perl. With Perly SMIL, Perl hackers can more quickly write programs that generate SMIL output. Perly SMIL can be downloaded free-of-charge.

1.5.4 SMILGen

An interesting addition to the SMIL GUI editing scene is SMIL*Gen*, a RealNetworks product developed and distributed as free-of-charge and open source. It provides an XML-oriented GUI, facilitating creation of XML constructs in general, accounting for the possibilities and restrictions of individual DTDs and schemas, and with some SMIL 1.0- and 2.0-specific features built directly in. It is more general purpose than template-based SMIL 1.0 editors, but requires more XML and SMIL expertise. It doesn't have the intricate SMIL 2.0-specific interface that GRiNS has — but then, SMILGen is free-of-charge.

1.5.5 MAGpie

American public television's National Center for Accessible Media (NCAM) has developed *MAGpie* for the creation of closed-captions and audio descriptions. MAGpie makes it easier to get the timing information from the media to which captions and descriptions are synchronized. MAGpie generates captions and descriptions in SMIL 2.0 code. It comes with an embedded GRiNS previewer.

1.5.6 GRiNS

The industrial-strength power tool for SMIL 2.0 authoring is GRiNS, by Oratrix. GRiNS provides graphic user interfaces for viewing and editing the spatial and often intricate temporal structure of SMIL 2.0 presentations. The authoring environment also provides integration and playback of individual media components and portions of SMIL presentations. GRiNS gives performance feedback (providing network bandwidth analysis for multiple connection speeds and user profiles) and it exposes all of the SMIL language. Like its player counterpart, GRiNS is a complete SMIL 2.0 implementation. It can output code for the SMIL 2.0 Language profile, the 3GPP Mobile profile and XHTML+SMIL. Like most power tools, GRiNS is useful for the more expert authors of larger presentations, but it can have a higher learning curve than simple text editors. The GRiNS editor can be downloaded with a several week free-of-charge trial period. After the trial expires, a license needs to be purchased.

1.6 SMIL and Other Specifications

The potential of multimedia on the Web is tremendous. Even the most conservative commentators realize that the introduction of audio/video assets as first-class Web objects can have a major impact on the way that people will consume information and entertainment in the future. Not surprisingly, SMIL is not alone in the multimedia standardization space. Often, multimedia standards are characterized by their content, rather than their composition. In this sense, there has been some confusion as to how SMIL relates to these other formats.

1.6.1 CMIF

In 1991, CWI in the Netherlands began a research project on network hypermedia. Late that year, CMIF (the CWI Multimedia Interchange Format) for synchronized multimedia was published that contained the seminal elements of what would later become SMIL. CMIF supplied the general timing semantics, structure, content control, layout, linking and interaction facilities that would be used in the SMIL language. (Some of these facilities made it into SMIL 1.0, others in SMIL 2.0.) Many of CMIF facilities were 'enhanced' by the committee-driven standardization process. (Some of these enhancements were also improvements!) The CMIF player/editor later formed the basis for the Oratrix GR*i*NS environment.

1.6.2 Dynamic HTML

Dynamic HTML (D-HTML) was introduced as a way of introducing local time and animation effects into a static HTML Web page. While some of the animation primitives in SMIL 2.0 resemble the functionality of some uses of D-HTML, SMIL's scope is much broader than the local nature of D-HTML.

1.6.3 Flash

Macromedia's *Flash* is a proprietary content media type that is primarily used for small animations. In contrast, SMIL 2.0 is not a content media type, in the sense that it does not define any particular type of media, such as vector or raster images, videos, text or audio data. Instead of media content, SMIL describes media *composition*. A SMIL presentation can include Flash objects.

SMIL has a number of advantages over proprietary formats such as Flash. One is that it is fully XML-based — it is able to describe adaptive content, and a single file can be targeted to several different target platforms, such as broadband, Web and mobile. The format is also truly open — no one company controls its destiny.

1.6.4 MPEG-4

MPEG-4 is a family of protocols that cover a wide range of media-related concerns, but not a specific solution to any one class of media presentation. It is often stated that the biggest competitor for SMIL 2.0 is MPEG-4. While it is tempting to be drawn into a feature-by-feature comparison, most of SMIL 2.0 and MPEG-4 are actually very complementary.

The major differences between MPEG-4 and SMIL lie in the approach to document structuring and in the separation between structure and content. MPEG-4 is essentially a final-form description of a presentation. It is saved in a binary format, contains extensive control information, and directly contains all of the media content of the presentation. A SMIL document provides a specification of the high-level and detailed synchronization, layout and content control requirements, but it contains no data — the actual media items are included by reference. As with Flash, the combination of content and control can provide a more precise implementation of a presentation, but the separation of content and control can provide a more flexible and reusable presentation architecture.

Both SMIL and MPEG-4 use a profile-based architecture. The profile architecture of MPEG-4 is significantly more complex than SMIL's, resulting in a wide variability in the components that are actually implemented in any particular MPEG-4 player. MPEG-4 also carries with it substantial licensing issues, as much of its component standards contain intellectual property that must be licensed from the IP owners. SMIL 2.0, on the other hand, has been implemented under a royalty-free agreement with its developers.

During the development of SMIL 2.0, close cooperation was maintained with a portion of the MPEG-4 community. Since MPEG-4 is a binary-encoded standard, it was felt that SMIL 2.0 could be used as the text-format for MPEG-4 presentations. The result is the coordinated development of SMIL 2.0 and MPEG-4 through the *XMT (eXtensible MPEG-4 Textual Format)* specification. Here, MPEG-4 encodes low-level objects, while SMIL 2.0 encodes high-level, XML-based object composition.

1.7 Summary and Conclusion

SMIL 2.0's release makes full-fledged multimedia accessible to every user, every author, every implementer and to the infrastructure of the Web itself. It is emerging as a major force in making the existing Web and its various interfaces more animated, engaging, accessible and informative.

SMIL 2.0 is widely supported and distributed. The full-powered SMIL 2.0 Language profile is supported in the Web multimedia mainstay RealOne and the open-source Ambulant players. The 3GPP SMIL profile is supported on a wide range of telephone and PDA devices. XHTML+SMIL is supported in Internet Explorer, the world's most widely distributed network browser. SMIL timing with graphics in SVG is available in the Adobe and Corel SVG players. Large-scale SMIL 2.0 presentation design and maintenance is available through GRiNS, while several template-based editing systems are available for making smaller presentations.

The purpose of this chapter has been to introduce you to the SMIL environment. All of the presentations discussed in this chapter are available on the book's Web site. This site also contains a list of links to SMIL-related products and services. We suggest that you try to experiment with our demonstration examples and that you then move on to our next chapter, which looks at the structure of the SMIL format.

1.8 Further Resources

W3C Audio/Video Pages

The W3C keeps an up-to-date SMIL Web site with information on players, editors and tutorials at: `http://www.w3.org/AudioVideo/`.

SMIL Players and Editors

Our book's Web site has pointers to various SMIL tools and a downloadable version of the Ambulant SMIL 2.0 player. See: `http://www.XmediaSMIL.net/` .

Vendor SMIL Pages

Many SMIL player vendors have pages that contain SMIL documentation, including example documents and tutorials.

2

Understanding SMIL 2.0 Code

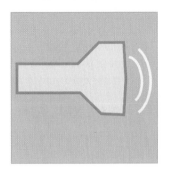

This chapter provides a reader's guide to the structure and contents of SMIL presentations. By walking through a complete SMIL example, we'll introduce the main concepts and concerns that you will encounter when you first start making SMIL multimedia documents.

We start with a brief review of basic XML language constructs. We then describe an example presentation (*Flashlight*) and give an overview of SMIL functionality, based on six functional categories:

- SMIL *structure*: the basic framework for encoding SMIL presentations;
- *media content*: the constructs for referencing external media objects;
- *layout*: the facilities for managing rendering resources;
- *timing*: the core control constructs for temporal structuring;
- *linking:* the constructs for link-based navigation and interaction; and
- *adaptivity*: the tools for tailoring presentations to the environment.

Together, these categories form the *what*, *where*, *when*, *how* and *for whom* of SMIL. We end with a description of Flashlight in various SMIL profiles.

After you finish this chapter, you should have a broad reading knowledge of SMIL 2.0. This will get you ready to build your own presentations using the in-depth information presented in the body of this book.

2.1 Understanding XML Structure

XML, or the *eXtensible Markup Language*, is the meta-language for SMIL (and other Web formats, including XHTML). It is a language that describes how other languages should be structured. An XML definition does not, in and of itself, tell you anything about the meaning of any part of a language — it is simply a set of common conventions for language designers.

There are three concepts to be mastered when learning an XML language:

- understanding the *elements* that the language defines,
- understanding the *attributes* that the language defines for those elements, and
- understanding the kind of *references* within (and outside) the document that the language supports.

This section will introduce you to enough of XML to let you understand the *Flashlight* SMIL example later in this chapter. It will also give you most of the details you need to read any SMIL example in our book. If you are hungry for more information on XML, see the references at the end of this chapter.

2.1.1 XML Elements

The basic unit of XML is the *element*. An XML document consists of a set of nested element definitions. The first element in an XML document, at the top of this tree, is called the *root* element.

XML elements consist of a case-sensitive name with no embedded spaces; they are delimited in XML code by *angle brackets*, the '<' and '>' characters. You may not have any white space between the left angle bracket and the name of the element.

The following fragment shows the element <img>.

```
<img ... >
```

Here, img is the element's *generic identifier*. An element's generic identifier is unique: all elements with the same generic identifier refer to the same XML element definition. An element will usually have one or more attributes associated with it; these are discussed later in this section.

Quick Tip

Since SMIL is strict XML, all identifiers are case-sensitive. Thus, all of the following refer to different elements:

    `<img>, <Img>, <iMg>, <imG>, <IMg>, <iMG>, <ImG>, <IMG>`.

SMIL only allows lower-case generic identifiers for elements: `<img>`.

Technically, the <img> element shown above is not complete because it only indicates that the <img> element *begins*. This is the element's *start-tag*. To make it a complete element, you also need to define an *end-tag*. XML provides two types of end tags: one for use with empty elements that have no content, the other for (nested) elements with content.

Empty Elements

When an XML element is *empty*, this means that all of the information associated with that element is specified using only the element's generic identifier and its attributes (if any). It doesn't mean that it has no attributes or that the element doesn't reference content! The end-tag for an empty element is represented by the '/' character just before the right angle bracket in the element's definition (with no embedded spaces):

```
<img ... />
```

One of the characteristics that separates SMIL from XHTML is that a SMIL file does not contain media content: it *references* media content. Media object elements in SMIL point to a file containing media data, but they do not contain the data itself. This includes the `<text>` element! Occasional use of embedded media is allowed, but this content is placed in an element via one of its attributes. For now, consider all media object references to be empty in XML's sense of the word.

Elements with Content (Including Nested Elements)

Many elements in an XML language have content. This content is in the form of a nested containment of elements. This nested containing of elements allows the building of a hierarchical structure for a document. In the following example, our `<img>` element is put inside a `<body>` element:

```
1  <body>
2    <img attributes ... />
3  </body>
```

By placing these tags around the image element, we indicate that `<body>` contains the content `<img>`. In all cases of nesting, the nested time container is closed by repeating the parent element tag, preceded with a '/', as in line 3.

Most of SMIL's timing and control elements can contain any number of other elements, and each child element can itself contain *child* elements, continuing to any degree of depth. In this manner, the *tree*-shaped *hierarchical* containment structure of XML elements — or the element tree — can become quite large and complex. Some minimal variants of SMIL Basic place restrictions on the depth of nesting to one level, but more recent versions of mobile SMIL profiles have removed this restriction.

Quick Tip

Since SMIL is strict XML, all start tags must be matched by end tags. If you don't do this, a SMIL parser must reject your file.

2.1.2 XML Attributes

Each element may have zero or more *attributes*. An attribute assigns a value to a parameter of the element. **All values for attributes must be quoted**!

In our growing SMIL example, we add a timing attribute to the `<img>` element as follows:

```
<body>
  <img dur="3s" ... />
</body>
```

Here, we assign a value of "3s" to the attribute named dur of the `<img>` element. Note that XML doesn't assign a meaning to the attribute name or the value — it simply specifies the syntax. SMIL assigns the meaning duration to the attribute dur.

Attribute names are case sensitive and are not allowed to contain embedded spaces. Not all attributes will be used in all elements; the XML specification is used to define which attributes are associated with which elements.

Complex languages like SMIL tend to have many attributes. Some of these attributes are the same as corresponding attributes in other XML languages, others are slightly different, and yet others are totally new. One of the most difficult tasks for the designers of SMIL was to balance the need to reuse common attribute names and to still make clear the distinctions between SMIL's use of an attribute name and, say, HTML's use of the same name. In the chapters below, we'll point the major differences between SMIL and other XML languages as needed.

SMIL has many attributes, so it uses long, descriptive names to help clarify the SMIL code. Unfortunately, long names — like *systemdefaultlanguage* — are hard to read. When SMIL 1.0 was designed, hyphens were used to make long attribute names more readable: *system-default-language*. By the time SMIL 2.0 was released, hyphens had fallen from favor and camel casing was used to clarify attribute names: *systemDefaultLanguage*. It is important to understand that the user can't choose between camel casing or hyphens — this is a choice that was made by SMIL's language designers.

> **Quick Tip**
>
> Most of SMIL 1.0's hyphenated attribute names have been deprecated in SMIL 2.0 and replaced with camel-case equivalents. You can still use the old names — which means that SMIL 1.0 files still play on a SMIL 2.0 player — but new files should use the new names.

2.1.3 XML References

This sections describes XML's facilities for specifying internal resources, external files and portions of external files.

Internal References

XML elements in different parts of the same document can refer to each other by using *ID (unique identifier)* and *IDREF (unique identifier reference)* attributes. An ID attribute gives its element a unique name. ID attributes typically have the name "id". An IDREF attribute allows an ID defined elsewhere in the document to be used in an element. For example, consider the following fragment:

```
<region id="title" ... />
  ...
<body>
  <img dur="3s" region="title" ... />
</body>
```

In this fragment, a <region> element has the unique identifier attribute id with a value *title*. Only one element in the entire document can use this particular ID attribute value. The `<img>` element can refer to this region by using the IDREF attribute `region` with the value *title*.

External Files

Sometimes external files play a role in XML documents. SMIL presentations, for example, often use external files to define the media content that plays within a multimedia presentation. XML documents refer to external files by assigning their locations as values for certain attributes. For example, assume a image file named *Title.png* exists that contains the words "The GR*i*NS Flashlight". We would reference this file from our SMIL presentation as follows:

```
<region id="title" ... />
...
<body>
  <img dur="3s" region="title" src="Title.png" />
</body>
```

The `src` attribute is recognized by SMIL as being a URI. This attribute's value can be the name of a file, a pathname for the file in the local file system, or a location on the Web. In the example, the contents of this image file are displayed for three seconds.

Portions of External/Internal Files

The external and internal references just discussed can be combined to refer to portions of external files. Such references are usually constructed as attribute values containing the location of an external XML file, followed by a '#' character, then followed by an IDREF of an XML element within that file. The same technique can be applied to internal references, with the exception that the file name is not used. If, for example, we wanted to define an internal link anchor reference to the *intro* section of the current SMIL file, we'd say:

```
<region id="title"/>
...
<body>
  <a href="#intro">
    <img dur="3s" src="Title.png" region="title" />
  </a>
  ...
  <par id="intro">
    ...
  </par>
</body>
```

The behavior of links and the behavior of SMIL are not determined by the XML syntax. Instead, the XML syntax is used to describe elements and attributes in a clear and unambiguous manner in an external specification that also specifies behavioral properties.

As we will see, SMIL has a wealth of options for defining temporal attributes that control the activation of elements and media content.

2.2 *Flashlight*: A SMIL Example Presentation

Now that we've discussed the basics of XML, it is time to look at a detailed SMIL example: *Flashlight*. *Flashlight* is based on an interactive multimedia user's guide; it touches on all the major areas of SMIL 2.0 functionality.

The Structure of Flashlight

The presentation schematic for the *Flashlight* presentation is illustrated in Figure 2-1. Here we see that *Flashlight* consists of a set of structured segments that describe how to set up and use the device. The opening segment consists of a logo and a main image, both of which are shown in parallel with an audio track and a set of text captions. The entire content of the opening segment is accompanied by an image that contains link anchors for navigation.

The second segment shown in Figure 2-1(b) illustrates how to put batteries in the flashlight. The segment is structured very much the same as Figure 2-1(a), except that the main image is replaced by a more complex sub-structure.

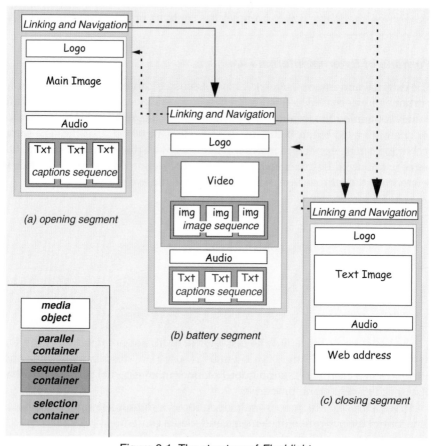

Figure 2-1. The structure of *Flashlight*.

This sub-structure, contained in a red selection box, lets the player decide if either a video object is shown or if the video is to be replaced by a sequence of images. (In this presentation, the images will be shown instead of the video object if the bitrate of the network connection is determined by the player to be below about 34Kbps.) As with the first segment, a logo is shown and a set of text captions accompany an audio voice track. Once again, a navigation bar is shown that allows the user to jump to another section.

The third segment of the presentation shows the logo and contains three interior media objects: a main image (containing styled text), a Web address and an audio track. (Since the main image gives all of the important information in text form, a separate captions sequence is not required.) The Web address has an anchor attached to it so that users can click through to the Web site for extra information (and a chance to purchase the flashlight itself.)

At any time during the presentation, a user may navigate to the section that is of interest via a set links on the linking menu bar. (Some of the links are shown in the image) When a link is followed, the presentation context changes to the new subject material — the old context goes away. This is not always necessary: sometimes a new context will augment rather than replace content.

The Runtime View of Flashlight

Once the presentation structure is defined and the media assets are created, the flashlight presentation can be rendered on a SMIL player. One such rendering is shown in Figure 2-2: this figure shows three snapshots of the presentation, one for each main segment. If we had played flashlight in another SMIL player, the outer window will be different (that is, the menu bars and the skin of the player interface will be customized by the player manufacturer), but the content of the presentation should be the same. If it is used on a different type of device, some of the content may be scaled or ignored, depending on device characteristics.

The following sections look at the general structure of the Flashlight example and then consider the consequences of playing the presentation on different classes of SMIL 2.0 players.

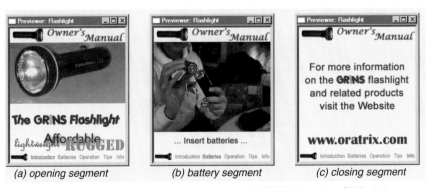

(a) opening segment　　(b) battery segment　　(c) closing segment

Figure 2-2. Display of *Flashlight* using the GR*i*NS Player for SMIL 2.0.

Flashlight SMIL 2.0 Code

Example 2-1 shows the SMIL 2.0 code written for the SMIL 2.0 Language profile for a subset of the *Flashlight* presentation. If this code seems overwhelming, look back at the presentation schematic on page 26. (If it *doesn't* seem overwhelming, perhaps you should look at it again!) In order to reduce the complexity of this example, we've only included three subsections in the code of *Flashlight*. The entire presentation is available on our book's Web site.

```
1  <!DOCTYPE smil PUBLIC "-//W3C//DTD SMIL 2.0//EN"
                    "http://www.w3.org/TR/REC-smil/SMIL20.dtd">
2  <smil xmlns="http://www.w3.org/2001/SMIL20/Language">
3    <head>
4      <meta name="title" content="Flashlight"/>
5      <meta name="generator" content="GRiNS for SMIL 2.0, win32 build 153"/>
6      <meta name="author" content="Jack Jansen and Dick Bulterman"/>
7      <layout>
8        <root-layout id="Flashlight" backgroundColor="#ffffcc" width="240"
                  height="269"/>
9        <region id="Title" left="0" width="240" top="0" height="29"/>
10       <region id="Image" left="0" width="240" top="29" height="180"
                  z-index="2"/>
11       <region id="Text" left="0" width="240" top="209" height="42"
                  fit="meet"/>
12       <region id="Buttons" left="0" width="240" top="251" height="15"/>
13       <region id="Logo" left="0" width="240" top="169" height="42"
                  z-index="3"/>
14       <region id="Sound"/>
15     </layout>
16     <transition id="fade1s" type="fade" dur="1s"/>
17   </head>
18   <body>
19     <par>
20       <img region="Title" src="M/title.gif"/>
21       <seq>

         <!-- This is the opening segment. -->

22         <par id="Intro">
23           <img id="button-intro" region="Buttons" src="M/b-intro.gif">
24             <area id="AIB" href="#Bat" sourcePlaystate="stop"
                    coords="99,0,139,15"/>
25             <area id="AIM" href="#MI" sourcePlaystate="stop"
                    coords="220,0,237,15"/>
26           </img>
27           <par>
28             <img id="I-picture" region="Image" src="M/lamp1.jpg"
                    transIn="fade1s"/>
29             <img region="Logo" fill="freeze" src="M/FL.gif"
                    transIn="fade1s"/>
30             <audio id="I-Welcome" region="Sound" src="M/Welcome.mp3"/>
31             <seq id="description" begin="2">
32               <img id="lightweight" region="Text" dur="1s" fill="transition"
                    src="M/lw.gif" transIn="fade1s"/>
33               <img id="affordable" region="Text" dur="1s" fill="transition"
                    src="M/af.gif" transIn="fade1s"/>
34               <img id="durable" region="Text" dur="2s" fill="freeze"
                    src="M/du.gif" transIn="fade1s"/>
35             </seq>
36           </par>
37         </par>
```

Example 2-1. The SMIL 2.0 Language profile code for *Flashlight*.

```
<!-- This is the Batteries segment. -->
```
```
 1   <par id="Bat">
 2    <img id="buttons-battery" region="Buttons" src="M/b-batteries.gif">
 3     <area id="ABI" href="#Intro" sourcePlaystate="stop"
         coords="39,0,91,15"/>
 4     <area id="ABM" href="#More" sourcePlaystate="stop"
         coords="220,0,237,15"/>
 5    </img>
 6    <par>
 7     <switch>
 8      <video id="B-vid" region="Image" src="M/Bat.avi" transIn="fade1s"
         transOut="fade1s" systemBitrate="34400" />
 9      <seq>
10       <par>
11        <img id="BI-ccw" region="Image" dur="5s" src="M/cCW.jpg"/>
12        <audio id="BA-CCW" region="Text" src="M/cCW.mp3"/>
13       </par>
14       <par>
15        <img id="BI-insert" region="Image" dur="8s"
           src="M/Insert.jpg"/>
16        <audio id="BA-insert" region="Text" src="M/Insert.mp3"/>
17       </par>
18       <par>
19        <img id="BI-CW" region="Image" src="M/cw.jpg"
           transIn="fade1s"/>
20        <audio id="BA-CW" region="Text" src="M/cw.mp3"/>
21       </par>
22      </seq>
23     </switch>
24     <seq>
25      <img id="B-ccw" region="Text" dur="5s" src="M/ccw.gif"/>
26      <img id="B-in" region="Text" dur="8s" fill="transition"
         src="M/insert.gif" transIn="fade"/>
27      <img id="B-cw" region="Text" src="M/cw-sm.gif"
         transIn="fade1s"/>
28     </seq>
29    </par>
30   </par>
```
```
<!-- This is the Closing segment. -->
```
```
31   <par id="More">
32    <img id="b-MI" region="Buttons" dur="50s" src="M/b-moreinfo.gif">
33     <area id="AMI" href="#Intro" sourcePlaystate="stop"
         coords="39,7,91,26"/>
34     <area id="AMB" href="#Bat" sourcePlaystate="stop"
         coords="99,6,139,25"/>
35    </img>
36    <par>
37     <img id="moreinfo" region="Image" src="M/moreinfo-F.gif"/>
38     <audio id="Thanks" region="Text" src="M/Thanks.mp3"/>
39     <a href="http://www.oratrix.com/" >
40      <img id="wlink" region="Text" dur="indefinite" src="M/www.gif"/>
41     </a>
42    </par>
43   </par>
44   </seq>
45  </par>
46  </body>
47 </smil>
```

Example 2-1. The SMIL 2.0 Language profile version of *Flashlight (continued)*.

2.2.1 The Head and Body Sections

Example 2-2 gives an outline form of the *Flashlight* document. All SMIL documents for the SMIL Language profile (including Mobile SMIL) adhere to this structure, so it can be used as a standard text template.

```
 1  <!DOCTYPE smil PUBLIC "-//W3C//DTD SMIL 2.0//EN"
                    "http://www.w3.org/TR/REC-smil/SMIL20.dtd">
 2  <smil xmlns="http://www.w3.org/2001/SMIL20/Language">
 3   <head>
     ...
17   </head>
18   <body>
     ...
83   </body>
84  </smil>
```

Example 2-2. The basic structure of a SMIL presentation.

Line 1 of Example 2-2 defines the document type to be used by the XML parser for the SMIL document. Note that line 1 forms a single XML statement, but that it ends with a single right angle bracket — not a "/>"! Line 2 identifies the host language of this document as SMIL. The <smil> element is used in every type of SMIL document in which SMIL is the host language. In order to differentiate between, say, a SMIL 1.0 document and a SMIL 2.0 document, line 2 also has an XML namespace identifier attribute (xmlns):

```
xmlns="http://www.w3.org/2001/SMIL20/Language"
```

This namespace specification is required in SMIL 2.0 host language documents, whether they are based on the SMIL Basic profile or the full SMIL 2.0 Language profile (or somewhere in between). Some SMIL files may contain additional namespace declarations; these are used to identify any extensions to SMIL that are required by the document. A SMIL player can then determine if these extensions can be supported. If an additional or non-standard namespace is used in a presentation, the DOCTYPE declaration either must be removed or it must be updated to point to a new DTD that will recognize the namespace additions. The default DOCTYPE declaration may only be used with the standard SMIL namespace definition.

Lines 3 through 17 contain the SMIL <head> section. This section contains definitions that are not part of the temporal flow of the presentation. Among the elements you can expect to find in the <head> are: <meta>, <layout> and <transition>. The <head> section is optional.

Lines 18 through 83 define the SMIL <body> section. This section contains the media and timing control elements in the SMIL specification. The <body> is technically optional, but a SMIL presentation without a <body> is seldom useful. While most XML languages contain a <body> section, SMIL's <body> has an extra feature: it also defines a sequential timing container, just like a SMIL <seq> element. This means that all of the top-level contents of the <body> are evaluated as a temporal sequence by the SMIL player.

The following sections discuss the contents of the <head> and <body> sections in detail. Since, however, the <transition> element from SMIL 2.0 is difficult to place in our partitioning of concepts, we will consider it here before moving to the rest of SMIL. Line 16 of our example contains a definition of a transition resource:

```
16   <transition id="fade1s" type="fade" dur="1s"/>
```

This line defines a named transition (in this case, *fade1s*) which can be used in any media object reference in the body of the presentation. The definition on line 16 does not cause a transition to occur — it simply defines all of the parameters associated with a potential transition in one place. The transition can be applied to a particular media object by adding an attribute for an input or output transition (or both) to an object. For example, line 8 contains the following video reference:

```
45        <video id="B-vid" region="Image" src="M/Bat.avi" transIn="fade1s"
          transOut="fade1s" systemBitrate="34400" />
```

Line 8 defines both an input (transIn) and an output transition (transOut). Since both reference the same transition definition on line 8 (*fade1s*), both will have the same transition behavior. This form of indirect attribute assignment reduces the complexity of the specification. Indirect attribute assignment is also used for SMIL layout and for aspects of SMIL content control.

> **Quick Tip**
>
> SMIL allows you to define transitions on all types of media; keep in mind that on some platforms, placing transitions on certain types of intensive media (such as video) can be computationally expensive: it may look great on the desktop, but it may put off users on mobile devices.

2.2.2 Media Content

The 'I' in SMIL stands for *"Integration"* — SMIL does not create media, but rather integrates multiple media that already exist into a single presentation. The primary SMIL construct for retrieving media content is the <ref> element. The <ref> specifies a general object reference. In order to aid reading of a SMIL document, most profiles allow <ref> to have the synonyms <img>, <video>, <audio>, <text>, <animation> and <textstream>. The SMIL language does not enforce that an object referenced via a synonym is of the type suggested by the tag (for example, that an <img> tag actually references an image) — that's why all of these element identifiers are only synonyms to <ref>.[1]

Line 20 contains a simple reference to a media object:

```
20   <img region="Title" src="M/title.gif"/>
```

---

1 Versions of the 3GPP Mobile profiles required that only the synonyms be used instead of <ref> and that the type of the element (i.e., img) match the encoding of the media.

This line requests that the media file `title.gif` is shown in the layout region *Title*. One interesting aspect of this example — from a timing and synchronization perspective — is that the display request does not contain any start or end times, or any duration! Unlike a lot of presentation languages, SMIL can often compute these times based on other information in the specification. This makes creating and maintaining a presentation easier than if every object had its timing explicitly specified.

Lines 20, 23-26, 28-30, 32-34, 2-5, 8, 11-12, 15-16, 19-20, 25-27, 32-35 and 37-38 and 40 all define media object references. Most references will have attributes to define the source of the media (`src`) and a layout region for rendering the media (`region`). They may also include attributes for specifying transitions or alternative content, or explicit timing information when necessary.

It is important to remember that the SMIL file contains no actual media content — it only contains pointers to content. This makes the SMIL file small and it allows it to be processed independently of any content.

> **Quick Tip**
>
> When an *alt* attribute is used in a SMIL document, its content is never rendered directly in the presentation. Instead, the contents may be used by some players to identify content in a mouse-over balloon, but this is optional behavior. SMIL content control elements should be used to specify alternative content for media objects.

2.2.3 Layout

Players based on the SMIL 2.0 Language profile (including 3GPP SMIL and SMIL Basic) use SMIL Layout. Players that implement other profiles usually support CSS layout. Both approaches provide control over object placement and scaling.

The general layout and positioning model used in the *Flashlight* example is shown in Figure 2-3. SMIL supports the notion of a top-level container window (called either the *root-layout* or *topLayout*, which contains one or more regions. Each region defines a rectangular collection of pixels and a region stacking order (called the *z-index*). In profiles supporting hierarchical layout, the layout section may also support a region hierarchy within parent regions. (This is useful if the parent's position is animated.) Each region can have default behavior specified for media object clipping and scaling, and in most profiles it is also possible to specify centering and registration points for media in regions. SMIL also provides support for audio layout, but this support is not extensive.

SMIL layout is geared to the placement of media objects in a fixed viewing environment. That is, unlike an HTML page which can be resized without impacting content, a SMIL presentation layout is usually very media centric. As a result, SMIL Layout has only indirect support for specifying window border widths and text placement options. (CSS has much more extensive support for

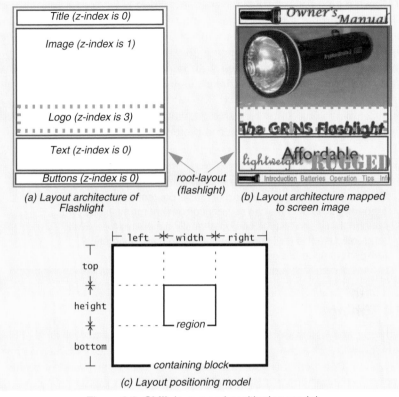

(a) Layout architecture of Flashlight

root-layout (flashlight)

(b) Layout architecture mapped to screen image

(c) Layout positioning model

Figure 2-3. SMIL layout and positioning model.

these.) While this limitation can sometimes be frustrating, it does help keep SMIL Layout simple enough to be used on low-power devices.

Example 2-3 shows the layout specification for our sample presentation. The layout contains the root-layout container window (called *Flashlight*) and six media rendering regions. Some of the regions are assigned an explicit stacking order, others take the default of their parent (in this case, the default for the root

```
7   <layout>
8     <root-layout id="Flashlight" backgroundColor="#ffffcc" width="240"
              height="269"/>
9     <region id="Title" left="0" width="240" top="0" height="29"/>
10    <region id="Image" left="0" width="240" top="29" height="180"
              z-index="2"/>
11    <region id="Text" left="0" width="240" top="209" height="42"
              fit="meet"/>
12    <region id="Buttons" left="0" width="240" top="251" height="15"/>
13    <region id="Logo" left="0" width="240" top="169" height="42"
              z-index="3"/>
14    <region id="Sound"/>
15  </layout>
```

Example 2-3. Layout section for *Flashlight*.

is '0'). Each region contains positioning information when screen space is used; audio regions do not have positioning information in SMIL 2.0. Note that the region *Logo* is spatially embedded on top of the region *Image*. Any content rendered in *Logo* will overlay the content in the overlapping part of *Image*.

Most of the attributes associated with regions are self-explanatory. (If you can't explain them to yourself yet, take a look at Chapter 6: *SMIL Basic Layout*.) One attribute that is new is `fit`: this attribute specifies how over- and under-size media objects are rendered. (A value of *meet* means: scale the media in such a way that it fills the region completely.)

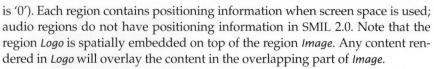

> **Quick Tip**
>
> SMIL supports dynamic resizing of media content to the shape of the rendering window. This can be very convenient for multi-platform support, but it can also be computationally expensive for a SMIL renderer. Use this facility with caution if you plan to target low-performance devices.

2.2.4 Timing

The timing and synchronization functional group represents the core of SMIL 2.0 functionality. The group is divided into 19 modules, each of which defines a collection of XML elements and attributes that control some aspect of timing.

For any content within a timing element (whether a media object or structure container), the primary issues to be addressed are:

- when does the element begin?
- how long is it active?
- what happens to it when it is no longer active?
- are there other (non-timing) conditions that cause an element to begin or end?

These questions are "answered" by specifying a set of timing attributes and elements. The timing attribute values are applied to SMIL's temporal elements or to other elements and their children.

Timing Attributes

SMIL 2.0 has an extensive set of attributes to control timing, most of which carry reasonable defaults so that basic timing and synchronization operations can be accomplished easily. Note that not all of the SMIL 2.0 profiles support all of the attributes, and the syntax of defining and setting the attribute values may vary. This being said, a design objective of SMIL 2.0 was that each attribute should have a well defined semantic that remains constant across profiles.

Timing Elements

Although SMIL defines a large set of timing attributes, it only introduces three timing elements: `<seq>`, `<par>` and `<excl>`. All three elements represent timing containers: they influence how the timing of their children is defined.

A `<seq>` (sequential) container specifies that its children get processed sequentially: each child, whether it contains media or hierarchical structure, is processed when its predecessor ends. The following excerpt from Example 2-1 shows the top-level sequential behavior in our *Flashlight* presentation:

```
21    <seq>
22      <par id="Intro">
23      . . .
37      </par>
38      <par id="Bat">
39      . . .
67      </par>
68      <par id="More">
69      . . .
80      </par>
81    </seq>
```

The sequential container on line 21 indicates that each of its children (in this case, three `<par>` containers) are to be processed sequentially.

A `<par>` element specifies that its children play in *parallel*. Actually, this is a simplification of SMIL behavior: a `<par>` really says that the default behavior of its children is that they all share a common parent timeline with a common default begin at the start of the `<par>`, but that this default can be changed via SMIL's timing attributes. The `<par>` is the most general SMIL container. The following excerpt from Example 2-1 shows the parallel behavior of one of the `<par>` groups in *Flashlight*. Two images and one audio fragment are rendered starting at the default time of the beginning of the container. Two seconds later, an embedded sequential container becomes active. The `<par>` ends when the last element in the container ends.

```
27    <par>
28      <img id="I-picture" region="Image" src="M/lamp1.jpg"
            transIn="fade1s"/>
29      <img region="Logo" fill="freeze" src="M/FL.gif"
            transIn="fade1s"/>
30      <audio id="I-Welcome" region="Sound" src="M/Welcome.mp3"/>
31      <seq id="description" begin="2">
32        <img id="lightweight" region="Text" dur="1s" fill="transition"
            src="M/lw.gif" transIn="fade1s"/>
33        <img id="affordable" region="Text" dur="1s" fill="transition"
            src="M/af.gif" transIn="fade1s"/>
34        <img id="durable" region="Text" dur="2s" fill="freeze"
            src="M/du.gif" transIn="fade1s"/>
45      </seq>
46    </par>
```

An `<excl>` (or *exclusive*) element is very much like a `<par>`, with one major exception: at most one of the children of the `<excl>` can be active at one time. The easiest way to think about an exclusive container is that it is a `<par>` in which all of the children have conditional begin times. (Usually, this condition is a mouse-click.) When one child is selected, any other child that was playing is immediately de-activated. If another child is selected, it replaces its predecessor. When no child is active, the `<excl>` container ends (unless it has attributes that extend its life). Since `<excl>` is advanced SMIL functionality that is not supported by all SMIL profiles, we defer a discussion until Chapter 13: *Advanced SMIL Timing Behavior and Control.*

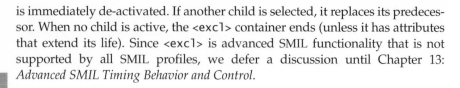

2.2.5 Linking

The `<excl>` construct illustrates one form of interactivity in a SMIL presentation. The `<excl>` is useful for controlling the activation of a piece of code conditionally, but there are other forms of interaction that are also useful. SMIL linking provides facilities for presentation *navigation* and *branching*: users can move around in the presentation, and they can grab extra information (sometimes from outside the scope of the document) for conditional inclusion into the presentation.

SMIL's primary linking constructs are, as in HTML, the `<a>` element (and its `href` attribute) and the `<area>` element (which gives linking control within an object). Both have very similar meanings to their HTML counterparts except for one major extension: both can add the notion of time to a link.

Links — or more correctly, *anchors* — can have a duration specified during which they are active. In this way, an object can have several links associated with it while the underlying object is active. Timed anchors also control the state of the entire source presentation: when a link is followed, the original document can be paused, replaced, or simply left to keep on running.

Linking is a very powerful feature for adding navigation and conditional content activation facilities to a presentation. Unfortunately, not all SMIL implementations support full SMIL linking functionality completely, so make sure you test your SMIL file carefully on all candidate players.

Two types of linking are shown in *Flashlight*. The following fragment shows internal linking using the `<area>` element:

```
23    <img id="button-intro" region="Buttons" src="M/b-intro.gif">
24      <area id="AIB" href="#Bat" sourcePlaystate="stop" coords="..."/>
25      <area id="AIM" href="#MI" sourcePlaystate="stop" coords="..."/>
26    </img>
```

Line 23 contains a reference to an image. There is no `begin` or `end` attribute defined for this object, so it lasts as long as other objects in the same `<par>` element.[2] Lines 24 and 25 contain `<area>` anchors that are defined as children of this object. Each anchor is defined to cover a certain part of the buttons bar at the bottom of the display area. If an anchor is selected, control is passed to the named part of the document as if a fast-forward or fast-reverse operation had taken place. The behavior of area-based links is similar to the equivalent HTML construct, with the exception that the state of the initial presentation can be explicitly manipulated via the `sourcePlaystate` attribute. Following the link also has a defined temporal behavior and influences the presentation timeline.

---

2 This is a simplification of what really goes on when elements have no timing.

A second type of link is shown in the following code fragment:

```
76      <a href="http://www.oratrix.com/" >
77        <img id="wlink" region="Text" dur="indefinite" src="M/www.gif">
78      </a>
```

Line 39 shows an anchor that is wrapped around the entire object rather than being defined as part of an object's rendering space. There are no spatial constraints and no explicit playstate settings.

Links in SMIL are similar to those in HTML in most respects, except that SMIL adds a description of the temporal consequences of links. It also provides a set of timing attributes that can be applied to links. Consider the following fragment, which extends the behavior of *Flashlight*:

```
<img id="button-intro" region="Buttons" src="M/b-intro.gif" dur="20s" >
    <area id="AIB" href="#Bat" begin="5s" dur="10s"
    sourcePlaystat="stop" coords="99,0,139,15"/>
</img>
```

The anchor named *AIB* now starts its active period 5 seconds after the image begins; the anchor is then active for 10 seconds. If someone clicks on the image anytime before the first 5 seconds, nothing happens. If someone clicks on the image after 15 seconds (that is, after the 5 second start delay and the 10 second active period of the anchor), nothing happens. But, if the anchor is selected during its 10 second active period, the control will flow to the target of the anchor (in this case, the anchor *Bat*).

Quick Tip

SMIL linking provides facilities that, with a bit of practice, simulate nearly all forms of interactive behavior. That's good, because many low-power SMIL profiles that don't support the <excl> element do support linking!

2.2.6 Adaptivity

On the Web, each document is available to essentially the entire world. It is also available to users that have special needs, such as the blind or the deaf. SMIL contains a suite of content control elements that simplify the task of supporting a worldwide, diverse audience by integrating multiple content streams in a single document.

The <switch> element is the most important SMIL element for adaptivity. At most one child of each <switch> element may be selected for inclusion in the presentation. Each child of the <switch> is evaluated by checking the state of a SMIL *test attribute* against the value of that variable in the SMIL player. The first child that is determined appropriate for playing is played. If none of the children is appropriate, then none is played.

To see how the <switch> works, consider the following fragment from Example 2-1:

```
44    <switch>
45      <video id="B-vid" region="Image" src="M/Bat.avi" transIn="fade1s"
          transOut="fade1s" systemBitrate="34400" />
46      <seq>
47       <par>
48        <img id="BI-ccw" region="Image" dur="5s" src="M/cCW.jpg"/>
49        <audio id="BA-CCW" region="Text" src="M/cCW.mp3"/>
50       </par>
51       <par>
52        <img id="BI-insert" region="Image" dur="8s" src="M/Insert.jpg"/>
53        <audio id="BA-insert" region="Text" src="M/Insert.mp3"/>
54       </par>
55       <par>
56        <img id="BI-CW" region="Image" src="M/cw.jpg" transIn="fade1s"/>
57        <audio id="BA-CW" region="Text" src="M/cw.mp3"/>
58       </par>
59      </seq>
60    </switch>
```

The <switch> on line 7 contains two top-level children: the <video> element on line 8 and the <seq> on line 9. The <video> element on 8 contains the systemBitrate attribute, which says: if the system bitrate has been determined (by the player) to be at least 34Kbps, then consider this switch child to be available. The SMIL player will use the first <switch> child that it determines is available for activation. Note that line 9 does not contain a system test attribute: this means that it is always an acceptable candidate. In this presentation, the image/audio sequence will only be played if the bitrate test for video failed.

System test attributes are usually found on children of a <switch>, but SMIL 2.0 also supports *in-line test attributes*. In-line test attributes provide a means for conditional acceptance of individual elements (or element trees) of SMIL, while switch-based content control provide a way of specifying alternatives within a document.

2.2.7 Putting it All Together

Now that we've looked at all the major components of the SMIL presentation, we can take a look at the presentation as a whole. You may want to refer back to Example 2-1 while we walk through the total presentation.

Lines 3 through 17 define the SMIL head section, in which the layout of the presentation is defined and in which any transitions are given. This information is used by reference in the rest of the presentation. The layout consists of five main windows and one audio region. The transition specifies a one-second fade.

The body of the presentation starts on line 18. The entire presentation consists of a sequence of three parallel elements. The first parallel element defines an image that is presented in parallel with two other images, an audio file, and a sequence of three images. This structure is repeated with minor modifications

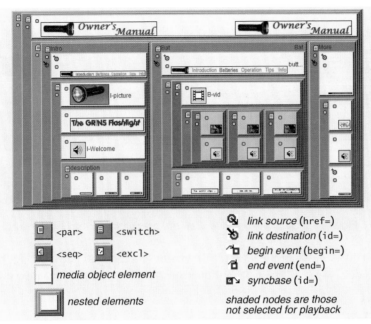

<par> `<par>` <switch> `<switch>`

<seq> `<seq>` <excl> `<excl>`

media object element

nested elements

link source (`href=`)

link destination (`id=`)

begin event (`begin=`)

end event (`end=`)

syncbase (`id=`)

shaded nodes are those
not selected for playback

Figure 2-4. Structure View of *Flashlight* from the GR*i*NS Editor for SMIL 2.0.

in the other two parallel components. The structure group on line 1 contains the linking image, and then either a video sequence or a set of images and audio. (The choice depends on the evaluation of the switch element.) This is played in parallel with a sequence of three images on line 24. The final parallel group contains a linking image in parallel with a combination of an image and audio on line 73, and an external linking image on line 78.

One interesting way to look at a SMIL presentation is to focus on its structure. Here, we are interested in the big picture, rather than any of the timing details of the individual media objects. Figure 2-4 shows a structure-only representation of *Flashlight*, as rendered in the GR*i*NS Editor. This view uses colors to show the nested presentation components, but it doesn't show any of the timing details. An advantage of the GR*i*NS approach is that, for example, the red block in the center of the image can show the state of a `<switch>` element. In this case, the video is selected and the image/audio sequence is darkened to indicate that it is inactive.

You should compare the structured view provided by the GR*i*NS Editor with the presentation schematic diagram presented in Figure 2-1 on page 26. Both use an encapsulated view of the structured presentation as a collection of nested time containers and media objects.

Time can also be integrated into a structured representation. Figure 2-5 shows the GR*i*NS structured timeline: here, objects are scaled to their duration (when known), but it is still possible to focus on the presentation structure.

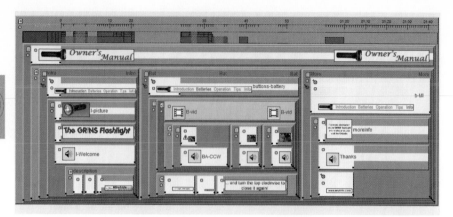

Figure 2-5. StructureTimeline View of *Flashlight* from the GRiNS Editor

Note that the status of the <switch> element has changed between Figure 2-4 and Figure 2-5: now the image/audio sequence is active and the video is inactive.

2.3 Encoding *Flashlight* in Different Profiles

The examples of *Flashlight* in the previous section focused on the SMIL 2.0 Language profile. In this section, we look at transformations of *Flashlight* for use with other profiles.

2.3.1 SMIL Mobile Profiles

There are several SMIL profiles in use on mobile telephones. The most restrictive version of SMIL (and one which is actually sub-SMIL in terms of adherence to the SMIL standard) is the Multimedia Messaging System (or MMS). At present, the most complete mobile version of SMIL 2.0 is found in the 3GPP's SMIL specification. This is supported in Nokia's 6600 handset.

Many early multimedia telephones support the MMS language, version 2. This language restricts a presentation to containing a sequence of media objects, with each object containing a single image, a single text caption and a single audio file. (Not all media objects are required.) This is too restrictive for our *Flashlight* example, but it does work for less complex applications.

> **Quick Tip**
>
> Visit the http://www.XmediaSMIL.net to find MMS-2 compliant demos.

The entire *Flashlight* example of Example 2-1 can be viewed without major modification on a 3GPP SMIL compliant device (version 5 or later). 3GPP SMIL version 4 and earlier imposes substantial restrictions on SMIL structure and should probably be avoided. Note that 3GPP used to label their SMIL support with an explicit version number (such as 3GPP PSS5 SMIL), but the version number has been removed in current 3GPP nomenclature.

The 3GPP SMIL client is essentially a SMIL Basic engine with extra support for events and for transitions. The changes that would need to be made to *Flashlight* in order to be fully 3GPP SMIL compliant are discussed in the following sections.

Head and Body Sections

All 3GPP SMIL documents require the standard SMIL namespace declaration, as shown below:

```
<smil xmlns="http://www.w3.org/2001/SMIL20/Language" >
```

If a specific document needs a particular feature from SMIL 2.0 (such as transitions, which may not be implemented in all versions of mobile clients), the following expanded namespace definition could be used:

```
<smil xmlns="http://www.w3.org/2001/SMIL20/Language"
      xmlns:pss5="http://www.3gpp.org/SMIL20/PSS5/"
      systemRequired="pss5" >
```

This definition defines a namespace variable (*pss5*) that is a shorthand for the entire 3GPP/PSS5 namespace string. The `systemRequired` attribute informs the SMIL player that it must understand all of the definitions of the 3GPP SMIL namespace to correctly process the document. This can be handy if your SMIL document may be used on a variety of clients (not all of which comply with the full standard). In general, however, it is not necessary to include a specific 3GPP namespace declaration.

The body section includes a transition definition. Transitions are supported by 3GPP in version 5 or later, but not in PSS4 or earlier. 3GPP SMIL supports a limited set of transition types: only *barWipe*, *irisWipe*, *clockWipe*, *snakeWipe*, *pushWipe*, *slideWipe* and *fade* are required. This limitation is hardly severe — if you use any more transition types, your viewers will probably go crazy anyway. (*Flashlight* only uses *fade*.)

The rest of the body section of Example 2-1 conforms to 3GPP SMIL. Keep in mind, however, that mobile terminals benefit from small file sizes: the smaller the size, the faster the setup within the handheld device. The only place to really be able to save on SMIL file size is in the use of SMIL's meta-data. *Flashlight* only uses three lines of meta-data — for a total of about 150 characters — but since this meta-data is typically not used by a 3GPP Player, other files with lots of meta-data could be stripped before being published. (This is true for PC players, too, but the setup time on desktop systems is rarely a factor.)

Media Content

3GPP SMIL supports audio, video, images and text, but it does not support all types of media within these types. All 3GPP players should support AMR audio, H.263 Video, MIDI, GIF, JPEG, and plain text. *Flashlight* uses GIF and

JPEG images, so these present no problems. For the most restrictive implementations, the AVI video and MP3 audio would need to be converted to the 3GPP corresponding formats, but most 3GPP SMIL devices will probably contain a RealOne SMIL engine. This means that either RealAudio/RealVideo can be used (for optimal performance) or that the media can be left in its original encoding.

Layout

Flashlight uses layout facilities that are compatible with 3GPP SMIL. The outer window size in the original presentation is 269 pixels high and 240 wide. This is acceptable for many smaller devices (such as PDAs), but it may be too large for the smaller resolutions of mobile telephones.

There are several alternatives available for making the presentation compatible with all devices:

- *Resize the base presentation*: you could survey all mobile devices and create a layout that is no bigger than the most restrictive presentation environment. This is very safe, but it can lead to frustration among users who have purchased fancier devices (or users of desktop SMIL players).

- *Use device default layout*: if no layout section is defined in a presentation, the SMIL player can place objects where it thinks they fit best. While this sounds attractive, it usually results in all content being stacked on top of all other content. The result is rarely pleasing (or useful).

- *Explicitly allow objects to be scaled*: SMIL provides values for object placement that allow media to be scaled. While this is potentially very useful, small devices will often have trouble when scaling images and (especially) video. (With lots of video, the presentation will probably last longer than the battery!)

- *Define multiple layouts using* SMIL *content control*: this is the most useful way of handling multiple devices. SMIL provides a wealth of facilities for providing alternative layouts within one presentation.

While a complete discussion of using multiple layouts within a presentation will have to wait until Chapter 12: *Advanced Layout Topics*, the code fragment in Example 2-4 provides an overview of how SMIL handles layout diversity. This example contains two layout sections within a common switch statement. The first section contains the standard layout, which has been designed for a display area of 269 pixels high and 240 pixels wide (or greater). If this room is available, then the base layout will always be used. If a smaller display is available, a second layout is used. This layout is defined for a 4::3 display and uses relative values instead of absolute positioning. It also allows certain media to be scaled. Note that rather than using the id attribute to define region names, the regionName attribute is used. This allows multiple layouts to be defined that create regions with the same names.

```
<switch>
  <layout systemScreenSize="269x240">
    <root-layout id="Flashlight" backgroundColor="#ffffcc"
                 width="240" height="269"/>
    <region regionName="Title" left="0" width="240" top="0" height="29"/>
    <region regionName="Image" left="0" width="240" top="29"
            height="180" z-index="1"/>
    <region regionName="Text" left="0" width="240" top="209"
            height="42"fit="meet"/>
    <region regionName="Buttons" left="0" width="240" top="251"
            height="15"/>
    <region regionName="Logo" left="0" width="240" top="169"
            height="42" z-index="3"/>
    <region regionName="Sound"/>
  </layout>
  <layout systemScreenSize="200x175">
    <root-layout id="Flashlight-A" backgroundColor="#ffffcc"
                 width="175" height="200"/>
    <region regionName="Title" left="0" width="100%" top="0"
            height="15%"/>
    <region regionName="Image" left="0" width="100%" top="15%"
            height="60%" z-index="1"/>
    <region regionName="Text" left="0" width="100%" top="75%"
            height="20%" fit="meet"/>
    <region regionName="Buttons" left="0" width="100%" top="95%"
            height="5%"/>
    <region regionName="Logo" left="0" width="100%" top="70%"
            height="20%" z-index="3"/>
    <region regionName="Sound"/>
  </layout>
</switch>
...
 <img region="Title" src="M/title.gif"/>
```

Example 2-4. Mobile layout section for *Flashlight*.

In the body section, a reference to a region is made. The player will select the appropriate layout for the device used during playback.

Timing

Flashlight is fully 3GPP SMIL compatible: it only uses the <par> and <seq> timing elements (and not the unsupported <excl>) and it makes use of only standard timing attributes.

Linking

3GPP SMIL supports the internal and external linking used in *Flashlight*. The only modification necessary might be to the content displayed in the external Web page:

```
<a href="http://www.oratrix.com/" >
  <img id="wlink" region="Text" dur="indefinite" src="M/www.gif">
</a>
```

Not all 3GPP players will have full XHTML support, and not all will have screens that are large enough to handle generic Web content.

One other potential problem for supporting *Flashlight* is the use of multiple linking targets within <area> elements:

```
<img id="button-intro" region="Buttons" src="M/b-intro.gif">
  <area id="AIB" href="#Bat" sourcePlaystate="stop" coords="..."/>
  <area id="AIM" href="#MI" sourcePlaystate="stop" coords="..."/>
</img>
```

The problem is not a lack of SMIL support for <area>, but rather a (potential) problem with the mobile device's UI: it may not have a pointer device that can easily be navigated over items. In general, use of the <a> element is safest, but this does introduce extra overhead in handling (and positioning) multiple images for linking use.

Adaptivity

3GPP SMIL supports the <switch> element as used in *Flashlight* (and in the enhanced layout section just discussed). No further modifications are necessary. One consideration that may be worthwhile is to add additional content control to address the needs of small devices. For example, the presentation could be modified to augment the bandwidth related <switch> statement with one that considers display size as well:

```
<switch>
  <video id="B-vid" region="Image" src="M/Bat.avi" transIn="fade1s"
         transOut="fade1s" systemBitrate="34400" systemScreenSize="269X240"/>
  <seq>
    ...
  </seq>
</switch>
```

Here, the <video> will only be activated if the bitrate is 34400 (or greater) and the screen size is at least 269x240.

Other Considerations

The use of 3GPP SMIL can definitely be classified as emerging. It is likely that there will be a high degree of non-uniformity across devices until the market settles on various devices and screen sizes. You should experiment carefully or use authoring tools that explicitly support a diverse set of devices.

2.3.2 SMIL 1.0 Profile

The *Flashlight* example is not a simple SMIL example, but its complexity does not come from extensive use of new features in SMIL 2.0. In fact, just as with Mobile SMIL, nearly all of the functionality in the example was available in the first versions of SMIL 1.0.

Unfortunately, this does not mean that you can give a SMIL 2.0 file to a SMIL 1.0 player and expect to get predictable results — that is, SMIL 2.0 is usually not downward compatible with SMIL 1.0. The inverse *is* true: nearly all SMIL 1.0 documents can be played in a SMIL 2.0 player, and nearly all can be converted to SMIL 2.0 by adding a SMIL 2.0 namespace definition.

In the following sections, we quickly look at the changes that need to be made to have *Flashlight* run on a conventional SMIL 1.0 engine.

Head and Body Sections

SMIL 1.0 does not require the use of an XML namespace declaration. (Why? Because SMIL 1.0 is older than namespaces.) Having a namespace — even an incorrect one — typically won't hurt, except that if you use a SMIL 2.0 namespace with a SMIL 1.0 document, a SMIL 2.0 player is required to test (and reject!) your SMIL 1.0 document.

In addition to removing the namespace, you should remove the transition element definition, since SMIL 1.0 doesn't support transitions.

Media Content

All of the media content and related attributes used in *Flashlight* can also be used by a SMIL 1.0 player with the exception of transition specifications. Each of these need to be removed from the specification.

Layout

The layout definition of the version of *Flashlight* in Example 2-1 is SMIL 1.0 compatible. Note that the use of `regionName` (see page 43) is not supported by SMIL 1.0.

Timing

Flashlight uses only SMIL 1.0 timing elements and attributes.

Linking

Flashlight uses the `<a>` and the `<area>` elements to specify link anchors. The `<a>` element is supported by SMIL 1.0. The `<area>` element was called the `<anchor>` element in SMIL 1.0, so this name needs to be changed. The linking attributes and functionality remain the same.

Adaptivity

Flashlight uses adaptivity elements and attributes that are essentially compatible with SMIL 1.0, with the exception of the various system test variable names. Consider the following code fragment of a modified line 45 (see page 29):

```
<video id="B-vid" region="Image" src="M/Bat.avi"
       system-bitrate="34400" system-screen-size="269X240"/>
```

Other Considerations

With the above changes, *Flashlight* will play on a SMIL 1.0 player. Keep in mind that not all SMIL 1.0 players supported SMIL functionality equally well.

2.3.3 XHTML+SMIL Profile

In order to make a version of *Flashlight* in the XHTML+SMIL profile, we need to change the basic encoding of the document and to replace SMIL layout with CSS layout functions. Example 2-5 shows one transformation from the SMIL 2.0 Language profile to HTML+TIME.[3]

At first glance, the contents and structure look very different from that shown in Example 2-1, but on closer inspection, the similarities are much greater than the differences. The elements and attributes share essentially the same names and the method of defining and manipulating temporal objects within the presentation is also very similar.

The following paragraphs provide an overview of the modifications and limitations of XHTML+SMIL for *Flashlight*.

```
 1  <!DOCTYPE HTML PUBLIC "-//W3C//DTD HTML 4.0 Transitional//EN">
 2  <html xmlns:t="urn:schemas-microsoft-com:time">
 3   <head>
 4    <style>
 5     .time {behavior: url(#default#time2)}
 6     .R-root-layout {position:absolute;overflow:hidden;
                left:0;top:0;width:240;height:269;background-color:#ffffcc}
 7     .R-Title {position:absolute;overflow:hidden;
                left:0;top:0;width:240;height:29;}
 8     .R-Image {position:absolute;overflow:hidden;
                left:0;top:29;width:240;height:180}
 9     .R-Buttons {position:absolute;overflow:hidden;
                left:0;top:251;width:240;height:15}
10     .R-Text   {position:absolute;overflow:hidden;
                left:0;top:209;width:240;height:42}
11     .R-Sound {}
12    </style>
13    <?IMPORT namespace="t" implementation="#default#time2">
14   </head>
15   <body>
16    <div id="Flashlight" class="R-root-layout">
17     <t:seq>
18      <t:par>
19       <t:img src="M-HT/title.gif" class="R-Title"/>
20       <t:seq >
21        <t:par id="Intro" >
22         ...
45        <t:/par>
46        <t:par id="Bat">
47         <t:par>
48          <t:switch>
49           <div class="time" timeContainer="par">
50            <t:video id="B_vid" src="M-HT/Bat.avi"
                  systemBitrate="56120" class="R-image"/>
51            <t:transitionFilter type="fade" subtype="crossfade"
                  dur="1" targetElement="B_vid" begin="B_vid.begin"
                  mode="in" from="0" to="1"/>
52            <t:transitionFilter type="fade" subtype="crossfade"
                  dur="1" targetElement="B_vid" begin="B_vid.end-1"
                  mode="out" from="0" to="1"/>
53           </div>
```

Example 2-5. Excerpt from *Flashlight* as an HTML+TIME presentation.

---

3 The bulk of this version was generated by the GRiNS/SMIL 2.0 Pro editor. Hand-editing may yield a different structure.

```
54     <t:seq>
55       <t:par>
56         <t:img id="BI_ccw_m" src="M-HT/CCW.jpg" class="R-image"/>
57         <t:audio id="BA_CCW" src="M-HT/cCW1.mp3" class="R-Sound"/>
58       </t:par>
59       <t:par>
60         <t:img id="BI_insert_m" fill="transition"
               src="M-HT/Insert.jpg" class="R-Image"/>
61         <t:audio id="BA_insrt" src="M-HT/Insert1.mp3" class="R-Sound"/>
62       </t:par>
63       <t:par id="m31">
64         <div class="time" timeContainer="par">
65           <t:img id="BI_CW" src="M-HT/cw.jpg" class="R-Image"/>
66           <t:transitionFilter type="fade" subtype="crossfade"
                 targetElement="BI_CW" dur="1" begin="BI_CW.begin" ... />
67         </div>
68         <t:audio id="BA_CW" src="M-HT/cw1.mp3" class="R-Sound"/>
69       </t:par>
70     </t:seq>
71     </t:switch>
72     <t:seq>
73       <t:img id="B_ccw" dur="6s" src="M-HT/ccw.gif" class="R-text"/>
74       <div class="time" timeContainer="par">
75         <t:img id="B_in" src="M-HT/insert.gif" dur="8s"
               fill="transition" class="R-text"/>
76         <t:transitionFilter type="fade" subtype="crossfade"
               targetElement="B_in_m" dur="1" begin="B_in.begin" .../>
77         <t:par id="m31">
78           <div class="time" timeContainer="par">
79             <t:img id="BI_CW" src="M-HT/cw.jpg" class="R-Image"/>
80             <t:transitionFilter type="fade" subtype="crossfade"
                   targetElement="BI_CW" dur="1" begin="BI_CW.begin" ... />
81           </div>
82           <t:audio id="BA_CW" src="M-HT/cw1.mp3" class="R-Sound"/>
83         </t:par>
84       </t:div>
85     </t:seq>
86     <t:seq>
87       <t:img id="B_ccw" dur="6s" src="M-HT/ccw.gif" class="R-text"/>
88       <div class="time" timeContainer="par">
89         <t:img id="B_in" src="M-HT/insert.gif" dur="8s"
               fill="transition" class="R-text"/>
90         <t:transitionFilter type="fade" subtype="crossfade"
               targetElement="B_in_m" dur="1" begin="B_in.begin" ... />
91       </div>
92       <div class="time" timeContainer="par">
93         <t:img id="B_cw" src="M-HT/cw-sm.gif" dur="3s"
               fill="transition" class="R-text"/>
94         <t:transitionFilter type="fade" subtype="crossfade"
               targetElement="B_cw" dur="1" begin="B_CW.begin" ... />
95       </div>
96     </t:seq>
97     </t:par>
98     </t:par>
99     <t:par id="More">
100    ...
129    </t:par>
130    </t:seq>
131    </t:par>
132    </t:seq>
133  </div>
134  </body>
135</html>
```

Example 2-5. Excerpt from *Flashlight* as an HTML+TIME presentation (*Continued*).

Head and Body Sections

As with most XML languages, the head section contains general declarations that are used for file parsing and processing, while the body section contains the 'meat' of the content. We consider the major changes in these sections in the paragraphs below.

The new host language for the document will become HTML, since the only implementation of this profile is Microsoft's HTML+TIME. The <html> element contains a reference to Microsoft's *time* namespace; this namespace (which is given the shorthand definition '*t*') contains all of the information required to parse the HTML+TIME structure.

```
 2  <html xmlns:t="urn:schemas-microsoft-com:time">
 3    <head>
 4      <style>
 5        .time {behavior: url(#default#time2)}
 6        ...
12      </style>
13      <?IMPORT namespace="t" implementation="#default#time2">
14    </head>
```

In order to make *Flashlight* HTML+TIME compliant, several fundamental declarations need to be made in the <head> section. The most important ones are the CSS declaration of the *time* behavior on line 5 and the association of the *time2* implementation of HTML+TIME with the *t* namespace on line 13. (The *time2* behavior is the second implementation of HTML+TIME; this implementation supports the bulk of SMIL 2.0 functionality.) The <head> section also contains a number of CSS definitions that are used for layout — more on this in the Layout section below. Note that HTML+TIME does not place transition definitions in the head section.

The structure of the body section is a mix of standard HTML and HTML+TIME extensions. Each of the elements in the body that are to be interpreted as HTML+TIME have the prefix <t:>. This lets the parser (and the browser) know that SMIL 2.0 functionality should be associated with the element rather than HTML behavior. In order to understand the distinction between HTML and SMIL (HTML+TIME) code, consider, the following fragment:

```
 17   <t:seq>
 18     <t:par>
 19       <t:img src="M-HT/title.gif" class="R-Title"/>
 20       <t:seq >
 21         ...
130       <t:seq >
131     <t:par >
132   <t:seq >
```

All of these statements are preceded with the *t* namespace qualifier. The <t:par> and <t:seq> elements are obviously SMIL related; they have no HTML equivalents. The <t:img> element on line 19 is an example of an element which has an HTML equivalent type (that is, HTML also has its own <img> element, with an HTML-defined structure and behavior). The <t:img>

specification says that the SMIL definition should be used instead of the HTML one.

One of the challenges of constructing a hybrid HTML/SMIL implementation is the definition of overall temporal control of a presentation. In documents written for the SMIL Language profile, it is clear that a single temporal scope governs the entire document. HTML has no corresponding single temporal scope — each cluster of HTML+TIME specification defines an independent local timeline. Various parts of the HTML code are delineated by the HTML <div> element. This element is used to define the scope of an encapsulated timeline with the HTML file.

Media Objects

Media objects are referenced using the standard SMIL media elements. As expected, the use of each media reference (such as audio or video) is prefaced with the "*t:*" namespace qualifier. (See lines 19 and 57 for examples.) If transitions are used on media items, these are implemented using XHTML+SMIL's transition filters. Each transition (input or output) gets its own transition filter specification, which are bundled together with the associated media object in a parallel element.

```
49      <div class="time" timeContainer="par">
50          <t:video id="B_vid" src="M-HT/Bat.avi"
                systemBitrate="56120" class="R-image"/>
51          <t:transitionFilter type="fade" subtype="crossfade"
                dur="1" targetElement="B_vid" begin="B_vid.begin"
                mode="in" from="0" to="1"/>
52          <t:transitionFilter type="fade" subtype="crossfade"
                dur="1" targetElement="B_vid" begin="B_vid.end-1"
                mode="out" from="0" to="1"/>
53      </div>
```

In this fragment, a video object (on line 50) is given an input transition (on line 51) and an output transition (on line 52). All three of these statements are bundled into a separate timeline defined by the <div> on line 49. (This <div> defines a <par> time container; while it is valid to use a <t:par> element instead, this does not work in HTML+TIME's implementation.)

Layout

HTML+TIME does not use SMIL 2.0 Layout. Instead, it uses CSS to position objects. The use of CSS is especially handy for text, but CSS absolute positioning can also be applied to emulate SMIL's Basic Layout functionality. In CSS terms, each of these definitions define a class that can be used when positioning a media item. The class is referenced in a manner similar to the SMIL region attribute:

```
19          <t:img src="M-HT/title.gif" class="R-Title"/>
```

In our example, several CSS definitions are grouped in the style section; these define areas that correspond to SMIL's layout regions:

```
4    <style>
5       ...
6       .R-root-layout {position:absolute;overflow:hidden;
                 left:0;top:0;width:240;height:269;background-color:#ffffcc}
7       .R-Title {position:absolute;overflow:hidden;
                 left:0;top:0;width:240;height:29;}
8       .R-Image {position:absolute;overflow:hidden;
                 left:0;top:29;width:240;height:180}
9       .R-Buttons {position:absolute;overflow:hidden;
                 left:0;top:251;width:240;height:15}
10      .R-Text  {position:absolute;overflow:hidden;
                 left:0;top:209;width:240;height:42}
11      .R-Sound {}
12    </style>
```

Matters of syntax aside, there are no fundamental differences in layout capabilities for the translation of *Flashlight* into XHTML+SMIL.

Timing

XHTML+SMIL provides full support for SMIL 2.0 timing elements. This means that the <par>, <seq> and <excl> elements and their attributes are all supported. XHTML+SMIL supports interactive, event-based timing and also all other major aspects of SMIL time functionality.

This being said, HTML+TIME's implementation of XHTML+SMIL does not always manage the functionality within time containers in a predictable manner. Very often, local timelines need to be defined (using the <div> element to define a <par>, <seq> or <excl> time container) instead of being able to use the <t:par>, <t:seq> or <t:excl> elements. If you experience timing problems in implementing an HTML+TIME document, we suggest you experiment with both forms until you get the desired behavior.

Linking

The XHTML+SMIL specification provides full support for SMIL's temporal linking capabilities. Unfortunately, the HTML+TIME implementation provides no support for temporal linking. This means that all linking within a document to 't:' qualified elements will not work. Only the HTML <area> element (not the <t:area> element) are supported in HTML+TIME, but even these elements cannot be used to jump inside a time container. The reasons for this are complex: SMIL linking requires that substantial state information gets saved (or generated) regarding the state of the target element at the time the link is activated. Without having some notion of global time, it is very difficult to construct the appropriate state description.

The following fragment gives a description of how linking could be handled within an XHTML+SMIL application. (We use the '*xs:*' namespace qualifier in order not to confuse the fragment with the HTML+TIME implementation.)
(Note that SMIL does not require a map element definition, since all of the information needed is contained in the area elements that are children of the <t:img> element.)

```
<xs:img id="buttons_battery_m" src="M-HT/b-batteries.gif"
    class="R-Buttons" dur="20s"/>
  <xs:area id="ABI" href="#Intro" sourcePlaystate="stop"
    shape="rect" coords="39,0,91,15">
  <xs:area id="ABM" href="#More" sourcePlaystate="stop"
    shape="rect" coords="220,0,237,15">
<xs:/img>
```

The lack of linking support in HTML+TIME can, in part, be compensated by structuring the presentation as multiple children of an `<t:excl>` element and then applying event-based timing. We discuss this further in Chapter 13: *Advanced SMIL Timing Behavior and Control.*

Adaptivity

As XHTML+SMIL (and HTML+TIME) provide support for SMIL's basic content control functionality, no substantial changes need to be made to the *Flashlight* application. (See line 48 for an example of the use of the `<switch>` element.) In-line use of text attributes on individual HTML elements is not allowed because HTML has no notion of the `<switch>` element.

One area where SMIL and HTML layout differ is the ability to provide aliases for layout region/class names using the `regionName` attribute. This has a consequence for supporting multiple layouts within a single HTML+TIME document: since the name of the CSS class definition is fixed, it is not possible to define alternative layouts in a style section that use the same class names in each definition. As a result, it is not possible to have the document select a layout at parse time that is then applied to the document at execution time. This means that if multiple layouts need to be supported, multiple specifications of media objects need to be made each time a variable class would be referenced, all of which would have to be wrapped inside of a SMIL `<switch>` element.

Other Considerations

Microsoft's HTML+TIME implementation (using the *time2* behavior) is a solid attempt at integrating SMIL functionality within an existing HTML framework. Our impression is that while the implementation is not fully debugged, the general XHTML+SMIL approach may prove to be very useful in the future. The fact that it is integrated into the world's most wide distributed browser means that it is certainly worthwhile to investigate SMIL support within HTML using HTML+TIME (although such support will only work in Microsoft's IE-5/6 implementations).

> **Quick Tip**
>
> Example 2-5 focuses on the overall specification of the presentation and zooms in on the detailed specification of the Battery section; if you want to see the complete presentation, visit http://www.XmediaSMIL.net.

2.4 Summary and Conclusions

The purpose of this chapter has been to introduce the structure of SMIL 2.0 by walking though a complete SMIL 2.0 example. The application we selected represents a non-trivial collection of elements and attributes. It supports complex SMIL layout structures and it makes use of a variety of SMIL time containers.

The chapter also presented a translation of this example in to various SMIL 2.0 profiles, including the full SMIL 2.0 Language profile and its SMIL Basic, 3GPP SMIL and SMIL 1.0 versions. We also looked at creating an XHTML+SMIL version of the demonstration by looking at an implementation using Microsoft's HTML+TIME language.

The first SMIL applications you will write will probably only use a small subset of the features and concepts presented in this chapter. Still, by looking at a large SMIL presentation, we expect that you will have a better idea of how the various pieces of the SMIL language fit together.

Parts Two and Three of this book review each of the elements and attributes provided in this section — plus several constructs that we didn't cover here. Now that you have a general idea of how SMIL works, you can work through the various chapters in this book to get a complete idea on how you can work with SMIL 2.0.

Before jumping into the details of the language, we provide an additional background chapter next. This chapter reviews the essential elements of the Web architecture that are relevant to most SMIL presentations. If you are familiar with the Web, you can start with Chapter 4, but a review of common terminology and architecture can be helpful if you aren't exactly sure of the differences between language and protocols, or the distinctions among servers, networks and clients.

2.5 Further Resources

XML

Extensible Markup Language (XML) 1.0 (Second Edition), Tim Bray, Jean Paoli, C.M. Sperberg-McQueen and Eve Maler (eds), W3C Recommendation, 10 February 1998, `http://www.w3.org/TR/REC-xml`.

HTML

XHTML 1.0: The Extensible HyperText Markup Language (Second Edition), Steven Pemberton, (ed. chair), W3C Recommendation, 1 August 2002, `http://www.w3.org/TR/xhtml1`.

Namespaces in XML

Namespaces in XML, W3C Recommendation, `http://www.w3.org/TR/REC-xml-names/`.

SVG

Scalable Vector Graphics (SVG) 1.0 Specification, Jon Ferraiolo (ed.), W3C Recommendation, 4 September 2001, `http://www.w3.org/TR/SVG`.

URI

RFC 2396: Uniform Resource Identifiers (URI): Generic Syntax, Tim Berners-Lee, Roy Fielding, Larry Masinter, IETF (Internet Engineering Task Force), 1998, `http://www.ietf.org/rfc/rfc2396.txt`.

XML Base

XML *Base,* Jonathan Marsh (ed.), W3C Recommendation, 27 June 2001, `http://www.w3.org/TR/xmlbase/`.

3
Local and Streaming Media

SMIL allows you to take one or more media objects and integrate them into a single multimedia presentation. From SMIL's perspective, the location of the media — whether local or spread across the Web — is not particularly important. From a designer's perspective, however, there is a big difference between information that is stored locally and information that needs to be fetched from half-way across the network, especially when multiple media streams need to be synchronized.

This chapter gives background information on local and streaming media issues. It will help you understand the general organization issues that impact all media presentations. We begin with a discussion of media types and media formats. We then discuss conventions for referencing local and remote media. We conclude with a discussion of synchronization and streaming media issues.

Very little in this chapter involves the particular elements and attributes of SMIL. (These are the subject of the rest of this book.) Instead, we focus on understanding the basic — and potential problems and pitfalls — of media organization that will help you make more effective presentations.

3.1 Classification of Media

Most viewers of multimedia presentations would probably say that there are two kinds of multimedia media data: *fast* and *slow*. (This is a tremendous improvement over what users would have said a few years ago: *slow* and *loading*.) Presentations with "fast" assets load quickly and run seamlessly. Presentations with "slow" assets take forever to load and then rarely run without stopping or pausing. Unfortunately — or, perhaps fortunately — not all Web users experience the same network performance. Depending on the connections available, the same piece of media may load very quickly or very slowly.

Media engineers typically take a more technical approach to classifying media. Within this world, there are two media classes: *discrete* and *continuous*.

- *Discrete media*: media in which there is no inherent duration associated with presenting the media. Discrete media includes images, text and most (structured) graphics. Discrete media can be very large (such as a 1600x1024x32 image of a landscape) or it can be very small (such as a one-bit GIF image).

- *Continuous media*: media in which time plays an essential role. Continuous media includes audio, video and some animated graphics. A piece of continuous media usually consists of an ordered set of discrete media components, each of which is usually called a frame or a sample. Continuous media objects can be very large (such as 4 minutes of 1600x1024x32 video) or it can be relatively small (such as a 4 second sound file that is encoded at a very low bitrate).

Table 3-1 provides an overview of the sizes of various discrete and continuous media objects. Some media are hybrid types: an SVG (or Flash) animation consists of a timed sequence of discrete images. Since animations are typically fetched as a single block, they are usually treated as discrete media.

For a media perspective, there is no direct relationship between a media type (continuous or discrete) and a user's performance experience. It is tempting to think of continuous media as always presenting more resource use problems within a multimedia presentation than discrete media, but this is not necessarily true: discrete media typically needs to be presented all at once, while continuous media can be fetched and presented in semi-autonomous blocks. A large image may be "slower" than the same-sized streamed video object. Continuous media does present one problem that is not encountered with discrete media: continuous media requires strict inter-frame synchronization to ensure that media playback is "correct". (A video or audio object will lose its semantic meaning if information is not rendered at a constant rate.)

Media Type	Media Class	Size (Kbytes)
Text (1 pg, raw)	Discrete	5.1
Text (1 pg, formatted)	Discrete	51.2
Color image (256x256)	Discrete	65.5
Color image (full screen)	Discrete	3,100.1
Audio sequence (10 seconds)	Continuous	160.0
Audio sequence (1 minute)	Continuous	10,500.2
Video sequence (short)	Continuous	70,000.4
Video sequence (long)	Continuous	151,500.3

Table 3-1. Typical media object types, classes and sizes.

3.2 Media Formats and Encodings

One of the common frustrations for many new users of SMIL is that the language does not contain a default set of media formats that are supported by all SMIL players and browsers. There are several reasons why SMIL was forced to be media-agnostic: first (and foremost), at the time SMIL was specified, there was no set of common continuous media formats that were available on all platforms without some form of server or licensing restrictions. The W3C did not want to force organizations implementing SMIL to adopt proprietary media formats, especially if these were not freely available. Of course, the fact that several companies on the SMIL standardization committee each had commercial interests that precluded the definition of a common set of media types didn't help, either! (The problems of standardizing on media were also true for SVG and HTML, but since these formats make little or no use of continuous media, the issue was not as obvious as with SMIL.)

The media-agnostic nature of SMIL does not mean that the selection of media formats is not a key media concern. The main reason that media formats are important is that, in raw form, both discrete and continuous media are typically too large to efficiently retrieve, transfer and process across a digital network. Even a relatively small raw image of 320x240x8 bits can result in significant transfer times across low- and moderate-speed networks. They also require lots of storage space on network servers and clients. As a result, various forms of compression have been developed for different media types. The following sub-sections consider compressed media formats for both discrete and continuous media.

3.2.1 Media Formats for Compressed Discrete Media

The typical types of discrete media found in multimedia presentations are photographic images, computer-generated (artificial) images, animated images and text. While many formats for each of these media objects exist, there are several formats that have taken on the role of *de facto* standards that are supported by most SMIL players and browsers. The choices are summarized in Table 3-2.

| SMIL Profile | Player/ Browser | Images | | | Text |
		Photo	Artificial/ Bitmap	Vector/ Animation	
SMIL Language	RealOne	JPEG	PNG, GIF	Flash, SVG	RealText, Plain
	Ambulant	JPEG	PNG	SVG	Plain
	GRiNS	JPEG	PNG	Flash, SVG	Plain
SMIL Mobile	MMS-2	JPEG	GIF	---	Plain
	3GPP	JPEG	PNG, GIF	SVG-Tiny	Plain
SMIL 1.0	QuickTime	JPEG	PNG, GIF	Flash	QuickText
XHTML +*SMIL*	IE-6 (HTML+Time)	JPEG	PNG, GIF	Flash, SVG	Plain, HTML

Table 3-2. Preferred discrete media, per profile and player.

Photographic Images

JPEG (a compression standard developed by the Joint Pictures Expert Group) is currently the most widely used image format across the Web for photographic images. It has excellent compression characteristics that can be tailored to meet the needs of the image content. While compression ratios of between 10:1 to 50:1 are common with JPEG, this compression comes at a price: JPEG has a lossy compression algorithm, which means that at higher compression rates, the resulting image can be considerably less crisp and clean than the original. In practice, for Web uses this is rarely a problem unless the compressed image is resized (made larger) as part of a SMIL scaling operation. Since nearly all image processing packages — and all digital cameras — support JPEG, it should be the primary choice for photographic image media.

Another popular format for images is TIFF (the Tagged Image File Format). TIFF images have the advantage that they provide a loss-less encoding of the original image (which is useful if the image is to be resized), but even compressed TIFF files often are too large for use in Web-based multimedia.

Artificial Images

Where JPEG is useful for photographs, it is often less optimal for computer-generated bitmaps that contain simple geometries and large fields of solid colors. (Screen-dumps or images generated from raster data are typical examples.) For these images, the PNG (Portable Network Graphics) format is usually a better choice. PNG also supports complete and partial transparency — allowing an image to be overlaid or blended on top of another media object. PNG is an open, royalty-free format that is supported by nearly all SMIL renderers and image manipulation packages.

Another standard for bitmap images is GIF (the Graphic Image Format). GIF files are well-known and widely used, but unless you need the animation facilities in GIF that allow sequences of sub-images, it is not a particularly good format for future use. GIF uses licensed technology which may impede its implementation in some SMIL renderers.

Vector-Based Animated Images

Unlike bitmaps, which contain all of the bits rendered in the image, a vector format describes shapes based on end-points, line segments, line thickness and fill colors. As a result, vector files describe how an image is to be generated rather than containing a painted version of the image itself. This often makes the size of vector images small — and, more importantly, it provides an ability to resize the image without quality loss.

There are two formats in wide use that support vector-based images: SVG and Flash. SVG is an open standard from W3C (the same people who brought you HTML and SMIL), while Flash is a closed standard that is controlled by Macromedia. Both SVG and Flash are usually supported in SMIL players via plug-in renderers. Many small devices are committed to supporting the SVG-Tiny profile.

A choice between SVG and Flash will most often rest on philosophical rather than technical grounds. While Flash encodings can be more compact than SVG — this because Flash uses a binary rather than text encoding format — some SMIL players/browsers provide native implementations of SVG, which means that parts of the timing of the SVG media can be controlled using SMIL's constructs. The ultimate choice between the formats will often rest on the availability of plug-in renderers for each format within a SMIL player/browser.

An alternative to both SVG and Flash is MPEG-4. MPEG-4 is a complete media encoding and scheduling solution that contains aspects of functionality found in both SMIL and SVG/Flash. Unlike SMIL, which uses a user-editable open format, MPEG-4 packages all media content in a closed, final-form format. In practice, mixing the use of SMIL and MPEG-4 is probably not very useful, although there are advantages to transforming SMIL into MPEG-4 and vice versa.

Plain and Formatted Text

In theory, text would seem like a very portable, ubiquitous media type. In practice, rendering formatted text in many media players is a difficult and resource consuming task that is usually minimally supported. The main reason for this is that the support for scalable fonts and text-based re-flow of content based on dynamic margins is very resource intensive. For all practical purposes, formatted text data is usually encoded as an image in PNG or GIF format. Small amount of incidental text can be encoded directly in the player's base font, but this is the exception rather than the rule on other than very small devices.

Alternatives for formatting text are the use of SVG or XHTML. Both of these solutions require activating external renderers. For this reason, unless lots of text is presented in the presentation, image encoding of text is usually used in the SMIL Language and Mobile profiles. Implementations of the XHTML+SMIL profile are much more suited to including large amounts of text. Note that the use of text for captions is typically done by treating text as a continuous media object. See *Timed Text* on page 61.

3.2.2 Media Formats for Compressed Continuous Media

The typical types of continuous media found in multimedia presentations are video clips, audio files and timed text. There are several formats available for each of these media types, but unlike discrete media, there has been little standardization in the use of continuous media. The principal barriers to standardization remain technology licensing issues and format compatibility with proprietary streaming media servers.

Apart from the issue of standardization, the primary distinguishing factor for the processing of continuous media is the transfer model used by the format. As we discuss more fully in *Accessing Media Within a SMIL Presentation* on page 65, two alternatives exist: a *download-and-play* model and a *streaming* model. While most streaming media servers can provide some measure of streaming support for nearly all media types, these servers often work best when they stream the — often proprietary — formats that were specially developed for the server.

In the following discussion, we consider both download-and-play and streaming media formats.

Audio

There are dozens of download-and-play audio formats but only relatively few streaming audio formats that can be used in a wide range of media players. The audio format selected will be driven by the type of platform being used and the type of audio being encoded. Table 3-3 lists the major formats supported by platform and player at the time this book was written. Note that many mobile players will support proprietary media formats (such as RealAudio or Windows Media) if the service provider has made special technology licensing deals with either RealNetworks or Microsoft.

SMIL Profile	Player/ Browser	Speech Audio		Music Audio	
		Download-and-Play	Streamed	Download-and-Play	Streamed
SMIL Language	RealOne	MP3	RealAudio	MP3	RealAudio, MP3
	Ambulant	MP3	Ogg Vorbis	MP3	Ogg Vorbis
	GR*i*NS	MP3	.rm, .wmf	MP3	.rm, wmf
SMIL Mobile	MMS-2	AMR	---	MIDI	---
	3GPP	AMR	--	MIDI	Impl. Dependent
SMIL 1.0	QuickTime	AIFF	AIFF	MP3	MP3
XHTML +SMIL	IE-6 (HTML+Time)	WAV	WM	MP3	WM

Table 3-3. Preferred audio media, per profile and player.

Video

As with audio, video can be either downloaded in its entirety before use or it can be streamed to a player/browser. While many video formats exist, the most common formats across the Web are: MPEG-1/2/4, AVI and RealVideo. Table 3-4 provides an overview of the primary and secondary formats available on major platforms as of the writing of this book. Note that MPEG-based formats can use a variety of codes and support a range of bitrates. Not all players may support all variants.

Timed Text

As mentioned above, most incidental text in multimedia presentations (such as headings and titles) will be formatted as bitmap images. An exception to this is the use of timed text for captions. Captioning has often been embedded within video media objects (so-called closed captions), but SMIL allows multiple caption objects to be specified within a media file as peer-level media objects. The advantage of this approach is that captions can be supported in multiple languages or at multiple levels of detail, and that the end-user can choose whether — and which — captions are visible.

Most of the solutions supported for captioning of content have been proprietary. Of these, *RealText* (developed by RealNetworks), *QuickText* (developed by Apple Computer) and *SAMI* (supported by Microsoft) are the most widely used. In mid-2002, the W3C started an activity on standardizing on a common timed-text format based on general SMIL timing constructs.

Table 3-4 provides a summary of timed text options available under various platforms and profiles. For those organizations participating in the W3C Timed Text activity, this format has been listed as a secondary format under the name TTF.

SMIL Profile	Player/ Browser	Video		Timed Text
		Download- and-Play	Streamed	
SMIL Language	RealOne	MPEG-2	RealVideo	RealText, TTF
	Ambulant	Div-X	Div-X	TTF
	GRiNS	MP4	.rm	.rt
SMIL Mobile	MMS-2	---	---	---
	3GPP	H.263	Impl. Dependent	Impl. Dependent
SMIL 1.0	QuickTime	MPEG-2	MPEG-4	QuickText
XHTML +SMIL	IE-6 (HTML+Time)	AVI	MPEG-4	SAMI

Table 3-4. Preferred video and timed text media, per profile and player.

3.2.3 Tools for Creating Media

The most time consuming part of making multimedia presentations is usually creating the media objects, not the SMIL file. While a detailed consideration of media creation is beyond the scope of this book, Table 3-5 lists a number of tools and software packages that can be used to create and edit media.

Media	Type	Formats	Software Tools	Hardware Tools
Images	Photo	JPEG, TIFF	Adobe Photoshop, miscl image editors	Dig. Cameras, Scanners
	Artificial	PNG, GIF		Scanners, tablets
	Vector	SVG Flash	Adobe Illustrator, Corel Draw Macromedia Flash	--
Text	Plain	txt (X)HTML	text editor Dreamweaver, Go Live!	--
	Timed	RealText, SAMI	Magpie	proprietary
Audio	Download	mp3, wav, aiff	SoundForge, MediaCleaner	Microphone, mixer panel, equalizers
	Streaming	RealAudio		
Video	Download	MPEG, AVI	Adobe Premiere, MediaCleaner	Dig. Video Camera Firewire
	Streaming	RealVideo WMV		

Table 3-5. Representative media creation tools.

3.3 URIs: Locating and Naming Media Objects

Once media objects have been created, they need to be named and placed at a location somewhere in the distribution environment. The *URI (Uniform Resource Identifier)* is a standardized syntax for identifying and locating such resource. SMIL, and other W3C Recommendations such as HTML and SVG, often use URIs as values for attributes that locate information, typically for presentation to the user. Figure 3-1 shows the basic components of a URI. The three core components of an Internet URI are the *scheme*, which states the protocol to use for transferring the media object, the *server*, which gives the name of the computer holding the media, and the *path*, which says where on the server the media is stored.

In this section, we go over three types of URIs: URIs to files stored on the local computer, URIs to resources stored across the Internet and URIs that are relative to a shared base location.

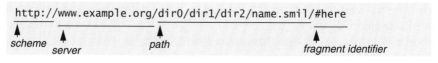

Figure 3-1. The basic components of a URI

3.3.1 Local URIs

The simplest type of URI specifies a file on the file system local to the browser. Such a local system path-name has the URI scheme prefix "file://", followed by a third slash and the path (without a server) to ensure that URI processors recognize it as a local path-name. (Note that the server name is included between the second and third slashes, but because this name is blank, it takes up no space!) If desired, a name of localhost may be used.

Presentations that use local file URIs are not portable — they only work on computers with the given files. This is fine for local presentations not using the Web, such as overhead presentations for groups or presentations distributed on CD-ROMs. However, SMIL presentations posted on the Web for playback at any location should not use local file URIs.

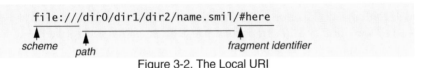

Figure 3-2. The Local URI

3.3.2 Remote URIs

Internet URIs can locate any object on the Web from anywhere on the Web. They are crucial for presentations that can play from any connected computer. In the bullets below, we discuss how URI schemes, servers and paths are used with remote URIs:

- *URI schemes*: The scheme of a URI states what protocol is being used to transfer the file or resource from the server to the browser. The server computer needs to know not just what to send, but how to send it, and the scheme tells the server how. The most commonly used transfer protocol on the Web is HTTP (Hypertext Transfer Protocol); this is a download-and-play protocol. This protocol goes with the URI prefix "http://".

  As a multimedia format, SMIL often incorporates streaming media, for which a streaming protocol is required. The streaming protocol most often used is RTSP (Real Time Streaming Protocol); this protocol allows incremental downloading and playback of media. This protocol goes with the URI prefix "rtsp://".

- *URI servers*: The second component of a typical URI is the server name. This is the name of the computer on the Internet that holds the media being retrieved. It tells the browser which computer on the Internet it must communicate with to get the media item.

- *URI paths*: The server uses the path to determine what from its system to send. This path is typically a path-name for a directory or file on the server's local file system. It can, however, be instead another type of string that the server can process to determine a media item to return.

- *URI fragment identifiers*: Fragment identifiers are placed after the '#' characters in the path name; they locate portions, or fragments, of files. Their typical use in SMIL is as named components of XML files, particularly HTML, SMIL and SVG. The effect of loading a named fragment of any of these files for display is that the whole presentation is loaded and its presentation state is "forwarded" to the located fragment. (How this "forwarding" occurs depends on the format). Fragment identifiers are not part of the URI.

Some players allow URIs to be extended with embedded parameters. SMIL has a separate mechanism to support such parameter passing, as described on page 65.

3.3.3 Relative URIs

The URIs presented up to now have been *absolute URIs*. An absolute URI by itself contains all the information needed to locate its resource from anywhere on the Web. *Relative URIs* are incomplete addresses that are applied to a base URI to complete the location. The portions omitted are the URI scheme and server, and potentially part of or all of the URI path as well.

The primary benefit of using relative URIs is that documents and the directories containing them can be moved or copied to other locations without requiring changing the URI attribute values within the documents — easing Web site maintenance. (However, these particular benefits assume the default behavior of relative URI paths.)

There are three types of relative URI specifications in SMIL: *internal URI references*, *relative paths* and xml:base *paths*.

- *Internal URI references:* URIs that begin with '#' characters are internal URI references. Such a reference locates some portion of the current document, unless overridden by an xml:base attribute assignment.

- *Relative URI paths:* Relative URI paths are typically used as a short means of locating media files stored in the same directory as the current document, or in a directory close to it. They often consist of just the filename (optionally with a fragment identifier into that file). They can also have a relative directory path before the filename.

- xml:base *paths:* By default, the base URI for a relative URI is the location of the current document. The xml:base attribute overrides this default: it explicitly sets a base location from which relative paths can be constructed. Use of this attribute enables, for example, the media for a presentation to be loaded from a media repository somewhere else on the Web than the SMIL document's site. Thus, no matter where on the Web the SMIL presentation is copied or moved to, it will get its media content from the same repository. Furthermore, if the media repository is moved, then only changing the single xml:base assignment is necessary to update the referencing of multiple src and href attributes.

```
hello.txt
file:///hello.txt
http://www.example.org/hello.txt
rtsp://www.example.org/hello.rm
data:,Greetings!
```

Example 3-1. Valid URI constructs for locating and referencing media.

Example 3-1 provides examples of URI structures. The SMIL-related aspects of URI use are discussed in Chapter 5: *Referencing Media Objects*.

3.3.4 Passing Parameters in URIs

The purpose of a URI is to locate and identify a network resource, such as a media object. In practice, simply pointing to a media object is often not enough to activate an efficient transfer between a server and a client. Many network protocols allow extensions to the URI to support the passing of transfer control parameters. These often are structured as query strings (that is, they contain a '?' followed by a set of expressions such as: lang=NL). These strings are placed at the end of the location of the resource. SMIL defines the <param> element to provide a more structured means of passing parameters to media servers (or to other parts of a presentation). For details, see *<param>* on page 252.

3.4 Accessing Media Within a SMIL Presentation

The continuous and discrete media objects used in a SMIL presentation can be stored on the same computer as the SMIL player (this is called *local media*) or it can be stored on a server somewhere across the network (this is *remote media*). All media is accessed via a URI (a uniform resource identifier). Local media is usually accessed via the local file system. Remote media can be accessed via a network file system, or via a streaming server.

3.4.1 Local access to media

It is tempting to think of local media as being fast and free (in the resource-use sense of 'free'), but this is only the case for desktop systems with large local disks. For systems within limited local storage, media assets can also be placed on local removable storage devices (such as CD-ROMs), but doing so will result in media that takes longer to load and access than would be the case on a local disk.

On mobile devices, such as PDAs and telephones, local access is further limited by the fact that storage size is severely limited, and the fact that the storage space that is available is relatively slow. (Slower devices typically use less battery power.)

While most SMIL presentations will be constructed to use remote media, local storage can provide an attractive alternative in some situations:

- *CD-ROM distribution*: the oldest media presentations were CD-ROM based, but even modern presentations (such as games or encyclopedias) are often distributed via hard-copy media. This is done for both commercial reasons (to protect the contents) and because of performance constraints.
- *Pre-loaded distribution*: for some applications, such as music, movies or hourly sports/news summaries, an interesting distribution model is pre-loaded local storage. Here, the entire presentation (plus assets) are pre-loaded onto a portable device (such as a PDA or higher-end telephone) over a possibly long period of time — overnight, or while the device sits passively in a desktop cradle. The presentation can then be accessed locally by the user while away from the network connection — such as on a bicycle, in a car or on an airplane.

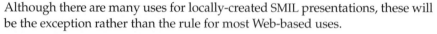

Although there are many uses for locally-created SMIL presentations, these will be the exception rather than the rule for most Web-based uses.

3.4.2 Remote Access to Media

SMIL was originally created to manage the presentation of media assets in a network environment. This involves integrating an architecture for standard resource naming (that is, providing a way to reference media objects) and defining a set of temporal and spatial rules for governing when and where the presentation client presents those objects. Given the diversity of Web information servers, client playback environment and the heterogeneity of the Internet itself, SMIL also gave early attention to facilities for customizing a presentation so that it can adapt to the resources and restrictions present when the SMIL file is activated.

Individual assets can be downloaded in their entirety during a presentation, or they can be fetched incrementally via a streaming server. Without streaming, remote access combines all the disadvantages of the local media (a lot of space is required to hold complete copies of media) with the disadvantages of the network (you need to wait a long time before all your media is present). For single media presentations — presentations that consist of a single audio or video file — some of the local storage and network delay problems can be minimized by using highly compressed formats, but this approach does not scale well if the presentation has lots of media components. It also isn't optimal for wireless and low-resource devices, because the transmission delay can still be substantial for whole media and the storage requirements too taxing for the device.

We consider various remote access issues in the following sections.

The Network Infrastructure

From the perspective of the user, there are two important aspects of the connection to 'the network': the speed of the connection itself and the connection model, or the method in which the user is attached to the infrastructure.

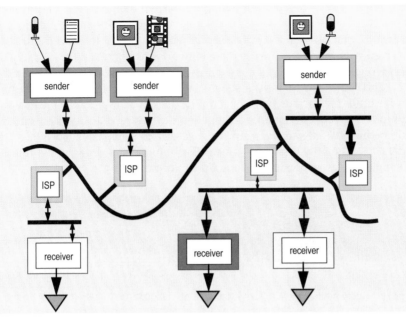

Figure 3-3. An overview of the network environment.
(The [Internet] backbone is not as homogeneous as shown.)

For remote multimedia, two connection models have dominated: one is where each client has direct internet connection (perhaps via a private local area network) and the other is the indirect connection to the network through a modem and a (wireless) telephone line. In both cases, a local internet service provider (ISP) connects the user to the network: this ISP can cache multimedia data — usually under contract with an information provider — or it can simply provide pass-through access to information that is transferred via a hierarchy of ISPs.

For most purposes, the connection through multiple levels of ISPs is transparent to the user, but it brings with it a performance penalty: the greater the number of intermediate ISPs, the greater the delay that is generated through the network. (For a typical connection from Amsterdam to Cambridge, England, it is not unusual to go through 15 levels of connections between the source and destination.) For non-trivial presentations, there may be several data paths through the network active concurrently. For example, a piece of video may come from a server in California, but the associated Dutch subtitles may come from a site in Amsterdam. The delay characteristics of each connection will likely vary considerably.

The transfer speed of any one connection is determined by the *available* bandwidth of each of the active network links and the processing power of both the source and destination to service any single request. For some transfers, even a very fast connection will not improve the perceived performance from server to client *if* the server is not able to process all requests adequately. On the other hand, even a very fast server will not be able to provide adequate perceived response if the intermediate network link(s) are not free to carry the data involved.

A bandwidth comparison is shown in Table 3-6 along with the resulting transfer times for various types of complex data. It is important to realize that the future expected acceptance of wireless devices as delivery platforms for multimedia will effectively result in a return to connection speeds of the mid-1990's. The only justifiable conclusion that one can draw is: the Internet will remain heterogeneous for a long time to come.

Data Type	Size (Kbytes)	Access Time			
		Mobile Modem[a]	ISDN[b]	Cable Modem[c]	ADSL[d]
Text (1 pg, raw)	5	0:00:01.71	0:00:00.42	0:00:00.01	0:00:00.00
Text (1 pg, formatted)	51	0:00:21.39	0:00:05.34	0:00:00.10	0:00:00.05
Color image (256x256)	65	0:00:27.30	0:00:06.83	0:00:00.15	0:00:00.07
Color image (full screen)	3,100	0:21:50.72	0:05:27.50	0:00:07.25	0:00:03.50
Audio sequence (10 sec.)	160	0:01:06.66	0:00:16.43	0:00:00.41	0:00:00.16
Audio sequence (1 minute)	10,500	0:58:40.00	0:14:39.12	0:00:23.43	0:00:11.73
Video sequence (short)	70,000	6:28:53.34	1:37:12.75	0:02:46.31	0:01:17.78
Video sequence (long)	151,500	42:00:00.00	9:58:51.67	2:52:48.73	1:23:20.00

Table 3-6. Comparative speeds of transfer technologies.
[a] Assuming a 28.8Kb Modem with an average transfer rate of 3KByte/second.
[b] Assuming a 128Kb Modem with an average transfer rate of 14KByte/second.
[c] Assuming a 4Mb Modem with an average transfer rate of 450KByte/second.
[d] Assuming a 8Mb Modem with an average transfer rate of 900KByte/second.

Network Protocols and Media Access

The current Internet can be partitioned by the protocols it uses to transfer information among its constituent computers. These are TCP (the *Transport Control Protocol*) and IP (the *Internet Protocol*). All computers that connect to the Internet use these protocols, which were developed in the late 1960's and early 1970's to handle (relatively) small amounts of text-based network traffic.

The early Internet was used to send files and e-mail messages as bulk, batch transfers. When the Web became popular in the mid-1990's, the Internet began to be used for massive on-line access to formatted information. This informa-

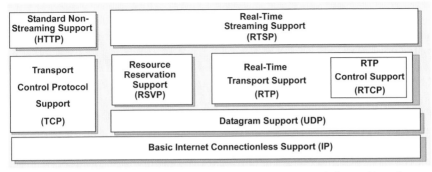

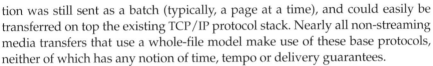

Figure 3-4. Types and relationships among network protocols for multimedia.

tion was still sent as a batch (typically, a page at a time), and could easily be transferred on top the existing TCP/IP protocol stack. Nearly all non-streaming media transfers that use a whole-file model make use of these base protocols, neither of which has any notion of time, tempo or delivery guarantees.

When the first multimedia computers arrived in the early 1990's, it became clear that new protocols were needed to guide continuous data from servers to clients. In order to address these needs, several new protocols were developed to provide support for streaming media. IP is still in wide use, and remains the dominant backbone protocol of the Internet. Above IP in the protocol stack comes a very simple protocol for packaging user data called *user datagram protocol*, UDP. (UDP is also a first-generation Internet protocol that has regained favor because of its lightweight nature.) Above these are streaming protocols: the *real-time streaming protocol* RTSP, the *resource reservation protocol* RSVP, and the combined *real-time transfer* and *real-time control protocols* RTP/RTCP. The full protocol stack is summarized in Figure 3-4.

Using these protocols, a server can request a guaranteed amount of bandwidth to be reserved before a transfer starts (using RSVP), then package the information for 'real time' transfer using RTP/RTSP and then allow information to be incrementally given to the user via RTSP. At present, some form of each of these protocols is in use.

Unfortunately, these streaming protocols have brought new problems to the Internet. Consider RSVP. Without going into detail on how the protocol works, it is obvious that the notion of resource reservation presents a concern for the various hub ISPs that make up the Internet backbone. The core issue is that if one customer says "please reserve 5% of your capacity for me for my use in the (near) future", the hub ISP has a major problem: it has no guarantee that the server will actually use the reserved bandwidth and it has no way of deciding among reservation requests when they arrive. For this reason, substantial use of resource reservation will not be seen across the generic Internet very soon. The resource reservation potential for mobile and wireless units is greater. This is a consequence of the lower bandwidth available at the device (meaning that without some sort of resource management, the entire infrastructure will collapse) and the fact that more of a substantial portion of the delivery infrastructure is managed by single, large entities who can impose their own management policies.

Another problem comes with RTP and RTCP. Unlike TCP, UDP and IP, RTP/RTCP are *framework* protocols. RTP does not specify how to move data between a server and a client in 'real time', it simply defines how a server and client are to format their requests. There is no guarantee that all servers and clients will support the same dialects of RTP and RTCP, which may make the protocols useless for the general Internet community. Considering the time it has taken for TCP/IP to become standard parts of computer system support, it may take some time before general end-to-end support for continuous media is available.

Streaming servers and streaming media encoding

While generic support for streaming media using open protocols seems to be a distant vision, special proprietary implementations of streaming media support dominate Internet media use. These implementations typically combine proprietary media compression implementations with proprietary implementations and extensions to basic RTP/RTSP/RTCP protocols. The proprietary nature of these implementations guarantees a high-degree of end-to-end compatibility for users of the media formats, but it also provides a lock into various media player vendors such as Apple, Microsoft and RealNetworks. This makes it difficult for third party media players and media infrastructures to break into the Internet infrastructure.

3.5 Summary and Conclusion

The SMIL specification makes very little demands on the data types and protocols used to transfer media between clients and servers. At the same time, since it imposes no restrictions, it also can't provide guarantees that every SMIL player will be able to play every SMIL presentation. This situation may be a short-term problem. The wireless market is providing a measure of openness in the multimedia protocol market. These vendors, who compete based on connect time instead of media encoding, want to have a wide-open network for data (but they want the delivery pipeline to be as closed as possible!). If the wireless world is able to have a major commercial impact, it may also result in a more open desktop Internet as well.

3.6 Further Resources

HTTP Specification

Hypertext Transfer Protocol, Version 1.1. W3C RFC-2616, June 1999.
`http://www.w3.org/Protocols/rfc2616/rfc2616.html`.

IP Specification

Internet Protocol (IP). IETF RFC-791, September 1981.
`http://www.ietf.org/rfc/rfc0791.txt`.

TCP Specification

Transmission Control Protocol (TCP). IETF RFC-793, September 1981.
`http://www.ietf.org/rfc/rfc0791.txt`

UDP Specification

User Datagram Protocol (UDP), IETF RFC-768, August 1980.
`http://www.ietf.org/rfc/rfc0768.txt`

RSVP Specification

Resource ReSerVation Protocol (RSVP) -- Version 1 Functional Specification, IETF
RFC-2205, September 1997. `http://www.ietf.org/rfc/rfc2205.txt`

RTP Specification

A Transport Protocol for Real-Time Applications (RTP), IETF RFC-3550, July 2003.
`http://www.ietf.org/rfc/rfc3550.txt`

RTSP Specification

Real Time Streaming Protocol (RTSP), IETF RFC-2326, April 1998.
`http://www.ietf.org/rfc/rfc2326.txt`

Ambulant Player

For information on the SMIL 2.0 compatible Ambulant player, see:
`http://www.ambulantPlayer.org/Player/`.

GRiNS Player

For information on the SMIL 2.0 compatible GRiNS player, see:
`http://www.oratrix.com/`.

Quicktime Player

For information on the SMIL 1.0 compatible QuickTime player, see:
`http://www.apple.com/quicktime/`.

RealNeworks RealOne Player

For information on the SMIL 2.0 Language Profile compatible RealOne player, see: http://www.real.com/.

HTML+TIME Browser

For information on the SMIL 2.0 XHTML+SMIL compatible HTML+TIME player, see:
http://msdn.microsoft.com/library/default.asp?url=/workshop/author/behaviors/reference/time2/htime_node_entry.asp.

Part Two

Basic SMIL Constructs

This part covers the basic functionality of SMIL 2.0. The elements and attributes described in chapters 4 through 9 probably will constitute 90% of the standard SMIL use. Nearly all of the material in this part can be used with the SMIL Language profile (including desktop and mobile SMIL) and — with the exception of layout — with XHTML+SMIL as well.

Topics Covered

Chapter 4 takes an in-depth look at the overall structure of a SMIL presentation. We describe the elements and attributes that are needed to encode the framework of a presentation in the various SMIL profiles. We also look at the XML facilities available to make a SMIL presentation future-proof.

Chapter 5 considers the inclusion of media assets in a presentation. It describes how media are classified, how they are referenced and how they are controlled from within a SMIL presentation. We look at the various types of media references supported by SMIL and the timing consequences of adding media to presentations.

Chapter 6 describes the basic facilities supported by all SMIL 2.0 Language profile versions for creating and managing presentation layout. We look at the layout elements and attributes in the head section and then consider how these elements can be applied to various types of media.

Chapter 7 provides a description of the temporal control of media objects within a SMIL presentation. We look at the basic time containers used by SMIL and then consider the basic set of timing attributes available to SMIL authors. This chapter covers the timing assets most used in basic SMIL presentations, in all SMIL profiles.

Chapter 8 describes the linking facilities in SMIL. It starts with a discussion of how links are used in HTML and then contrasts this with the time-driven linking facilities available in SMIL 2.0. It considers how SMIL defines anchors and link attributes and illustrates how SMIL linking can be used for message passing and activation.

Chapter 9 provides an overview of basic content control facilities within a SMIL presentation. It starts with background information on content selection and then describes the elements and attributes that SMIL provides that allow a presentation to be tailored to the needs of the network infrastructure and the target player.

 Chapter 10 concludes this part with a discussion of the visual transitions provided in SMIL 2.0. We begin with examples of transition effects and then look at how transitions can be defined. We then look at the elements and attributes provided by SMIL for basic and in-line specification of transitions for all media.

Goals

By the time you complete this part, you should be able to author presentations that make use of all of SMIL's basic multimedia presentation structuring facilities. You will also be able to understand and maintain SMIL presentations written by others for the various SMIL 2.0 profiles. The key to this part is that we only consider attributes and elements that are widely supported by SMIL's various players and profiles.

Prerequisites

In order to get the most out of this part, you should have read and understood the material in Part One of this book. You should also be able to open an existing SMIL presentation and send it to one of the major SMIL players for rendering.

4
SMIL Structure

This chapter provides an overview of the facilities provided by SMIL to encode the basic document structure. While most SMIL constructs define specific aspects of interactive multimedia presentation, a few constructs function to hold the others together. These constructs define a SMIL presentation's *structure*, and typically belong to the SMIL 2.0 Structure Module. We discuss these "structure bearing" constructs in the following subsections.

We begin this chapter with a quick review of basic SMIL structure issues. We then look at the element and attributes provided to support SMIL structure. We strongly recommend that you read Chapter 2: *Understanding SMIL 2.0 Code* before you start with the material in this chapter.

SMIL structure isn't very exciting: no fancy demos or intricate examples. Still, if the structure part of your presentation isn't right, you'll never see a bit of media data on the screen!

4.1 SMIL Language Structure Issues

Documents that use SMIL as their host language (such as presentations built for mobile telephones or the RealOne desktop player) require a framework in which the various parts of the SMIL declaration can be placed. As with most XML languages, this framework consists of some specification glue and two main document sections: the *head* and the *body* sections.

Chapter 2 gave a general example of a SMIL presentation. The document structure used in that presentation is reproduced here in Example 4-1. Line 1 specifies a *document type declaration*; this defines an XML class of the document that provides the name and location of the DTD to which the document con-

```
1 <!DOCTYPE smil PUBLIC "-//W3C//DTD SMIL 2.0//EN"
                        "http://www.w3.org/TR/REC-smil/SMIL20.dtd">
2 <smil xmlns="http://www.w3.org/2001/SMIL20/Language">
3  <head>
    . . .
17 </head>
18 <body>
    . . .
83 </body>
84 </smil>
```

Example 4-1. The basic structure of a SMIL presentation.

forms. This document type declaration also states that "smil" is the type of the document's top-most element.

> **Quick Tip**
>
> Although many players support a default document type declaration, you should get in the habit of defining the document type declaration explicitly. This will future-proof your presentations.

The document type declaration is followed by the root of the XML document tree. For SMIL documents, this is the <smil> element, as shown on line 2. The <smil> element is not optional for SMIL host language documents, and may only be used in profiles that are legal derivatives of the SMIL 2.0 (and 1.0) Language specification. The <smil> element is usually also used to identify optional parts of a document through XML *namespace* declarations.

The <smil> element contains at most two children: one <head> element and one <body> element (lines 3 and 18 of Example 4-1.). The <head> element is used to encode general parts of the specification that are either processed externally or are referenced in the body section. The <body> element is the base of the SMIL timing structure.

4.2 SMIL Structure Elements and Attributes

This section considers SMIL's structure elements. We start with a closer look at the document type declaration (which is actually not really an XML element, but a reference to the type of document being processed) and then consider the three elements defined by the SMIL structure module.

4.2.1 SMIL Document Type Declarations

As a meta-language, SMIL represents a family of XML-defined formats. Each of these family members is, from the XML perspective, a separate document class, and thus has a separate document type declaration at the beginning of each of its documents. Examples 4-2, 4-3 and 4-4 present the four main document type declarations that you are likely to find when working with SMIL documents.

```
1 <!DOCTYPE smil PUBLIC "-//W3C//DTD SMIL 2.0//EN"
                "http://www.w3.org/TR/REC-smil/SMIL20.dtd">
```

Example 4-2. Typical starting line for native SMIL documents.

```
1 <!DOCTYPE svg PUBLIC "-//W3C//DTD SVG 1.0//EN"
              "http://www.w3.org/TR/2001/REC-SVG-20010904/DTD/svg10.dtd"
```

Example 4-3. Typical starting line for SVG documents.

```
1 <!DOCTYPE html PUBLIC "-//W3C//DTD XHTML+SMIL //EN"
                "http://www.w3.org/2001/SMIL20/WD/xhtmlplussmil.dtd"
```

Example 4-4. Typical starting line for XHTML+SMIL documents

```
2 <smil xmlns="http://www.w3.org/2001/SMIL20/Language">
```

Example 4-5. Typical host language line for native SMIL documents.

Each DOCTYPE declaration contains the name of the XML root element used to encode SMIL functionality: this is *smil* for languages based on SMIL 1.0 or on various profiles of the SMIL 2.0 Language specification (including desktop and mobile SMIL), *svg* for SMIL animation functionality embedded in the SVG language, and *html* for SMIL 2.0 functionality included in a XHTML+SMIL-compliant player.

The DOCTYPE specification also includes the name and location of the document type definition (DTD) specification that the player's parser should use to process the file containing SMIL functionality. The DOCTYPE should match the profile specified and any extensions. The default DTD for each profile may only be used if no namespace or custom extensions have been applied.

The mechanisms used to define document classes are *Document Type Definitions (DTDs)* and *Schemas*. The DTD is the older type of document class specification. Schemas, which are more descriptive, are gradually replacing DTDs. Since SMIL was developed just between the DTD and Schema eras, SMIL defines its syntax using both.

4.2.2 SMIL Top-Level Structure Containers

This section describes the <smil>, <head> and <body> elements.

Element: <smil>

Every native SMIL document has a <smil> element as its root. The element indicates that the document is a SMIL *host language document*, and not a media-based SMIL document such as XHTML+SMIL or SVG. The <smil> element's place in SMIL structure is shown in Table 4-1.

<smil>		Profiles			
attributes	core	L	M	B	1
	xmlns				
children	<head>	L	M	B	1
	<body>				

Table 4-1. The <smil> element's place in SMIL structure.

The content of the <smil> element is always the same: first one <head> element, followed by one <body> element, and that's it. Like all SMIL elements, the <smil> element can have attributes drawn from SMIL *core attribute set*. (See page 80.) In addition, the <smil> element uses the xmlns attribute: the namespace declaration specifies which elements and attributes the document supports, and where a definition of these attributes can be found. There will always be a namespace definition for the base SMIL functionality; you may also need to include namespaces for each set of extension attributes in a document.

Examples 4-5, 4-6 and 4-7 show how SMIL functionality is defined for the major different host language specifications using SMIL. The namespace definitions for these contain a URI pointing to the location where the namespace is defined, optionally preceded with a namespace qualifier that can be used to

```
2 <svg xmlns="http://www.w3.org/2000/svg">
```

Example 4-6. Typical host language line for native SVG documents.

```
2 <html xmlns="http://www.w3.org/1999/xhtml"
        xmlns:smil="http://www.w3.org/2001/SMIL20">
```

Example 4-7. Typical host language line for native XHTML+SMIL documents.

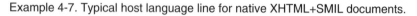

identify elements and attributes as belonging to the (non-default) namespace. For example, the XML namespace declaration in Example 4-7 defines two namespaces: the (default) HTML namespace and the *smil* namespace. All SMIL elements and attributes in the HTML document will be prefixed with the *smil* tag to identify them as being SMIL-specific. For example, the SMIL <par> element could be specified in an XHTML+SMIL document using the starting lines in Example 4-7 as:

```
<smil:par>
```

instead of the

```
<par>
```

used in SMIL host language documents.

Note that SVG documents containing SMIL animation do not need to reference the SMIL 2.0 specification, since SMIL animation functionality in SVG is included in the SVG specification.

> **Quick Tip**
>
> Players that support SMIL 2.0 functionality are required to enforce namespace use. If you don't specify a namespace, then your presentation will usually default to SMIL 1.0 elements and attributes — this is usually not what you want! To avoid this, always specify the correct XML namespace.

Element: <head>

The <head> element contains descriptive information about the presentation as a whole and defines resources for use throughout the presentation. It contains definitions for transitions and custom test attributes, meta-data about the presentation as a whole and the presentation's spatial layout. The <head> element structure and contents is shown in Table 4-2.

The <head> element accepts only the core set of SMIL attributes (see page 80).

<head>		Profiles			
attributes	core	L	M	B	1
parents	<smil>	L	M	B	1
children	<layout>			B	1
	<switch>		M		
	<transition>	L			
	<customTest>				
	<meta>		M	B	1
	<metadata>				

Table 4-2. The <head> element.

```
<head>
  <meta/>
  <customTest/>
  <meta/>
  <metadata/>
  <meta/>
  <layout> .. </layout>
  <meta/>
  <transition>
<head>
```

Example 4-8. Ordering of child elements in the <head>.

Note that the <head> element — in addition to meta-data, layout, transitions and custom tests — also accepts the SMIL <switch> element as a child. The <switch> can be used to encode multiple layouts within one document.

The order of top-level children in the <head> element is defined by the SMIL DTD. Example 4-8 shows the required order for the SMIL 2.0 Language profile. Only the SMIL 2.0 Language profile (including 3GPP SMIL and SMIL Basic) make use of the SMIL <head> element. Of these, SMIL Basic and 3GPP SMIL do not accept the meta-data or custom test child elements.

Element: <body>

The <body> element and its children define the structure and semantics of the presentation — its media content, timing, interaction and adaptivity. The <body> element's structural context is shown in Table 4-3.

The <body> element accepts all of the core attributes common to SMIL elements. It also contains general timing attributes — this is because the <body> is not only a structure element, but also an alias for the <seq> element. The <body> element can also be used to specify default fill behavior for all of its children. (We discuss the fill and timing attributes in chapters 6 and 7, *Layout* and *Basic Timing*.)

The SMIL 2.0 Language profile accepts all of <body>'s parent and child elements. XHMTL+SMIL accepts most child elements (except <prefetch> and <brush>). The most restrictive versions of SMIL Basic do not support <animation>, <prefetch>, <excl> and <brush> elements as children.

<body>			Profiles				
attributes	*core*						
	general timing		L	M	B	1	H
	fill						
	media description						
parents	<smil>		L	M	B	1	
children	media	media object			B	1	H
		<brush>		M			
	time	<par> <seq>			B		
		<excl>					H
	control	<switch>	L		B		
		<prefetch>		M			
		<a>			B		
		BasicAnimation					H

Table 4-3. The <body> element.

4.2.3 Core Structure Attributes

With the exception of the xmlns attribute discussed on page 77, the <smil>, <head> and <body> elements do not take any special attributes. Since they — like all other SMIL elements — accept a standard set of core attributes, we discuss these here.

The *core* attributes in SMIL are id, xml:base, title, alt, longdesc, class and xml:lang[1]. Each core attribute defines some aspect of the element's place in the XML structure and is independent of any particular aspect of multimedia presentation behavior. They are called "core" because they can be applied to all SMIL elements.

attribute	value	Profiles		
id	unique identifier	M	B	
title	CDATA			1
alt	CDATA			
longdesc	CDATA	L		H
class	CDATA			
xml:base	URI	M	B	
xml:lang	language tag			

Table 4-4. The Core Attributes

Attribute: id

Most XML document classes have an id (unique identifier) attribute, which makes elements referable to from IDREF attribute assignments. Such references have more specific meaning within some SMIL constructs, such as for assigning regions to media, hyperlinking within SMIL documents, and synchronization, as we saw in the example in Chapter 2. We discuss the full details of SMIL-specific semantics of id attributes for certain elements later in the book when those elements are discussed.

Attribute: xml:base

The xml:base attribute allows external file references to share a common base *uniform resource identifier* (URI). A URI defines a storage address somewhere across the Web. The use of the xml:base attribute facilitates authoring and maintenance by letting URI values be short and portable.

4.2.4 Core Attributes for Accessibility

The remaining core attributes, title, alt, longdesc, class and xml:lang, all apply to media description, and so we discuss these in full detail in Chapter 17: *Meta-Information, Media Description and XML Accessibility*.

4.2.5 Namespace Attributes

The elements and attributes accepted by a document are defined in the document's language specification. This set can be extended using XML *namespaces*.

---

1 The SMIL specification does not include the xml:lang attribute as among the core attributes. However, since any element can have one, we include it with the core attributes in this book for simplicity.

Attribute: `xmlns`

Namespaces are collections of XML-defined constructs, typically with a common theme (such as multimedia). Namespace syntax and processing are defined by the W3C Recommendation *Namespaces in* XML. Namespaces allow document classes to combine constructs from multiple sources. SMIL family languages use constructs from SMIL, as specified by the inclusion of the SMIL namespace, but they may use constructs from other namespaces as well.

The root element of every SMIL family document, whether it is native SMIL or media-based, has an `xmlns` attribute assignment. This attribute declares the default XML namespace used in the document's class — that is, it states the primary collection of XML-defined constructs the class uses. The attribute's value is most often the URL (Uniform Resource Locator) identifying where the namespace is officially defined. This attribute's assignment is typically fixed for a given format, so authors can start their presentations by just copying the code for the format of their choice, without worrying about the deeper intricacies of namespaces.

The most common namespace declarations for common SMIL profiles are shown in Example 4-5 through Example 4-7.

Some documents get constructs from more than one namespace. Constructs in these documents must clarify which namespace defines that construct. For SMIL 2.0 implementations, this is only an issue for the HTML+TIME implementation of the XHTML+SMIL profile. Here, both HTML and SMIL namespaces need to be declared. Example 2-5 in Chapter 2: *Understanding SMIL 2.0 Code* shows several examples of mixed use of namespaces; in that example, the SMIL functionality was defined using Microsoft's *t:* namespace identifier.

The "`xml:`" prefix

The "`xml:`" prefix refers to a special, generic namespace for use in all XML. It indicates that its construct is defined for inclusion in all XML document classes. Use of this prefix requires no `xmlns` assignment. SMIL has two constructs that use the "`xml:`" prefix: `xml:base` and `xml:lang`. These are each defined outside of SMIL and are used in all SMIL profiles, SVG and HTML.

Non-Standard Namespace Extensions

Some SMIL players and browsers extend the SMIL specification with their own document element, attributes or attribute values. These constructs are identified as coming from the application's extension by having that application's namespace prefix. Of course, constructs from one application are not guaranteed to be supported by other players or browsers.

Example 4-9 provides a namespace declaration line and a code example for a RealOne namespace-based extension to SMIL. In theory, constructs that contain a namespace qualifier should be ignored by SMIL players that do not understand or support the construct: they should not cause the document to be con-

```
<smil xmlns="http://www.w3.org/2001/SMIL20/Language"
    xmlns:rn="http://features.real.com/2001/SMIL20/Extensions">
...
<img src="bigButton.gif" rn:backgroundOpacity="50%" .../>
```

Example 4-9. Extension namespace definition used in the RealOne player.

sidered invalid SMIL. In practice, players such as RealOne refuse to play documents containing unknown namespaces.

Note that the default SMIL DOCTYPE should not be specified when using the RealOne player, since the SMIL DTD does not include RealOne extensions.

4.3 Summary and Conclusion

SMIL is the XML encoding of features for integrating and synchronizing multiple media. As such, it is a collection of elements and attributes that each define a particular aspect of multimedia presentation. These aspects include locating or defining of the media that is integrated, laying the media out on the screen and controlling other aspects of its playback, timing when the media are played and how they are synchronized with each other, how the user can interact with the presentation to affect its progression, and how the presentation adapts to varying situations. This chapter provided the broad introduction and background needed for learning about SMIL constructs in more detail and incorporating any SMIL construct into a presentation.

4.4 Further Resources

XML

Extensible Markup Language (XML) 1.0 (Second Edition), Tim Bray, Jean Paoli, C.M. Sperberg-McQueen and Eve Maler (eds), W3C Recommendation, 10 February 1998, http://www.w3.org/TR/REC-xml.

HTML

XHTML 1.0: The Extensible HyperText Markup Language (Second Edition), Steven Pemberton, (ed. chair), W3C Recommendation, 1 August 2002, http://www.w3.org/TR/xhtml1.

SVG

Scalable Vector Graphics (SVG) 1.0 Specification, Jon Ferraiolo (ed.), W3C Recommendation, 4 September 2001, http://www.w3.org/TR/SVG.

URI

RFC 2396: Uniform Resource Identifiers (URI): Generic Syntax, Tim Berners-Lee, Roy Fielding, Larry Masinter, IETF (Internet Engineering Task Force), 1998, `http://www.ietf.org/rfc/rfc2396.txt`.

XML Base

XML *Base*, Jonathan Marsh (ed.), W3C Recommendation, 27 June 2001, `http://www.w3.org/TR/xmlbase/`.

5
Referencing Media Objects

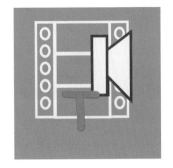

"Integration" is SMIL's middle name. SMIL does not define any media itself — it defines the glue that holds media together in multimedia presentations. SMIL's *BasicMedia* module and its constructs, the media object elements and the `src` and `type` attributes, provide the doorways though which media is brought into SMIL document structure. SMIL can define a bit of its own media with the `<brush>` element, which paints color on an area of the display and makes it a media object in its own right.

This chapter describes the basic alternatives for identifying the media objects to be contained in a presentation. We won't discuss layout or timing issues yet — these come in later chapters — but we will review everything you need to understand how SMIL references external media objects.

5.1 Partitioning Content and Control

A SMIL specification contains elements and attributes that allow media objects to be located and scheduled for presentation. (It also defines how linking and overall resource control can be integrated across the media items.) The SMIL specification *does not* define how the actual media is to be formatted. For SMIL implementations where SMIL is the host language (such as those based on the Language and Mobile profiles), there is a strict separation between the control information in the SMIL file and the content in media objects. For implementations of SMIL where another language serves as host (such as XHTML or SVG), the separation between content and control is less strict. The advantage of having a strict separation between content and control is that the SMIL file remains small: this allows the file to be parsed and handed off to the scheduler with a minimum of extra bits. (This is obviously important for small devices.) The advantage of mixing control elements and content is that a presentation can be easier to hand-edit: everything is in one file and the mixed control/content conventions that are used in HTML are maintained. For presentations that are largely text-based (such as those using the XHTML+SMIL profile), mixing control and content makes sense. For presentations that focus on images, audio and video, the separation of content and control is much more useful. The ultimate choice is more philosophical than technical.

```
1 <smil>
2   <head>
3    ...
4   </head>
5   <body>
6    ...
7    <text src="file:///hello.txt" type="text/plain" ... />
8    ...
9   </body>
10 </smil>
```

(a) using <text> and an external media object

```
1 <smil>
2   <head>
3    ...
4   </head>
5   <body>
6    ...
7    <ref src="http://www.example.net/hello.txt" type="text/plain" ... />
8    ...
9   </body>
10 </smil>
```

(b) using <ref> and an external media object

```
1 <smil>
2   <head>
3    ...
4   </head>
5   <body>
6    ...
7    <text src="data:,Greetings!" type="text/plain" ... />
8    ...
9   </body>
10 </smil>
```

(c) using <text> and an embedded media object

Example 5-1. Partitioning control and content in the SMIL Language profile.

In order to understand the various options that SMIL provides for identify-ing media objects, look at the three code fragments in Example 5-1. All of these examples use the SMIL Language profile — this is because SMIL profiles that use another host language (such as HTML) will use that language's media ref-erencing primitives. In each example, we want to display the text: Greetings!

In Example 5-1(a), we see the typical case for including media in a SMIL pre-sentation. The element <text> specifies a media object reference, the location and type of which are given by the src and type attributes. The actual text string is placed inside the referenced file. (Note that the src attribute uses con-ventional URI syntax. Please review *URIs: Locating and Naming Media Objects* on page 62 for a discussion on URIs.)

Example 5-1(b) shows a subtle variant of the SMIL example, in which the <text> element has been replaced by the <ref> element. Functionally, these two fragments are identical: in the full SMIL Language profile, the <text> ele-ment is simply a synonym for <ref>. (More on this starting on page 88.)

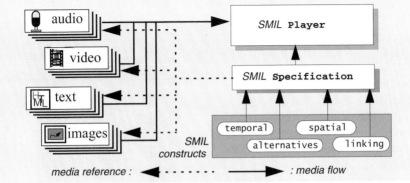

Figure 5-1. SMIL architecture.

Although most media used in a SMIL presentation will be referenced as an external object, it is also possible to embed media directly in the SMIL file. Example 5-1(c) gives an example of this using a *data* URI: the src attribute starts with the characters data:, (including the ',' !), followed by the actual content of the media.[1] For short text strings, this is a convenient mechanism, but for a 10MB piece of video, it is not particularly appropriate!

The basic architecture of SMIL in the SMIL Language profile is presented in Figure 5-1. The SMIL specification contains references to media (and other control information), but the media itself is located in external files.

We close our discussion on separating content and control with an example of non-SMIL. Many new users to SMIL expect that the following code fragment should be valid:

```
...
<text>
   Greetings!
</text>
...
```

It is important to realize that *this is not valid* SMIL. Whatever the merits of such a structure, it is not supported in the SMIL 2.0 Language profile. In other profiles, such as XHTML+SMIL, the <text> element is not used, but embedded content using the <P> element (and its equivalents) is more common.

---

1 The data URI can also accept parameters before the actual data. Since the separator character for these parameters is a comma, a final comma is expected before the actual data encoding starts. This is why the comma is required in the data string.

5.2 SMIL Media Object Elements and Attributes

The SMIL specification's media object modules define three sets of elements for referencing and controlling media objects in a presentation: *media object elements*, a *media object initialization element* and a *brush element*. Of these, the media object elements and the brush element represent basic SMIL functionality and are discussed in this chapter. The media object initialization element (which is named param) is advanced SMIL functionality and is treated in Chapter 11: *Subsetting and Extending Media*.

SMIL's media object elements are defined in the SMIL *BasicMedia* module. This module also defines the src and type attributes. All SMIL profiles include the *BasicMedia* module. The <brush> element is defined in the *BrushMedia* module. This module also defines the color attribute. Only the SMIL Language profile makes use of the *BrushMedia* module.

The XML structure of the media object and brush elements is shown in Table 5-1.

5.2.1 Media Elements

This section defines the media object elements in SMIL.

Element: <ref>

SMIL defines one media object element to specify which media objects are included in a presenta-

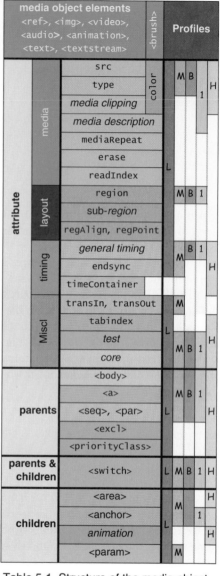

media object elements <ref>, <img>, <video>, <audio>, <animation>, <text>, <textstream>	<brush>	Profiles
attribute – media — src		M B · 1 · H
type	color	M B 1 H
media clipping		
media description		
mediaRepeat		
erase		
readIndex		L
attribute – layout — region		M B 1
sub-*region*		
regAlign, regPoint		
attribute – timing — *general timing*		M · B 1
endsync		H
timeContainer		
attribute – Miscl — transIn, transOut		M
tabindex		L
test		M B 1 · H
core		M B 1
parents — <body>		
<a>		M B 1 · H
<seq>, <par>		L · H
<excl>		
<priorityClass>		
parents & children — <switch>		L M B 1 H
children — <area>		H · M · 1
<anchor>		M · 1
animation		L · H
<param>		M

Table 5-1. Structure of the media object elements

tion: the <ref> (reference) element. In order to make reading SMIL files easier, the language also defines six synonyms for <ref>: <img>, <video>, <audio>, <animation>, <text> and <textstream>. These seven elements are identical in every way except for their names — they take the same attributes, can have elements of the same types for parents and children, and behave the same. In fact, these elements are totally interchangeable.

The SMIL Language profile uses different names as an authoring convenience (so that someone can read the SMIL file and understand what is going on), but they are not used by the SMIL player to determine the type of media content. This means that a (perverse!) author could use a <video> element to reference a file containing audio media. While not recommended, this works because a SMIL player is not allowed to use the name of the media object element to determine media types. Instead, either the type attribute or the media server should determine the type (and inform the player).

One exception to the flexible use of media element names applies to some mobile implementations of SMIL. In order to minimize parsing and processing overhead, these implementations often require that only an appropriately typed media object element be used in a SMIL file. These restrictions and the general rules for determining media types are discussed on page 92.

The placement of a media object element in the <body> element hierarchy determines *when* (and *if*) it gets played. We'll spend much of the rest of this book discussing the many intricacies of how this is determined. But for now, here's a (very) short summary how the type of a media object element's parent helps determine when it plays:

- <body>, <seq> — before or after its siblings
- <par> — along with its siblings
- <switch>, <excl>, <priorityClass> — instead of its siblings
- <a> — in response to user interaction

The potential child elements of media object elements play a variety of roles in relation to the media. The <a> and <area> elements (and <area>'s deprecated SMIL 1.0 equivalent <anchor>) make portions of the media item "clickable" by the user — the user can activate these portions of the media to make the presentation lead elsewhere. The <param> element specifies particular modifications to the media for its playback in the presentation. Child animation elements define animations, or progressive changes in the presentation structure, that occur while the media plays. The <switch> element gives alternative specifications of these other elements. We describe all these element types in full detail later in the book.

As shown in Table 5-1, all of the media object references can accept a large number of attributes. Of these, only a few deal with media object selection: src, type and various media clip attributes. Each of these are described in *Media Object Attributes* on page 90. All of the other attributes that are available are discussed in other chapters in this book.

Element: <brush>

The <brush> element is just like a media object element except that it defines a fill color for a rendering region rather than an external media resource. Since it doesn't refer to external media, the <brush> element doesn't need the src and type attributes. However, since it defines color display internally, it has an attribute other media object elements don't: color.

The code fragment in Example 5-2 illustrates the use of the <brush> element. A rendering space (in this case, a SMIL layout region named *window1*) is defined in line 2. The brush element in line 4 says: take the specified color (in this case, *blue*) and use it to fill the entire referenced region (in this case, *window1*).

Valid definitions for the color attribute are discussed on page 95.

```
1  ...
2  <region regionName="window1" ... />
3  ...
4  <brush color="blue" region="window1" ... />
5  ...
```

Example 5-2. Use of the <brush> element.

5.2.2 Media Object Attributes

Media object elements have many attributes, as shown in Table 5-1, which define various aspects of how media get presented in SMIL. These include the source and type of the media and (for <brush>) the rendering color. They further specify the subset of the media object to be integrated by selecting portions of the located media file and making modifications to its own intrinsic timing. The layout attributes other than region define fine-tuning of spatial positioning unique to the media object that go beyond what is specified for it in the document layout as a whole. General timing attributes fine-tune when the media item plays beyond the broader synchronization defined for it by its parent. The attributes transIn and transOut define visual transitions that occur on the media as it starts and finishes. The user can use multiple taps on the tab key to highlight different media objects with tabIndex. Finally, the test attributes help determine if the media should be elected for presentation to a given user.

This section focuses on those attributes that relate directly to the selection of the media object. We start with the source attribute, then consider the type attribute and then discuss attributes for defining sub-parts of a media object. We close with a discussion of the color attribute.

Attribute: src

The src (source) attribute gives the location of a media item to be retrieved for integration into a presentation. As in HTML, its value is a URI. Unlike HTML, SMIL's src attribute can reference any media type.

The src attribute will typically reference an external file containing either a single media object or a composition of media objects in some high-level encoding. (An HTML file containing text and images, a SMIL file containing a sub-presentation or a Flash file containing an animation are three examples of higher-level compositions.) As a language, SMIL does not place any restrictions on the media object identified in the `src` attribute, but certain SMIL players may have local restrictions on the types of media they can support. For example, mobile SMIL players may not support full HTML media, and XHTML+SMIL browsers may not support RealMedia proprietary datatypes. See Chapter 3: *Local and Streaming Media* for a discussion of media encoding issues.

Example 5-3 illustrates the use of the `src` attribute for typical cases in the SMIL Language profile. The reference on line 4 illustrates the fetching of an MPEG video via the RTSP streaming protocol. Note that both the SMIL client (your player/browser) and the media server need to support RTSP for this transfer to be successful. The reference on line 5 illustrates the fetching of an SVG animation. The transfer is controlled using the HTTP protocol, which means that the entire file will need to be downloaded before rendering can begin — assuming, of course, that the SMIL player supports the SVG format. The reference on line 6 illustrates the fetching of a local audio file. Line 7 also fetches a file that is located in the same directory on the same host as was the SMIL file. Although this is a valid use of the `src` attribute, it is only recommended if you are sure the relative location of the media won't change. Line 8 illustrates the use of a data URI to encode information directly into the SMIL file. If this is used, make sure you only use it with small amounts of media to avoid generating very large SMIL files.

The references on line 4 through 8 represent standard use cases for SMIL. The reference on line 9 illustrates another aspect of SMIL behavior: the `src` attribute is an optional part of a media object specification. If no `src` attribute is given, this is not an error — although, at first glance, it is pretty useless! If a media object reference is made to an object without a corresponding source file, no media is fetched (obviously), but the reference fully participates in the timing structure of the presentation. In effect, line 9 defines a temporal delay in the presentation of 10 seconds.

```
 1 ...
 2  <body>
 3    ...
 4    <ref src="rtsp://www.example.net/meAndMyDog.mpg" ... />
 5    <animation src="http://www.example.net/ourAddress.svg" />
 6    <audio src="file:///myCar.mp3" ... />
 7    <image src="myGarage.jpg" ... />
 8    <text src="data:,Hi Mom!" ... />
 9    <video dur="10s" />
10 ...
11 </body>
12 ...
```

Example 5-3. Uses of the `src` attribute in the SMIL Language profile.

Attribute: type

Once the player identifies and acquires a media object, it needs to know how to render it. In order to do this, the player selects either an internal or external rendering engine that is compatible with the format of the media. The SMIL player will contain a set of preferences that indicate which rendering engine should be used for each media type. The question is: how does the player know what kind of media is stored in the file.

The primary means of stating this is with MIME Media Types (or, more simply, *mimetypes*). A mimetype is a character string that defines the class of media (audio, video, image, text, application) and a media encoding type (such as jpeg, mpeg, RealVideo, etc.). For each media object used in the SMIL player, someone or something has to associate a mimetype with a media object. Table 5-2 defines common mimetype definitions.

Mimetypes may be *registered* or *informal*. Registered mimetypes are controlled by the Internet Assigned Numbers Authority (IANA). Informal mimetypes are not registered with IANA, but are defined by common agreement; they usually have an "x-" before the media type name.

Media Class	MIME Type
audio	audio/basic
	audio/mp3
	audio/mpeg
	audio/vnd.rn-realaudio
	audio/x-aiff
	audio/x-mp3
	audio/x-ms-wma
	audio/x-pn-realaudio
	audio/x-realaudio
	audio/x-wav
video	video/mpeg
	video/msvideo
	video/quicktime
	video/vnd.rn-realvideo
	video/x-msvideo
	video/x-ms-wmv
image	image/bmp
	image/gif
	image/jpeg
	image/png
	image/svg-xml
	image/tiff
	image/vnd.rn-realflash
	image/vnd.rn-realpix
	image/x-cmu-raster
	image/x-emf
	image/x-rgb
	image/x-wmf
text	text/html
	text/plain
	text/vnd.rn-realtext
composite	application/vnd.rn-realmedia
	application/x-shockwave-flash
	application/smil
	application/xhmtl+smil

Table 5-2. Common *mimetype* definitions.

The mimetype association for a media object can be made by:

- *the local computer's operating system*: each operating system typically keeps a table that associates mimetypes with part of a media object's name (usually a three- to five-character suffix, such as "txt" or "smil");
- *the user*: a user can define preferences in the player to associate media object names with mimetypes;
- *the author*: the designer of the presentation can explicitly state the mimetype of the media object, perhaps overriding the default processing that is associated with a particular name; or

- *the server*: the mimetype can be supplied by the media server when the object is transferred. (If it is local media, then the operating system can assign a mimetype.)

While associating a mimetype with a piece of media may seem like a pretty simple operation, there are all sorts of complexities involved. For example, some protocols may allow content substitution, so that what you get may not be exactly what you requested. The type of the media may also be unknown at author time, and it may be so new that the operating system may not know about it either.

SMIL defines a set of rules for mimetype association that distributes responsibilities across several parties. The general approach used is:

- If the transfer protocol defined in the src attribute is RTSP, then the value of the type attribute will be used to select an appropriate version of the request media object on the server. If no such object exists, the server returns what it thinks is an appropriate media object (and gives its type).

- If another transfer protocol is used (such as HTTP or FTP), the value of the type attribute takes precedence over any other means to determine the media type.

- For other protocols, the value of the type attribute should take precedence unless the protocol itself identifies a particular media type.

After the SMIL specification was published, updates to the standards for Web transfer protocols defined new precedence rules for determining mimetypes. These rules essentially suggest that the player should always trust the transfer protocol to identify the correct mimetype. Only if the protocol explicitly neglects to provide a mimetype should the value of the type attribute be used — and only if no type attribute is available should the file type suffix be used to determine media type. Note that in no cases may the name of the media element (text, audio, video, etc.) be used to distinguish media type.

Example 5-4 illustrates the use of the type attribute for typical cases in the SMIL Language profile. Line 4 illustrates how, using the RTSP protocol, the type can be used to select among various media encodings on the server. Line 5 illustrates how, using the HTTP protocol, the SMIL type attribute can be used to override that default association of a media object's file extension. Line 6 shows how the media element name (text) is ignored and overridden as a GIF image.

```
1  ...
2  <body>
3    ...
4    <video src="rtsp://www.example.net/myDog" type="video/mpeg" ... />
5    <audio src="http://www.example.net/myCar.txt " type="audio/mpeg" ... />
6    <text src="data:image/gif;base64,0x0aef7edb1dcab2abcd...ffc2" ... />
7    ...
8  </body>
9  ...
```

Example 5-4. Uses of the type attribute in the SMIL Language profile.

As of the writing of this book, the future treatment of mimetypes by new SMIL players was still under discussion. For standard media types (such as *.jpeg* or *.txt*) there will probably be little problem, but if your application integrates new media types or new transfer protocols, you should check the fine-print of your SMIL player's documentation.

Attribute: clipBegin and clipEnd

The attributes presented thus far allow a media object to be identified and, optionally, associated with a media type. For many simple uses of media, these are all the (media) attributes that you will need to start playing media in your presentation. In some presentations, however, you may not want to play an entire media object. Instead, you may want to play only a particular fragment. SMIL supports this via the media clipping attributes that are defined in SMIL's *MediaClipping* module.

Playing a subset of a media object typically only makes sense for continuous media, such as audio and video. You can identify the media object you want to take the clip from by using the src attribute. You can then specify the place where the clip is to be using the clipBegin attribute. (If no clipBegin is specified, the object always starts at the beginning.) You can also specify the end of a clip by using clipEnd. (If no clipEnd is defined, then the media object plays to completion.)

The only major issue to be resolved when using clipBegin and/or clipEnd is: how do you specify the temporal point of the beginning/end of the clip? Do you use seconds (or minutes, or hours) or do you identify individual samples (or frames) in the source media? SMIL lets you do both.

Example 5-5 illustrates the use of the clipBegin and clipEnd attributes for typical cases in the SMIL Language profile. For purposes of example, assume that the video *myDog.mpg* is 60 seconds long. Line 4 shows a clip that starts 20 seconds into the video and then plays to the end. (The metric *npt* stands for "normal play time".) It says: start rendering the video 20 seconds into the video's normal play time. Line 5 also starts about 20 seconds into the

```
1  ...
2  <body>
3    ...
4    <video src="rtsp://www.example.net/myDog" type="video/mpeg"
           clipBegin="npt=20s" ... />
5    <video src="rtsp://www.example.net/myDog" type="video/mpeg"
           clipBegin="smpte-25=0:00:19:01" ... />
6    <video src="rtsp://www.example.net/myDog" type="video/mpeg"
           clipEnd="npt=40s" ... />
7    <video src="rtsp://www.example.net/myDog" type="video/mpeg"
           clipEnd="smpte-30-drop=0:00:39:24" ... />
8    <video src="rtsp://www.example.net/myDog" type="video/mpeg"
           clipBegin="20s" clipEnd="40s" ... />
9    ...
10 </body>
11 ...
```

Example 5-5. Uses of the clipBegin/clipEnd attributes
in the SMIL Language profile.

video, but in this case, it identifies a particular frame in the video using the SMPTE/PAL encoding format "smpte-25". (In this example, the second frame of the 20th second is selected — that's pretty precise for a dog!) Line 6 and 7 show how the end of the clip can be identified using both NPT and SMPTE encodings (in this case, using SMPTE/NTSC notation). Line 8 shows that, when no timing metric is given, 'npt' is assumed.

If the NPT metric is used (or implied), its value is a SMIL clock value. These are defined in Chapter 14: *Advanced SMIL Timing Attributes*. SMPTE encodings are a bit more complex; see Chapter 11: *Subsetting and Extending Media* for a description.

There are some important performance and licensing implications of using `clipBegin` and `clipEnd` in a presentation. First, identifying a short media fragment (such as a 10 second clip out of a two hour video) will not necessarily mean that only 10 seconds of video are transferred between the server and the client. Since `clipBegin` and `clipEnd` are SMIL attributes (not transfer protocol attributes), it could well be that the entire video is transferred across the network and then only a short fragment played on the local machine. (Some players and protocols may be able to optimize this performance, but this is a player issue, not a SMIL issue.) Second, if you are accessing media from a pay-per-view server, you may still be charged for a complete media access even if only a short part of the media is used.

Quick Tip

In SMIL players that support the full SMIL 2.0 specification, both the attribute names `clipBegin` and `clip-begin` (as well as `clipEnd` and `clip-end`) must be supported. `clip-begin` and `clip-end` are the SMIL 1.0 names for the media clip attributes. Note also that SMIL 1.0 did not default its clip metric to 'npt'; strictly speaking, clip-end="10s" is an invalid specification.

Attribute: color

The `color` attribute of the `<brush>` element and the `backgroundColor` attribute in `<region>` specifies a color that is to be displayed. The syntax of the values is illustrated in Figure 5-2. *Color values*, the only practical values of the `color` attribute, are described next.

A *color value* can be the name of a color, the numeric definition of a color or a color setting on the user's Web browser. The syntax of the color values is illustrated in Figure 5-2.

Color Names. SMIL, and the Web as a whole, establish 16 color names as short cuts for defining colors. These color names are shown in Figure 5-2. Be careful when using color names because some Web browsers use additional non-standard color names that other browsers may not recognize — make sure to use only one of these 16 standard names when using color names.

RGB Color Specifications. The Web presentation standards share not only the 16 color names but also the means of defining all of the colors the Web can present. This scheme is based on the use of *red*, *green* and *blue* as the primary colors for creating color combinations. From these primary colors comes the name of the scheme: *RGB*. An RGB specification states how much of each primary color is used in making the color defined. The intensity levels of the primary colors are stated in Web color definitions with three primary color coordinates. There are three ways to state these three coordinates: *percentage triplets*, *decimal triplets* and *hexadecimal notation*, described below. Of these, hexadecimal notation is the most often used and the most frequently recommended, since it is the most compact and is completely precise.

- *RGB percentage triplets*: The most easily learned way to define colors on the Web is with *RGB percentage triplets*. These state what percentage of each primary color is mixed into the color shown. These consist of the letters "*rgb*" followed by a pair of parentheses, known as *RGB functional notation*. In between these parentheses, there are three percentage values. Each is a number, either integer or floating point, from 0 to 100, followed by a percent sign. These percentage values are separated by commas followed by optional white space characters, which typically consist of a single space.

- *RGB decimal triplets*: A more precise way to specify a desired Web color is with an *RGB decimal triplet*. RGB percentage triplets can be inaccurate for color representation because not all percentage values correspond with one of the 256 8-bit values computers use for color. RGB decimal triplets have the same syntax as RGB percentage triplets, except that the three coordinates are not percentages but integers in the range from 0 to 255, and that they are, of course, not followed by percent signs. This numeric range of 256 different values ensures that each RGB decimal triplet corresponds directly with one possible computer display color, and vice-versa.

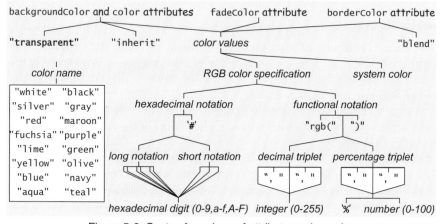

Figure 5-2. Syntax for values of attributes using color

- *RGB hexadecimal notation:* The most concise, most common, and most highly recommended color definitions are in *RGB hexadecimal notation.* They have the same accurate one-to-one correspondence that RGB decimal values have, but with fewer characters. RGB hexadecimal notation typically consists of seven characters, though a short form usable for some colors consists of only four characters. RGB hexadecimal notation always begins with a '#' followed by six hexadecimal numbers. Hexadecimal notation uses 16 "digits" that increase from '0' to '9' and then from 'A' to 'F' or 'a' to 'f'.

  For the full seven-character notation, called *long notation,* two of these hexadecimal digits are used for each primary color coordinate. The first digit puts you in a neighborhood of 16 adjacent primary color intensities, and the second chooses one of these 16. The four-character *short notation* for RGB hexadecimal consists of a '#' followed by three or six hexadecimal digits, one for each primary color coordinate. The trade-off of this shorter notation is that it defines fewer colors.

System Colors. The color attribute can also be assigned any of the *system colors* defined by CSS. These colors are not set by the author but by the user, or by the browser on behalf of the user. System colors enable users to set a color scheme for their presentations that best suites them, perhaps by being tailored to their visual disabilities. They also allow presentations to blend in with the system's and windowing environment's color scheme. In SMIL, use of system colors provides visual consistency when integrating CSS-styled media that also uses system colors. Authors should be careful when using both system colors and author-defined colors. System colors can vary considerably from user to user and in some cases may clash with the colors set by the author. Similarly, system colors may clash with colors set in visual media integrated into the SMIL presentation.

5.3 Timing Consequences of Media Object Use

Whenever a media object is added to a SMIL specification, it is assigned a duration. The value of this duration depends on a number of factors. For continuous media objects such as audio or video, the intrinsic duration of the media is used if this can be determined by the player. (This information is often — but not always — stored in the header of the media object.) For discrete media objects, the duration of the object defaults to 0 seconds, which is not very long. It may seem strange that a media object is assigned a duration of 0 seconds: if an author wanted a 0 second object, it would seem simpler to not specify any media at all! For a SMIL perspective, using 0 seconds makes perfect sense: first, if you didn't use 0, what else would you use? Second, SMIL makes a distinction between an object's *timing duration* and its *rendering duration.* (By default, an object with duration of zero will stay visible until its time container ends.) Both of these topics are discussed in detail in Chapter 7: *Basic SMIL Timing.*

5.4 Summary and Conclusion

The *BasicMedia* module and its constructs, the media object elements and the `src` and `type` attributes, locate media and place it in SMIL presentation structure. The `src` attribute states where the media is and how to download it. The `type` attribute lets the browser choose the right process for rendering the media into the presentation. A media object element's placement in the body tree determines much of when and if the media object is played. Other attributes of a media object element determine the rest of the object's timing. The *BasicMedia* module is used by SMIL 1.0 and all SMIL 2.0 profiles. Unique to the SMIL Profile, the *BrushMedia* module and its constructs, the <brush> element and its `color` attribute, allow the SMIL author to define rectangles of color as media objects.

5.5 Further Resources

URIs

RFC 2396: Uniform Resource Identifiers (URI): Generic Syntax, Tim Berners-Lee, Roy Fielding, Larry Masinter, IETF (Internet Engineering Task Force), 1998, `http://www.ietf.org/rfc/rfc2396.txt`.

Relative URIs

RFC 1808: Relative Uniform Resource Locators, Roy T. Fielding, IETF (Internet Engineering Task Force), *June 1995*, `http://www.ietf.org/rfc/rfc1808.txt`.

XML *Base*

XML *Base*, Jonathan Marsh (ed.), W3C Recommendation, 27 June 2001, `http://www.w3.org/TR/xmlbase/`.

SVG

Scalable Vector Graphics (SVG) 1.0 Specification, Jon Ferraiolo (ed.), W3C Recommendation, 4 September 2001, `http://www.w3.org/TR/SVG`.

HTML

XHTML 1.0: The Extensible HyperText Markup Language (Second Edition), Steven Pemberton, (ed. chair), W3C Recommendation, 1 August 2002, `http://www.w3.org/TR/xhtml1`.

CSS

Cascading Style Sheets, Level 2, Bert Bos, Håkon Wium Lie, Chris Lilley and Ian Jacobs (eds), W3C Recommendation, 12 May 1998, `http://www.w3.org/TR/CSS2`.

6

SMIL Basic Layout

Layout states *where* on the screen each piece of visual media is shown and *how* audio objects are rendered when activated. A presentation's layout defines the visual "style" or "look and feel" of the composite combination of all of its media objects. Layout is important because it adds the semantic organization that helps a viewer absorb the multiple content streams inherent in a multimedia presentation quickly and efficiently.

SMIL layout is concerned with the relative placement of (multiple) media objects, but not the internal formatting of any of the individual objects. Explicit layout facilities exist in SMIL because the temporal and lexical structure of a SMIL document typically has no direct relationship with the spatial structure of the presentation. The placement of each object in a presentation is usually driven more by media centric concerns (such as having video and images appear in predictable places) than with any inherited properties based on the lexical place within the document of the media object. This makes SMIL fundamentally different than, say, HTML or most text documents.

This chapter presents the core facilities of SMIL layout. These include the elements and attributes that control presentation layout, and the way that SMIL separates layout specification from layout use. We will also consider alternatives to SMIL layout in a presentation, including SMIL's default layout rules and the ability to use alternative layout languages. If you don't care about the models, jump to page 104 for the basic concepts of SMIL 2.0 layout.

6.1 An Overview of Layout Concepts

There are several different strategies appropriate for multimedia layout. In order to understand some of the alternatives, consider the multimedia presentation shown in Figure 6-1. Here we see a hypothetical news broadcast, which is made up of several elements: there are several static icons and labels, there is a place for video and graphics, there is room for (optional) captions, and there is a ticker tape area that is intended to keep viewers with shorter attention spans engaged throughout the presentation. The contents of any of the objects may change during the newscast — the studio video may be replaced with a remote report or the labels and captions may change over time — but the general visual structure will remain the same.

The Net News — broadband edition
all the bits fit to blit

Monkey's Uncle Found
in Remote Part of
Western Brasil

... The animal, with a tail about
15 cm (6") long, was found ...

found without motor ** Three thermal trees transplant

Figure 6-1. A SMIL presentation of a Web newscast.

In organizing the presentation's media objects, a designer can choose one of three general approaches:

- *Embedded Layout*: The first is to assume all layout concerns are defined by the underlying media items. With this strategy, all of the layout decisions are resolved at media creation time and then 'baked' into the presentation. This approach gives ultimate control to the presentation designer and no control (other than composite rendering) to the media player.

- *Dynamic Layout*: At the opposite end of the layout spectrum is the approach in which all layout is determined dynamically by the presentation environment, based on the structure of the document or the timeline of the presentation. This philosophy gives a controlling role in how a presentation is displayed to the viewer's media player at the expense of the presentation's designer.

- *Compositing Layout*: A compromise between dynamic and embedded layout is to consider a presentation as a composite of relatively autonomous objects (each using internal embedded or dynamic layout models) that are visually positioned into a composite arrangement by a presentation designer. This approach de-couples media contents from media placement, but it leaves the presentation designer in control.

Each of these approaches has their advantages and disadvantages.

The key advantage of using embedded layout is that a certain look-and-feel is guaranteed at production time. In terms of Figure 6-1, the components can be carefully formatted, and complex content models can be used to provide often stunning visual effects. A disadvantage of the approach is that it limits individual component reuse or easy content substitution: if you want to reuse the video or the ticker tape news in an other context, you are out of luck. (While this is seen as a disadvantage in Web terms, it is often viewed as a prime advantage by content owners who want final-form formatting and strict distribution control.)

The key advantage of dynamic layout is that all placement decisions can be made based on knowledge of the final rendering environment. Figure 6-2 shows two dynamic restylings of the presentation for a 2::3 aspect ratio instead of the original 4::3. Figure 6-2(a) uses a lexical algorithm, where a scaled background and the ticker tape are placed as peers, and the video, graphics, images and text are nested within these objects in a top-to-bottom order based on their order of appearance in the document's source file. Figure 6-2(b) illustrates a restyling based on a temporal algorithm: each successive media object is nested in order of temporal appearance in the presentation, with each new object presented with slight offset in origin and at the next-higher stacking level. Both approaches are very predictable, but both are pretty useless because neither the structure of the source document or the coarse timing of the presentation have a direct relationship with the spatial needs of the presentation. Dynamic styling has no idea of the semantics of the information presented, which means that the composite message conveyed by a particular placement of objects is lost or altered. The result is usually undesirable for presentations with more than one simultaneous media object.

The advantage of using compositing layout is that it provides the ability to combine autonomous objects into a 'new' whole, but it still provides a designer with total control over the coordinated (visual) composition of the objects. Since multimedia presentations have multiple, simultaneous objects, this coor-

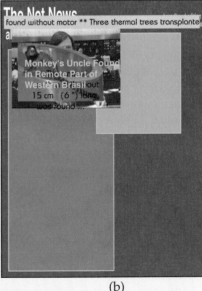

found without motor ** Three thermal trees transplante

Monkey's Uncle Found
in Remote Part of
Western Brasil

... The animal, with a tail about
15 cm (6") long, was found ...

found without motor ** Three thermal trees transplante

Monkey's Uncle Found
in Remote Part of
Western Brasil out
15 cm (6") long
was found ...

(a)   (b)

Figure 6-2. A dynamically transformed Web newscast.
(a): layout based on lexical structure, as shown in Example 6-1 on page 121;
(b): layout based on temporal order, as used by SMIL Empty Layout.

dination is essential to eliminating confusion in a presentation. At the same time, composition layout still provides the player with an ability to influence selection and — when appropriate — the rendering of individual objects. However, considering the processing expense of dynamically reformatting media such as audio, video and images, the restyling of media types other than text will be the exception, not the rule.

6.2 SMIL Layout Models

The initial proposals for SMIL layout were based on strict compositing model. From a graphic designer's perspective, the ability to directly influence layout within the presentation specification was seen as a great good. In terms of the W3C standardization process for SMIL 1.0, however, it was seen as a great problem. This debate, which centered on the definition of a special-purpose layout model within the SMIL specification rather than having SMIL apply CSS, resulted in a rather complex overall layout solution in SMIL when it was released in 1996. This section describes the basic layout facilities defined for SMIL 1.0 and then considers SMIL 2.0's extensions.

6.2.1 SMIL 1.0's Approach to Layout

SMIL 1.0 supported three forms of layout control:

- SMIL *Default Layout*: an implicit layout architecture based on a fully dynamic model that allowed the media player to make placement decisions. To obtain this model, a presentation excluded all layout definitions from the <head> element. SMIL 1.0 players were free to integrate their own layout constraint mechanisms — such as style sheets — but no major player offered this functionality.

- SMIL *Empty Layout*: an implicit set of dynamic layout rules based on a model in which objects are offset and stacked based on their temporal appearance in the document. (Figure 6-2(b) used the algorithm of SMIL Empty Layout.) To obtain this model, a presentation integrated the following empty layout declaration in the <head> section:

```
<head>
  <layout>
  </layout>
</head>
```

(See *SMIL Empty Layout Semantics* on page 117 for more details.)

- SMIL *Basic Layout*: an explicit layout architecture based on the compositing model that provided logical containers (regions) that could be used to define where and how related groups of media are rendered. To obtain this model, the following specification was included in the <head>:

```
<head>
  <layout>
  ...      <--! explicit layout definition -->
  </layout>
</head>
```

A design constraint for SMIL 1.0 Basic Layout was that it had to maintain compatibility with CSS-2 absolute positioning functionality. SMIL 1.0 layout was strongly-typed and enforced a one-to-one association of media with layout regions: each region could only be used to render a single type of media, and only one media object could be active in a region at a time. (A region could be used for several media items of the same type, but only one at a time.)

For presentations that consisted of a single media object — such as one video or a single audio object — SMIL Empty Layout provided a baseline layout solution. For more complex presentations, SMIL Basic Layout provided a reasonable way of providing the basic kinds of control necessary for multimedia. (Since SMIL Default Layout was totally player dependent, its use is discouraged.)

6.2.2 SMIL 2.0's Approach to Layout

The essence of SMIL 1.0 layout has been carried forward and expanded in SMIL 2.0. As with SMIL 1.0, profiles based on SMIL 2.0 do not need to provide explicit support for layout control. On the other hand, in languages where layout plays an important part of the presentation's specification, extensive new facilities have been provided to allow fine-grain control of how objects are placed on the rendering surface. Most of the restrictions on SMIL 1.0 layout were also removed.

SMIL 1.0's *Default* and *Empty* models are preserved in SMIL 2.0. As illustrated in Figure 6-3, SMIL 1.0's *Basic* model has been extended and modularized into four (optional) layout modules. These are:

- *BasicLayout*: this module defines the <layout>, <root-layout> and <region> elements, the region attribute, and various control attributes for SMIL regions. It provides core layout functionality that is backwards compatible with SMIL 1.0 layout.

- *AudioLayout*: this module defines the soundLevel attribute as an extension to the <region> element. In contrast to the module and attribute names,

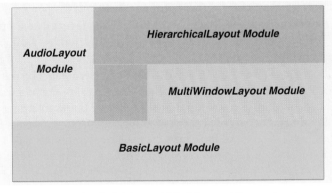

Figure 6-3. SMIL 2.0 Layout Modules and Dependencies

this module does not really define where audio is placed (for example, on which channel) or the absolute output level of the audio. Instead, it defines the relative value of the audio output.

- *MultiWindowLayout*: this module extends *BasicLayout* and allows multiple top-level windows to be defined and coordinated within one presentation context. It defines the `<topLayout>` element and the `open` and `close` attributes for managing the multiple windows.

- *HierarchicalLayout*: this module extends *BasicLayout* and *MultiWindowLayout*. It provides the ability to define layout overrides on the media definition element, it allows regions to be created dynamically within the presentation, and it allows content to be aligned relative to a set of registration points within the region.

All profiles that support SMIL Basic Layout will include the *BasicLayout* module. Only players that are based on the full SMIL 2.0 Language profile should be expected to offer complete support for all layout modules.

6.2.3 Summary of SMIL Layout Concepts

Before looking at the layout model in detail, we summarize some of the important concepts about SMIL's layout models:

- *Layout specification is optional in* SMIL: you don't have to use SMIL Basic (or Advanced) layout, but if you do use it in a player that conforms to the SMIL Basic or SMIL Language profiles, you are guaranteed to get SMIL's layout semantics;

- *Individual profiles may choose to extend or replace* SMIL *Basic Layout with other models*: the proposed XHTML+SMIL profile uses CSS layout, while some new profile may choose to define new layout models.

- SMIL *Layout is not constraint-based*: you don't define in terms of relationships among objects, you define layout in terms of one or more layout canvases. (There are some constraint based relationships defined in the *HierarchicalLayout* module.)

- SMIL *2.0's implementation of Basic Layout is backwards compatible*: it provides extra functionality above that in SMIL 1.0, but all players that support SMIL Basic Layout must be backward compatible and render SMIL 1.0 documents correctly.

- SMIL *Basic Layout and* CSS: all of SMIL 1.0 Basic Layout can be transformed into a CSS-2 equivalent notation, albeit in a less concise manner than is convenient for multimedia specifications. In SMIL 2.0, the mapping between SMIL layout and CSS is not complete, but equivalent forms exist for many standard operations. We look into the relationship between SMIL layout and CSS in Chapter 12: *Advanced Layout Topics*.

This chapter discusses the Basic Layout and Audio Layout support. Multi-Window Layout and Hierarchical Layout are discussed in Chapter 12.

6.3 SMIL Basic Layout Elements and Attributes

Some layout features are so fundamental that all types of multimedia use them. Most multimedia applications place visual media at various rectangular locations on a presentation space consisting of a single window. SMIL 2.0 Basic Layout defines this behavior. It acts as the foundation for all SMIL-defined layout, being required for the use of any of the other layout modules.

SMIL Basic Layout constructs are sufficient for the display of multimedia on small-screen, portable devices; SMIL Basic and 3GPP SMIL devices use only these constructs for their layout. XHTML+SMIL, on the other hand, does not use Basic Layout, but provides support for positioning constructs based on CSS's absolute positioning.

The elements that are used to define layout positioning support for SMIL 2.0 Basic Layout are:

- `<layout>`, which defines a collection of regions for the presentation;
- `<root-layout>`, which defines the overall window for the presentation;[1] and
- `<region>`, each of which defines an area in the display for placement of visual media or a container for the rendering of audio media.

A presentation may have zero, one or — if `<switch>` is supported — multiple `<layout>` elements. Within each `<layout>` element, zero or one `<root-layout>` elements and zero or many `<region>` elements may appear. Neither `<root-layout>` nor `<region>` have children in Basic Layout. Within a non-empty `<layout>` section, a presentation may define at most one `<root-layout>` element and it may define multiple `<region>` elements.

Figure 6-4 revisits the example of Figure 6-1 to show how the components in the news presentation can be mapped to the various elements in SMIL 2.0 Basic Layout. The news presentation defines a set of interior regions and an outer player window.

The layout definition begins with the specification of an over-all canvas container (the `<root-layout>`), which defines the boundaries of that presentation's rendering space. This container tells the SMIL player how large the composite presentation window will be. The player may enlarge this window with extra control interfaces or provides scroll bars, if these are required for the final rendering. Such extra space is outside of SMIL Basic Layout's control.

Inside the `<root-layout>` canvas are six rendering regions, labelled *B*, *V*, *G*, *H*, *C* and *T*. Each of the regions reserves a range of pixels that can be assigned to various media objects during the presentation. A region's stack level (called its z-index) will determine which bits are actually visible in case of overlapping use of region pixels. Each region has attributes for identification and control;

---

1 Note that while most SMIL 2.0 constructs use camel-case naming, SMIL layout uses the name <root-layout> instead of <rootLayout>. You must use the hyphenated form.

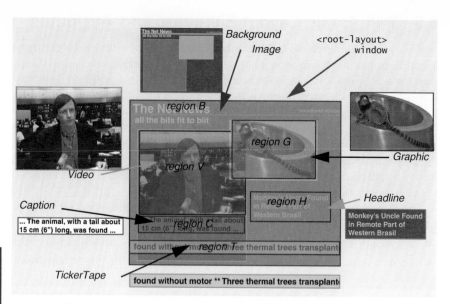

Figure 6-4. Layout Design for the Newscast Presentation

three sets of attributes are shown: the name, the size, and the z-index. (Other attributes are considered later.) By default, when a region is used to display a media object, the object is placed in the upper-left corner of that region.

> **Quick Tip**
>
> Not all mobile devices support scrolling of media within layout regions. Be careful not to rely on the mobile player to fit your media to the device's screen.

6.3.1 SMIL Basic Layout Elements

This section describes <layout>, <root-layout> and <region>.

Element: <layout>

The <layout> element specifies the placement rules for visual objects in a SMIL presentation. Most of this specification happens through its children, particularly through its child <region> elements. These elements define all placement of visual objects within the presentation window. A <layout> element can also have, optionally, one <root-layout> element child, which specifies the presentation window itself. All elements from the four SMIL 2.0 layout modules appear as descendants of <layout> elements, and most layout-related attributes appear in <layout> elements or their descendants. The <layout> element structure is shown in Table 6-1.

If a presentation has no `<layout>` element or if none of the type attributes are recognized, the player's internal default layout rules are used. If it has one empty `<layout>` section, then SMIL's empty layout rules are used. (They are described in *SMIL Empty Layout Semantics* on page 117.) If it has one non-empty `<layout>` section, then SMIL Basic Layout rules are applied, as discussed in this section. If it has multiple `<layout>` sections, then the first section that is recognized by the player based on a `<switch>` element evaluation is used. (See also Chapter 9.)

`<layout>`		Profiles			
attributes	type			B	1
	core		M		
	system test	L			
	customTest				
parents	`<head>`			B	1
	`<switch>`	L	M		
children	`<region>`	L	M	B	1
	`<root-layout>`				

Table 6-1. Structure of the `<layout>` element

Element: `<root-layout>`

The `<root-layout>` element defines the characteristics of the top level window in the presentation. There can be only one `<root-layout>` element within a layout section. This window is open during the entire presentation. The `<root-layout>` element is empty: it contains no `<region>` elements as children. (The `<region>` elements defining the regions to be placed in the `<root-layout>` window are siblings.) The `<root-layout>` structure is shown in Table 6-2.

`<root-layout>`		Profiles			
attributes	backgroundColor				
	width, height				
	core		M	B	1
	system test, skip-content	L			
	customTest				
parents	`<layout>`	L	M	B	1
children	none		M	B	1

Table 6-2. Structure of the `<root-layout>` element

As its hyphenated name suggests, `<root-layout>` is a holdover from SMIL 1.0, which has only single-window presentations. It is maintained for compatibility use in SMIL 2.0 and for use in SMIL Basic, which uses only one window. The `<root-layout>` element is still allowed in multi-window presentations, but usually should be replaced by <topLayout> in common use. (See Chapter 12: *Advanced Layout Topics* for details.) It may be useful as an authoring convenience indicating one window as the primary window, such as a central menu window controlling the rest of the presentation.

Element: <region>

The <region> element is the primary connection between media object elements and SMIL's layout structure. For most applications, each <region> element defines a container that is used to render one or more media objects. The regions may hold arbitrary content: audio, video, text, animations, images or arbitrary programs that render to a visual or audio region. SMIL does not restrict the types of content, although various SMIL players may provide support for only limited data types. The structure of the <region> element is laid out in Table 6-3.

A major change between SMIL 1.0 and SMIL 2.0 is that SMIL 2.0 regions can support the simultaneous rendering of multiple media objects (of arbitrary types). If only the *BasicLayout*

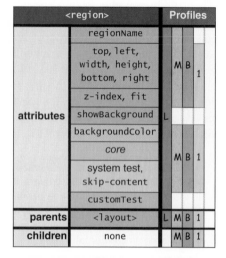

<region>		Profiles			
attributes	regionName				
	top, left, width, height, bottom, right		M	B	1
	z-index, fit				
	showBackground	L			
	backgroundColor				
	core		M	B	1
	system test, skip-content				
	customTest				
parents	<layout>	L	M	B	1
children	none		M	B	1

Table 6-3. The <region> element's place in SMIL structure

module is supported, this facility is of limited utility because there is no way of selectively positioning objects within the region, and thus information will be obscured. Selective positioning is provided via the sub-region positioning attributes in the *HierarchicalLayout* module. (See Chapter 12: *Advanced Layout Topics* for details.)

There are several types of attributes that apply to regions. These include the following groups:

- *referencing attributes*: these give the region a reference name;
- *positioning attributes*: these allow the region to be placed within the <root-layout>;
- *background attributes*: these define how parts of the region not containing media objects are rendered;
- *stacking and scaling attributes*: these attributes determine either how regions are placed relative to other regions, or how over-/under-sized media is placed within a region.

Each group of <region> element attributes is considered in the following sections.

6.3.2 Basic Layout Attributes Architecture

This section considers three sets of layout attributes, one for each of the layout elements defined in *SMIL Basic Layout Elements and Attributes* on page 105.

The attributes taken by each element are limited, except for the `<region>` element. The values that each `<region>` attribute can take are summarized in Table 6-4.

Class	attribute	value
Referencing	`regionName`	*name*
	`id`	*id*
Scaling	`z-index`	*integer* | `auto` | `inherit`
	`fit`	`hidden` | `scroll` | `fill` | `meet` | `slice`
Positioning	`width, height, top, left, bottom, right`	length-values | `auto`
Background	`backgroundColor`	*Color value*
	`showBackground`	`always` | `whenActive`
Audio	`soundLevel`	*number '%'*

Table 6-4. Attribute values of the `<region>` element.

6.3.3 `<layout>` Attributes

The `<layout>` element accepts the core SMIL attributes and — if supported by the profile — it also accepts attributes from the *SystemTest* module. It also accepts the `type` attribute, which is used to specify the layout mechanism to be used by the SMIL player.

If the `type` specification defined in a `<layout>` element is:

```
...
<head>
  <layout type="text/smil-basic-layout">
  ...
  </layout>
</head>
...
```

then SMIL's Basic Layout semantic are used. It is also possible to specify other layout models if the player supports these. If an invalid or unrecognized type definition is given, then the entire layout specification is skipped. (This will usually result in a presentation not being rendered at all, but this facility can be used as a brute-force method of selecting among alternative layout models.) If no `type` attribute is defined, then *text/smil-basic-layout* is assumed.

6.3.4 `<root-layout>` Attributes

The layout attributes available on the `<root-layout>` element control the size of the outer window and the color of the background.

```
...
<head>
  <layout type="text/smil-basic-layout">
    <root-layout id="Player-Window" width="640" height="480"
        backgroundColor="red"/>
    ...
  </layout>
</head>
...
```

Attribute: height and width

The size of a window is determined by its element's `width` and `height` attributes. The value of each attribute is always a number stating the given dimension in pixels, with an optional suffix of "*px*". This is an absolute specification of the window's size. If either of these attributes is not explicitly set, then the browser determines this dimension of the root window in any manner it sees fit. Thus, for predictable behavior across browsers, both of these attributes should always be assigned.

Attribute: backgroundColor

If the images you put on the screen do not cover all of the space or if a region is left empty for part of a presentation, the `backgroundColor` attribute determines how the unused space in the region is filled. When applied to the `<root-layout>` element, it sets the background for an entire presentation.

The `backgroundColor` attribute takes the same values as the `color` attribute. Its default value is *transparent*. Unless you are sure of the resulting behavior in the SMIL player, it is typically best to override this for the `<root-layout>` element (otherwise parts of the system background may appear). For reasons of compatibility with CSS-2, the `backgroundColor` attribute may also be given the value of *inherit*. While the intention of this facility is admirable, it is useless in practice, since none of the parent elements of `<root-layout>` accept a color-setting attribute.

> **Quick Tip**
>
> The `background-color` attribute is included in SMIL 2.0 for compatibility with SMIL 1.0. The attribute and its value are treated exactly as if it were a backgroundColor attribute. There is no reason to use this attribute in a new SMIL 2.0 presentation — backgroundColor should be used instead.

Other Attributes

The `<root-layout>` also accepts the core SMIL attributes.

6.3.5 `<region>` Referencing Attributes

There are two ways of naming a region: using `id` or with `regionName`. The choice depends on whether multiple regions need to be referenced by a single name.

Attribute: id

Like all SMIL elements, the `<region>` element can have an `id` attribute. For `<region>`, the `id` attribute has the special meaning that it can establish a name for that region. In SMIL 1.0, the `id` attribute was the only way of naming a region. Because of XML restrictions, each id must be unique. This means that presentations that have alternative layouts, or in which a single media object is to be rendered in multiple regions, need another mechanism to identify the target region. SMIL 2.0 introduced the `regionName` attribute for this purpose. As a result, the `id` attribute is only treated as a region name if no other region is assigned that same name via a `regionName` attribute.

Attribute: regionName

The `regionName` attribute takes an XML name string as a value, and makes this value the name of the region. Like the `id` attribute, it establishes its value as a means of referring to this element from another. Unlike the `id` attribute, this attribute does not have to be unique, and thus it enables multiple regions to share the same name. This is useful if you intend to have multiple layouts in a single presentation.

When resolving a region reference, a SMIL player will first see if one or more `<region>` elements exist that define a `regionName` corresponding to the reference name. If no `regionName` exists, the player will see if there is a `<region>` with an `id` attribute matching the reference name. If neither a `regionName` or an `id` is found, the reference is treated as an orphan. See *SMIL Empty Layout Semantics* on page 117 for more details on orphan processing.

> **Quick Tip**
> Since `regionName` is more flexible than `id`, you should use it when constructing presentations.

6.3.6 `<region>` Positioning Attributes

The primary use of the `<region>` element is *region positioning*. The region positioning attributes are `top`, `left`, `width`, `height`, `bottom` and `right`. They define rectangular areas in which visual media are displayed. The possible values of these attributes and their use is illustrated in Figure 6-5.

The positioning attributes are relative to the region's *containing block*, which is determined by the `<region>` element's parent. For the *BasicLayout* module (and for SMIL 1.0) the containing block is the root window — the region is

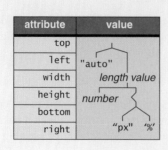
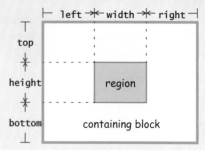

Figure 6-5. Region positioning attributes

placed in the root window, and the region's measurements are in terms of the root window. If you do not define region positioning attributes, the region fills up its containing block by default.

The values of the <region> element can contain percentages or pixel offsets. For Basic Layout and SMIL 1.0, these attributes do not directly specify the size of the window actually shown on the screen. Instead, they specify the size of the display area within this window. The window itself may also consist of the display area plus additional borders and scrollbars, increasing the total size of the window beyond the stated width and height dimensions. If a SMIL presentation is being written to cover the entire screen of a windowed environment, then this increased size should be taken into account. This additional size will vary between SMIL browsers and windowing environments.

The positioning attributes use *length values* to assign dimensions along the screen. To state a distance in terms of display screen pixels, make the value either a number by itself or a number followed by "px". To state the distance as a percentage of the maximum available distance, assign a number (from 0 to 100) followed by '%'. This syntax is illustrated in Figure 6-5. Length values can be assigned to the region positioning attributes. The length values used in SMIL have the same syntax as length values in HTML.

Attribute: top and left

These are the primary region positioning attributes; they place the top-left corner of an image the specified distance away from the top and left edge of the containing block using either pixel or percentage values. The region will extend to the containing block's right or bottom edge unless constrained by other region positioning attributes.

Attribute: width and height

These are the primary region sizing attributes. The width and height attributes take pixel and percentage values. If left is set, then a width pixel value puts the region's right that many pixels over from its left. A percentage value for width sets the region's width at that percentage of the containing block's width, making the region's right that far from the region's left. The same rules apply for using the `height` attribute with `top` to determine the region's bottom.

Attribute: bottom and right

Sometimes explicitly setting the `bottom` and `right` attributes is helpful, such as when these edges of the region relate strongly to other positions on the display. Their values state the distance between the region's lower-right corner and the bottom and right sides of the containing block, either as absolute pixels or as percentages of the containing block's dimensions. When used with `top` and `left`, the `width` and `height` attributes are unnecessary. In the absence of `top` and `left` attributes, the `width` and `height` attributes are applied to the bottom-left corner positioned by the `bottom` and `right` attributes. The value of a `bottom` or `right` attribute is ignored if both other region position attribute along the same dimension are assigned.

Value: *auto*

When specifying values for region positioning attributes, you'll never need to explicitly assign the value "auto". It states that the given dimension is calculated from the region's related dimensions and the containing block, as described above for each attribute. This construct comes from CSS, in which its more complex inheritance issues make the construct more of a concern to authors than in SMIL region positioning.

6.3.7 Background Attributes

You can set a color for the background of a region and you can control what happens to the region when it is not actively displaying content.

Attribute: backgroundColor

The `<region>` element has a `backgroundColor` attribute, which takes the same values as the `backgroundColor` attribute for `<root-layout>` elements. While we recommend against transparent window background colors for the `<root-layout>`, a `backgroundColor="transparent"` assignment is quite useful for regions since it prevents accidental blocking out of other images.

Quick Tip

For many presentations, it is usually advisable to assign a non-transparent background color for the `<root-layout>` and have all region backgrounds be transparent, allowing either other images or the window background to show through. Since this is the default assignment for the attribute, the most useful region background color is also the easiest to specify!

Attribute: showBackground

If the <region> element has a backgroundColor attribute, the showBackground attribute will determine when this background is shown. If the value is *always*, the background is always shown behind any content in the region. (This is even true when the region may not be referenced by any active media objects.) If the value is *whenActive*, the background will only be painted on pixels not in use with a region actually being referenced by a media object (including any hierarchical child regions.) The default value is *always*, but if you have lots of regions that are used only in certain parts of the presentation, you may want to use *whenActive*.

6.3.8 Stacking and Scaling Attributes

SMIL Layout provides two facilities for controlling the relative placement of media: the fit attribute controls how a media object is scaled to its window and the z-index attribute controls how windows are stacked relative to each other.

Attribute: fit

The fit attribute determines how media is scaled to the size of the region. This is only an issue if the media object is not the same size as the region into which it is being rendered. Figure 6-6 gives a summary of the options available in SMIL 2.0. In all cases, the top left corner of the media object is placed at the top left corner of the region. The value of fit determines the method with which images are resized for tailored integration into your presentations.

- fit="hidden": The default value for the fit attribute is *hidden*. In regions with fit="hidden", media objects are shown at their original size and shape, pixel by pixel. When an object is too short or narrow to reach both ends of its region, the background color fills the gaps. If the object extends beyond a region border, this extension is *hidden*, or cut off — the media object is cropped. The user cannot see the hidden portions of the object and has no means of accessing any link anchors associated with them.

- fit="scroll": The *scroll* attribute value of fit acts just like *hidden*, with one exception: the user is given a scrolling mechanism, such as a scroll bar, to access any part of the media object hidden beyond the region edge. A scroll bar will appear along either the right side or bottom of the region, or both, when the corresponding dimension of the display is too large. Some players may support other mechanisms for scrolling, such as mouse or voice interaction.

- fit="fill": While *hidden* and *scroll* preserve the original shape and size of the media object, the remaining values of fit can change the object's size for a tailored fit in the region. The value *fill* changes the size to make the media object fit exactly in the region, with no region background showing.

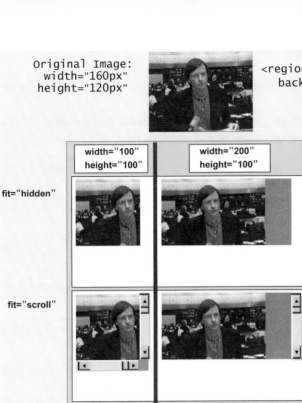

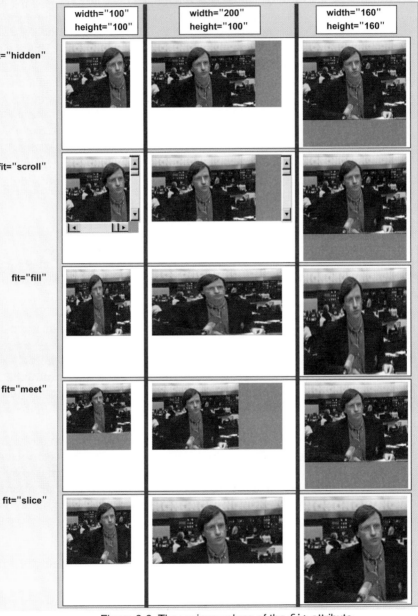

Figure 6-6. The various values of the `fit` attribute.

As a result, it can also change the rendered shape of the media — if the height/width ratio, known as the *aspect ratio*, of the media object and the region differ, the object will be squeezed and stretched to *fill* the region completely.

- fit="meet": To render the whole media object as large as possible without stretching it, use the *meet* value. This value starts the object at the upper left of the region and increases its size proportionally until it *meets* three of the region boundaries. If the object and region differ in aspect ratio, a bar of background will show along either the region bottom or right. This can be used to generate a *letterbox* effect.

- fit="slice": To fill the entire region without stretching the media object, use the *slice* value. This value starts the object at the upper left of the region and increases its size proportionally until it meets all four of the region boundaries. If the object and region differ in aspect ratio, a piece of either the image's bottom or right will be *sliced* off and hidden from the user.

Note that the manner in which the difference between the bottom and right sides of the media and region is handled varies with the fit attribute setting.

Attribute: z-index

SMIL lets you display some visual media in front of others, blocking parts or all of the media further back from view. This effect can be used, for example, to create a montage appearance of photos scattered on top of each other, or to have a background image with other smaller images on top of it. This feature is applied when two or more regions have overlapping positions defined. SMIL handles overlaps by giving all regions *z-index* stacking levels. When two regions overlap, the region with the higher z-index "covers" the other with its overlap. The z-index attribute's value is either a positive or negative integer, or zero. The higher a region's z-index attribute, the higher its stack level, and thus the further forward it appears on the screen. The z-index attribute in SMIL behaves as the z-index property in CSS, with a few exceptions that relate to timing. (The name z-index is used instead of zIndex for compatibility with both CSS and SMIL 1.0.)

When two regions overlap, everything shown in the region with the higher z-index covers this overlap. This includes any still or moving image displayed in the region, plus any region background color. Transparent areas of the covering region will not block underlying region content. Such transparent areas include transparent region background color as well as transparent portions of images displayed[2].

---

2 Some SMIL 1.0 players and many SMIL 2.0 Basic players may not be able to support z-index processing of high-performance media such as video. The direct use of low-level pixel mapping support may preclude the player's ability to process overlap information efficiently. Always test applications combining video with layered regions on target devices for compatibility.

When overlapping regions have the same z-index value, the region showing the most recently started media item will appear in front of the other. That is, any time a media object is presented, its region obscures any overlap with regions at the same z-index. A object started later in one of these other regions will then cover its overlap area with the first region. If displays begin simultaneously in overlapping regions with the same z-index, then the region defined lexically later in the SMIL code will appear foremost on the screen.

6.3.9 Referencing Regions from Media Objects

Media objects use a single attribute to reference layout regions.

Attribute: region

SMIL Basic Layout defines the region attribute as the mechanism used by media objects to reference one or more layout regions. The value of the region attribute typically refers to a <region> element in SMIL-defined layout based on the regionName or id (in that order), though it can also refer to the name of a rendering device in a <layout> element's alternative format, such as CSS.

6.3.10 SMIL Empty Layout Semantics

Media object elements without a resolved region name are *orphans*. Orphaned media are displayed according to the empty layout rules. This results in rendering orphaned object in the upper-left corner of the browser's main presentation window. Such media is not resized and can potentially fill the entire window, although some browsers may limit the space given to orphaned media to a fixed size (such as 100x100). When you see a media object unexpectedly appear outside the context of a defined region, it may be because it is orphaned.

6.4 SMIL Audio Layout Elements and Attributes

This section discusses SMIL's (minimal) support for audio.

6.4.1 Elements for Audio Layout

The *AudioLayout* module extends the functionality of the *BasicLayout* module's <region> element (see page 108) by adding a single new attribute: soundLevel. This module is specified separately from other Basic Layout support because some SMIL renderers may not be able to implement sound level manipulation.

6.4.2 Attributes for Audio Layout

The audio layout module defines one additional attribute for the <region> element: soundLevel.

Attribute: soundLevel

The soundLevel attribute allows the author to manipulate the relative output of an audio object. A typical use case is when the audio of a spoken-text object is reduced because a second spoken-text object (such as when audio captions are used) is presented in parallel.

Contrary to what you may expect, this attribute does not allow you to define an explicit output sound level as a decibel (dB) value. Instead, the soundLevel attribute takes a percentage value, which tells the player to play the sound at the defined percentage of the volume that would otherwise be used.

Setting the sound level to 100% tells the SMIL player to reproduce the sound at the same level it was saved

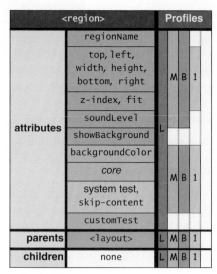

	`<region>`	Profiles			
attributes	regionName		M	B	1
	top, left, width, height, bottom, right		M	B	1
	z-index, fit		M	B	1
	soundLevel	L			
	showBackground	L			
	backgroundColor	L			
	core		M	B	1
	system test, skip-content		M	B	1
	customTest		M	B	1
parents	`<layout>`	L	M	B	1
children	none	L	M	B	1

Table 6-5. The complete `<region>` element's place in SMIL structure

in the media object. A value of 0% says to play the audio silently — but to still play it! A value of 200% will effectively double the recorded level of the audio, subject to hardware limitations. In all cases, the requested sound level is not the actual level of audio that will be produced via the output device on the player, since the user may independently set the volume control on the computer or on the physical speakers.

The default value of soundLevel is 100%. It is strongly recommended that you experiment with several values when explicitly setting the soundLevel attribute.

6.5 Examples Using SMIL Basic Layout

This section provides a number of examples of the use of SMIL Basic Layout. We start with the specification of a typical layout section, then consider how layout elements are referenced from the presentation body and conclude with an example of multi-target layout from within a single presentation.

6.5.1 Defining the `<layout>` Section

There are two cases of interest when defining a layout section in a presentation: layout for presentations with only a single media object active at one time and layout for presentations in which multiple media objects are active simultaneously.

Single Media Layout

Many simple SMIL presentations consist of a single streamed media object. It is tempting to ignore layout issues for these presentations, but this is not a good idea. In order to guarantee that a media object is shown in its (visual) entirety, a basic layout definition should be used. For a 240x180 video, the following layout section could be appropriate:

```
...
<head>
  <layout type="text/smil-basic-layout">
    <root-layout id="Example 1" width="240" height="200"
          backgroundColor="black"/>
    <region id="V" top="10" width="100%" height="180" z-index="1"/>
  </layout>
</head>
...
```

This will result in letterbox video layout: the layout will fill the width of the root layout and 10-pixel black bands will be shown on the top and the bottom of the player's window. While the root layout window and the video window could be made the same size, the use of the letterbox gives the view the impression that a widescreen video is being shown rather than a postage stamp.

Note that nothing in the layout definition restricts the media type of the contents. Note also that the values for various attributes can be mixed as percentages and pixel offsets. Finally, note that SMIL makes a distinction between the overall presentation window (the `<root-layout>`) and the rendering regions for a media objects.

Multimedia Layout

The following example shows a layout section that defines the six regions used in Figure 6-4 on page 106:

```
...
<head>
  <layout type="text/smil-basic-layout">
    <root-layout id="Example 2" width="640" height="480" />
    <region id="B" left="0" width="640px" top="0" height="480px" z-index="0"
        backgroundColor="red" showBackgrond="always"/>
    <region id="V" left="30" width="50%" top="90" height="50%" z-index="1"/>
    <region id="C" regionName="G" left="308px" width="257" top="57"
        height="160" z-index="2" backgroundColor="white" />
    <region id="H" left="370" width="55%" top="270" height="80" z-index="1"/>
    <region id="G" regionName="C" left="5%" width="300" top="335"
        height="60" z-index="2" backgroundColor="#cceeee"
        showBackground="whenActive"/>
    <region id="T" left="0" width="640" top="400" height="40" z-index="2"/>
  </layout>
</head>
...
```

In this definition, the root layout does not have a background color defined, but a separate background region is used (region *B*). While the body of the presentation will probably have a background image that is shown in this region, a separate background color is also defined — this makes sure that a predictable background is available if the background media object is not available. Since we always want to see the background, the showBackground attribute is defined to be *always*. (This is the default value; we use it for clarity.) The region labelled *G* may be used to hold an overlay graphic. We explicitly define the background to be white. Since the default functionality of always is explicitly defined, this white background will be available during the entire presentation, even when the region is not active — this is probably a bad idea. A better approach is the one shown for the region with the regionName of *C*: here, a background color is defined which will only be visible when the region is actually used to render the media content. If any part of the content is transparent, then the region's background color will show through rather than the background in the presentation. This usually gives a more controlled result.

Note that the author of this fragment is doing his best to make things interesting for the SMIL player: the region with the regionName of *G* has an id of *C*; *C* is also the regionName of the region with the id of *G*. A good SMIL player won't be fooled: a regionName will be associated with a region even if it has a different id. (Whatever the construction, all id's need to be unique.)

6.5.2 Supporting Multiple Layouts in One Presentation

In most of our examples, one layout section is defined that describes the layout geometry of the presentation. For some applications, supporting multiple layouts within the presentation is appropriate. You may want to have one layout that describes how a mobile client presents its information when it is docked and one for when the same presentation is accessed when the client is in its mobile mode. Another example is the layout approach used by the MMS mobile clients: two layouts are defined, one for landscape devices and one for portrait devices.

SMIL allows multiple layout specifications to be given and to be wrapped in a SMIL <switch>. We give an example of this in Chapter 9: *Content Selection and Control*.

6.5.3 Referencing Media in the Presentation

Once a layout section has been defined, the media content in the presentation can be directed to the appropriate regions using the region attribute:

```
   ...
      ...
    <par id="Story4" >
      <video id="Studio4"  region="V" src="rtsp://.../studio4.mpg"/>
      <img id="Graphic4" region="G" src="Uncle.png"/>
      <img id="Headline4" region="H" src="MonkeyHeadline.mpg"/>
      <ref id="Caps4" region="C" src="MkyCaps.ttxt" systemCaptions="true"/>
    </par>
   ...
```

This fragment shows how media elements can send multiple sets of information to the layout objects based on the timing structure of the presentation. The layout definition knows nothing about the presentation timing and the presen-

```
<?xml version="1.0" encoding="ISO-8859-1"?>
<!DOCTYPE smil PUBLIC "-//W3C//DTD SMIL 2.0//EN"
                "http://www.w3.org/TR/REC-smil/SMIL20.dtd">
<smil xmlns="http://www.w3.org/2001/SMIL20/Language">
<head>
  <layout type="text/smil-basic-layout">
    <root-layout id="What Cheer" width="640" height="480" />
    <region id="B" left="0" width="640px" top="0" height="480px" z-index="0"
        backgroundColor="red"/>
    <region id="V" left="30" width="50%" top="90" height="50%" z-index="1"/>
    <region id="C" regionName="G" left="308px" width="257" top="57"
        height="160" z-index="2" backgroundColor="white"
        showBackground="whenActive"/>
    <region id="H" left="370" width="55%" top="270" height="80" z-index="1"/>
    <region regionName="C" left="5%" width="300" top="335" height="60"
        z-index="2" backgroundColor="#cceeee" showBackground="whenActive"/>
    <region id="T" left="0" width="640" top="400" height="40" z-index="2"/>
  </layout>
</head>
<body>
  <par id="NewsMaster">
    <img id="Background" region="B" src="NewsBack1.png" />
    <ref id="ticker" region="T" src="feed.ttxt" />
    ...
    <par id="Story4" >
      <video id="Studio4"  region="V" src="rtsp://.../studio4.mpg"/>
      <img id="Graphic4" region="G" src="Uncle.png"/>
      <img id="Headline4" region="H" src="MonkeyHeadline.mpg"/>
      <ref id="Caps4" region="C" src="MkyCap.txt" systemCaptions="true"/>
    </par>
    ...
  </par>
</body>
</smil>
```

Example 6-1. SMIL code for Figure 6-4's layout.

tation timing does not know anything about the presentation layout: the two sections are orthogonal in terms of functions and features.

We can combine the layout and the referencing sections together into one presentation. Example 6-1 shows how the news presentation developed in Figure 6-4 could be implemented using SMIL Basic Layout.

6.5.4 Adjusting Rendering Properties

The following fragment shows how layout attributes can be used on SMIL media elements to control presentation rendering behavior:

The layout region *V* is given a size of 640 wide by 480 high. The default scaling algorithm specified with the fit attribute is *fill*, which means that the content in the presentation will be stretched in both directions to fit the display space.

In the body section, three media objects are presented in sequence. The first is a picture of a famous movie actor. While famous actors often like the idea of a face lift, they typically don't like to have their cheeks spread wide or their noses pulled down, so the default fit="fill" behavior will probably get you into trouble. Instead, set the fit value to *meet*: this scales the image to fill the space,

```
    ...
  <head>
    <layout type="text/smil-basic-layout">
      <root-layout id="Example 3" width="640" height="480"
          backgroundColor="red"/>
      <region regionName="V" width="640px" height="480px" fit="fill"/>
    </layout>
  </head>
    ...
  <seq id="FilmReviewsAndNews">
    <img id="First" region="V" src="actor.png" fit="meet" dur="5s"
        backgroundColor="0xff00bb"/>
    <video id="Second" region="V" src="movie.mpg" fit="hidden" />
    <text id="Third" region="V" src="review.html"dur="45s"/>
  </seq>
    ...
```

Example 6-2. Adjusting layout from the presentation <body>.

but it preserves the original aspect ratio of the media. Note that this actor's contract apparently specifies a particularly flattering background color, so the
media object also explicitly sets the backgroundColor attribute.

The second media object is the film itself. Because video is expensive to
reshape in real time, it is advisable to keep the object at its original size. You can
do this with a fit override value of *hidden*. If the video is smaller than 640x480,
the background will show. In Chapter 12: *Advanced Layout Topics*, we show
how advanced layout can be used to center the media in a window; this is not
supported in basic layout.

The final media object is an HTML review. Here, a scaling option to fill the
space is appropriate.

6.5.5 Rendering Multiple Copies of a Single Media Object

In addition to manipulating the size of a media object, SMIL also lets you target
multiple regions from a single media object. The regionName attribute is the
key to this functionality. Consider the following fragment:

```
<?xml version="1.0" encoding="ISO-8859-1"?>
<!DOCTYPE smil PUBLIC "-//W3C//DTD SMIL 2.0//EN"
                "http://www.w3.org/TR/REC-smil/SMIL20.dtd">
<smil xmlns="http://www.w3.org/2001/SMIL20/Language">
  <head>
    <layout type="text/smil-basic-layout">
      <root-layout id="Player-Window" width="1280" height="960"
          backgroundColor="red"/>
      <region regionName="V" width="640px" height="480px" fit="hidden"
          top="0" left="0" />
      <region regionName="V" width="640px" height="480px" fit="hidden"
          top="50%" left="0" />
      <region regionName="V" width="640px" height="480px" fit="hidden"
          top="0" left="50%" />
      <region regionName="V" width="640px" height="480px" fit="hidden"
          top="50%" left="50%" />
    </layout>
  </head>
  <body id="WallOfTVs">
    <video id="RobsFavorite" region="V" src="movie.mpg" fit="hidden"/>
  </body>
</smil>
```

In this infamous example, multiple regions have the same name (because they use the `regionName` attribute), so the media object is displayed in all the regions simultaneously. If, for whatever reasons, the player is unable to present the media object in all these regions, then the object will be shown in the region that was defined first in the SMIL code. For this reason, make sure the most important region for a multiply displayed media item is defined first in the code.

6.6 Summary and Conclusion

For the most part, SMIL layout defines the spatial arrangement of visual media on the screen. It establishes the windows used in a presentation, and what media gets shown in them. Within these windows, SMIL layout sets up regions for the different spaces media gets shown in. Layout constructs can adapt the size and shape of images to fit best in these allocated spaces. While elements from the SMIL Layout Modules typically hold the attributes for this positioning and adjustment, media object elements can assign these as well for further fine-tuning of individual image displays. In addition to this placement of visual media, SMIL layout also controls the relative volume of audio media played in a presentation.

The facilities discussed in this chapter form a base for layout functionality. SMIL 2.0 also supports a number of advanced layout features that make media positioning easier and more predictable. They also allow layout regions to be structured as a hierarchy of regions. (This is useful if you want to animate the position of multiple objects in a coordinated manner.) Finally, advanced layout also allows you to selectively create new regions dynamically on the media object reference line for increased positioning control. All of these features are discussed in Chapter 12: *Advanced Layout Topics*.

6.7 Further Resources

CSS

Cascading Style Sheets, Level 2, Bert Bos, Håkon Wium Lie, Chris Lilley and Ian Jacobs (eds.), W3C Recommendation, 12 May 1998.
`http://www.w3.org/TR/CSS2`.

HTML

XHTML 1.0: The Extensible HyperText Markup Language (Second Edition), Steven Pemberton, (ed. chair), W3C Recommendation, 1 August 2002,
`http://www.w3.org/TR/xhtml1`.

7

Basic SMIL Timing

SMIL timing defines when elements in a presentation get scheduled and, once scheduled, how long they will be active. The SMIL timing facilities are the core contribution of the SMIL standard: using the elements and attributes defined in the 19(!) timing modules, time can be integrated into any XML language.

Many multimedia authors are familiar with basic timing concepts. Tools to create individual media assets — such as video and audio objects — have long integrated some notion of timing when constructing and combining audio and video assets. Unlike most media editing, however, SMIL takes timing several steps further: in a SMIL-based document, every media object and nearly every structural element has a specific timing scope. While media timing plays an important role in determining the overall duration of a presentation, the structure of the document is also used to simplify and optimize the rendering of media presentations. SMIL timing defines a collection of elements that determine the relative start and end times of document objects and a collection of attributes that control the duration, persistence, repetition and accuracy of timing relations in a document. SMIL can be used directly as the host language for a document (as is done in the SMIL Language profile and in SMIL Basic), but it can also serve as the basis for integrating time-based coordination of otherwise static elements (as is done in SVG animation and in the XHTML+SMIL profile).

In order to understand SMIL and to use its facilities efficiently, this chapter starts with a discussion on the basic aspects of the SMIL timing model. We then discuss the basic temporal elements and attributes available with SMIL, plus some powerful extensions. We then provide some examples of how timing can be integrated into various SMIL-based presentations. Timing is a complex subject. For this reason, our discussion is centered around a series of small examples, each of which illustrates an important timing element or attribute.

> **Quick Tip**
>
> The best way to understand SMIL timing features is to construct small demonstration programs of your own and to play them on a SMIL player. The book's Web site has a set of initial demos to get you started.

7.1 SMIL Timing Model Basics

The timing model used by SMIL to specify the (relative) begin times of media objects and their durations is based on a *structured timing model*. This means that the nested presentation structure in a SMIL document — and not only hard-coded clock values — are used to define the high-level activation and synchronization of objects. For many simple SMIL documents, you will never have to explicitly specify a begin time or a duration of a media object: the SMIL player can figure all of these out at presentation time. Of course, if you want more precise control over your presentation (such as inserting delays or specifying interactive behavior), SMIL also provides more complex timing mechanisms.

In order to use SMIL effectively, it is important to understand several key principles of SMIL's timing and synchronization model. This section provides an overview of the concepts used by SMIL and it gives background information on why SMIL does things the way it does. Later sections provide more detailed information on all of SMIL's timing facilities. The timing model is covered in more detail in Chapter 13: *Advanced SMIL Timing Behavior and Control*.

7.1.1 A Simple Slideshow Presentation

We introduce the timing issues addressed by SMIL in terms of the slideshow presentation depicted in Figure 7-1. This presentation contains a single background image on top of which a sequence of slides is placed, each with an accompanying image containing a text label and an audio file containing spoken commentary. The presentation also contains a single background music object that is played throughout the presentation.

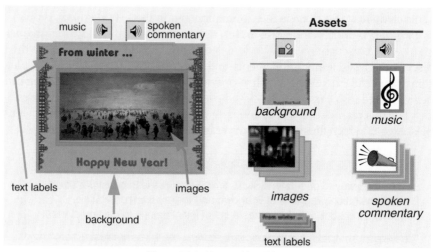

Figure 7-1. Happy New Year

The timing in this presentation is dominated by two objects: the background music object determines the duration of the total presentation and the spoken commentary objects are used to determine the duration of each of the image slides. This means that we have an outer time base for the entire presentation and a set of inner time bases for each slide in the presentation.

7.1.2 Media Object and Presentation Timing Definitions

A basic property of multimedia presentations is that they require some degree of temporal coordination among the objects being presented. The more complex a presentation — either in terms of number of simultaneous objects or number of synchronization control points — the greater the amount of control information required. SMIL uses *timing attributes* and *timing elements* to provide the activation and synchronization control information in a presentation. In general, timing attributes are used to control the timing behavior of media object and timing elements are used to control the behavior of the presentation as a whole.

Media Timing

As we saw in Chapter 3: *Local and Streaming Media*, multimedia presentations contain two types of media objects: *discrete* media and *continuous* media. Discrete media objects, such as the text labels, the background image and each of the slide images in Figure 7-1, have no implicit duration. If referenced in a SMIL file without any additional timing attributes, their duration will be 0 seconds — which is not very long. *Continuous* media, such as the background music object and each of the spoken commentaries in Figure 7-1, have implicit durations that are defined within their media encodings. If referenced in a SMIL file without any additional timing attributes, they will be rendered for the full duration defined by the object.

In our example, we want each slide image and the associated text labels to be displayed for a duration that is defined by the accompanying spoken commentaries. (Each slide/text/audio group will have different durations, since not all spoken commentary is equally long.) SMIL provides a range of attributes that allow the duration of objects to be explicitly defined and refined, and it provides a general inheritance model in which the durations of both discrete and continuous media can be obtained by the context in which a media object is presented in relation to other objects. This allows the durations of the images and text to match that of the spoken audio.

Presentation Timing

A SMIL file contains references to one or more of media objects and a set of timing primitives that determine when these objects get started relative to one another. The total timing of each of the media objects, plus any additional timing control defined in the SMIL file, determines the duration of the composite presentation. Sometimes this composite duration can be calculated in advance, but often it can't.

The basic timing of the slideshow presentation described in Figure 7-1 is deterministic: that is, we can determine the full timing in advance of the presentation's execution by evaluating the timing of each of the continuous media objects. It is important to understand, however, that our presentation is only deterministic if we ignore several potential presentation-time delays — these include any streaming delays associated with bringing the media object from a server to the presentation device, or any delays at the client associated with decoding and rendering individual media objects. For local presentations, such as CD-ROM multimedia, it is safe to assume that all the delays in the system can be predicted in advance and factored into the presentation timing. For Web-based multimedia, where the delays when obtaining media may be considerable (and unpredictable) and where there may be wide variability in the performance of end-user devices, assuming that presentations are fully deterministic is a dangerous strategy.

A presentation with uncertain timing characteristics is called *non-deterministic*. In addition to the network streaming delays discussed above, non-deterministic timing can also be the result of content substitution within the presentation or as a result of using interactive, event-based presentation timing. We discuss the impact of content substitution on timing in Chapter 9: *Content Selection and Control* and interactive timing in Chapter 13: *Advanced SMIL Timing Behavior and Control*.

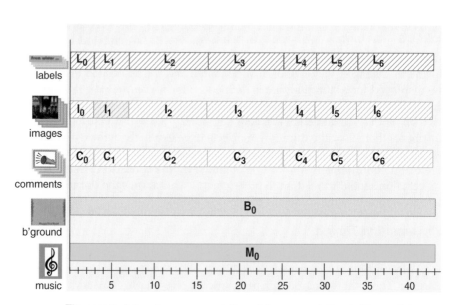

Figure 7-2. A timeline representation of the presentation in Figure 7-1.

SMIL and Timelines

A timeline metaphor is often used to model presentations. A timeline is a simple graph showing time on one axis and one or more media objects on the other axis. An example timeline, showing the elements and objects in Figure 7-1 is shown in Figure 7-2. This timeline shows the media sorted by layout: the left axis shows the various classes of media objects used, and the bottom axis shows the cumulative duration. We could have also defined separate lines for each media object, but this is usually less space efficient.

A timeline exposes the exact temporal relationships among media items. We can translate this to a text format by assigning explicit begin times for each media object and defining durations to discrete objects. One such encoding is the time-list structure of Example 7-1. The background audio and image objects (lines 1 and 2) are followed by the set of slide images (lines 3-9), the spoken commentary (lines 10-16) and the image-encoded text labels (lines 17-23). The begin times are determined by the duration of the spoken commentary objects. While Example 7-1 could be used as the basis for SMIL timing, this would be unwise. A better approach is to use structure-based timing primitives.

SMIL and Structure-Based Timing

The main advantage of the timeline model is that it is an easy-to-understand representation of continuous media objects under deterministic timing conditions. As such, it is a representation used often in video and audio media editors. Unfortunately, while deterministic timing is good for modelling video tape, it doesn't scale well to most Web environments: if one of the image objects arrives later than planned, or if the client is slow in rendering the audio, the timeline doesn't really help in maintaining order among objects. Things

```
 1  <audio id="M0" begin="0s"              ... />
 2  <img id="B0" begin="0s"   dur="43s"... />
 3  <img id="I0" begin="0s"   dur="3s"  ... />
 4  <img id="I1" begin="3s"   dur="4s"  ... />
 5  <img id="I2" begin="7s"   dur="9s"  ... />
 6  <img id="I3" begin="16s"  dur="9s"  ... />
 7  <img id="I4" begin="25s"  dur="4s"  ... />
 8  <img id="I5" begin="29s"  dur="5s"  ... />
 9  <img id="I6" begin="34s"  dur="9s"  ... />
10  <audio id="C0" begin="0s"             ... />
11  <audio id="C1" begin="3s"             ... />
12  <audio id="C2" begin="7s"             ... />
13  <audio id="C3" begin="16s"            ... />
14  <audio id="C4" begin="25s"            ... />
15  <audio id="C5" begin="29s"            ... />
16  <audio id="C6" begin="34s"            ... />
17  <img id="L0" begin="0s"   dur="3s"  ... />
18  <img id="L1" begin="3s"   dur="4s"  ... />
19  <img id="L2" begin="7s"   dur="9s"  ... />
20  <img id="L3" begin="16s"  dur="9s"  ... />
21  <img id="L4" begin="25s"  dur="4s"  ... />
22  <img id="L5" begin="29s"  dur="5s"  ... />
23  <img id="L6" begin="34s"  dur="9s"  ... />
```

Example 7-1. Time-list translation of the timeline in Figure 7-2

become even more troublesome if we don't know the implicit duration of the audio items when constructing the timeline or if the duration of the object changes over the lifetime of the presentation. (Since the SMIL file doesn't contain the media — it contains a pointer to the media — the timing and the update history of the media object are de-coupled from its use.) Finally, if we add content substitution or interactive timing to the presentation (such as having the follow-on slide begin on a mouse click rather than at a fixed time) the timeline representation loses almost all of its utility.

In order to provide a more realistic framework for Web documents, SMIL is based on a *structured* timing framework in which the structured relationships among objects can be used to define most timing. SMIL encodes its timing relationships by defining a logical timing hierarchy rather than an exact timeline. The hierarchy for Figure 7-1 is shown in Figure 7-3. Here we see a set of green logical parallel nodes (P_0-P_7) and one blue logical sequential node (S_0). The parallel components say: activate the sub-components together as a unit, and the sequential component says: activate the sub-components sequentially. The SMIL textual encoding of the presentation hierarchy is shown in Example 7-2.

While a timeline can state that objects I_2, C_2 and L_2 all start at 7 seconds into the presentation and that they each have a duration of 9 seconds, the SMIL hierarchy can state what is really going on logically:

- that objects C_i, I_i and L_i are to be treated as a logical group that get scheduled together (that is, they begin and end together);
- that the duration of I_i and L_i depend on the duration of C_i,
- that all three objects are to begin after object C_{i-1} — and, by extension, I_{i-1} and L_{i-1} — end.

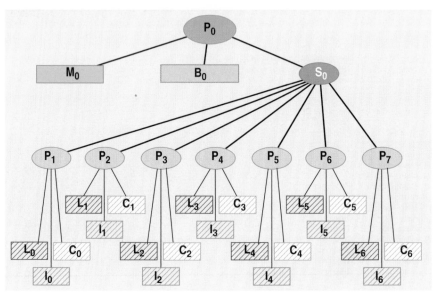

Figure 7-3. The SMIL hierarchy for Figure 7-1.

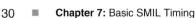

```
<par id="P0" >
 <audio id="M0"    ... />
 <image id="B0"    ... />
 <seq id="S0" >
  <par id="P1" >
   <img id="I0"    ... />
   <audio id="C0"  ... />
   <img id="L0"    ... />
  </par>
  <par id="P2" >
   <img id="I1"    ... />
   <audio id="C1"  ... />
   <img id="L1"    ... />
  </par>
  ...
  <par id="P7" >
   <img id="I6"    ... />
   <audio id="C6"  ... />
   <img id="L6"    ... />
  </par>
 </seq>
</par>
```

Example 7-2. SMIL structure for Figure 7-1.

Note that none of these relationships depend on the exact duration of any of the objects — you can construct a SMIL file before you know anything about the actual media being used.

A single timeline for one instance of a SMIL specification (that is, for one of the — potentially many — run-time uses of the presentation) can be constructed by combining the structured composition of objects with a model of the execution environment that contains information on the performance of the network connection, the preferences of the user, etc. A timeline based on the implicit media timings alone is not rich enough to model the various structured paths throughout a SMIL presentation.

7.1.3 Durations, Time and Timebases

One of the most powerful features of SMIL is a flexible time model in which various aspects of an element's behavior can be determined by the context in which it is being presented. In order to use this model, it is important to understand a number of temporal distinctions and constraints applied by the SMIL model. These include defining the active period of an element and defining the way that delays and relative starting/ending times can be expressed in a document.

Defining the Active Period of an Element

Most media formats require that the duration of all of the component media objects are explicitly defined. SMIL has several attributes that support direct duration definition, but it also provides attributes that allow you to specify or limit several layers of logical object durations. These layered durations, which are illustrated in Figure 7-4, are:

(a)
Implicit
Duration

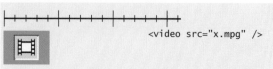

`<video src="x.mpg" />`

In this example, the *implicit duration* is 4 seconds.

(b)
Simple
Duration

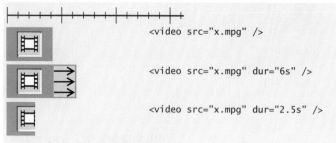

`<video src="x.mpg" />`

`<video src="x.mpg" dur="6s" />`

`<video src="x.mpg" dur="2.5s" />`

Implicit Duration modified by dur.

(c)
Active
Duration

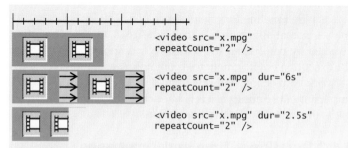

`<video src="x.mpg"`
`repeatCount="2" />`

`<video src="x.mpg" dur="6s"`
`repeatCount="2" />`

`<video src="x.mpg" dur="2.5s"`
`repeatCount="2" />`

Simple duration modified by a repeat count or duration.

(d)
Rendered
Duration

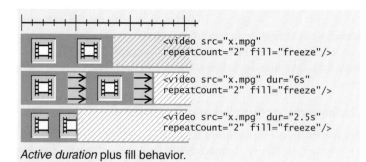

`<video src="x.mpg"`
`repeatCount="2" fill="freeze"/>`

`<video src="x.mpg" dur="6s"`
`repeatCount="2" fill="freeze"/>`

`<video src="x.mpg" dur="2.5s"`
`repeatCount="2" fill="freeze"/>`

Active duration plus fill behavior.

Figure 7-4. SMIL durations.

- *Implicit duration*: This is the duration of the media object as defined when the object was created. Most discrete media items have an implicit duration of 0 seconds; some quasi-discrete media — such as animated images — may have a longer duration, but they are modelled as having an implicit duration of 0 seconds. Continuous media objects have a duration that is equal to the temporal length of the object. Many media formats (but not all!) define the implicit duration explicitly in the media encoding. If this encoding is not available, the SMIL player typically will have to scan the entire object to determine its duration. (This can be a time consuming process.) Since a SMIL file does not contain the actual media, the SMIL timing model cannot make very many assumptions about an object's duration. This is why other logical timing durations have been defined within SMIL. Note that the implicit duration is also often called an object's intrinsic or inherent duration. See Figure 7-4(a).

- *Simple duration*: It is possible to modify an object's implicit duration with an explicit duration via SMIL's dur attribute. The result of applying an explicit duration (if any) to an object yields its simple duration. (If the implicit duration is not modified by a dur attribute, then the implicit and simple durations are the same.) The simple duration of an object may be longer or shorter than the implicit duration. Simple durations can also be defined to have special values that logically limit or stretch the duration of objects; these are the *media* and *indefinite* values, and are considered on page 135. See Figure 7-4(b).

- *Active duration*: SMIL defines a number of attributes that allow an element to be repeated. These attributes modify the element's simple duration, and the resulting repeated duration is called the object's active duration. If an element's simple duration is shorter than its implicit duration, only the first part of the element will be repeated. If the element's simple duration is longer than its implicit duration, the entire element plus the temporal difference between the implicit and simple durations will be repeated. (During this "extra" time, either nothing will be rendered or the final frame/sample of the media object will be rendered: the behavior depends on the media type.) The end attribute can be used to define when the active duration ends. If an element does not repeat, its simple and active durations are the same. See Figure 7-4(c).

- *Rendered duration*: The active duration of an element ends after its dur/end and repeat attributes have been applied. This does not mean that an object disappears at the end of its active duration. SMIL provides an attribute to control the persistence of an object after its active duration has ended: the fill attribute. If fill is set to *freeze*, the element will remain rendered until the end of its parent time container. If fill is set to *remove*, the object is removed from the screen as soon as its active duration ends. For discrete media with a fill="freeze" attribute, the object will simply be rendered as if its active duration was extended; for visual continuous media, the last frame or sample of the object will be rendered. (For an example, look at lines 17-19 in Example 7-2 on page 131: images I_6 and L_6 remain visible even though they have an active duration of 0 seconds because the effective default value for fill on these objects is *freeze*.)[1]

It is important to understand that each of these durations apply to every temporal element in SMIL. Every element has an implicit, simple, active and rendered duration. Luckily, most of these durations can be managed by the SMIL player, but understanding each of these durations, and their impact on presentation timing, can help you understand why a SMIL player behaves the way it does for your presentation.

Clock Values

Many timing attributes are based on clock values. These values can take several different forms, and they may serve as all or part of an attribute's time value. All clock values represent a relative time, and have meaning only within the context of a time container.

Clock values may be given in four general forms:

- *Full clock values*: These are times represented as a colon-separated list of hours, minutes, seconds and fractions of a second. (If you also need to specify days, months and years, use *wallclock timing* instead.) A full clock value of 5:22:19.94 means 5 hours, 22 minutes, 19 seconds and 940 milliseconds. (The fractional component is optional, all the others are required.) This is a relative time, and has meaning only within the context of a time container's *syncbase*. (Syncbases are described below.)

- *Partial clock values*: These are times represented as a short-hand notation containing minutes, seconds and (optionally) fractions of a second. A clock value of 11:10.95 means 11 minutes, 10 seconds and 950 milliseconds.

- *Timecount values*: These are numbers with an optional type string and an optional fractional component. An integer clock value with no type string (such as '10') implies a timecount in seconds; it is equivalent to '10s'. Allowed type strings are: "h", "min", "s" and "ms".

- *Wallclock values*: These are times represented in three parts: a date field, a time field and an (optional) timezone field. The format for the date field is: YYYY-MM-DD, followed by a required 'T' character. The time field is the same as in the full clock value, above. The timezone offset format, when used, is: {+|-}hh:mm; it specifies an offset from UTC. If a timezone offset is not given, the local time on the player's host is used. An example of wallclock time is: 2004-01-04T10:14:48.12+1:00.

SMIL also allows relative times within media elements to be specified in a time notation that is relevant to that media. This is considered in Chapter 14.

---

1 Our discussion in this chapter on the freeze and remove values for fill considers basic functionality. We discuss the details of fill more completely in Chapter 14: *Advanced SMIL Timing Attributes*.

Syncbases

Except in the special case of wallclock timing, every clock value in SMIL is relative to some other part of the document. The child elements of a parallel container are started relative to the start time of the parent, while the child elements of a sequential container are started relative to the end of their predecessor (except for the first child, which starts at the beginning of its parent). Every element in a SMIL specification has a specific temporal reference point: its *syncbase*. Most elements never have to explicitly specify their syncbase reference since the common SMIL time containers do this by default. Sometimes, however, an element may want to specify a non-default syncbase as its reference object. SMIL supports this functionality using *explicit syncbase timing*. An explicit syncbase is a named element (within the same host document) that has a temporal context, and which is not a child of the element in which it is being referenced. (This is less complex than it reads.) A syncbase timing reference contains a temporal event that is used as the scheduling base for the referencing object. This timing reference can be further modified with a clock value.

In order to fully appreciate the role of syncbase timing, we first need to consider the elements and attributes defined for less complex operations, but to give a taste of what's ahead, consider the SMIL fragment in Example 7-3.

```
1 <smil ...>
2 ...
3      <video id="a" src="a.mpg" />
4 ...
5         <img id="name" begin="a.begin+10s" end="a.end" src="name.png" />
6 ...
7 </smil>
```

Example 7-3. An overview of syncbase timing.

This example contains an element on line 3 that starts an associated video object. In some other part of the document, an image containing a text label is started 10 seconds after the video begins. The label remains visible until the end of the video.

Syncbase timing can be very complex and its use in simple documents is rare. Still, for certain applications, it can be a powerful construct.

7.1.4 Special Timing Values

SMIL defines two special timing values that can be used to specify the temporal context of an element. These are *indefinite* and *media*.

Value: *indefinite*

The indefinite value can be used to indicate that a timing dependency (either a begin/end time or a duration) is to be determined outside of the element in which the indefinite value appears. While many SMIL authors (and some SMIL implementers!) assume that indefinite is synonymous with "forever," it is really synonymous with "I have no local idea ...". As we will see later in this chapter, an attribute assignment of dur="*indefinite*" simply means that some other part of the SMIL specification — either the parent time container or some other element — will determine the element's duration. Only if no other part of the document constrains the duration will an indefinite value result in an unlimited duration, but even then, a value of indefinite can never result in a presentation that a user (or user agent) cannot end.

Value: *media*

The attribute value *media* can be applied to obtain the desired timing value directly from the associated media item. Although it is not often required to explicitly use the media value (mostly because this will be the default behavior), it is sometimes useful to set a duration or end time to *media* when you want to exert explicit control in complex timing situations. We will give examples of this value for the attributes begin, end, dur, max, repeatCount and repeatDur when these are discussed later in this chapter.

7.1.5 Interactive Timing and Events

In the normal course of processing, the activation hierarchy of a SMIL 2.0 document determines the rendering of document elements. The user can influence the elements selected by using SMIL 2.0 events. The event architecture allows document components that are waiting to be activated or terminated to actually start or stop. There are several uses of events allowed in SMIL 2.0, but perhaps the most important new semantic in the language is the combination of events and the begin/end attributes. In further combination with the <excl> element, events provide a very powerful mechanism for conditional content activation. Interactive timing is treated in Chapter 13: *Advanced SMIL Timing Behavior and Control*.

SMIL 2.0 also supports a rich hyperlinking architecture. Unlike links in XHTML, the fundamental concept of the SMIL link is that it models a temporal seek in a presentation. Rather than simply activating a target element, the target play state that is activated is identical to the state that the presentation would have been in if the target point had been arrived at 'naturally'. (One exception is that all event-based activation is ignored.) This means that all nodes temporally between the source and destination of the link need to be evaluated to see if they would have contributed to the final target play state. The temporal seeking and activation facility allows very polished presentation construction — but its implementation in the player is not for the faint-hearted! SMIL's linking facilities is the subject of Chapter 8: *Basic Linking*.

7.2 Basic SMIL Timing Elements

SMIL 2.0 extends the elements and attributes available for creating XML-structured multimedia presentations defined for SMIL 1.0. At the same time, SMIL 2.0 introduced a profile-based architecture in which various timing (and other

SMIL) components are made available to non-SMIL host languages. This section provides an overview of each of the elements and attributes available in all profiles that include any SMIL timing. They are defined in the SMIL *BasicTimeContainers* module. *BasicTimeContainers* is a stand-alone module that can be easily integrated into other languages.

A SMIL presentation is a structured composition of autonomous media objects. The high-level composition is achieved using three timing elements: the <par>, the <seq> and the <excl>. Of these, the <excl> is an advanced timing element that is not supported in all profiles. Therefore, we discuss it separately in Chapter 13: *Advanced SMIL Timing Behavior and Control*.

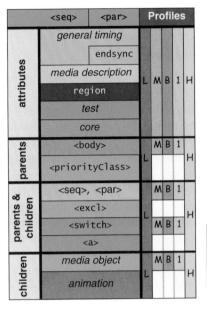

	<seq>	<par>	Profiles				
attributes	general timing						
		endsync					
	media description		L	M	B	1	H
	region						
	test						
	core						
parents	<body>			M	B	1	
	<priorityClass>		L				H
parents & children	<seq>, <par>			M	B	1	
	<excl>		L				H
	<switch>			M	B	1	
	<a>						
children	media object			M	B	1	
	animation		L				H

Table 7-1. Structure of the basic time container elements.

7.2.1 Basic Time Containers

The <par> and the <seq> elements form the core of SMIL timing and are discussed below.

Element: <par>

The most general of SMIL's timing containers is the <par>. The <par> defines a local time container that can be used to activate one or more child elements. The children of a <par> container are all rendered in "parallel". In terms of SMIL's timing model, this does not mean that they get rendered at the same time, but that they share a common syncbase defined by the <par> container. Any or all of the children may be active at any time that the parent <par> is active. The structural context of the <par> element is illustrated in Table 7-1.

```
<par>
    <img id="a" dur="6s" src="..."/>
    <img id="b" dur="4s" src="..."/>
    <img id="c" dur="5s" begin="7s" src="..."/>
</par>
```

<par> temporal context

Figure 7-5. SMIL's <par> timing element.

The basic timing structure of the <par> is illustrated in Figure 7-5. The default syncbase of the <par> is the beginning of the element. That is, by default all children of a <par> element start when the <par> itself starts. (This is illustrated by nodes "a" and "b".) As discussed below, timing attributes can be used to specify other begin times. By default, the <par> ends when the last child ends, although the exact ending behavior of the <par> is determined by the endsync attribute.

Element: <seq>

A relatively unique timing container is the <seq> element. The children of a <seq> are rendered in such a way that a successor child never can begin before its predecessor child completes. In other words, the syncbase of each child is the end of the active duration of its predecessor. A successor element may have an additional start delay, but this delay cannot resolve to be negative in relation to the end time of its predecessor. The <seq> ends when its last child has ended. Unlike the <par>, the <seq> does not support the endsync attribute: since there is only one child active at a time in a <seq>, there is no need to select among children to determine the container's end. The structural context of the <seq> element is illustrated in Table 7-1.

The basic timing structure of the <seq> is illustrated in Figure 7-6. The <seq> is especially useful when describing timing in a non-deterministic environment; by specifying that a set of elements logically follow one another, then a delay in one element can be easily passed to its successors.

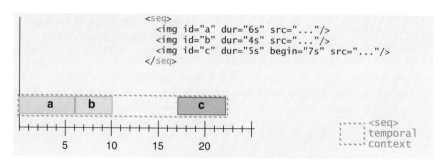

Figure 7-6. SMIL's <seq> timing element.

7.2.2 Nested Composition of Timing Elements

The basic time containers can be nested in a presentation hierarchy. That is, any child of either a <par> or <seq> (or <excl>) can be a simple media object or an embedded time container. As in SMIL 1.0, the hierarchy can represent relatively static presentation timing. The introduction of event-based activation/termination in SMIL 2.0 also allows a dynamic activation path to be defined. Most of the children of a time container will influence the timing behavior of that container, but some children — such as the <a> element, or the <switch> — are

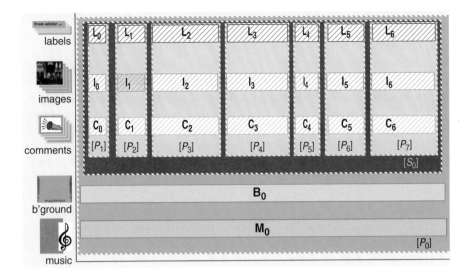

Figure 7-7. A structured timeline representation of the presentation in Example 7-2.

timing transparent. This means that they do not contribute to the determination of the container's duration.

Figure 7-7 illustrates the temporal composition of the example presentation in Figure 7-1 on page 126, based on the SMIL encoding in Example 7-2 on page 131. Note that the `<par>` and `<seq>` elements are nested as green and blue boxes, respectively. (The node labels of the structure containers are placed in brackets at the bottom of each container.) This type of structure presentation of multimedia documents — in which the structural relationships between objects are highlighted rather than the (often unknown) timing characteristics — was pioneered by the Oratrix GR*i*NS authoring environment.

7.3 Basic SMIL Timing Attributes

The *BasicTimeContainer* module of SMIL 2.0 defines the synchronization relationships available with temporal composition elements. The timing provided by the `<par>` and `<seq>` elements can be further refined by using a wealth of timing control attributes. Unlike other SMIL modules, where functionality is grouped in relatively broadly-based collections of elements and attributes, the partitioning used by SMIL timing is fine-grained. Functionality is spread across 19 timing modules, many of which contribute no more than a few values for attributes defined in other modules. The reason for such fine-grained partitioning is that complex, advanced timing is usually not needed by all languages that may want to reuse SMIL timing. By isolating functionality in collections of modules, language designers can flexibly determine the exact set of timing features that they wish to include (and specifically exclude!) in their adoption of

SMIL timing. This 'count me out' philosophy didn't hurt the SMIL standardization process, either.

The modules considered in this chapter are:

- *BasicInlineTiming*: The most basic collection of temporal attributes are grouped in the *BasicInlineTiming* module. These attributes define when an element begins and ends relative to the default syncbase defined by its parent time containers. While temporal composition elements define most timing based on logical structure, the inline timing attributes rely heavily on numerical values to determine an instant in a presentation. This module is supported by the SMIL Language profile, SMIL Basic, 3GPP SMIL, XHTML+SMIL and SVG.

- *BasicTimeContainers*: This module defines the timing elements `<par>` and `<seq>`, but it also defines two important SMIL attributes: `endsync` and `fill`. These attributes allow the structural timing defined by the elements to be refined, either by specifying which child out of a group of children controls the end of a parent container (this is the `endsync` attribute) or by allowing the perceived duration of an object — or collection of objects — to extend past its active duration (the `fill` attribute). All profiles and languages that support SMIL timing semantics will support these attributes.

- *MinMaxTiming*: Many SMIL timing attributes allow timing to be specified or modified within the context of an element's structural place in the document hierarchy. The *MinMaxTiming* module provides two attributes that provide control over the duration of an element outside the context of its temporal structure: the duration can be bound to a minimum duration or a maximum duration. The *MinMaxTiming* module is supported by the SMIL Language profile, SMIL Basic and XHTML+SMIL.

- *MultiArcTiming*: This module allows the begin and end attributes to accept a list of begin or end times. This can be useful for objects that are to be repeated, but it is especially useful for handling event-based timing.

- *SyncbaseTiming*: The *SyncbaseTiming* module allows the syncbase of an element to be explicitly defined relative to the beginning or the end of some other element in the document. (The basic time containers provide short-hand notations for syncbase timing; this module defines explicit control from elements that are not necessarily co-located.) The SMIL Language profile and XHTML+SMIL support this module

- *RepeatTiming*: The *RepeatTiming* module defines attributes that control the way in which elements are repeated. Where SMIL 1.0 had a unified — and often misunderstood — attribute for repeating elements, SMIL 2.0 introduces two attributes: `repeatCount` and `repeatDur`. This module is supported by the SMIL Language profile, SMIL Basic and XHTML+SMIL.

Given the high degree of interaction among the SMIL timing modules in defining and assigning attributes and attribute values, this chapter will not take a module-based approach for discussing SMIL timing. Instead, we look at

General Timing Control	Object Persistence Control
-begin	-fill
-end	-fillDefault
-dur	
	Extended Timing Control
Repeat Behavior Control	-endsync
-repeatCount	-min
-repeatDur	-max

Figure 7-8. Overview of timing attributes treated in this section.

timing attributes from a user perspective. Figure 7-8 gives an overview of the attributes to be discussed in this section and the classification of attributes that this chapter uses. Within each group, we discuss basic and advanced attribute use. The more esoteric uses of SMIL's basic timing attributes are discussed in Chapter 14: *Advanced SMIL Timing Attributes*.

7.3.1 General Timing Control Attributes

The general timing control attributes are: begin, dur and end. The begin attribute controls when a particular element starts, the dur attribute controls the element's simple duration and the end attribute controls the end of the active duration. (In general, begin+dur=end, but this is not always true.) The collection of general timing control attributes and values for the basic timing elements are shown in Table 7-2.

attribute	value			elements	Profiles
begin, end	begin/end			<prefetch>	
dur	clock value	"media"	"indefinite"	<a>, <area>	L M B 1 H
				<body>, <seq>	
				<par>	
				media object, <brush>	

Table 7-2. General timing control attributes.

All three of these attributes retain their behavior from SMIL 1.0. The principal SMIL 2.0 extension to begin and end is that these attributes now support a list of begin/end times instead of a single begin/end value. This is not particularly useful for simple SMIL applications, but it is very useful if a combination of SMIL's scheduled and event-based timing is used. (More on this in Chapter 13: *Advanced SMIL Timing Behavior and Control*.) Multiple begin/end times can also be useful if objects are to be restarted, as in animations.

Attribute: begin

Each of SMIL's time containers defines a default begin time for its children. The default for <par> is the start of that <par>, while the default for a <seq> depends on the lexical order of its children: the first child starts at the start of the <seq> and each successive child starts after the preceding child has ended. SMIL allows this default behavior to be overridden by the begin attribute. For simple uses, the begin attribute will contain a clock value. Usually, this clock value contains a non-zero positive temporal offset, such as:

```
begin="10"
begin="10s"
begin="0:10.0"
begin="0:00:10.0"
```

All of these values represent a begin delay of 10 seconds. Given a choice, you should probably use the second version, as it gives a reasonable balance between clarity and brevity.

Technically, a specification of:

```
begin="10s"
```

defines a 10 second delay from the implied syncbase of the element containing the begin attribute. (This is usually either the start of a parent <par> or the end of a predecessor child in a <seq>.)

Defining explicit syncbases. SMIL allows the syncbase used in the presentation to be explicitly defined for <par> elements by specifying an ID of the syncbase, and specifying a timing qualification of that syncbase (either begin or end). The following element specifies that an audio object starts 4 seconds after the end of an element named _snarf_:

```
<audio id="bazinga" begin="snarf.end+10s" ... />
```

In SMIL 1.0, the element with ID of _snarf_ had to be a peer of the _bazinga_ element. SMIL 2.0 relaxes this requirement: the element _snarf_ must be in the same document as _bazinga_, and it can't be a child of _snarf_, but there are no other restrictions. (The situation where _snarf_ and _bazinga_ are not peers is referred to as an _out-of-scope_ syncbase.) Note that SMIL 1.0 used a slightly different syntax for specifying syncbases; this format has been depreciated in SMIL 2.0.

In the SMIL Language profile (including SMIL Basic), explicit syncbases are rarely used in simple documents, but for other host languages (like those supporting the XHTML+SMIL profile), the use of explicit syncbases can be handy. This is because the host document provides no common temporal basis among its objects, so that you often need to define a common syncbase explicitly when coordinating content specified in different parts of the same document.

Specifying multiple begin times. In a SMIL 1.0 document, each element could specify at most one begin time. SMIL 2.0 allows multiple begin times to be defined. In general, an object will start as soon as any of its begin conditions are satisfied. It will also restart if a new begin condition is satisfied! For example, the following object will begin after a delay of 10 seconds from its default syncbase *and* 3 seconds after the start of *snarf*, unless it has had restrictions placed on its repeat behavior — it will not just start when the first begin condition in the list gets resolved:

```
<video begin="10s; snarf.begin+3s" ... />
```

The use of multiple begin times has a number of features and restrictions that are discussed in Chapter 14: *Advanced SMIL Timing Attributes*; these include ways of defining interactive starts of an object and restricting an object's restart behavior. For most simple SMIL documents containing only a single begin time, these restrictions are not important.

The begin *attribute and the* <seq> *element.* There is one restriction on the use of the begin attribute that *is* important for all SMIL documents: a <seq> time container may only have a single begin attribute value, and that value must contain a non-negative clock value. Multiple begin time lists are not allowed in a <seq>, and neither is explicit syncbase timing. In the following set of statements, line 5 is not valid SMIL, but lines 6 through 8 are valid and provide the same functionality as was intended in line 5:

```
 1  <par>
 2    <audio id="snarf" ... />
 3    <seq>
 4      <image begin="2s" dur="5s" ... />
 5      <img begin="snarf.end+2s" ... />    <!-- this is invalid SMIL! -->
 6      <par>                               <!-- this is valid SMIL -->
 7        <img begin="snarf.end+2s" ... />
 8      </par>
 9    </seq>
10  </par>
```

Line 5 is not valid because a child of a <seq> may not contain a syncbase offset. The <par> on line 6 begins a new temporal content: the <par> starts when the preceding image ends; it then delays the start of its child image until 2 seconds after the end of the *snarf* object.

Invalid begin times. An interesting final point is: what does a SMIL player do if you give it an improper begin time specification? Some of the rules for processing bad values are profile dependent, and others depend on the kind of begin attribute values being used. If you were to give this example to a generic SMIL player, it should refuse to play the entire document because of an error with the value of a begin attribute in a <seq>.

Attribute: dur

The dur attribute establishes the simple duration of an element. (Recall from Figure 7-4 on page 132 that the simple duration is the duration without repeat behavior.) When used with a media object, it defines how much of that media object will be used. When used with a time container, it defines a limit on the simple duration of that container. If the defined duration is longer than the time container or media object, temporal and rendering padding will result.

For all media object references, the default value for dur is media. For time containers, the default value for dur is the simple duration of the children of that container. When a value is explicitly specified, a non-zero, positive clock value is usually used.

The dur **attribute and** fill**.** Once the simple duration specified by dur ends, the associated element will either repeat (if repeat behavior has been specified) or become a candidate for removal from the player's list of rendered objects. Whether it is actually removed depends on the value of the fill attribute, as discussed on page 147.

The dur **attribute and indefinite timing.** It is also possible to assign the value of *indefinite* to dur; this means that the simple duration is explicitly defined to be indefinite, and that the active duration and the element's end moment will be taken from the temporal context of the presentation.

Examples. The following two SMIL statements result in an element with a simple duration of 0 seconds:

```
<img src="image.png" ... />
<img src="image.png" dur="media" ... />
```

The following statement is actually invalid SMIL, but many SMIL players also accept it as a means to specify an element with a simple duration of 0 seconds:

```
<img src="image.png" dur="0" ... />
```

(This is invalid because the specification explicitly says that the clock value of the dur attribute must be greater than 0.)

The following (short) presentation illustrates the behavior of the *indefinite* duration value:

```
<smil ...>
  <body>
    <img src="image.png" dur="indefinite" ... />
  </body>
</smil>
```

The image will be rendered and the simple duration will be set to indefinite. This will result in the active duration being set to the further timing context of the presentation. Since no other timing context is explicitly provided, the image will be rendered "forever".

If we extend the presentation above a bit, we can see some additional behavior of the SMIL timing model:

```
1 <smil ...>
2   <body>
3     <par>
4       <img src="image.png" dur="indefinite" ... />
5       <video id="V1" src="ten-sec-video.mpg" ... />
6     </par>
7   </body>
8 </smil>
```

In this example, the <par> on lines 3 through 6 renders an image and a 10 second video. The simple duration of the image is indefinite and the simple duration of the video is 10 seconds. After 10 seconds, the simple duration of the video ends, but the indefinite duration of the image means that unless something else in the presentation explicitly limits the duration, the presentation will not end. (The default behavior of the video is that the last frame will be shown during the entire period after 10 seconds.)

We now replace line 5 with the following:

```
5    <video id="V1" src="ten-sec-video.mpg" dur="10s" ... />
```

The result is that since the video now has an explicit duration, it no longer has default fill semantics, and the last frame is not shown for the remainder of the presentation. (Only the image is shown.)

We next replace line 3 with the following:

```
3    <par endsync="V1"/>
```

The result is that even though the image on line 4 has an indefinite duration, the <par> will end when the video on line 5 ends. The timing context for the indefinite is determined by the context of the parent.

This section has illustrated the behavior of dur on media objects, but all of the examples also apply when dur is defined for time containers such as <par> and <seq>. The only real difference is that an assignment of dur="media" is not allowed for time containers; in this case, the duration assignment will be ignored.

Attribute: end

A SMIL element ends at the end of its active duration. This is determined by either the element's content or the parent time container. An element can also specify a non-default end time via the end attribute. The end attribute is very similar to the begin attribute. Rather than repeating all of the begin's properties here, please make sure you've read the section on begin above before continuing with this section.

The end attribute provides explicit control over the end of the active duration. As with begin, the end can specify a single clock value or an explicit syncbase (with optional clock value offset), or a list of values. (There are also other values allowed; these are covered in Chapter 14: *Advanced SMIL Timing Attributes*.) Unlike the begin attribute, there is no restriction on the use of end with <seq> elements. Note that even if multiple end times are specified, the associated element will end only once — this is when the first end condition is met.

Examples. The following fragment gives examples of the use of the end attribute:

```
1    <video src="one-hour-video.mpg" end="25s" ... />
2    <video src="one-hour-video.mpg" end="1:00:15" ... />
3    <video src="one-hour-video.mpg" end="snarf.end" ... />
4    <video src="one-hour-video.mpg" end="35s; snarf.end+5s" ... />
```

In line 1, the one-hour video is cut short after 25 seconds. In line 2, the active duration of the one-hour video is extended by 15 seconds. In line 3, the video element ends when the element *snarf* ends (even if this is after 3 hours!). In line 4, the video element ends either after 35 seconds or 5 seconds after *snarf* ends, whichever comes first.

The examples above do not show a time context for each video reference. It is important to note that, unless an explicit syncbase is defined, the end attribute modifies the end time relative to the default syncbase of the element, not the duration of the media object.

Consider the SMIL fragment in Example 7-4. The default syncbase of the children of the <seq> in lines 3 through 7 is the end of the predecessor child. This means that:

- the video element on line 4 ends 25 seconds after the start of its syncbase (which is the beginning of the <seq>)
- the video element on line 5 ends one hour and 15 seconds after the start of its syncbase (which is the end of the element on line 4)
- the video element on line 6 ends one hour and 15 seconds after the start of its syncbase (which is the end of the element on line 5) — this is 5 seconds before the end of the video media object, because that object started being rendered 20 seconds after the start of its syncbase.

Make sure you understand why the end of the video element on line 6 occurs before the end of the video object: the end attribute does not modify the duration of the media object, but it modifies the end of the element containing the video object in relation to that element's syncbase.

Now, look at the <par> in lines 9 through 13 of Example 7-4. The start of the <par> on line 9 defines the default syncbase for the children of this <par>. This means that:

- the video element on lines 10 ends 25 seconds after the start of its syncbase (which is the beginning of the <par>)
- the video element on line 11 ends one hour and 15 seconds after the start of its syncbase (which is also the beginning of the <par>)

```
1 <smil ...>
2   ...
3   <seq>
4     <video src="one-hour-video1.mpg" end="25s" ... />
5     <video src="one-hour-video2.mpg" end="1:00:15" ... />
6     <video src="one-hour-video3.mpg" begin="20s" end="1:00:15" ... />
7   <seq>
8   ...
9   <par>
10    <video src="one-hour-video1.mpg" end="25s" ... />
11    <video src="one-hour-video2.mpg" end="60.25m" ... />
12    <video src="one-hour-video3.mpg" begin="20s" end="1.004167h" ... />
13  <par>
14  ...
15 </smil>
```

Example 7-4. The end attribute in relation to its syncbase.

- the video element on line 12 ends one hour and 15 seconds after the start of its syncbase (which, once again, is the beginning of the <par> on line 9) — as with the case on line 6, this is 5 seconds before the end of the video media object, because that object started being rendered 20 seconds after the start of its syncbase.

These examples all relate to a single video object, but the same syncbase-based evaluation of end times also holds true for any time container containing an explicit end attribute.

Combined Use of begin, dur and end

It is possible to combine the use of the begin, end and dur attributes on an element. Combining begin and dur usually results in obvious behavior, since they both relate to the simple duration of an object. Since the end attribute overrides the default end of the active (not simple) duration, the resulting behavior is not always obvious. The less obvious details are discussed when we look at advanced timing properties.

7.3.2 Object Persistence Attributes

Two attributes control the persistence of objects after they have completed their active duration: fill and fillDefault. In this chapter, we consider simple uses of fill behavior. More complex uses of these attributes are discussed in Chapter 14: *Advanced SMIL Timing Attributes*. The allowed values and related elements for fill are shown in Table 7-3.

attribute	value	Elements	Profiles				
fill	"freeze", "remove"	<par>, <seq>	L	M	B	1	H
		media object, <brush>					

Table 7-3. Basic object persistence attribute fill.

Attribute: fill

SMIL allows an object to remain visible after the end of its active duration by specifying a fill attribute. If fill is set to *freeze*, the object will remain visible until the end of its parent time container. If it is set to *remove*, the object is removed as soon as its active duration ends. The default for visual media is effectively *freeze*; fill has no meaning for audio media. There are some special cases for fill that allow the visibility of an object to extend past the active duration of its parent (such as when transitions exist). The value of fill also determines how long an object remains 'clickable' for linking and interaction. These cases are considered in Chapter 14: *Advanced SMIL Timing Attributes*.

If the fill attribute is applied to a time container, then the rendering state of all of the children (and descendants of the children) are set to their respective fill behavior at the moment the active duration of the container ends.

```
1 <smil ... >
2 <...>
3   <par id="outer">
4     <img id="label" src="label.png" dur="20s" />
5     <par id="inner" dur="15s">
6       <img   id="picture" src="image.png" dur="5s" fill="freeze" ... />
7       <video id="lady"       src="ten-sec-video.mpg" fill="remove" ... />
8     </par>
9   </par>
10  ...
11 </smil>
```

Example 7-5. The fill attribute.

The default fill behavior is *auto*. Determining the effective fill behavior can be complex, so we defer a complete discussion to Chapter 14: *Advanced SMIL Timing Attributes*. For most simple cases, we can use the rule that if an element explicitly defines a simple duration using dur, the effective default behavior of fill is *remove*. Otherwise, the simple duration is determined by the implicit duration of the element and the effective default fill behavior is *remove*.

Figure 7-5 illustrates fill behavior. The *outer* <par> element has an effective default fill behavior of *freeze*. Thus, when its children end, they will remain visible. The image *label* on line 4 has the default fill behavior of *remove* because of the dur. The *inner* <par> element has an effective default fill behavior of *remove*. The image *picture* has an explicit fill behavior of *freeze*, and the video *lady* has explicit fill behavior of *remove*. When the presentation starts, all media is active. After 5 seconds, *picture* ends its active duration but it stays visible because of the fill="freeze". The *lady* video ends at 10 seconds and the last frame is immediately removed. The *inner* <par> ends at 15 seconds, and removes all of its children (even the image *picture*). After 20 seconds the image *label* ends, as does the <par> *outer*, and the screen is empty.[2]

Now, assume we change line 5 to add an explicit fill="*freeze*":

```
<par id="inner" dur="15s" fill="freeze" >
```

In this case, the video *lady* is still removed after 10 seconds, but the image *picture* is displayed for the full 20 seconds (until the end of *outer*'s active duration.)

The fill *attribute and transitions.* When used with transitions, the fill attribute can also accept advanced values that can extend the simple duration (and the active duration) beyond the temporal scope of the parent time container. See Chapter 10: *Transition Effects* for details.

7.3.3 Extended Timing Control Attributes

SMIL 2.0 has two new attributes that provide extra duration control: min and max. These attributes can be used to define a lower or upper bound on the active duration of the containing element, regardless of that element's other

---

2 Note that some SMIL players keep the final state of the presentation rendered — this is a player implementation issue and has no relation to the presentation's composite fill behavior.

timing characteristics. As in SMIL 1.0, SMIL 2.0 also supports the ending of a time container via the endsync attribute. These three attributes, shown in Table 7-4, are discussed in this section.

attribute	value			elements	Profiles
min			"0"	<prefetch>	
max	clock value	"media"	"indefinite"	<a>, <area>	
				animation	L M B
				<body>, <seq>,	
endsync	"last", "first", "all"		IDREF to child	<par>, <excl>	1 H
				media object, <brush>	

Table 7-4. Extended timing attributes

Attribute: min

The min attribute can be used to specify an explicit minimum active duration on an element. It accepts either a clock value or "media" as values. The default value of min is "0", which is the same as saying that the value is unconstrained. The value *media* may only be used on media objects; its use says: the minimum duration is the implicit value of the media object. If used together with the max attribute, min must be less than or equal to the value specified for max.

The following statements give examples of the min attribute:

```
1 <video src="one-hour-video.mpg" min="25s" ... />
2 <video src="one-hour-video.mpg" min="0" ... />
3 <video src="one-hour-video.mpg" min="media" ... />
```

Statement 1 constrains the minimum active duration of the video element to 25 seconds. Line 2 illustrates default min behavior. Line 3 says that the minimum duration of the video element is the one-hour duration of the media object.

While syncbase timing cannot be used as a value for the min attribute, min can be used in conjunction with dur and end to produce interesting and occasionally useful results. Consider the following statement:

```
<video id="snarf" src="one-hour-video.mpg" min="25s"
       end="bazinga.end" ... />
```

If *bazinga* ends 15 seconds after the start of *snarf*, the duration of *snarf* will be extended for 10 seconds (to 25 seconds).

The following fragment shows the impact of min on a <par> with an explicit duration:

```
<par dur="10s" min="20s" >
  <video src="one-hour-video.mpg" ... />
  <img src="label.png" ... />
</par>
```

Without timing control, the video element would be active for an hour, and the label would be active for 0 seconds, and then be rendered for the next 60 minutes because of its default `fill="freeze"` behavior. The `min` attribute on the `<par>` says that its active duration is 20 seconds. The dur attribute on the `<par>` constrains the simple duration of the `<par>` to be 10 seconds. So, what really happens? After 10 seconds, the simple duration of the `<par>` ends, so the video and image have their timing context terminated. The `min` extends the active duration of the `<par>`, but since the simple duration has ended, only the default fill behavior is rendered: since this is *remove*, nothing is rendered for the 10 additional seconds of active duration.

Attribute: max

The `max` attribute can be used to constrain the maximum active duration of an element. It is similar to the min, except that an explicit value of indefinite can be specified. (This is also the default.)

The behavior of the max attribute is predictable, although finding relevant use cases can be a challenge. For example, consider the following statements:

```
<video id="a" src="one-hour-video.mpg" max="30s" end="bazinga.end" ... />
<video id="b" src="one-hour-video.mpg" end="30s; bazinga.end" ... />
```

The video element *a* will play for a maximum of 30 seconds or until the element *bazinga* ends (if this is earlier). The same behavior applies to video element *b*.

Attribute: endsync

Where `min` and `max` provide clock-value based constraints on element timing, SMIL provides the `endsync` attribute to provide logical control on timed objects. As in SMIL 1.0, if a `<par>` has multiple children, it can specify that the entire `<par>` ends when the first child ends, when the last child ends or when a named child ends. This attribute can be assigned to the `<par>`, `<excl>`, `<brush>`, and media object elements. (The use with `<brush>` and media objects is typically limited to animation.)

The following fragment illustrates `endsync` behavior:

```
<par endsync="snarf" >
  <video id="bazinga" src="video.mpg" ... />
  <audio id="snarf"   src="audio.mp3" ... />
</par>
```

The `<par>` ends when the *snarf* ends; if this is later than the end of *bazinga*, the last frame of *bazinga* will be frozen. The default value of endsync is *last*.

An element with the assignment endsync="*all*" waits for all of its children to play to completion at least once, regardless of whether they have scheduled or interactive begin times.

The behavior of the `endsync` attribute is intuitive, except when combined with the dur and/or end attributes. This is because having both an endsync and a dur or end will cause conflicting definitions of element duration. In order to resolve these conflicts, the following rules are applied by a SMIL player:

1) If dur and endsync are specified on the same element, the endsync is ignored. Thus, in the following example, the duration of *snarf* is 20 seconds:

```
<par id="snarf" dur="20s" endsync="b" >
   <video id="a" src="video.mpg" ... />
   <audio id="b" src="audio.mp3" ... />
</par>
```

2) If end and endsync are specified on the same element, the endsync is ignored. Thus, in the following fragment, the duration of *bazinga* ends when *snarf* ends:

```
<par id="bazinga" end="snarf.end" endsync="b" >
   <video id="a" src="video.mpg" ... />
   <audio id="b" src="audio.mp3" ... />
</par>
```

There are also some special cases of endsync behavior when used with repeated elements. We consider these below.

7.3.4 Repeating Objects and Sub-Structures

The default behavior of all elements is that they play once, for either an implicit or explicit duration. The SMIL 2.0 repeatCount attribute allows an iteration factor to be defined that acts as a multiplier of the object's simple duration. (The resulting duration is the active duration.) A special value *indefinite* is used to specify that an element is to be repeated continually until its (parent) timing context ends. The repeatDur attribute defines a duration for all of the repeated iterations. The repeat timing control attributes and values are shown in Table 7-5.

attribute	value		elements	Profiles
repeatDur	*clock value*		`<a>`, `<area>`	
			animation	
repeatCount	*decimal number greater than "0.0"*	*"indefinite"*	`<body>`, `<seq>`	L M B 1 H
			`<par>`, `<excl>`	
			media object, `<brush>`	

Table 7-5. Repeat control attributes.

Attribute: repeatCount

The repeatCount attribute makes the element's content sub-presentation or media object to repeat the stated number of times. Its value can be either a number or *indefinite*. A numeric value indicates the media object plays that number of times. Fractional values, specified with decimal points, can be used as well.

The following statement specifies that *snarf* is to be repeated 4.5 times:

```
<audio id="snarf"    src="audio.mp3"  repeatCount="4.5" ... />
```

If the associated audio file was 4 seconds long (its implicit duration), then the active duration of snarf is 18 seconds.

A repeat count may also be applied to time containers. As is shown in the following fragment, the simple duration of the container is repeated for the number of iterations specified by the repeatCount.

```
<par repeatCount="3" >
    <video id="bazinga" src="video.mpg" ... />
    <audio id="snarf"   src="audio.mp3" ... />
</par>
```

In this example, the active duration will depend on the implicit durations of the media items; the simple duration will be the maximum of *bazinga* and *snarf*. The active duration will be the simple duration times three.

A repeatCount is typically only useful on media with implicit timing, or on media with an explicit duration. Consider the following three statements:

```
1 <img id="bazinga" src="picture.png" repeatCount="3" ... />
2 <img id="snarf"    src="picture.png" dur="3s" repeatCount="3" ... />
3 <img id="rex"      src="picture.png" dur="indefinite" repeatCount="3"...  />
```

The element *bazinga* on line 1 has an implicit duration of 0 seconds; repeating the element doesn't change this. The element *snarf* on line 2 has a defined simple duration of 3 seconds; the active duration after the repeat is 9 seconds. The element *rex* on line 3 has an indefinite duration; as with a 0 duration, a repeat count doesn't alter the active duration.

If the repeat count is set to be *indefinite*, then the playback repeats until the element is stopped by its temporal context.

Attribute: repeatDur

The repeatDur attribute is similar in most respects to repeatCount, except that a duration is given instead of a multiplier. It states that the element is to repeat its playback until the specified duration has passed.

The following statement specifies that *snarf* is to be repeated for 15 seconds:

```
<audio id="snarf"    src="audio.mp3"  repeatDur="15" ... />
```

The actual number of time that the audio object is repeated depends on its duration. If the audio object's implicit duration is 3 seconds, it will repeat 5 times. If its implicit duration is 15 seconds, it will be played once. If its implicit duration is 25 seconds, only the first 15 seconds will be played.

As with all elements, a timing constraint on a parent container will limit the active duration of the children. As a result, in the following fragment, the audio object will be rendered for 25 seconds:

```
<par dur="25s">
    <audio id="snarf"    src="audio.mp3"  repeatDur="100s" ... />
</par>
```

Combing Repeat Behavior with Other Timing Attributes

It is possible to combine either `repeatCount` or `repeatDur` with other timing attributes. The resulting timing usually results in predictable behavior for simple cases, but sometimes the differences in manipulating the simple, active and rendered durations within one element can lead to SMIL statements that are not always easy to understand.

The best advice that we can give is to make sure that you understand the differences between the various types of SMIL durations. This becomes vital if you work with interactive behavior in SMIL, or if you use multiple begin times on objects. If you plan to use SMIL Animation — or if you plan to make use of the SMIL repeat attribute — then a complete understanding of the SMIL timing model is essential. We suggest that you read the model section of this chapter and Chapter 13: *Advanced SMIL Timing Behavior and Control* very carefully. As a last resort, the SMIL specification can be consulted: there you will find 156 pages of information on the timing model alone.

7.3.5 Advanced Timing and Synchronization Attributes

SMIL 2.0 provides a collection of advanced attributes to control synchronization behavior and to facilitate integration of SMIL into other XML languages. While these attributes are discussed more fully in Chapter 14: *Advanced SMIL Timing Attributes*, we introduce them briefly here.

SMIL synchronization control attributes

In a perfect world, all of the defined timing in a specification would be implemented perfectly by a SMIL 2.0 player. Unfortunately, the world is not only imperfect — it is also unpredictable. In order to provide some measure of control in the face of unpredictably, SMIL 2.0 provides three high-level synchronization control attributes: `syncBehavior`, which allows a presentation to define whether there can be slippage in implementing the composite timeline of the presentation; `syncTolerance`, which defines how much slip is allowed; and `syncMaster`, which allows a particular element to become the "master" timebase against which all others are measured.

XML integration support

When used in a native SMIL 2.0 document (one in which the outer XML tag is `<smil>`), the nature and meaning of various timing elements is clear. When integrating SMIL timing into other XML languages, a mechanism is required to identify timing containers. The SMIL 2.0 specification does this using the `timeContainer` and `timeAction` attributes.

7.3.6 The General Timing Attributes

Some of the attributes from the timing and synchronization modules apply to many SMIL element types. These are grouped into the *general timing attributes*. These attributes are:

- begin, end, dur,
- repeat, repeatCount, repeatDur,
- restart, restartDefault,
- fill, fillDefault,
- min, max,
- syncBehavior, syncBehaviorDefault, syncTolerance, and syncToleranceDefault.

Perhaps the most important thing to remember about these attributes is that they may be applied to nearly all of SMIL's elements — not just to media objects.

7.4 Summary and Conclusion

Timing is the most important contribution of SMIL. This chapter introduces the basic constructs of SMIL timing. The basic time container elements <seq> and <par> specify SMIL's simplest temporal relationships: those of playing in sequence and playing in parallel. The basic in-line timing values of the *inline* timing attributes begin, end and dur set an element's timing as temporal offsets from the begin time it gets from its time container parent. Syncbase values for the begin and end attributes synchronize an element with the beginning or ending of other elements. The attributes repeatCount and repeatDur cause an element's media object to repeat its playback. If, after its start time, duration and repeated duration, the element ends before the end of its parent, the fill attribute defines the persistence of the element in SMIL's timing tree.

This chapter has considered the basic timing and synchronization attributes. While these cover a broad range of SMIL presentations, there is more to timing control than is presented here. The SMIL timing model also supports interactive and event based timing. These constructs are considered in Chapter 13: *Advanced SMIL Timing Behavior and Control*. (They include the <excl> element and various refinements to the begin and end timing attributes discussed in this section.) The attributes discussed here also have more esoteric values and uses. These are considered in Chapter 14: *Advanced SMIL Timing Attributes*. After experimented with the basic timing support in SMIL, you are encouraged to make more extensive use of SMIL timing by using the advanced features.

A summary chart of the attributes that provide basic timing control in SMIL 2.0 are shown in Table 7-6.

attribute	value			elements	Profiles
min	*clock value*	"media"	"0"		L M B 1 H
max	*clock value*			<prefetch>	
dur	*clock value*		"indefinite"		
begin, end	*begin/end*			<a>, <area>	
repeatDur					
repeatCount	*decimal number greater than "0.0"*			<body>, <seq>	
				<par>	
endsync	"last", "first", "all"	"media"	IDREF to child	*media object*, <brush>	

Table 7-6. Structure of the basic timing and synchronization attributes.

8
Basic Linking

Of all of the features and facilities available across the Web, probably the single most important is *linking* (or, as it is sometimes known, *hyperlinking*). Linking is the ability to define and activate a non-linear navigation structure within and across electronic documents. By following a link, you select the ordering of content that best meets your needs.

The popularity of HTML and the World Wide Web have given the concepts of linking broad acceptance and a place in technological history that Vannevar Bush probably never could have imagined when he first published the basic concepts of linking more than 50 years ago[1]. SMIL provides support for all of the basic HTML linking functionality that most Web users expect, meaning that SMIL authors can quickly integrate linking into their presentations. SMIL also provides a set of extensions to HTML linking that provide support for links in a temporal environment. In addition, SMIL's linking facilities provide a way to better separate the definition of the link's components from the actual media contents; this can make linking more manageable in a dynamic Web environment. Finally, SMIL also provides features that differentiate the two main uses of linking constructs: links for navigation and links for conditional activation of content.

This chapter explores the basic linking facilities in SMIL. We start with a review of linking concepts. We then briefly relate these concepts to how linking is supported in HTML and extend the discussion to cover the concepts available in SMIL 2.0.

8.1 An Overview of Linking Concepts

In its simplest form, a link is a pointer. It defines an address of a document and, optionally, an offset within that document. Of course, to be useful, the user needs to know that the link exists. This means that a mechanism is required in the originating document to indicate that a link is present. This is called a (source) *anchor*. If the link points to anything other than the beginning of the target document, then a (destination) anchor into the target is also required.

---

1 V. Bush, "As We May Think," The Atlantic Monthly, July 1945.

There are many ways to implement links and anchors. In a conventional book, you can create an anchor by circling some text or an illustration and then create a link by writing an address — such as the name of another book and a relevant page number — in the margin. When you follow this cross-reference type of link, you will replace one document with another. (You may want to turn down the corner of the page you are currently reading so that you can return to the source place easily; doing so creates a destination anchor for the way back.) Another model for a link is the footnote[2]: you can point to additional material that is not considered mainstream, with the expectation that the reader returns to the main flow after reading the note. A glossary is an example of a multi-source link, while an index is an example of a multi-destination link.

When circling text and scribbling addresses, the anchors and links were placed directly in the source material: the book. This is handy if you are the only user of the book, but it can also be a problem if the book has many users — or if the book isn't yours. In this case, it is sometimes useful to construct a separate list where you can define source and destination anchors and the associated links without corrupting the original document.

All of these issues and concepts also relate to electronic links, including those used in HTML. SMIL extends these ideas with *timed links*: links in which the source anchor may only be active for a limited period of time (say the first eight seconds of a presentation), or in which the target of the link may change during the rendering of the media object. Adding the concept of time to links provides many new possibilities — including auto-firing of a link after a fixed period of time, or limiting the amount of data that is rendered when a link is followed.

Before looking at the intricacies of timed links, we will start with a brief review of non-temporal links as implemented in HTML We then consider non-temporal and temporal links in SMIL.

8.1.1 Links in HTML

The use of links with text-based documents is usually called *hypertext*. Text provides a relatively simple linking environment: you can easily insert the link address and the source and destination anchors in the text document using a text editor. The browser then needs to be able to identify those places where a source anchor exists, and bingo: you have links!

The most prominent uses of links in hypertext documents are:

- *links for navigation*: by following a link, you are taken from one content 'focus' to another. The link is typically uni-directional, but a two-way link can also be defined. The source focus is usually replaced by the link, but the destination can also augment the source.

---

2 In a footnote, the source anchor is the footnote symbol or number. The address in the link is typically implied: either at the bottom of the page, at the end of a chapter or at the end of the document. A second link, taking you back to the original text, is implied at the end of the footnote.

- *links for activation*: by following a link, a follow-on part of a presentation is started. This can be used when structuring the presentation of lengthy, complex information. Activation links also provide a means of presenting alternative content with one local presentation flow.

- *links for message passing*: when following certain links, it is sometimes useful to present state information to the destination document. Both navigation and activation links can be supplemented with parameters provided by the user (or the user's browser).

Of these, the use of links for navigation (with or without message passing) is the most common form of HTML's hypertext links.

In the early days of the Web, "following a link" always meant replacing one page with another. It was only later that a new window could open on link traversal, and even later that the notion of a *frame* was introduced that allowed a destination to be placed within a relatively constant common context.

While the concepts of linking are pretty straight-forward, there are many approaches to hyperlink implementation that have been presented and (passionately) defended over the last fifty years. Since SMIL linking is nearly the same — but not identical! — to HTML linking, we will concentrate on their similarities and differences in the following sections.

Embedded Anchors and Links in HTML

One of the things that made HTML linking a huge success was its simplicity. An HTML <a> element is used to define both anchors (source and destination) and link addresses. Example 8-1 shows a simple HTML document that illustrates the basic concepts of HTML links. An HTML source anchor defines a span of content that is placed between the <a>...</a> elements (see lines 3, 4 and 5). The source anchor can span one character or an entire document, but it cannot overlap other source anchors.

An HTML destination anchor is defined by the 'name' attribute in the <a> element (line 6). The destination anchor may span a range of content (line 6), or it may identify a single point in the document (line 7).

```
1  <HTML>
2  <Body>
3    <P>Here is an <A href="#nearTheEnd"> anchor </A>.
     It points to a location within this document.</P>
4    <P>This is another
     <A href="http://www.w3.org/AudioVideo">anchor</A>.
     It points to an external document located at www.w3.org.</P>
5    <P>Here is a link containing a reference to a destination anchor
     <A "http://www.w3.org/TR/smil20/extended-linking.html
        #SMILLinking-Introduction">fragment</A>.
6    <P><A name="nearTheEnd">This</A> is the definition of a
     destination anchor.</P>
7    <A name="theEnd"/>
8  </Body>
9  </HTML>
```

Example 8-1. An HTML document showing link concepts.

An HTML link address can point to a destination anchor within the source document, a complete external document or a destination anchor within an external document. (Lines 3, 4 and 5 give an example of each type.) The link address is specified by the HREF attribute and consists of a URI and a fragment identifier, joined by the '#' connector. If the URI is not present, then the current source document is assumed. If the fragment identifier is not present, then the beginning of the document is assumed. If neither the URI or the fragment identifier are present, the beginning of the current document is also assumed.

External Anchors and Links in HTML

All of the anchors and links in Example 8-1 are specified within the source HTML document. If you want to add new links to the document (or replace old ones), you need to explicitly edit its content. While this has proven to be a simple and popular approach, it limits the reuse of the HTML text object. If the document being extended is not a shared resource, adding links means making a separate copy. This assumes, of course, that you are allowed to copy and modify the text. (For third-party audio and video objects, this is rarely the case.) It also makes it difficult to add links to media types that are not easily changed with a text editor.

Creating links in non-textual (or protected) media requires a facility for separating the anchor/link definition from the media object associated with the source anchors. (X)HTML supports external link specification via the <map> and <area> elements, as shown in Example 8-2. Line 1 references an image and uses the <map> named *mapNP* to define the various source anchors and link addresses that are active when the image is rendered. The browser will map the coordinates in each of the <area> specifications as overlays on top of the image and associate the link addresses with each area. Note that the shapes of the areas need not be rectangular. Note also that several images can reference the same map, but that areas within a map may not overlap.

```
 1  <p><img src="nicePicture.gif" usemap="#mapNP" alt="Nice Picture"></p>
 2
 3  <map name="mapNP">
 4  <area href="overview.html#start"
 5          alt="General Overview"
 6          shape="rect"
 7          coords="0,0,123,45">
 8  <area href="overview.html#quiz"
 9          alt="Did you get it?"
10          shape="rect"
11          coords="111,0,675,45">
12  <area href="review.html"
13          alt="A Reneral Review"
14          shape="circle"
15          coords="111,99,30">
16  <area href="summary.html"
17          alt="Final Words"
18          shape="rect"
19          coords="111,150,401,45">
20  </map>
```

Example 8-2. External links via <map> and <area>.

8.1.2 SMIL: Adding Time to Links

SMIL has taken many of the concepts of HTML linking, including the <a> and <area> elements. While these general concepts have been reused, SMIL provides its own specification of the <a> and the <area> elements within the SMIL namespace. This is because SMIL's model of separating content from document structure has required some changes to how the <a> and <area> elements have been defined.

SMIL defines a timing and synchronization model that can be used to influence many of the objects in a presentation. Links are no exception: the active period of an anchor and the temporal effects of following a link can be controlled directly or indirectly by the timing parameters associated with the object.

Time, Linking and Structure in SMIL

It is tempting to think about linking in a timed environment as simply a matter of jumping to a particular time moment in a presentation. For example, consider the newscast video shown in Figure 8-1. Let's suppose you want to add anchors and links so that you can jump from story to story in the video. If you add a source anchor to the video element at times t_{s1} through t_{sn}, and define a destination anchor at time t_d, following the link becomes a straight-forward process of moving the presentation's time pointer to t_d at the moment the link is activated.[3]

Upon closer inspection, however, the process is anything but simple. First, what we really want to do is to link *story 1* to *story 2*, and not necessarily the interval t_{s1} through t_{sn} to t_d. (Today's *story 1* may be 28 seconds long, but *story 1*

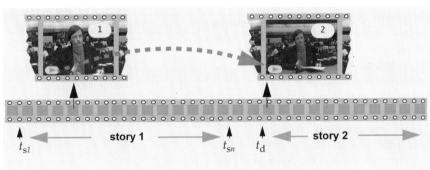

Figure 8-1. Links in a single media object.

---

3 In a streaming environment, this is not *so* simple: if the destination anchor has not been buffered at the player, there will be a delay in the presentation until enough of the video is sent from the server to allow streamed playback. This can happen for both forward and backward links. Linking backward in a 'live' video stream is theoretically possible, but jumping forward in a live stream presents some serious (meta)physical problems that are outside of SMIL's scope!

tomorrow may be 90 seconds long!) Also, when we navigate in the video, we also navigate along the sound track. Our video encoding has encapsulated sound, but if it had multiple sound tracks — or an animated ticker-tape running under the image — each would need to be repositioned independently.

SMIL provides the multimedia author with unprecedented flexibility in defining a reusable link architecture. It does this because SMIL links are based on the presentation's structure, not a single timeline. This flexibility means that the same SMIL document, with the same linking definitions, can be used for many different versions of the document. In our news example, the logical linking structure of navigating from *story 1* to *story 2* is totally independent of the duration of each of the stories. It also means that any other media object active will also be linked, so that a consistent presentation state is preserved.

8.2 SMIL Basic Linking Elements

This section describes the two elements defined in the *BasicLinking* module. They are: <a> and <area>.

Element: <a>

The <a> element's structure is laid out in Table 8-1. Like HTML, SMIL uses the <a> element to define a source anchor and a link address. Unlike HTML, SMIL does not use the <a> element to define a destination anchor — instead, the XML ID of the target object is the specification for the destination. The link address is a URI with an optional fragment name connected with a '#'; it is essentially the same as in HTML.

SMIL uses the <a> element as a *whole-node anchor*: it acts

<a>		Profiles					
attributes	*LinkingAttributes*						
	href						S
	begin, end, dur, *repeat timing*, min, max	L	B	M	1	H	
	system test, customTest						
parents	<body>,<priorityClass>	L	B	M	1	H	
parents & children	*time container*	L	B	M	1	H	
	<switch>						
children	*media object*, <brush>		B	M	1		
	<prefetch>	L				H	
	animation						S

Table 8-1. Structure of the <a> element.

as a wrapper around the associated object. An example of SMIL's use of the <a> element is shown in Figure 8-2. When the media object *Video1* is played, the entire object is wrapped with an anchor containing a link to the destination anchor named *part1* of another SMIL presentation named *Example.smil*. Note that when the link is followed, default SMIL behavior is that the entire source presentation is replaced with the destination presentation — not just the element that contains the source anchor.

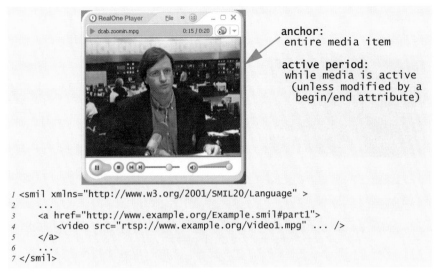

```
1  <smil xmlns="http://www.w3.org/2001/SMIL20/Language" >
2      ...
3      <a href="http://www.example.org/Example.smil#part1">
4          <video src="rtsp://www.example.org/Video1.mpg" ... />
5      </a>
6      ...
7  </smil>
```

Figure 8-2. Use of the <a> element in SMIL.

Element: <area>

The <area> element defines a source anchor and a link address. Just as SMIL's <a> element (and unlike HTML), the destination anchor associated with the link is the XML ID of the target object; this may be an ID in the same document or an external URI with optional fragment name. The structure of the <area> element is shown in Table 8-2.

	<area>		Profiles				
	LinkingAttributes						
	href						S
attributes	begin, end, dur, repeat timing, min, max	L	B	M	1	H	
	system test, customTest						
parents	media object	L	B	M	1	H	
children	none.	L	B	M	1	H	

Table 8-2. Structure of the <area> element

Where SMIL's <a> element is a whole-node anchor, the <area> element defines an anchor that applies to only a part of the media object. This 'part' can be spatial (like the HTML <area> element), but it can also be temporal: <area> can be used to define an anchor that is only active for a part of an object's duration. Unlike HTML, the <area> element is not defined as content of a <map> element, but as content of a media object. The <map> element does not exist in SMIL.

An example of SMIL's use of the <area> element is given in Figure 8-3. The <area> *a1* provides conventional HTML functionality in a SMIL document; it is active during the entire active duration of the media object. The <area> *a2* is

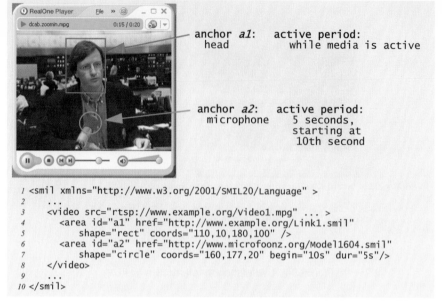

```
 1 <smil xmlns="http://www.w3.org/2001/SMIL20/Language" >
 2     ...
 3     <video src="rtsp://www.example.org/Video1.mpg" ... >
 4         <area id="a1" href="http://www.example.org/Link1.smil"
 5             shape="rect" coords="110,10,180,100" />
 6         <area id="a2" href="http://www.microfoonz.org/Model1604.smil"
 7             shape="circle" coords="160,177,20" begin="10s" dur="5s"/>
 8     </video>
 9     ...
10 </smil>
```

Figure 8-3. Use of the <area> element in SMIL.

only active for the five seconds starting at the 10th second of the video. If the video is shorter than 10 seconds, *a2* is never active.

In order to appreciate the structured and temporal linking options that SMIL presents, consider the two methods of defining a linked-news structure. The first method uses a single video object in parallel with a sound track, while the second method uses multiple video/audio object combinations.

Figure 8-4 shows a video containing two timed anchors, each of which is defined in an <area> element. In both cases, the entire viewing area is used for the anchors. If the link is activated within the first 28 seconds, the video presentation is set so that rendering continues from the 36-second point. Not only the video's rendering time is adjusted, however: the accompanying audio track is also set so that it renders from the 36-second point onward. (The reason for this is explained below.) The activation times are hard-coded into the presentation. This approach is useful if the video object is static — that is, if the same video object is used every time the presentation plays.

Figure 8-5 shows another approach. Here, the link addresses are not set to the XML ID's of the video, but to structure containers containing logical combinations of the presentation. The advantage of this approach is that the timing of each anchor is independent of the document structure. The entire presentation's structure can be reused with new media objects without change. When combined with SMIL's content control facilities, this approach becomes even more powerful. By wrapping a <switch> element around the audio, you could support multi-lingual audio or a combination of audio and text captions, without having to adjust presentation timing.

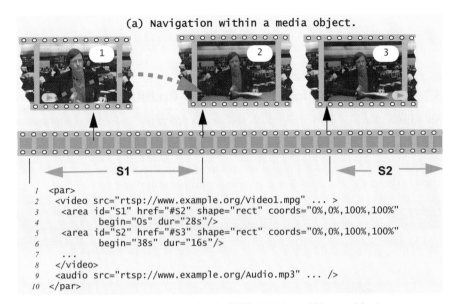

(a) Navigation within a media object.

```
1   <par>
2     <video src="rtsp://www.example.org/Video1.mpg" ... >
3       <area id="S1" href="#S2" shape="rect" coords="0%,0%,100%,100%"
4              begin="0s" dur="28s"/>
5       <area id="S2" href="#S3" shape="rect" coords="0%,0%,100%,100%"
6              begin="38s" dur="16s"/>
7       ...
8     </video>
9     <audio src="rtsp://www.example.org/Audio.mp3" ... />
10  </par>
```

Figure 8-4. Linking strategies in SMIL: Linking within an object.

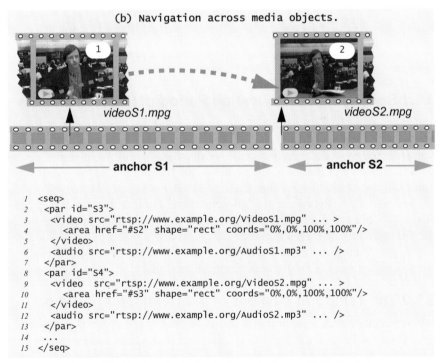

(b) Navigation across media objects.

```
1   <seq>
2     <par id="S3">
3       <video src="rtsp://www.example.org/VideoS1.mpg" ... >
4         <area href="#S2" shape="rect" coords="0%,0%,100%,100%"/>
5       </video>
6       <audio src="rtsp://www.example.org/AudioS1.mp3" ... />
7     </par>
8     <par id="S4">
9       <video  src="rtsp://www.example.org/VideoS2.mpg" ... >
10        <area href="#S3" shape="rect" coords="0%,0%,100%,100%"/>
11      </video>
12      <audio src="rtsp://www.example.org/AudioS2.mp3" ... />
13    </par>
14    ...
15  </seq>
```

Figure 8-5. Linking strategies in SMIL: Linking across objects.

Element: <anchor>

SMIL 1.0 used the <anchor> element to specify partial node anchors. This element is still available in SMIL 2.0, but since the <area> element offers the same functionality, the <anchor> element has been depreciated.

8.2.1 SMIL Basic Linking Attributes Architecture

As enumerated in Table 8-3, SMIL defines a range of link-related attributes. These attributes define how a link is activated, when it is activated, where it is activated, and the impact of link activation on the source and destination presentations. Each of these aspects are addressed in this section. The attributes apply to both the <a> and <area> elements, unless otherwise noted.

attribute	value		elements	Profiles				
				M	B	1	H	S
href	URI							
sourcePlaystate	"play", "pause"	"stop"						
destinationPlaystate								
show	"new", "replace"		<a>, <area>		L	1		
external	"true", "false"							
target	name of display environment							
sourceLevel, destinationLevel	non-negative percentage, "100%"							

Table 8-3. Linking attributes overview.

8.2.2 Specifying the Activation Period of Source Anchors

SMIL timing can be used to restrict the active period for a link construct. In Figure 8-4, the <area> element with ID *S1* specifies that the associated anchor is active during the first 28 seconds of the video (line 4) and the <area> element with ID *S2* specifies that its anchor is active for 16 seconds, starting 38 seconds into the video object (line 6). Outside this period, no anchors are active.

SMIL allows the definition of a link activation period on the <a> and <area> elements. Both types of anchors are timing-transparent: they do not influence the timing of the SMIL presentation.

No new linking attributes are required to support this behavior; the <area> elements accepts all of SMIL's basic timing attributes.

8.2.3 The Temporal Moment of the Destination Anchor

Where specifying the duration of a source anchor is usually straight-forward, specifying the behavior of following a link to a destination anchor can be very complex. This complexity arises out of the nested time structure of SMIL documents: when a destination object is activated, then all of the other media objects that are also specified to be rendered must also be activated. The details of such activation are actually part of the chapter on SMIL timing, but the basic rule is:

When a link is specified to a point in a destination document that is not the (temporal) beginning of that document, then the link needs to be implemented as if it were a 'fast-forward' across the effective timeline of the target document up to the destination anchor. All parts of the presentation that would be active if the presentation had reached destination anchor without linking must also be present (and in the same state) if it reaches this point via linking.

This statement looks pretty simple, but it has tremendous temporal consequences for the SMIL presentation scheduler. Since not all of the timing attributes of each of the media objects and the SMIL `<par>`/`<seq>` structure are defined statically, the scheduler needs to compute the effective state of the presentation so that all of the media items (and the progress into those items) are displayed just as if the document had been allowed to be played from the beginning. If this computation is not done efficiently, it can severely impact the duration of following a link!

The rules for determining the temporal moment of the destination of the link can be summarized as follows:

- *Destination is already active*: If the destination of the link is already active, the element is effectively restarted. The temporal moments of all of its peer and ancestral elements are also effectively reset based on the begin time of the link destination.

- *Destination is inactive, begin time is resolved*: If the begin time of the destination is resolved (that is, if it has a defined begin time because of explicit or implied timing semantics or if the begin time was resolved based on an earlier traversal of the link), then the presentation seeks to that temporal moment. The temporal state of the peers and ancestors is also realigned to match the temporal moment of the link destination.

- *Destination is inactive, begin time is unresolved*: This is the most complex case. If the destination is not active and if it has an unresolved begin time (it is waiting on an event or it has `begin="indefininte"` defined), the scheduler has to bubble up the document tree to find the first resolved parent. This time is applied to each of the children until the link destination is reached. The resolved begin time is applied to the link destination and it is saved by the scheduler for potential reuse in resolving this link (or any link that targets a child of the destination) in the future. The pseudo-resolved begin time for the link may be reset if a parent restarts or if some other condition exists that causes a new effective begin time to be defined.

There are special case rules that are applied for interactive timing. Since these rules require more background on SMIL events, we return to this topic in *Linking, Events and SMIL Timing* on page 290.

8.2.4 Attributes for Link Anchor Geometries

The shape and coords attributes can be used with <area> to specify geometry.

Attribute: shape

The <area> element has — as in HTML — a shape attribute. to specify the shape of an anchor. Permissible values are: *rect, circle* and *poly.* The shape attribute is applied to the underlying media object after this object has been scaled (based on SMIL Layout constructs) but before the media is clipped onto the viewing region. This can result in part of the shape being set outside the viewable area of the media.

Attribute: coords

The size and position of the anchor defined by the shape attribute is determined by the coords attribute. They are similar to HTML's shape and coords attributes.

The mapping of the coordinates given in the <area> to the source image and the containing regions occurs as follows:

1) The origin of the coordinate space for the anchor (that is, the 0,0 point) is placed at the upper-left corner of the image, not of the region into which the image is rendered. If the media object has been offset within the region (by using SMIL Layout's sub-region positioning), care needs to be taken to make sure that the anchor is correctly specified relative to the object. If a 320x240 media object is placed at an offset of 15 pixels from the top and 30

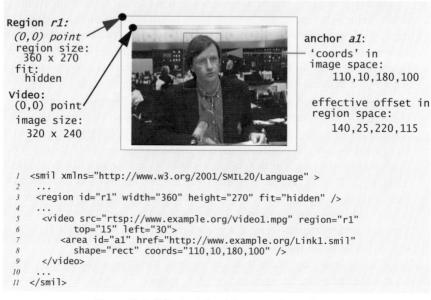

Figure 8-6. Offset origin of the coords attribute.

pixels from the left, the center point of the anchor's coordinates (160x120) will actually be placed at a region offset of 190, 135 in region space. This will normally not present a problem unless you want to overlay another object within the same visual space or if the image is scaled by the player for rendering. (See Figure 8-6.)

2) In order to remain consistent with HTML, SMIL defines that the pixel values used in the <area> correspond to the resolution of the display device (usually the screen) rather than to the media object's dimensions. Thus, if a 320x240 video is scaled to a 300x200 region of screen pixels with fit="*meet*" (that is, the entire object is scaled proportionally so that the full media object is visible), the coordinates of the image's center should be (133, 100) and *not* (160,120). (See Figure 8-7.)

Region *r1:*
region size: 300x200
fit: meet

Video:
original size: 320x240
scaled size: 266x200

anchor *a1:*
'coords'
(in region space):
    92,8,180,83

effective offset
(in media space):
    110,10,180,100

```
1   <smil xmlns="http://www.w3.org/2001/SMIL20/Language" >
2   ...
3   <region id="r1" width="300" height="200" fit="meet" />
4   ...
5     <video src="rtsp://www.example.org/Video1.mpg" region="r1" >
6       <area id="a1" href="http://www.example.org/Link1.smil"
7             shape="rect" coords="92,8,180,83" />
8     </video>
9   ...
10  </smil>
```

Figure 8-7. Display scaling and coords behavior.

3) If a portion of an image is not visible (because it is larger than the region size and the image is not scaled), it may be possible to specify a range of pixels that is outside the region. A typical case of this happening is when percentage values are used to specify the coordinates in the <area>. If this happens, the anchor is defined relative to the image (because of rule 1), but since it is outside of the display area, these pixels cannot be resolved (because of rule 2) and thus the anchor will not be selectable. If an anchor falls partially in the region and partially out of the region, only that area within the region is selectable. (See Figure 8-8.)

The rules for mapping coordinate values to visual display space represent a compromise between reusing existing HTML functionality and working with SMIL layout rules. For profiles that do not support SMIL layout, this is not a problem. Unfortunately, these profiles often have only limited SMIL linking support. More information on spatial cropping is provided in Chapter 11: *Subsetting and Extending Media.*

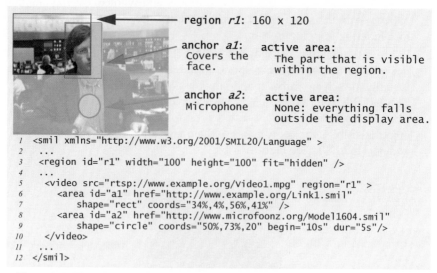

```
1    <smil xmlns="http://www.w3.org/2001/SMIL20/Language" >
2    ...
3    <region id="r1" width="100" height="100" fit="hidden" />
4    ...
5      <video src="rtsp://www.example.org/Video1.mpg" region="r1" >
6        <area id="a1" href="http://www.example.org/Link1.smil"
7           shape="rect" coords="34%,4%,56%,41%" />
8        <area id="a2" href="http://www.microfoonz.org/Model1604.smil"
9           shape="circle" coords="50%,73%,20" begin="10s" dur="5s"/>
10     </video>
11   ...
12   </smil>
```

Figure 8-8. The shape and coords attributes within the SMIL <area> element.

8.2.5 Attributes to Control the Playstate After Activation

When a link is activated (followed) in a SMIL presentation, the SMIL timing and synchronization rules specify the temporal state of the link's destination. But what happens then? Does the new document start playing, or does it wait for you to request that it starts? And what happens to the state of the original presentation? Does it get replaced, does it get paused or does it simply keep on playing? SMIL Basic Linking provides a collection of attributes that control both the original (source) document and the new (destination) document.

SMIL 2.0 uses three attributes to control the state of the source and destination presentations when a link is followed: *destinationPlaystate, show* and *sourcePlaystate.* Note that in order to maintain compatibility with SMIL 1.0, both *show* and *sourcePlaystate* can influence the behavior of the source presentation after a link is activated. When both are specified, the value of the *show* attribute has precedence over *sourcePlaystate.*

The specification of behavior for the source and destination presentations is generally only relevant for linking to external documents. Special rules for source and destination states exist if the source and destination anchors are in the same SMIL file; in this case, the destination always replaces the source.

Attribute: destinationPlaystate

This attribute specifies the state of the presentation containing the destination anchor. It can be set to *play* or *pause.* (The default is play.) If paused, user interaction in the player controlling the destination anchor will need to be used to play the presentation.

Attribute: show

This attribute specifies how the source and destination presentations are handled. The show attribute was the only control attribute in SMIL 1.0; for SMIL 2.0 implementations, two values are supported: *new* and *replace*. If the value of show is *new*, then both the source and destination presentations will be active after following the link. (They will most likely be activated in separate player instances, if the implementation supports this.) If the value of show is *replace*, then the source presentation is paused and — if supported by the player — its current state is saved for possible reactivation later. The destination presentation then replaces the source in the original player instance.

Attribute: sourcePlaystate

This attribute controls the behavior of the source presentation after a link is activated. It allows the following values: *play, pause* and *stop*. If *play* is specified, the source presentation continues playing. If *pause* is specified, the source presentation pauses at the point the link is activated; when the destination presentation completes, the source presentation should resume. If *stop* is specified, the source presentation is terminated.

8.2.6 Other Linking Control Attributes

SMIL provides a set of attributes that control when a link is activated, where the presentation containing the destination anchor is rendered, and the volume levels of the source and destination when a link is activated. SMIL also supports HTML's alt, tabindex and accesskey linking attributes, although it redefines them for use in the SMIL namespace. All of these attributes apply to both SMIL's <a> and <area> elements.

Some of the attributes below are defined in other XML languages as well as in SMIL. SMIL provides a uniform container model for (media) content in which the SMIL document may embed content in other formats, or other formats may embed SMIL content. For example, you could construct a SMIL presentation that contains an HTML object, or you could construct an HTML presentation that contains a separate SMIL document that gets rendered via a plug-in player. It could be that the outer, containing document defines an anchor and link address on top of an anchor/link defined in the embedded document. In such cases, the link defined by the containing (outer) document has precedence over the link in the embedded (inner) document.

If an embedded document contains a — non-conflicting — anchor/link, then activating this link impacts that embedded document only: SMIL 2.0 does not have an architecture that allows the embedded link to influence the containing document.

Attribute: actuate

SMIL allows links to be activated by user interaction (as in HTML), or it allows links to be activated automatically. Link activation is controlled by the `actuate` attribute. The *onRequest* value for `actuate` specifies that the link is followed using the human interaction interface of the player. The *onLoad* value specifies that the link is activated at the moment that the active duration of the object containing the link begins. (The name *onLoad* is somewhat of a misnomer, since objects can be loaded by the player well in advance of the start of their active duration. While *onStart* might have been a wiser choice, the name was used for historical HTML reasons.)

Attribute: target

The `target` attribute controls where the destination is rendered upon activation. SMIL's use of the HTML `target` attribute allows a destination presentation to be placed in a named SMIL region or an HTML frame; the identifiers used across regions and frames must be unique.

Attribute: external

The `external` attribute controls the type of application that is used to render the destination after it is activated. The SMIL `external` attribute specifies how the destination is processed: if it has a value of *true*, an external renderer of a type appropriate for the type of the media object will be used, and if the value is *false*, the destination will be opened by the same application as was used for the source presentation — this will usually be the SMIL player. The default is *false*. If a value of *true* is used, then the implementation environment (not the SMIL standard) determines which application should render the media object.

Attribute: sourceLevel and destinationLevel

Two attributes control the audio levels of the source and destination presentation after a link has been activated. The `sourceLevel` attribute takes a percentage value and applies it to the cumulative volume of the source presentation. The `destinationLevel` attribute takes a percentage value and applies it to the volume of the destination presentation.

Attribute: alt

This attribute specifies a text string which may be used by a user agent to identify an anchor. While it can be used in the context of linking, it is not defined as part of the *LinkingAttributes* module, but is part of the *MediaObjects* module (see Chapter 17: *Meta-Information, Media Description and XML Accessibility*).

Attribute: tabindex

The value of this attribute is an integer. It specifies a selection ordering of a set of anchors that are active (in the sense of SMIL timing). User agents may support tab-based selection of anchors — that is, they may support the use of the tab key to cycle through a set of active anchors — any one of which can then be selected by an appropriate UI device, such as a mouse or an enter key. The use of this attribute is identical to its HTML counterpart, except that only those SMIL elements that are in their active period (that is, being rendered or in their freeze period) are included in the tabbing order.

Attribute: accesskey

The value of this attribute defines a keyboard character or device rocker button that can be used to activate a link. If there is a conflict between the definition of an access key between the SMIL presentation and a media object in that presentation — for example, if an HTML object is being presented in a SMIL presentation, and both lay claim to the 'K' key — then the SMIL presentation will process the key and actuate the link. If the embedded content specifies an access key that is not in conflict with a SMIL definition, then the associated link is followed within the embedded content. If two anchors within a SMIL document share the same access key, the one rendered in a SMIL region having the highest z-index stacking order dominates.

8.3 Other Uses of Links in SMIL

The SMIL linking examples presented up to this point have concentrated on using linking for navigation. As we discussed earlier in this chapter, linking is also often used for activation control and message passing. We will briefly consider these uses in the following paragraphs; more advanced activation control is considered in the sections on SMIL timing and the exclusive element <excl>.

8.3.1 SMIL Linking and Activation Control

Where the use of linking for navigation allows the focus of a presentation to be set to some non-linear piece of content, the use of linking for activation control typically allows a follow-on part of a presentation to be delayed until some explicit user action takes place. SMIL 2.0 introduced interactive timing in the begin and end attributes to manage this efficiently. SMIL 2.0 also introduced the <excl> element for managing presentation-wide activation control. Since, however, not all SMIL 2.0 profiles support interactive timing or the exclusive construct, some designers may still need to use linking to manage a minimal form of presentation interactivity.

Figure 8-4 and Figure 8-5 considered two methods for managing a mix of navigation and activation control: both methods allowed a user to click on a 'next' icon to advance to the following story in a news presentation. In those examples, if the link was not followed, the next story would be reached when the current one ended. Two other examples of activation control are shown in Figure 8-9. Here we see a user's manual for a flashlight. The user is given some complex instructions (in this case, how to open the top), at which point the presentation pauses on line 8 until the user clicks on the anchor over the *Continue* button.

Line 8 in Figure 8-9 uses *lazy activation control*: if the user does not click within 90 seconds, the presentation continues on its own. This may be appropriate for some situations, but in others it may be more appropriate to give an open-ended delay. (The *findBatteries* segment starting on line 11 is one example: for some users, finding the correct batteries may require a trip to the store!) Line 15 gives a potential solution: the duration of the image containing the anchor is set to *indefinite* rather than to a fixed time period.

The specification of indefinite durations can be useful, but also dangerous. Many SMIL authors assume that indefinite means forever, but this is not correct. A duration of indefinite really means: forever, or the end of the parent time container, which ever comes first. Consider the following fragment, which is a variant on lines 11 through 17 of Figure 8-9:

```
...
<par id="findBatteries" endsync="v">
    <video id="v" src="findCorrectBatt.mpg" ... />
    <img id="I1" src="findCorrectBatt.png" ... />
    <a href="insertBatteries">
        <img id="I2" src="Continue.png" dur="indefinite" .../>
    </a>
</par>
...
```

In this example, the duration of the *findBatteries* <par> is determined by the duration of the video *V*. This is because the image I1 has no explicit duration, and the image I2 will stay active only until the resolved end time of its parent (the <par>).

While the use of linking for interaction is most prevalent in SMIL 1.0 documents or for applications targeted to light-weight SMIL 2.0 profiles, this facility

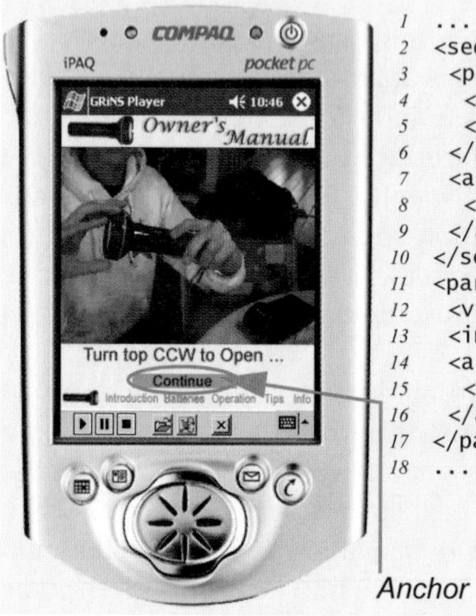

```
1   ...
2   <seq id="a">
3       <par>
4           <video src="turnTopCCW.mpg" ... />
5           <img src="turnTopCCW.png" ... />
6       </par>
7       <a href="#findBatteries">
8           <img src="next.png" dur="90s" .../>
9       </a>
10  </seq>
11  <par id="findBatteries">
12      <video src="findCorrectBatt.mpg" .../>
13      <img src="findCorrectBatt.png" ... />
14      <a href="#insertBatteries">
15          <img src="next.png" dur="indefinite".../>
16      </a>
17  </par>
18  ...
```

Anchor

Figure 8-9. Using linking for activation control.

should be used sparingly. One of the most expensive operations that a SMIL player must perform is the dynamic calculation of the effective playback time of a link target, and the subsequent scheduling of all of the media that must be active at that point. Low-performance SMIL platforms may not be able to process these calculations in a viewer-friendly manner. If at all possible, SMIL interactive timing should be used instead.

8.3.2 SMIL Linking and Message Passing

Early in the development of HTML, authors discovered that linking was a handy way of sending arguments, parameters and state information to and from servers. The typical mechanism for passing these messages in HTML looked like:

```
http://example.org/people/publick/show.php4?persnr=554
```

The '?' character designated application-specific information that was piggy-backed onto the link address. Overloading a link address with additional information is typically considered "not done" within the hypertext research community, but it was considered as a "we have no other choice" mechanism by the development community.

The stricter separation between content and structure in SMIL has had the positive side-effect that overload of link addresses is rarely used. This is not because SMIL removes all need for message passing, but more because a SMIL document typically sends extra parameters to media objects via the <param> element that is specified as content to the media object reference rather than their URI's.

8.4 Summary and Conclusion

This chapter has covered the basics of SMIL's temporal linking facilities. SMIL's linking support provides both short-cut anchors for entire nodes via the <a> element, and extensive support for partial-node anchors via the <area> element.

Not all SMIL 2.0 profiles implement SMIL linking functionality, and (unfortunately) not all players that include linking functionality do so correctly. This is due to the nature of SMIL 2.0 linking: the ability to faithfully produce a destination link context for timed media is, simply put, hard. It can consume considerable resources and it can make demands on media codecs that are not trivial to implement.

Designers interested in using SMIL linking to control activation of media objects should strongly consider SMIL's event-based interaction facilities. These facilities, which center around the use of the <excl> element, are discussed in Chapter 13: *Advanced SMIL Timing Behavior and Control.*

8.5 Further Resources

HTML

XHTML 1.0: The Extensible HyperText Markup Language (Second Edition), Steven Pemberton, (ed. chair), W3C Recommendation, 1 August 2002, http://www.w3.org/TR/xhtml1.

XLink

XML Linking Language (XLink) Version 1.0, Steven DeRose, Eve Maler and Ron Daniel Jr. (eds), W3C Recommendation, 27 June 2001. http://www.w3.org/TR/xlink.

9
Content Selection and Control

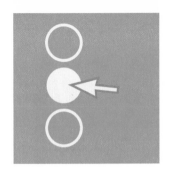

SMIL's content selection capabilities allow a presentation to be tailored to meet the needs of diverse runtime environments. This can include selecting between high/low-bandwidth content or choosing among media objects based on a viewer's language preference. From a user's perspective, the selection can be passive — the player can decide which content is appropriate without ever having to ask the user — or it can occur under the user's direct control. (The method that selection is exposed is based on the implementation of the SMIL player.) SMIL places all of the content control primitives within the same SMIL document, meaning that a wide range of users (and user devices) can be accommodated from within a single source file.

This chapter looks at the basic content control facilities in SMIL 2.0. We begin with background information on content selection and then look at the content control elements and attributes available in all SMIL profiles. We finish with an example of how content control can be integrated into SMIL presentations. Chapter 16: *Extended Content Control* considers advanced content control primitives that may not be available in all profiles or all players.

9.1 Content Selection: Rationale and Scope

This section considers some operational aspects of delivering a multimedia presentation in a networked environment. We start with looking at assumptions about the runtime environment and then consider adaptation techniques.

9.1.1 Understanding the Runtime Environment

In the early days of desktop multimedia, a presentation designer could make many assumptions about the runtime environment that would be available when the content was presented. For example, consider a CD-ROM published in 1994 filled with images from London's National Gallery collection.[1] Along with requiring a multimedia PC with mouse, 4MB of RAM and 1MB of disk space, it contained the following set of installation and system requirements:

- a physical CD-ROM drive, plus CD-ROM extensions for the operating system, which met the following restriction: *In order to run properly, Art Gallery*

---

1 Microsoft Art Gallery, Microsoft Home Disc 220-052-002. © 1994 Microsoft Corporation.

requires an MPC-compatible CD-ROM drive. An MPC-compatible drive "has an average seek time of less than one second and can transfer data from the compact disc at 150K per second while using less than 40% of the CPU bandwidth".

- a VGA+ (640x480) display with 8-bit color depth, with the following caveat: *In 16-color mode the paintings will not display correctly. You may run in higher resolutions than 256-colors but there will be no improvement of the picture quality and the performance will probably slow down. Animations will not run in any mode except 256-color.*

- an audio card and speakers or headphones, with the following restrictions: *Please note that Art Gallery requires an MPC-compatible sound board to be installed and is not intended to run with drivers which use the PC internal speaker, such as the unsupported "PC Speaker" driver. Such a driver will not, in most cases, play any sounds and if the driver setup option "Enable Interrupts" is not checked, your system may crash.*

(Evidently, art lovers in 1994 had to be pretty fond of their computer, too!)

After inserting the CD-ROM, the installation script tested if all required components existed. If not, you were not able to view any part of the presentation. Once you got past these tests, you got an interactive multimedia overview of paintings, as shown in Figure 9-1.

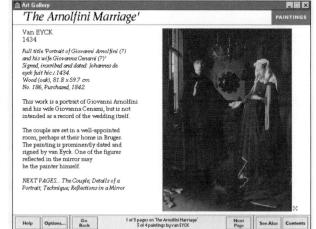

Figure 9-1. Excerpt from the *Microsoft Art Gallery*.
(Content © 1994 Microsoft Corporation.)

System Requirements

The point of this example is to show that the CD-ROM's designers could be very specific about the presentation environment they required at runtime. Once multimedia started to migrate to Internet-based delivery, many unpredictable factors entered into the presentation equation. If we revisit these requirements with 21st Century eyes, it is interesting to see if life for a modern multimedia designer has gotten any easier:

- The limitation to a specific class of processors and a minimal amount of memory seem archaic in an age of giga-hertz CPUs and hundreds of megabytes of memory. Or is it? Does your multimedia telephone support the memory and processing power requirement listed for *Art Gallery*?

- A fixed amount of disk storage is required to hold the basic executable for the presentation. Do all potential Web clients for presentations allow such intermediate storage, and will all users allow you to write on their disks?

- An interactive pointing device is required to view the presentation. What happens if there is no mouse, or if your user has no hands available?

- With the advent of the Web as a distribution medium, the need for particular CD-ROM requirements has been replaced with the need to know the end-to-end performance available between the server holding your media and the user's computer. Is the 1994 limitation of less than 1 second seek time and a sustained transfer rate of 150K/sec. realistic for current Web and mobile devices — and what happens if it isn't?

- If one of your viewers has just spent half a month's salary for a top-of-the-line display with ultra-high resolution and support for millions of colors, will a presentation that uses only 256 colors make *you* look like a cheapskate? What happens if other users want to view your presentation using run-of-the-mill mid-range display hardware — do they wind up waiting forever because you are sending bits that will never be seen?

- The *Art Gallery* CD-ROM had specific device requirements for audio hardware. Current Web presentations may require specific media types. Do you expect that all systems will support your media types, or will you provide some fall-back media types 'just in case'?

- What happens if your audience doesn't speak English (the language used in *Art Gallery*), or if they do speak English but they prefer UK English usage? Will you need to create separate copies per language — and how much effort is required to keep these multiple presentations consistent?

Web-based multimedia presentations provide unprecedented opportunities to share your messages with hundreds of millions of users world-wide, but it brings with it the challenge of meeting the needs of a diverse set of largely unknown users. The better you are at meeting their needs, the broader the reach of your message. As a content author, you can always create a simple presentation that assumes your users/clients will be able to view all of the data objects that you send them. You can also take a broader view by specifying some alternatives to either individual objects or to entire sub-parts of the presentation. Such alternatives can be based on presentation resources (for example, on a slow connection, it may be wise to substitute a slide-show presentation for a piece of video), or the choice may be based on natural language (for example, having both English and Spanish versions of an audio and/or a set of text messages available within the same document).

Content Control and Accessibility

One of the historical reasons to support alternate content is to help users who, for whatever reason, cannot accept certain data formats — such as audio for a deaf user, or video for a blind user, or high-resolution information for a user attached to a low-resolution computer. Unfortunately, many designers still view supporting the "format disabled" as a luxury and give presentation accessibility little priority. As the Web expands its reach, it is important to realize that making presentations accessible must become a key design concern.

Along with legal requirements that mandate support for a broad user community, it is vital to understand that accessibility is not an "us *vs.* them" issue: all of us are unable to accept certain types of media at certain times, depending on our work or use situations. For example, if you are working without headphones in a shared office space, you may be unable to accept audio information, even if there is nothing wrong with your hearing — the circumstances simply don't allow you to disturb others around you! Likewise, if you are driving your car at top speeds down the highway, you should probably have your eyes glued to the road and not to your portable display — in this case, you are as media-blind as someone who can't see anything at all. Perhaps more pragmatically, if you want to address a wide range of users on a wide range of devices, it is key that you plan diversity into your presentation. If not, you just won't be able to deliver your message with full impact.

9.1.2 Techniques for Creating Adaptive Presentations

There are four approaches to customize information in a presentation:

1) A minimum set of performance, device and user characteristics could be assumed, and the entire presentation could be architected for the needs of this lowest common denominator.

2) Multiple presentations can be created, one for each quality level. The user then selects the presentation of choice at runtime.

3) Each presentation could be over-specified to include all of the potential media items for all potential uses, and the media player at the client could be used to make an appropriate selection.

4) The presentation specification acts as a control file that contains pointers to all of the potential alternatives, but only those actually used by a specific user would be sent from the server to the client.

Option (1) is illustrated in Figure 9-2. It provides a manageable solution to meeting the needs of the designer and the user, but it rarely results in compelling content. People with connections or equipment below the baseline will be disenfranchised, while people with more than the baseline will be presented

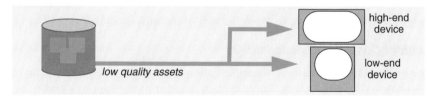

low quality assets

high-end device

low-end device

Figure 9-2. Option 1 — Sending all users the same media content.

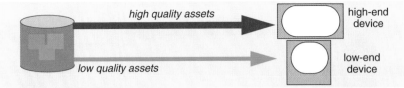

Figure 9-3. Option 2 — Have users select appropriate content explicitly.

with an inferior presentation. Designers could get away with this approach when everyone had 1994-style hardware, but as the Web moves to portable devices (and as high-end users begin to demand high-end content), a one-size-fits-all approach is a dead-end solution.

Option (2), shown in Figure 9-3, shifts the responsibility of making an 'appropriate' selection to the user, who gets presented with choice of presentations or formats. Unfortunately, this means that multiple copies of a presentation need to be made and maintained. It also assumes that a user knows how to make an appropriate selection. Option (2) is better than nothing, but is not very extensible: if users need to select among 7 languages, three network connection speeds and twelve different types of display devices, they may spend more time selecting options than viewing content!

Option (3), illustrated in Figure 9-4, is a disaster in the making. If you package content for, say, high-speed connections together with content for low-speed connections, you wind up overloading a minimal link and effectively reducing the bandwidth available for high-end users. This may seem like a crazy solution, but it is the one that had been adopted by most of the proprietary formats (such as MPEG-4 and Real Networks' *SureStream* technologies).[2]

SMIL uses alternative (4), which is illustrated in Figure 9-5: it allows a designer to specify a collection of alternatives for use during the presentation, but it doesn't send copies of each of the various datastreams across the network — it allows a SMIL player to select one or more alternatives at runtime depend-

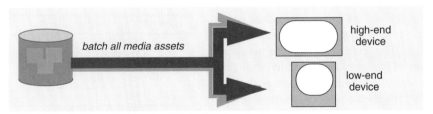

Figure 9-4. Option 3 — Send all media to all users, and have player select locally.

---

2 Special purpose processing by proprietary protocols at the server and the client can reduce the effective datarate used in some of these formats, but accessing a composite datastream without such protocol support can greatly increase the amount of data set and significantly reduce the quality of the presentation.

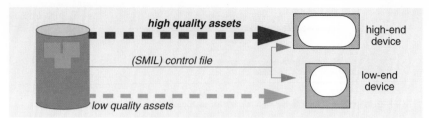

Figure 9-5. Use a control file to present alternatives for selection and then send only the media objects necessary.

ing on the (dynamic or static) setting of user and system preferences on the client system. SMIL also does this in a 'declarative' way: it doesn't hide the selection in scripts or proprietary encodings, but it makes selection a first-class citizen in the language.

9.2 Content Control Elements and Attributes

SMIL provides several elements and attributes for defining the conditional or selective inclusion of media objects. These primitives are defined in SMIL's content control modules. Most of the basic selectivity primitives are defined in the *BasicContentControl* module, and are covered in this chapter. These are the system test attributes and the <switch> element. More advanced content control facilities are discussed in Chapter 16: *Extended Content Control*.

9.2.1 SMIL Basic Content Control Elements

SMIL defines one element for use with basic content control: <switch>.

Element: <switch>

The <switch> element establishes a collection of alternatives for a sub-presentation. Each child of the element is one alternative. At most one child of a <switch> element is selected for playback. The <switch> has the semantic that its contents are evaluated in lexical order; when the first element with a test attribute that evaluates to *true* is found, the corresponding element is played. Once any of the elements is selected, the search for a suitable candidate stops. While at most one child element of the <switch> is played, that child may be very complex and can contain

<switch>		Profiles				
attributes	custom test					
	system test	L	M	B	1	H
	core					
parent	<head>	L	M			
parent or child	media object					
	time container	L	M	B	1	H
	<a>					
	<switch>					
child	<layout>					
	<area>	L	M	B	1	
	<prefetch>					H

Table 9-1. Structure of the <switch> element.

```
<switch>
    <video systemBitrate="128000" src="video.mpg" region="Main" />
    <seq systemBitrate="128000" >
        <img dur="5s" src="image0.png" region="Main" />
        <img dur="4s" src="image1.png" region="Main" />
        <img dur="9s" src="image2.png" region="Main" />
    </seq>
</switch>
```

Example 9-1. The SMIL <switch> statement.

multiple media objects and other embedded <switch> statements. If none of the elements evaluate to *true*, then nothing is played.

An example of the use of the <switch> element is given in Example 9-1. The <switch> element has two children: a <video> object and a <seq> element. At runtime, the children of the <switch> are tested in lexical order (that is, they are tested in the order in which they appear in the text of the SMIL file). If the player-determined bitrate is 128,000 bps or higher, the video plays. If the bitrate is less than 128,000 bps but at least 56,000 bps, the image sequence gets played. (If the bitrate is lower than 56,000 bps, nothing gets played.)

It is important to realize that the test attribute is placed on the *children* of the <switch> and not on the <switch> element itself. If the test attribute is placed on the <switch>, then the player will try to determine whether the <switch> element should be evaluated rather than its contents. Consider what happens if the player encounters the following attribute when the bitrate has been determined to be 64,000 kbps:

```
<switch systemBitrate="128000">
    ...
</switch>
```

The answer: nothing. The entire <switch> is skipped because it contains a test attribute that says to only look at this element if the bitrate is greater than 128,000 kbps, which it isn't (it was only 64,000 kbps). Placing a test attribute on the <switch> element is usually only useful if the <switch> is itself a child of a parent <switch> construct.

If one of the elements in the <switch> does not contain a test attribute, it will always evaluate to TRUE. Used correctly, this is a powerful feature. It is often desirable that a <switch> contains a candidate element that will always play if nothing else does. This gives a default semantic to the <switch>. An example of the use of a default element is shown in Example 9-2. Here, if the bitrate is

```
<switch>
    <video systemBitrate="128000" src="video.mpg" region="Main" />
    <seq systemBitrate="128000" >
        <img dur="5s" src="image0.png" region="Main" />
        <img dur="4s" src="image1.png" region="Main" />
        <img dur="9s" src="image2.png" region="Main" />
    </seq>
    <text dur="10s" src="summary.txt" region="Main" />
</switch>
```

Example 9-2. Setting a default behavior in a <switch> statement.

below 56,000 bps, the text object will play because it does not contain a test attribute, thus it will always be used unless something lexically higher in the <switch> evaluates to *true*. The default alternative should always be placed last in the selection list.

> **Quick Tip**
>
> The SMIL specification does not specify when the <switch> should be evaluated. Most players will evaluate the <switch> dynamically, at the temporal moment (time) that it is encountered in the presentation. Some players — such as HTML+TIME — evaluate the switch when the file gets parsed and essentially will remove non-selected elements from the presentation before it starts.

9.2.2 SMIL Basic Content Control Attributes Architecture

The basic selection primitive in SMIL is the *test attribute*. A *test attribute* consists of an attribute and a value. A SMIL player sets values for all system test attributes based on user interaction or a player configuration file. If a particular test attribute is referenced within the presentation, its value is compared to the current setting of that test attribute in the SMIL player. If the values are the same, the element containing the attribute is included in the presentation. If it is not the same (that is, if it evaluates to *false*), then the element (and its content) is not included in the presentation.

SMIL distinguishes between *system test attributes* and *custom test attributes*. The system test attributes listed in Table 9-2 are fully defined in the SMIL 2.0 specification and are available across all SMIL implementations. Custom test attributes do not have pre-defined meanings; they may be tailored to the needs of the application. System and, when supported, custom test attributes may be

		attribute	elements	Profiles				
system test attributes	user	systemLanguage		L	M	B	1	H
		systemCaptions						
		systemAudioDesc						
		systemOverdubOrSubtitle					1	
	environment	systemBitrate	all except <head>, <body>, <customTest>, <meta> and <metadata>	L	M	B	1	H
		systemScreenDepth						
		systemScreenSize						
	resources	systemCPU		L	M	B		H
		systemOperatingSystem						
		systemComponent						
		systemRequired					1	

Table 9-2. Structure of the system test attributes

placed on almost all elements — more elements than any other attributes except the core attributes.

The following sections consider all of the system test attributes supported by SMIL 2.0. We do so by classifying attributes as relating to *user, environment* or *resource* test attribute classes. Note that test attributes are not only applied to media content, but can be used to selectively include entire presentation sub-parts. We begin with a discussion of the in-line use of test attributes. We defer a discussion of custom test attributes to Chapter 16: *Extended Content Control.*

9.2.3 In-Line Use of System Test Attributes

Most of the examples using system test attributes up to this point have been in the context of evaluating alternatives within the <switch> element. In SMIL 1.0, this was the only place that a test attribute could be used. SMIL 2.0 relaxes this requirement by allowing test attributes to be placed on any statement (inside or outside a <switch>). The element containing the test attribute would then be evaluated for conditional inclusion.

As an example of the use of in-line test attributes, consider the following example, in which two equivalent methods are shown for selecting a video media object to be played if the bitrate of the network connection at the time of the presentation (as measured by the player) is at least 128,000 bits per second:

```
<video systemBitrate="128000" src="video.mpg" />
...
<switch>
    <video systemBitrate="128000" src="video.mpg" />
</switch>
```

In both cases, if the bitrate was less than 128,000 bps, the entire <video ... /> element is ignored. Selecting between the <switch> and in-line forms is often a matter of convenience, especially if complex nested alternatives are used. (In these cases, use of the <switch> can lead to a combinatorial explosion of alternatives.)

If you want to select one of a set of objects, you might be tempted to use the following approach:

```
1   <par>
2       <video systemBitrate="128000" src="video.mpg" />
3       <seq systemBitrate=" 64000">
4           <img dur="5s" src="image0.png" />
5           <img dur="4s" src="image1.png" />
6           <img dur="9s" src="image2.png" />
7       </seq>
8   </par>
```

This fragment highlights a common misconception of applying in-line test attributes: if the system bitrate is at least 128,000 bps (as measured by the player), then the video on line 2 is played; otherwise, if the bitrate is at least 64,000 bps, then the sequence of images on lines 3 through 7 is played.

This is not correct. If the bitrate is 128,000 bps, it is also 64,000 bps. Thus, in this example, the image sequence plays if the bitrate is between 64,000 bps and 127,999 bps, and both the images and the video will be displayed if the bitrate is 128,000 bps or greater. You may think that changing the <par> to a <seq> would do the trick, but it doesn't: it simply sets the presentation to be sequential rather than in parallel.

In general, you should only use in-line test attributes when you want to conditionally include a single element — not select among a set of alternative elements. To do the latter, you should wrap the alternatives in a <switch> element.

9.2.4 User-Related System Test Attributes

SMIL defines four user-related system test attributes. These are:

- systemLanguage,
- systemCaptions,
- systemAudioDesc, and
- systemOverdubOrSubtitle.

Table 9-3 describes the attributes and supported values of the user-related system test attributes.

		attribute	value(s)
system test attributes	user	systemLanguage	list of language tags
		systemCaptions	"on", "off"
		systemAudioDesc	
		systemOverdubOrSubtitle	"overdub", "subtitle"

Table 9-3. User-related system test attributes

Attribute: systemLanguage

The systemLanguage attribute allows a SMIL player to select content based on language preferences in the document. The value of the systemLanguage attribute is a comma-separated list of language tags. Each language tag consists of a two-character primary language tag, optionally followed by a dash and language sub-tag. Language sub-tags are typically two-character country and region codes representing local dialects of the languages.

Standard use of systemLanguage is illustrated in the following fragment:

```
1  <switch>
2    <audio systemLanguage="en-uk" src="..." />
3    <audio src="..." />
4  </switch>
```

If the language preference set in the player is UK English, the audio object on line 2 gets selected. Otherwise the audio object on line 3 is played.[3]

When a tag in the user preferences language list is identical to a tag in the `systemLanguage` attribute value, the element using the tag is selected. If the user has a language tag consisting only of a primary language tag with no dialect sub-tag, this constitutes a match with any `systemLanguage` tag with that prefix and any sub-tag. If the `systemLanguage` value contains both a primary language tag and a dialect sub-tag, the user agent must have had that dialect tag explicitly defined.

Please read this paragraph again: it has the following consequences:

```
1  <switch>
2    <audio systemLanguage="en-uk" src="..." />
3    <audio systemLanguage="en-us" src="..." />
4    <audio systemLanguage="en" src="..." />
5    <audio src="..." />
6  </switch>
```

If a user's player has been set to prefer UK English (*en-uk*), the <switch> element will select the audio object on line 2. If US English (*en-us*) is preferred, the audio object on line 3 will be played. If the user has selected any kind of English (that is, only the primary language tag *en*), the audio object on line 2 will be selected (not line 4, since a match with line 2 happens first!). If any language other than English or any English dialect other than *us* or *uk* has been set, the default audio on line 5 is played. The audio on line 4 should never get selected by a conforming SMIL player.

Attribute: systemCaptions

The `systemCaptions` attribute allows content to be logically labelled as a caption. The allowed values are *on* and *off*. The `systemCaptions` attribute is typically used to determine if caption text gets displayed, although nothing in the SMIL standard requires that it be explicitly related to text captions.

The following fragment illustrates the use of `systemCaptions`:

```
<par>
  <video src="video.mpg" .../>
  <switch>
    <text systemCaptions="on" src="captions.rt" ... />
  </switch>
</par>
```

> **Quick Tip**
>
> In normal use, only a specification of `systemCaptions="on"` is typical. Another, less typical use is specifying `systemCaptions="off"`; this has its element play only if captions were **not** requested.

---

3 The primary language tag for English is *en* and the sub-tags for US and UK English are *us* and *uk*, respectively.

Attribute: systemOverdubOrSubtitle

Another option for captioning is to label content as being a sub-title or an over-dub media object. An systemOverdubOrSubtitle="overdub" assignment sets an element as containing dubbing. Such an element is only selected for playback if the user has stated a preference of dubbing over subtitles. The *subtitle* value declares the element content as containing subtitles, to be played only if the user prefers subtitles. The systemOverdubOrSubtitle attribute has no default value. If the attribute is not assigned to an element, then the user's preference between dubbing and subtitles has no impact on the element's selection.

Consider the following fragment, which combines several test attributes:

```
1 <par>
2   <video src="video.mpg" ... />
3   <par systemCaptions="on">
4     <audio systemOverdubOrSubtitle="overdub" src="..." />
5     <textstream systemOverdubOrSubtitle="subtitle" src="subtitles.ttf"/>
6   </par>
7 </par>
```

The outer <par> on line 1 schedules a video element on line 2 and an inner <par> on line 3. The inner <par> is only evaluated if the systemCaptions preference has been set. Assuming that the value is 'on', two objects are considered for activation. An audio stream on line 4 is played if a preference for overdub has been defined, while a timed text object is played if a preference for subtitles has been set. If neither preference has been set, no captions get played.[4]

> **Quick Tip**
>
> SMIL does not perform checks on the media objects to ensure that subtitles are text or that overdub objects are audio. While this may seem strange, it gives the designer lots of flexibility in performing content substitution.

Attribute: systemAudioDesc

The systemAudioDesc attribute can also be used to define conditional content. It is intended to be used to include audio captions in a presentation. (A typical use case is to include audio captions for the blind that describe the contents of an image.) The systemAudioDesc accepts the values *on* and *off*. As with systemCaptions, the value is typically set to *on* if the attribute is used; select-ing the value *off* states that an associated element should only be used if system audio descriptions were explicitly asked to be excluded.

The following example shows how the systemAudioDesc attribute can be used in conjunction with an <excl> element; this allows a main presentation to

---

4 This example actually is a simplification of what really needs to happen to support dynamic subtitles or captions, since the media renderer for the video needs to know to reduce its sound level if the overdub option was selected.

be paused while captions are played. (See Chapter 13: *Advanced SMIL Timing Behavior and Control* for a description of the <excl> element and a more extended description of the following fragment)

```
1 <excl dur="indefinite">
2   <priorityClass peers="pause">
3     <video src="video.mpg" begin="0s" ... />
4     <audio src="audio1.mp3" begin="10s" systemAudioDesc="on" ... />
5     <text src="story2.txt" begin="30s" dur="20s" systemAudioDesc="on"
         ... />
6   </priorityClass>
7 </excl>
```

In this example, an <excl> time container starts on line 1, containing a priority class of 3 peer objects (lines 2 through 6). In a nutshell, this construct says:

- Start rendering the video object on line 3 (since it has a hard begin time of the start of the <excl>.
- At 10 seconds into the video, if the systemAudioDesc preference is *on*, the audio object will pause the video. Assume it lasts 5 seconds.
- At 15 seconds, the video resumes (if it had paused).
- At 30 seconds, if systemAudioDesc is *on*, a text object pauses the video.
- At 50 seconds, the video continues to completion.

Each time the video pauses, a media object can explain something about the content to a user who has requested extra detail.

9.2.5 Environment-Related System Test Attributes

SMIL 2.0 defines three environment-related system test attributes. These are:

- systemBitrate,
- systemScreenDepth, and
- systemScreenSize.

Unlike user-related attributes, the value of these attributes within the SMIL player can be expected to be set by the player architecture based on some form of direct measurement. In certain situations — such as presentation development — it can be handy to explicitly set values for these attributes in the player, so that various design choices can be tested.

Attribute: systemBitrate

The systemBitrate attribute can be used to specify a minimum number of bits per second in network bandwidth that must be available for the element to be selected for playback. The value is a single integer representing an effective bitrate. SMIL does not define how the bitrate should be measured, or when it is measured (dynamically or statically). As a result, this attribute can provide only crude control over available network resources.

In this fragment, both the <par> and the <seq> element have a systemBitrate attribute. If the bitrate is less than 64000 kbps, neither the video nor the collection of slides will be played.

		attribute	value
system test attributes	environment	systemBitrate	integer > 0
		systemScreenDepth	
		systemScreenSize	'x'-split pair of integers > 0

Table 9-4. Environment-related system test attributes

```
1    <switch>
2      <video systemBitrate="128000" src="video.mpg" />
3      <seq systemBitrate="64000">
4        <img dur="5s" src="image0.png" />
5        <img dur="4s" src="image1.png" />
6        <img dur="9s" src="image2.png" />
7      </seq>
8    </switch>
```

Attribute: systemScreenDepth

The systemScreenDepth attribute can be used to specify the minimum number of bits the screen's color palette that must be available for the element to be selected for playback. The value is an integer.

In the following fragment, the video on line 2 will play if the screen depth has been determined to be at least 8 bits deep. If the bit depth is less than 8 bits but at least 2 bits, the video on line 3 will be played. If the screen depth is less than two bits, then no video is played.

```
1    <switch >
2      <video region="image" src="away8.avi" systemScreenDepth="8"/>
3      <video region="image" src="away2.avi" systemScreenDepth="2"/>
4    </switch>
```

Attribute: systemScreenSize

The systemScreenSize attribute specifies the minimum length in pixels of the screen needed in each dimension that is required for the current element to be selected. The value defines a screen height and screen width (in pixels, expressed as integers) of the following form: systemScreenSize="480X640", where height is given first. (The 'X' between the height and width is capitalized and is placed without leading or trailing spaces.)

The screen size attribute is often useful when selecting among layouts. One example of how this could be used is in selecting between the two standard MMS layout options: one for a portrait screen and one for telephones that use landscape displays. The code in Example 9-3 is adapted from the MMS con-

```
1   ...
2   <switch>
3     <layout systemScreenSize="352X144"> <!-- landscape -->
4       <root-layout width="352" height="144" />
5       <region regionName="Image" width="176" height="144" />
6       <region regionName="Text" width="176" height="144" left="176"/>
7     </layout>
8     <layout systemScreenSize="176X216"> <!-- portrait -->
9       <root-layout width="176" height="216" />
10      <region regionName="Image" width="176" height="144" />
11      <region regionName="Text" width="176" height="72" top="144"/>
12    </layout>
13  </switch>
14  ...
15  <par>
16    <img src="myDog.png" region="Image" />
17    <text src="Shaggy.txt" region="Text" />
18  </par>
19  ...
```

Example 9-3. Selecting among layouts using the <switch> statement.

formance specification. It shows two layout definitions, each defining two regions and a root layout.

In this example, the SMIL player on the mobile device will presumably know its display architecture and make a choice among the layout options. Note that each layout specification makes use of the regionName attribute rather than an id attribute to identify the region. In this way, the references to each region on lines 15 and 16 do not need to be aware of the layout architecture. (For more information on the regionName attribute, see page 111.)

(The independence of layout and the body structure shown in Example 9-3 is rare. Usually, some form of conditional structuring of media will be required in the body that will mirror the various layout choices.)

As a final note: the MMS standard will not allow the fragment in Example 9-3 to be processed. MMS does not support <switch> elements, system test attributes or the regionName attribute.

9.2.6 Resource-Related System Test Attributes

The resource-related system test attributes are used to determine if various system characteristics are available. The test attributes in this group are:

- systemCPU,
- systemOperatingSystem,
- systemComponent, and
- systemRequired.

The player will typically set the internal values for these attributes directly without user interaction, although some players may allow users to define explicit values for these attributes for testing purposes.

Table 9-5 provides an overview of the various resource-related attributes and their accepted values.

attribute		value
systemCPU		"alpha" "arm" "arm32" "hppal.1" "m68k" "mips" "ppc" "rs6000" "vax" "x86"
systemOperatingSystem		"aix" "beos" "bsdi" "dgux" "freebsd" "hpux" "irix" "linux" "macos" "ncr" "nec" "netbsd" "nextstep" "nto" "openbsd" "openvms" "os2" "osf" "palmos" "qnx" "sinix" "rhapsody" "sco" "solaris" "sonly" "sunos" "unixware" "win16" "win32" "win9x" "winnt" "wince" "unknown"
systemComponent		white space-split list of URIs
systemRequired		white space-split list of namespaces

The left spanning labels read "system test attributes" and "resources".

Table 9-5. Resource-related system test attributes

Attribute: systemCPU

The systemCPU attribute specifies a particular hardware architecture that must be available when a presentation is played. The SMIL 2.0 specification suggests an initial list of values for this attribute. (See Table 9-5.) Individual players and browsers may support additional values for other types of CPUs.

This attribute can be used to determine if a particular media type could be played on a particular platform:

```
1   <switch >
2     <video region="image" src="away.slo" systemCPU="x86"/>
3     <video region="image" src="away.avi" />
4   </switch>
```

While this approach seems harmless enough, some Web users are concerned that this test might give away valuable information on their operational environment to a server that monitors media object use. For this reason, the systemCPU attribute also accepts a value of *unknown*: this lets the element play only if the user has requested that the attribute's resource remain private.

While the intent of this value is noble, it is only a partial privacy solution which has cumbersome semantics. For example, consider the following element:

```
1   ...
2     <video region="image" src="rtsp://www.example.org/niceVideo.mpg"
          systemCPU="unknown"/>
3   ...
```

While one might expect that this video would play on any system, it will actually only be selected on players that have had the type of their CPU set explicitly to *unknown*.

Attribute: systemOperatingSystem

This attribute specifies a particular software architecture that must be available when a presentation is played. The SMIL 2.0 specification suggests an initial list of values for this attribute. (See Table 9-5.) Individual players and browsers may support additional values for other types of operating systems.

The following fragment illustrates the use of `systemOperatingSystem`:

```
1  <switch >
2    <video region="image" src="away.divx" systemOperatingSystem="linux"/>
3    <video region="image" src="away.avi" systemOperatingSystem="win32"/>
4    <video region="image" src="http://www.example.org/away.jpg" />
5  </switch>
```

This attribute also supports the value of *unknown,* with all of the advantages and limitations discussed under `systemCPU`.

Attribute: systemComponent

The `systemComponent` attribute accepts as its value a list of URIs separated by white space characters (spaces, tabs and newlines). Each URI denotes a browser software component, typically renderers for particular media, that is needed to present the current element. The browser must support all of the components listed in order to play the element.

The following fragment can be used to ensure that *mpg* video is supported by a version of a player for a given document.

```
1  <smil xmlns="http://www.w3.org/2001/SMIL20/Language"
2       systemComponent="http://www.ambulantPlayer.org/supportedMedia/mpg">
```

A disadvantage of using `systemComponent` is that SMIL browsers typically don't support a standard list of component names. A list of URIs that may work on one browser may not be accepted by another, even though the named media renderer is actually supported by both systems.

Quick Tip

Before using `systemComponent` with a mobile SMIL player, check the documentation carefully to make sure of the URIs that the player accepts. Given the evolving nature of cross-device support, this is a non-trivial exercise.

Attribute: systemRequired

The `systemRequired` attribute contains a list of white space-separated namespaces. Each namespace listed defines elements and attributes that the element and its sub-presentation may use. Such a namespace could identify a module from SMIL 2.0 or an extension beyond the SMIL 2.0 standard. A player must support all of the namespaces listed in order to play the element.

The following fragment shows a typical use of `systemRequired`:

```
1  <smil xmlns="http://www.w3.org/2001/SMIL20/Language"
2       xmlns:pss5="http://www.3gpp.org/SMIL20/PSS5/"
3       systemRequired="pss5" >
```

Here, an extension namespace is defined that corresponds to 3GPP SMIL for mobile devices. By using `systemRequired`, we are insisting that the player understands the implementation model defined by the namespace URI before executing the document. The advantage of this is that the player can choose to reject a document at parse time, rather than waiting to be confronted with an unsupported element or attribute value at some time during the presentation. (Of course, you should use this only if the extensions are really required: if you use only standard SMIL, your presentation may be rejected even though you never use an unsupported construct.)

The use of SMIL 2.0 module namespaces in the `systemRequired` attribute is a primary component of SMIL Basic's scalability framework. The scalability framework lets SMIL Basic presentations put SMIL 2.0 constructs outside SMIL Basic in elements with the constructs' modules indicated by the attribute. Players supporting the extra features will play these elements.

9.2.7 SMIL 1.0 Test Attribute Support

All system test attributes from SMIL 1.0 were deprecated and replaced with SMIL 2.0 attributes with camel cased names. (The hyphenated names may still be used, but this is not recommended.) Each of these SMIL 2.0 attributes takes the same values and encodes the same behavior as its deprecated predecessor.

The deprecated SMIL 1.0 system test attributes are listed in Table 9-6 with their SMIL 2.0 replacements.

deprecated	replacement
system-language	systemLanguage
system-overdub-or-caption	systemOverdubOrSubtitle
system-captions	systemCaptions
system-bitrate	systemBitrate
system-screen-size	systemScreenSize
system-screen-depth	systemScreenDepth
system-required	systemRequired

Table 9-6. The deprecated SMIL 1.0 system test attributes with their SMIL 2.0 equivalent replacements

9.2.8 Static and Dynamic System Test Attribute Evaluation

There are two approaches to evaluating attributes: *static* and *dynamic*. With static evaluation, the value kept by the player for each test attribute is determined once (either at parse time or when the presentation starts) and is not updated. Dynamic evaluation allows the current value of a player's test attribute to be used; this can result in differing behavior in, for example, a repeat loop. The choice between static and dynamic is a player implementation issue — the SMIL standard allows both mechanisms to be supported.

9.3 Examples Using SMIL Content Control

We finish this chapter with a complete design example that ties together the concepts of SMIL's content control attributes. Our example is related to the *Flashlight* presentation discussed in Chapter 2: *Understanding SMIL 2.0 Code*.

Suppose you are a multimedia designer and that you receive the following requirements for a new presentation:

- create an illustrated Web owner's guide for a new flashlight,
- target the presentation for two versions of a hand-held PDA device (one slow model, one fast), at several levels of available network bandwidth, and
- make the presentation so that both customers in the United States and the United Kingdom can 'relate' to the content.

Let's look at how SMIL's content selection facilities can help manage this task.

9.3.1 Media and Presentation Design

The first step in any design process is to identify your target audience. In this case, the audience is on both sides of the (North) Atlantic ocean. While there are many similarities between the United States and the United Kingdom, there are also a few important differences. Perhaps the most important (al least for this example!) is this: if you say "flashlight" to most people in the UK, they will have no idea that you are talking about a handheld device that gives off light. (In the UK, they call this sort of thing a *torch*.) On the other hand, if you say "torch" to a US audience, it will likely conjure up images of that thing being held high in the right hand of the Statue of Liberty in New York Harbor — which the English spell *Harbour*. Still, the differences are not all that great, and after eating a bagel with orange marmalade to get in the right multi-cultural mood, you decide that a single presentation with some content customization should work.

After looking through some existing user manuals to get some design inspiration, you write some voice-over text and create a few images that show how the device works. Just when you think you are ready to make the final design, you learn that the manufacturer wants video included in the presentation. Since the customer has paid a pretty penny/pence for the expensive/dear flashlight/torch, the manufacturer wants your presentation to shine, too. Still, knowing that the available bitrate to the PDA might be limited, you wisely decide to take a few images from the video and whip up a quick slideshow as an alternative to the video when the connection is less than about 100Kbps.

Before creating the assets, you add one nice touch to the presentation: instead of providing only audio voice-overs, you add an option for captions (in both dialects of English) so that users can also view the owner's guide while working in noisy environments. This is also very user-friendly for any deaf clients.

After completing the artwork and text, you wind up with the following collection of assets:

- two sets of audio tracks, one with a US English voice, and one from the UK,
- two sets of graphics (one with *Torch* and the other with *Flashlight*),
- one set of videos and several image extractions for a slideshow,
- two sets of background images with text labels, and
- two sets of captions.

After a pass by the legal department, you are ready to create the presentation.

9.3.2 The Structure of the Presentation

Figure 9-6 shows the opening views of each of the presentations. On the left is a PDA version for the US market and on the right is the PDA version with content for the UK market .

(a) US market   *(b) UK market*

Figure 9-6. Two views of the Flashlight/Torch Owner's Manual.

The presentation consists of five sections:

- Introduction (with a *Welcome and Thank You* pitch),
- Batteries (with type information and, in the US version, legal disclaimers),
- Operation (with information on turning on/off the device),
- Tips & Tricks (with helpful information for daily use), and
- More Info (with links to the company's Web sites in the US and the UK).

The basic structure of the presentation is shown in Example 9-4. The (common) background of the presentation is defined in line 7. Since none of the background text uses contentious spelling, you can get away with one image. Each of the sections of the presentation is displayed in sequence, all in parallel with the background.

Each section of the presentation will pointers to media assets plus various SMIL control elements and attributes to enable dynamic content selection.

```
1  <smil xmlns="http://www.w3.org/2001/SMIL20/Language">
2    <head>
3      <.../>
4    </head>
5    <body>
6      <par>
7        <img region="Background" src="media/title.gif"/>
8        <seq>
9          <par id="Intro">
10            <.../>
11          </par>
12          <par id="Batteries">
13            <.../>
14          </par>
15          <par id="Operation">
16            <.../>
17          </par>
18          <par id="Tips">
19            <.../>
20          </par>
21          <par id="More-Info">
22            <.../>
23          </par>
24        </seq>
25      </par>
26    </body>
27  </smil>
```

Example 9-4. General flow of *Flashlight/Torch*.

9.3.3 Using SMIL to Define the Adaptive Presentation

Let's consider how SMIL's basic selection mechanisms can be applied in the flashlight/torch example. We consider three moments during the presentation, and give an indication of some of the content choices made during the design phase. In Figure 9-7, we see a part of the *Operation* segment. In the left portion, the assets active in the US market version are shown: a US voice-over, a slide-show, and US captions. In the UK version, a UK voice is used, a video is being

Figure 9-7. The *Operation* section of *Flashlight/Torch*.

Figure 9-8. The *Tips & Tricks* section of *Flashlight/Torch*.

shown instead of the slideshow (presumably because more bandwidth was available at the time the presentation was shown) and captions are turned off.

In Figure 9-8, we see a part of the *Tips & Tricks* segment. The left portion continues to use US market version audio, but now it shows video instead of slides. Meanwhile, the quality of the UK link may have decreased, because it is now showing slides instead of video. Note that both presentations make use of a common text label under the visual media object. (This is evidently important information that the designer doesn't want the user to have go unnoticed.)

In Figure 9-9, we see a fragment of the final part of the presentation: the closing image, each customized for a particular language, and a text field showing the two Web sites related to this presentation. If a US market user clicks the Web address in that presentation, a link is made to the US Web site. If a UK user follows the link associated with the UK image, the UK Web site is activated.

Figure 9-9. The *More Info* section of *Flashlight/Torch*.

The structure of each of the segments is similar in this presentation, so Example 9-5 looks in detail at the *Tips & Tricks* segment. (Some simplifications have been made to make the code readable. In particular, the linking information has been removed.)

The *Tips* section consists of a sequence of two parallel blocks. The first block warns that only the correct battery types should be used. The <switch> in lines 3 through 11 allows either a video or a sequence of images to be selected, based on the systemBitrate test attribute on line 4. (If this evaluates to *false*, then the sequence starting on line 5 will always be selected, since it has no test attribute.) In parallel with the visual media, a second <switch> selects either US or UK market audio. Finally, a captions image will be displayed if the systemCaptions setting in the player is set to *on*. (If not, no captions will be shown and this element will be ignored.)

The second part of the *Tips* section contains a segment warning that, for best results, the light should be pointed away from the user. This section consists of the parallel presentation of a captions image on line 30 (in this case, non-optional), plus a sequence containing a combination of images and video in lines 19 through 25, followed by an audio selection in lines 26 though 29. (Note that if the presentation is being played on a player that is set for anything other than US or UK languages, no audio will be played at all.)

```
1   <seq id="Tips">
2     <par id="Correct-Batteries">
3       <switch>
4         <video region="image" src="batt.avi" systemBitrate="128000" />
5         <seq>
6           <img region="image" dur="1s" fill="freeze" src="b-1.gif"/>
7           <img region="image" dur="1s" fill="freeze" src="b-2.gif"/>
8           <img region="image" dur="1s" fill="freeze" src="b-3.gif"/>
9           <img region="image" dur="2s" fill="freeze" src="b-4.gif"/>
10        </seq>
11      </switch>
12      <switch>
13        <audio region="audio" src="Batt-US.mp3" systemLanguage="en-us"/>
14        <audio region="audio" src="Batt-UK.mp3" />
15      </switch>
16      <img region="caption" src="c-batt.gif" systemCaptions="on" />
17    </par>
18    <par id="Point-Away-Advice" dur="5.5s">
19      <seq>
20        <img region="image" dur="2s" fill="freeze" src="away-key.jpg"/>
21        <switch systemBitrate="128000">
22          <video region="image" src="away8.avi" systemScreenDepth="8"/>
23          <video region="image" src="away2.avi" systemScreenDepth="2"/>
24        </switch>
25      </seq>
26      <switch>
27        <audio region="audio" src="Res-US.mp3" systemLanguage="en-us"/>
28        <audio region="audio" src="Res-UK.mp3" systemLanguage="en-uk"/>
29      </switch>
30      <img region="captions" src="point-away.gif"/>
31    </par>
32  </seq>
```

Example 9-5. Structure of the *Tips & Tricks* section.

Look closely at the sequence in lines 19 through 25. It starts with an image, which is presented for 2 seconds and is then frozen on the screen for the duration of the parent time container (in this case, 5.5 seconds). After two seconds, the next element in the <seq> is evaluated: this is the <switch>. Note that this <switch> will only be further evaluated if the *systemBitrate* is found to be 128000 bps or greater at the time the evaluation takes place. If this is *true*, then the children of the *<switch>* are checked in turn. If the screen depth of the player is 8 bits or greater, then the first video is played. If the screen depth is 4 bits or greater (but less than 8 bits), the second video is played. If the screen depth is less than 4 bits, nothing is played. (Although not directly related to selection, studying this fragment leads to the following question: if the 8-bit video is 4 seconds long and the 4-bit video is 5 seconds long, what is the duration of the *Point-Away-Advice* <par>?)

The use of a test attribute on the <switch> element, as shown on line 21, determines whether the <switch> itself is evaluated. You should work through this example to understand all of the possible execution cases covered by lines 18 through 31.

9.4 Summary and Conclusion

The *BasicContentControl* module provides all of the system test attributes functionality from SMIL 1.0 (albeit using camel-case naming instead of hyphenated names). The major addition of SMIL 2.0 is to allow test attributes to be used in-line (that is, outside of the <switch> element).

The advantage of the system test attribute approach is that it allows SMIL players and SMIL authors to have a common set of test variables that can be used to create adaptive presentations. The disadvantage of this approach is that the set of system test attributes supported by SMIL 2.0 is fixed in the standard. If you want to test on, for example, the desire to have detailed content rather than summary content, then the standard set of attributes don't help. To solve this problem, SMIL 2.0 offers custom test attributes, defined in Chapter 16: *Extended Content Control*.

9.5 Further Resources

Language Tags

Tags for the Identification of Languages, Harald T. Alvestrand, RFC 1766, UNINETT, March 1995.
`ftp://ftp.isi.edu/in-notes/rfc1766.txt`.

Primary Language Tags

ISO CD 639/2:1991. Code for the Representation of Names of Languages: alpha-3 Code, International Organization for Standardization (ISO), 1991.
`http://lcweb.loc.gov/standards/iso639-2/langhome.html`.

Language Sub-tags

ISO 3166:1999. Codes for the representation of names of countries and their subdivisions, International Organization for Standardization (ISO), 1999.
http://www.iso.ch/iso/en/prods-services/iso3166ma/index.html.

10
Transition Effects

When SMIL 1.0 was released in 1998, it provided a host of facilities for scheduling and placing visual media on the user's display device. One of the features that was noticeably absent, however, was any ability to have images (or other visual media) cross-fade from one image to the next. Although certain proprietary media formats such as *RealPix* supported fades and simple animations on images, there was no general mechanism for defining how visual content could 'flow' into the presentation.

SMIL 2.0 corrects this deficiency. It provides a comprehensive mechanism for specifying *transition effects* on visual media. A transition effect is a behavior on a media object that defines how that media object is rendered with respect to content already active. SMIL provides both a simple means of specifying begin and/or end transitions on media and a more powerful mechanism for providing arbitrary rendering control during the active duration of a media object.

Strictly speaking, the transition effects facilities in SMIL are advanced material because not all SMIL profiles guarantee transitions support. (This limitation applies to the simplest versions of SMIL Basic and sub-SMIL languages such as MMS-2.0.) Now that the 3GPP has adopted the use of SMIL transitions in newer versions of the Mobile SMIL specifications, however, transitions have entered the mainstream of SMIL features.

This chapter describes SMIL's transition effect facilities. We begin with a short discussion of how transition effects can be modelled and then show by example how SMIL integrates transition effects with timing and display primitives. We then discuss the — sometimes tricky — timing considerations for providing transitions support in many situations. We follow with a detailed discussion on how transition features can be applied to documents in the SMIL Language and XHTML+SMIL profiles. We close with a description of the transitions supported by SMIL 2.0.

10.1 Concepts and Models of Transition Effects

Most everyone who owns a television or who has seen a Powerpoint presentation is familiar with the notion of a transition effect: an existing media object (such as an image or a video) is incrementally replaced by a second media object. During this incremental replacement process, either the original or the new object can be deformed in some way (geometrically or in terms of opacity), but the goal is always the same: rather than have a single change-over moment from one object to the next, the change-over is done gradually.

This section explores some of the fundamental concepts associated with transition effects and looks at a number of conceptual models that are used to implement transitions. (If you are simply interested in getting your SMIL transitions to work quickly, you can go right to section *Examples Using SMIL Transition Effects* on page 221.)

10.1.1 Basic Transition Effects Concepts

In its simplest form, a transition effect defines a visual or aural relationship between two objects. The transition can be used to define how a new object B starts relative to an existing object A, or how an existing object A ends relative to the start of a new object B. Objects A and B can be either actual media objects (such as images, text strings, audio objects or video sequences), or one of them can be (a part of) the presentation background. Several examples of visual transitions are given in Figure 10-1.

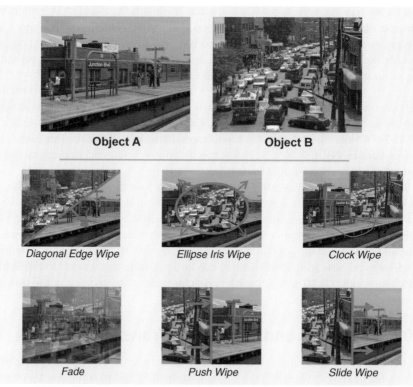

Figure 10-1. Examples of transition effects from Object A to Object B.
(Red lines have been added to indicate transition boundaries and direction.)

In addition to identifying the objects involved in the transition, all transition effects have a number of properties that control the transition. These are:

- *Type*: SMPTE, the Society of Motion Picture and Television Engineers, define 4 major types of transitions: *edge wipes, iris wipes, clock wipes* and *matrix wipes*. SMIL also supports three other types of transition effects: *fades, push wipes* and *slide wipes*. It is possible to add new types of transitions to the collection used by SMIL.

- *Sub-type*: nearly all transition types can be further divided into sub-types that provide additional control over the transition effect. For example, the fade transition has the sub-types: *cross-fade, fade-from-color* and *fade-to-color*.

- *Start time*: conceptually, there are many ways to define the begin moment of the transition. As we will see, SMIL uses a time that is relative to the target media object's start or the end time.

- *Duration:* transitions with short durations happen quickly; transitions with long durations occur slowly. Varying the duration can set the effect or mood you want to create.

- *Progress range*: the progress range defines how much of the transition effect is to be shown during the transition. A transition can consist of a full effect (such as a full fade from background to the target object), or a partial effect (such as fading from, say, 25% to 80%).

- *transition repeat values*: a set of vertical and/or horizontal repeat factors. These allow a transition to be scaled to a portion of the display area and then repeated horizontally or vertically.

The inherently temporal nature of transitions means that a period of time needs to be allocated to the duration of the transition effect. As we will see, defining this temporal interval is not always easy, especially when designing interactive presentations.

10.1.2 Transition Models

While the basic concepts that need to be supported for transitions are fairly uniform, there are several underlying models that can be used to define how transitions are implemented in a given language. In this section, we review four of these models. Of the first three, all are related in some way to how SMIL produces transition effects; understanding the differences in approaches can help you make more effective use of SMIL's facilities.

The Baker's Oven Model

Perhaps the easiest way to attach a transition effect to a media object is to open a media editor and "bake" the transition effect directly into the source media object. Probably the most common effect that gets baked into media is a few seconds of fade-out at the end of a pop music song. (Inserting this effect is almost always easier than composing a convincing ending!) In this case, one of the media objects is the source music and the other is silence. For video, we

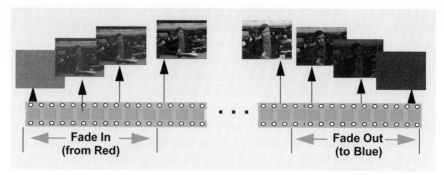

Figure 10-2. Baking transition effects into a media object.

could use a single media object and the (possibly transparent) background color or we could define a transition effect between two video clips.

The process of creating baked transition effects is illustrated in Figure 10-2. Here we see that a video object is altered to begin with a fade from a solid red background and then end with a fade to a solid blue background. If we knew which media object preceded or followed this one, we could have also created cross fades from one video to the next.

Baking transitions into media is a heavy-weight solution since it involves changing the actual object. This makes the process harder to un-do and it makes it more difficult to reuse the media object in different contexts. It also is usually impossible to bake transitions into non-temporal objects such as images. Not unimportantly, if you don't own the media object, altering it to include transitions is usually a violation of copyright.

The Switcher's Hand Model

The earliest implementations of non-baked transition effects were based on the analog mixing of two signals. A person sitting at a switching device with a selector knob and progress lever could cause one signal stream to be transitioned into another. We call this the *Switcher's Hand* model.

The switcher's hand model is illustrated in Figure 10-3. Sources *A* and *B* are fed into a mixer; a selector knob determines the type of transition effect (in this case, a cross-fade) and a progress lever determines how much of each source is visible. Similar mixing devices are common for audio media.

The advantage of this model is that it is easy to implement in hardware and that, with a skilled operator, it works effectively and smoothly. The disadvantages of the model include that it is difficult to create new types/sub-types of transitions and that most operators only have two hands (thus the complexity of the transitions is limited). With the advent of programmable switch boxes, many different types of effects can be selected and many incoming media streams can be combined — but operators still have only two hands!

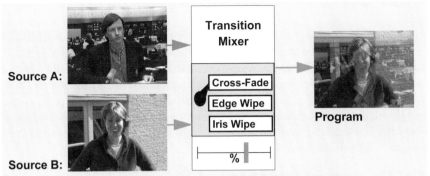

Figure 10-3. Modelling transitions as a mixing filter.
A cross-fade is selected and the wipe slide has 35% of Source A and 65% of Source B displayed the result as its output.

The Painter's Canvas Model

A more flexible approach to inserting transitions is to apply the effect on the rendered version of a media item rather than on the object itself. Just before an object gets displayed, a transition effect can be defined relative to the existing background. This approach is often called the *Painter's Canvas* model.

The top part of Figure 10-4 illustrates the Painter's Canvas model. A red background area, representing all or part of the presentation's background, is combined with a new media object to create an updated background. The new object is incrementally applied over the duration of the transition effect. When the new object is added, it can be transformed in size or shape and then incrementally mixed in with the existing canvas. The bottom part of Figure 10-4 shows this incremental progress over a three second period. To obtain a smooth

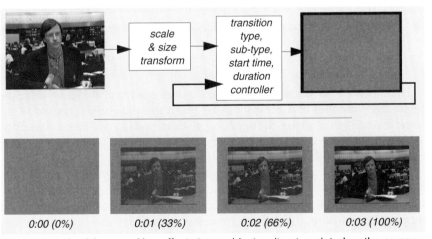

Figure 10-4. Applying transition effects to an object as it gets painted on the screen.

transition, approximately 10 intermediate images per second need to be created.

The painter's canvas model is easy to implement and easy to understand. (It formed the basis of the RealNetworks *RealPix* format.) Still, it has some disadvantages. First, there is usually no notion of an object's original identity once it has been placed on the canvas. This means that while it is easy to fade an object into a scene, it is very difficult to fade a particular object *out* of a scene. A second problem is that the painter's canvas does not fully describe what happens when the background itself changes during the transition (such as when you fade an image onto a video background).

The SMIL Animation Filter Model

SMIL uses a transitions model that has aspects of the switcher's hand and the painter's canvas models. (It also supports baked transitions via the media renderers.) The key aspects of SMIL's support for transitions are:

- A transition is defined as an interaction between a renderable target media object and (a part of) the presentation background.

- The target media object can be a single media object (such as an image or a video) or, depending on the profile, a container object that holds renderable media (such as an HTML <div> or <span>). It cannot not be a time container that groups renderable media, such as a <par> or <seq> element.

- The background consists of a media object (or background color) that is active in the display area referenced by the target object. For the SMIL 2.0 Language profile, this is usually a SMIL Layout region, but it can be any rendering surface in any layout model that is associated with the media. (Unlike the Painter's Canvas model, the background can contain active media that can change during the transition).

- The timing of the transition's target media object (its start and end times and its duration) are used as a *timebase* for the transition effect.

- The transition is modelled as a black box that takes as input: transition type, sub-type, duration and a start/end progress value. A computed progress value defines the progress through the transition. *It is this progress value that is animated (changed) by the transition implementation.*

The schematic of the SMIL transitions model is shown in Figure 10-5. The begin and end times of the transition are taken from the timing context of the target media item. As we will see, SMIL provides both a style-like specification of transition behavior and an in-line behavior specification where the transition is defined as the child of the target media item.

The SMIL transitions effects implementation does not require a particular type of layout implementation. This means that the facilities in the transitions effects modules can be applied to any XML language that needs transitions support. For purposes of this book, however, we will consider transitions using SMIL Layout and CSS-based layout in XHTML+SMIL implementations.

Target Media:

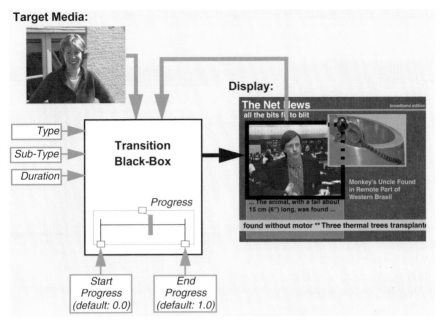

Figure 10-5. SMIL transitions model.
A target media object is combined with a (portion of) the display space. A transition type, sub-type and duration are given to the transitions black box. The progress through the transition is determined based on an intermediate progress value.

10.1.3 Basic and Inline Transitions

SMIL provides two sets of elements and attributes: a short-hand transitions implementation called SMIL *Basic Transitions* and a more control-oriented version called SMIL *Inline Transitions*. In general, SMIL 2.0 Language players will support the *Basic Transitions* elements and attributes, while XHTML+SMIL players will support *Inline Transitions*. (SMIL players may support both basic and in-line transition formats, but this is not typical.)

10.2 Basic Transitions Elements and Attributes

The SMIL *BasicTransitions* module defines one element and seven attributes for defining transition templates and two attributes for associating transition templates with target media elements. In addition, several type-specific attributes are provided to control the behavior of individual effects.

This section considers the behavior of basic transitions. These are nearly always implemented in SMIL 2.0 Language players, including mobile SMIL implementations that support transition effects.

10.2.1 Basic Transition Elements

This section discusses the `<transition>` element.

Element: <transition>

The `<transition>` element's structure is laid out in Table 10-1. This element, which is usually specified in the `<head>` element, allows a transition template to be defined. Each template must have an id attribute so that it can be referenced from within the `<body>` section.

There may be an arbitrary number of `<transition>` elements in the `<head>` section of a document. Each element defines a single transition template. The definitions do not need to be unique (except for the id value of each template).

Each `<transition>` element may have a `<param>` element as a

<transition>		Profiles
attributes	type	L M
	subtype	
	startProgress	
	endProgress	
	direction	
	type-specific	
	dur	
	skip-content, test, core	
parents	<head>	L M
children	<param>	L M

Table 10-1. Structure of the <transition> element.

child; this allows new transitions with new control attributes to be specified.

In addition to the attributes shown in Table 10-1, additional attributes may be allowed for the control of specific transition types.

10.2.2 General Attributes for Basic Transitions

The *BasicTransitions* module uses five attributes to define a transition template. The dur attribute is usually also required, although the default value of one second may be used. The transitions element also must include an XML ID and it may include the skip-content, test and core attributes.

Attribute: type

In the context of transitions, the type attribute is used to specify the general transition. The type attribute is required. If the named type is not supported by the player, the transition is ignored. Note that this is not an error condition, since implementations are free to ignore transitions. The following fragment illustrates the specification of a transition type:

```
<transition id="X1" type="barWipe" ... />
```

The section *Transition Classes, Types and Sub-Types* on page 230 lists the set of transition types as defined in the SMIL 2.0 specification. This list contains transitions defined by SMPTE and a set of SMIL-specific transformations. (While the table groups transitions by class, the class name is not used in the type attribute; use only the type value names.)

Implementations that support transitions are required to provide support for the following transition types: *barWipe*, *irisWipe*, *clockWipe*, and *snakeWipe*. The *fade* transition type is not required, but it is generally supported by all implementations that support transitions.

Attribute: subtype

The `subtype` attribute provides transition-specific control. There are over 100 sub-types specified for transitions, all of which are specific to the transition type used. The following fragment illustrates the specification of a transition sub-type:

```
<transition id="X1" type="barWipe" subtype="leftToRight" ... />
```

There is a default sub-type defined for each transition type. Only the default sub-type for the four required transitions types must be supported by implementations that support transitions. If an unknown sub-type is specified (or if no sub-type is specified), then the default for the type will be used.

Attribute: dur

This attribute specifies the duration of the transition. The value of this argument must be a SMIL clock value. The default duration is one second. The following fragment illustrates the specification of a transition duration:

```
<transition id="X1" type="barWipe" subtype="leftToRight"
     dur="2s" ... />
```

SMIL does not support a speed attribute for transitions. Instead, the duration attribute can be used to define fast or slow transition effects: a transition with a short duration will occur relatively quickly, while a transition with a long duration will occur relatively slowly.

Note also that the duration of the transition does not modify or influence the duration of the object associated with the transition. If the object ends before the transition completes, the active duration of the object *is not* extended.

Attribute: startProgress

By default, a transition starts at the beginning of its effect. The `startProgress` attribute allow an alternative start state of a transition to be defined. This attribute is a real number in the range of 0.0-1.0. The default value is 0.0. The following fragment illustrates the specification of a transition start state:

```
<transition id="X1" type="barWipe" subtype="leftToRight"
     dur="2s" direction="reverse" startProgress="0.4" ... />
```

A value of 0.4 corresponds to a start progression state of 40%.

Attribute: endProgress

The `endProgess` attribute defines the end state of a transition. It is a real number in the range of 0.0-1.0. The default value is 1.0. The end progress value must always be greater or equal to the start progress value. If start/end progress are equal, the transition remains fixed at the defined progress value for the duration of the transition. The following fragment illustrates the specification of a transition start state:

```
<transition id="X1" type="barWipe" subtype="leftToRight"
    dur="2s" direction="reverse" startProgress="0.4"
    endProgress="0.8" />
```

A value of 0.8 corresponds to an end progression state of 80%.

Attribute: direction

This attribute specifies the direction of the transition (not the direction of rendering of the media object!). Legal values are *forward* or *reverse*. The provision of the direction attribute is a by-product of the animation-based implementation of transitions. The following fragment illustrates the specification of a transition direction:

```
<transition id="X1" type="barWipe" subtype="leftToRight"
    dur="2s" direction="reverse" ... />
```

This example specifies that the left-to-right bar wipe should occur in reverse: from right-to-left.

On the surface, the direction attribute would seem to double the number transitions available (one in the forward direction, one in the reverse). In practice, however, the attribute is less useful than it may seem: most of the geometric transitions already have forward and reverse behavior defined (such subtype="rightToLeft"), and for non-geometric transitions — such as a fade — there is no meaningful notion of a reverse transition. The direction attribute is useful as a shorthand option when copying transition definitions.

10.2.3 Type-Specific Attributes for Basic Transitions

SMIL provides a mechanism for defining a transition type and sub-type. For those transitions that need extra arguments, two additional mechanisms are provided: the fadeColor attribute and the (general purpose) <param> element.

Attribute: fadeColor

The fadeColor attribute can be used in the special case that the transition type is *fade* and the transition sub-type is either *fadeFromColor* or *fadeToColor*. In this case, the fadeColor attribute specified the color to be the source or destination fade color. The value is a SMIL color value, with a default of *black*.

The following fragment illustrates the use of the fadeColor attribute:

```
<transition id="X1" type="fade" subtype="fadeFromColor"
    dur="2s" fadeColor="red" />
```

If the type and sub-type are not *fade* and *fadeFromColor*/*fadeToColor* (respectively), then this attribute is ignored.

Support for the `fadeColor` attribute can be seen as a pure convenience function. It is interesting to note that this convenience function is provided for a non-required transition!

Using the <param> Element

Other than a fade color, none of the transitions defined in the SMIL 2.0 specification allow the specification of additional arguments. In order to support new or custom transitions, however, the SMIL `<param>` element can be used to pass attributes to the transition processor. The following fragment illustrates the use of the `<param>` element in the context of transitions:

```
<transition id="S1" type="colorBurst" subtype="magentaRocket">
    <param name="numberOfBursts" value="9" />
</transition>
```

In this example, a new transition type named *colorBurst* has been implemented in a special-purpose SMIL player. It supports the *magentaRocket* transition sub-type. This transition type accepts an argument that defines how many rocket heads are included in the transition (in this case, 9).

The use of the `<param>` element does not give any extra control over the standard set of transitions, and it is only useful for players in which the desired transition is actually supported. For more information on the structure and use of the `<param>` element, see *Initialization Attributes for Media Objects* on page 251.

> **Quick Tip**
>
> If you define a transition that may not be supported in all players, make sure you define a fall-back transition type in the instance list of transitions. (See the *transIn* and *transOut* attributes, below.)

10.2.4 Attributes for Integrating Basic Transitions

Once a transition has been defined in the `<head>` section, it can be referenced in the `<body>` using the `transIn` and/or `transOut` attributes. While the intention of these attributes is to specify input and output transitions, this is not really what they do: they actually state whether the transition effect should be associated with the beginning or the end of a media object. (The nature of the effect will determine if it is inherently input or output related.) A better set of names might have been `transBegin` and `transEnd`.

Attribute: transIn

The `transIn` attribute specifies that the associated transition is to be scheduled at the beginning of the rendering of the media object. It can be added to any media object reference. In the SMIL 2.0 Language profile, it only applies to visual content. The value of the `transIn` attribute is a semicolon-separated list of transition names (each of which were defined in the presentation head section). The first transition in the list that is recognized and supported by the implementation will be used. transIn may be used together with transOut.

Attribute: transOut

The transOut attribute specifies that the associated transition is to be scheduled at the end of the rendering period of a media object. It can be added to any media object reference. In the SMIL 2.0 Language profile, it only applies to visual content. The value of the transOut attribute is a semicolon-separated list of transition names (each of which were defined in the presentation head section). The first transition in the list that is recognized and supported by the implementation will be used. transOut may be used together with transIn.

Examples of Using transIn and transOut

Example 10-1 provides an example of how SMIL basic transitions are defined and integrated. Two transitions are defined: *f2s* (a 2-second fade up from color) and *S1* (a special transition type). The behavior in this example is as follows:

- On line 15, a video is started that fades in from a red background. This is not the background color of region *v* (which is blue), but the fade color defined in the transition. The last frame of the video will be frozen beyond the temporal scope of object *A* because of the fill="transition".

- On line 16, an image is started and displayed for 4 seconds. If the player supports the *colorBurst* transition, it will be used. If not, the fade transition will be used (unless fade is also not supported). Since the last frame of the video on line 15 was held for use with the transition, this frame forms the background of the transition effect. Note that the image element does not

```
 1 <smil ...>
 2  <head>
 3   ...
 4   <region id="v" backgroundColor="blue" ... />
 5   ...
 6   <transition id="f2s" type="fade" subtype="fadeFromColor"
        dur="2s" fadeColor="red" />
 7   <transition id="S1" type="colorBurst" subtype="magentaRocket">
 8    <param name="numberOfBursts" value="9" />
 9   </transition>
10   ...
11  </head>
12  <body>
13   ...
14   <seq>
15    <video id="A" src="a.mpg" transIn="f2s" fill="transition" region="v"/>
16    <img id="B" src="b.jpg" transIn="S1; f2s" region="v" dur="4s" />
17    <video id="C" src="c.mpg" transIn="S1" transOut="f2s" region="v" />
18   </seq>
19   ...
20  </body>
21 </smil>
```

Example 10-1. SMIL basic transitions integration.

have a `fill="transition"` attribute value defined. As a result, it will be removed from the screen at the end of its active duration.

- The video object on line 17 starts with a *colorBurst* transition (if available). The transition will use the region's blue background as the basis for this transition — this is because `fill="transition"` was not defined on the preceding element. At the end of the video, the fade transition will be applied. As defined on line 6, the *f2s* transition will fade content from the target media object into the presentation from a red background.

  The behavior of this transition will be as follows:

  — two seconds before the end of video C on line 17, the transition starts;

  — since the transition is a *fadeFromColor,* the region *v* will be painted in red (the fill-from color) at the moment the transition starts;

  — the red fill color will fade away during two second duration of the transition, incrementally making the video — which was already active — visible; and

  — just as the video ends, its final frame is fully exposed.

(This behavior, while interesting, is probably not very useful other than to help understand exactly how transitions are supported.)

The *transition* value of the `fill` attribute provides essential functionality for supporting transitions in a `<seq>`. Details are given in *SMIL Timing and Transitions* on page 226.

In designing transition effects, it is important to realize that the transition definition is only a hint to the implementation. The fact that a transition exists does not lengthen or shorten the active duration of the base media object, nor does it impact the scheduling of any of the other objects in the presentation.

In addition to the attributes discussed in this section, Basic transitions also accept a set of transition modifiers. Since these are also used with *Inline* transitions, we defer a discussion of transition modifiers until the section *Modifying Basic and Inline Transitions* on page 221.

10.3 Inline Transitions Elements and Attributes

Profiles that support the SMIL *InlineTransitions* module will implement the `<transitionFilter>` element. This element, which is closely related to the behavior provided by SMIL Animation, allows for detailed and fine-grained specification of transition effects. At present, only the XHTML+SMIL profile supports this element; it is *not* supported by the SMIL 2.0 Language profile.

10.3.1 Inline Transition Elements

This section defines the `<transitionFliter>` element.

Element: <transitionFilter>

The <transitionFilter>'s structure is laid out in Table 10-2. It supports attributes for the specification of general transition properties, as well as timing and animation control attributes. The transition filter element is typically used as a child of a media object element, but it can also be used as a stand-alone element that references a target media object. The transition filter can also accept the <param> element as a child.

<transitionFilter>		Profiles
attributes	transition attributes	
	timing attributes	
	animation attributes	H
	integration attributes	
	skip-content, *test*, *core*	
parents	*media objects*	H
children	<param>	H

Table 10-2. Structure of the <transitionFilter> element.

10.3.2 General Attributes for Inline Transitions

SMIL's *InlineTransitions* module defines three attributes that may be used to define a transition filter's behavior: type, subtype, and mode.

Attribute: type

The type attribute is used to specify the general transition. The type attribute is required. If the named type is not supported by the player, the transition is ignored. Note that this is not an error condition, since implementations are free to ignore transitions. The following fragment illustrates the use of type:

```
<transitionFilter type="barWipe" ... />
```

The tables in *Transition Classes, Types and Sub-Types* on page 230 list the set of transition types as defined in the SMIL 2.0 specification. This list contains transitions defined by SMPTE and a set of SMIL-specific transformations. (While the table groups transitions by class, the class name is not used in the type attribute; use only the type value names.)

Implementations that support transitions are required to provide support for the following transition types: *barWipe, irisWipe, clockWipe,* and *snakeWipe.* The *fade* transition type is not required, but it is generally supported by all implementations that support transitions.

Attribute: subtype

The subtype attribute provides transition-specific control. There are over 100 sub-types specified for transitions, all of which are specific to the transition type used. The following fragment illustrates the specification of a transition sub-type:

```
<transitionFilter type="barWipe" subtype="leftToRight" ... />
```

There is a default sub-type defined for each transition type. Only the default sub-type for the four required transitions types must be supported by implementations that support transitions. If an unknown sub-type is specified (or if no sub-type is specified), then the default for the type will be used.

Attribute: mode

A transition can be defined to be an *input* or *output* effect. Input effects use the background as the primary rendering object and then incrementally bring in the target media object; output transitions use the target media object as the initial rendering source and then gradually transition in the background. Legal values for mode are *in* and *out*.

```
<transitionFilter type="fade" subtype="fadeFromColor"
     mode="in" ... />
```

The *BasicTransitions* module defined the transIn and transOut attributes to define when a transition should start relative to the target media object. The transition filter element's mode attribute — although it appears to be similar — defines whether a transition has an input or output effect, but says nothing about when the transition get scheduled. To control the start time, use the begin attribute (see below).

10.3.3 Timing Attributes for Inline Transitions

The timing attributes for controlling the start, duration and end of the transition filter are: begin, dur, and end. Transition filters may also accept the repeatCount and repeatDur attributes. (For a complete discussion on all values for these attributes, see Chapter 14: *Advanced SMIL Timing Attributes*.)

Attribute: begin

The begin attribute determines the start time of the transition effect. The default is 0 seconds (the beginning of the associated media object.) Begin timing may be complex, since it may involve relative or interactive timing.

The following fragment illustrates the use of the begin attribute:

```
<video src="a.mpg" >
    <transitionFilter type="fade" subtype="fadeFromColor" mode="in"
         fadeColor="red" begin="3s"/>
</video>
```

In this example, the fade begins three seconds after the associated media object has started. After playing normally for three seconds, the display will become red and the associated object will be come incrementally visible again over a period of one second (the default duration of the transition).

Attribute: dur

The dur attribute defines the duration of the transition effect. The default duration of a transition effect is one second.

Attribute: end

The end attribute explicitly specifies an end time for transition effect. The end timing may be complex, since it may involve relative or interactive timing.

Attribute: repeatCount

Usually, a transition is applied once to a media object. If a transition effect is not specified as a child of a media object, it can occasionally be useful to repeat transition effects. A repeat count can be given using the repeatCount attribute.

Attribute: repeatDur

As with repeatCount, the repeat duration of a stand-alone transition filter can be specified using the repeatDur attribute.

10.3.4 Animation Attributes for Inline Transitions

Transition filters accept five animation-related attributes: from, to, by, values and calcMode. Since the meaning of these attributes are identical to those defined by SMIL Animation, we will only summarize their behavior here. For more details, see Chapter 15: *SMIL Animation*.

Attribute: from

By default, a transition starts at the beginning of its effect. The from attribute allows an alternative start state of a transition to be defined. This attribute is a real number in the range of 0.0-1.0. A value of 0.4 corresponds to a start progression state of 40%. The default value is 0.0. The from value is ignored if the values attribute is also present.

The following fragment illustrates the specification of a transition start state:

```
<transitionFilter type="fade" subtype="fadeFromColor" mode="in"
    fadeColor="red" begin="3s" from="0.4"/>
```

This attribute is similar to the startProgress attribute of SMIL Basic Transitions discussed on page 211.

Attribute: to

The to attribute defines the end state of a transition. It is a real number in the range of 0.0-1.0. The end value must always be greater or equal to the from attribute value. If from/to attribute values are equal, the transition remains fixed at the defined progress value for the duration of the transition. A value of 0.8 corresponds to an end progression state of 80%. The default value is 1.0. The from value is ignored if the values attribute is also present.

The following fragment illustrates the specification of a transition end state:

```
<transitionFilter type="fade" subtype="fadeFromColor" mode="in"
        fadeColor="red" begin="3s" from="0.4" to="0.8" />
```

This attribute is similar to the endProgress attribute of SMIL Basic Transitions discussed on page 211.

Attribute: by

The by attribute specifies a increment value for use in determining the progress of the transition effect. It is a real number representing an incremental percentage; legal values are a single value in the range 0.0-1.0. This attribute is ignored if the values attribute is present. The following fragment illustrates the specification of a increment value:

```
<transitionFilter type="fade" subtype="fadeFromColor" mode="in"
        fadeColor="red" begin="3s" from="0.4" end="0.8" by="0.2"/>
```

Attribute: values

This attribute contains a semicolon separated list of values to be used to determine the progress of the transition effect. The processing of the values (whether absolute or incremental) is determined by the calcMode attribute. Legal values are a set of real numbers, each between 0.0-1.0.

The following fragment illustrates the specification of a values list:

```
<transitionFilter type="fade" subtype="fadeFromColor" mode="in"
        fadeColor="red" begin="3s" values="0.0;0.33;0.66;1.0"/>
```

Attribute: calcMode

The values defined with the values attribute can be interpreted as either a set of discrete steps or as a set of interpolation points. Legal values are *discrete* and *linear*. The default mode is *linear*, which provides for a smooth set of steps between the points defined in the values list. Unlike the use of calcMode with SMIL Animation, the *paced* mode is not supported for transition filters. The following fragment illustrates the specification of a calculation mode:

```
<transitionFilter type="fade" subtype="fadeFromColor" mode="in"
        fadeColor="red" begin="3s" values="0.0;0.33;0.66;1.0"
        calcMode="linear"/>
```

10.3.5 Type-Specific Attributes for Inline Transitions

As discussed for Basic Transitions, SMIL provides two mechanisms for defining type/sub-type specific attributes: fadeColor and the <param> element.

Attribute: fadeColor

The fadeColor attribute can be used in the special case that the transition type is *fade* and the transition sub-type is either *fadeFromColor* or *fadeToColor*. In this case, the fadeColor attribute specified the color to be the source or destination fade color. (In all other cases, `fadeColor` is ignored.) The value is a CSS color value, with a default of *black*. The following fragment illustrates the use of the `fadeColor` attribute:

```
<transitionFilter type="fade" subtype="fadeFromColor" mode="in"
    fadeColor="red" />
```

Using the <param> Element

In order to support new or custom transitions, the SMIL <param> element can be used to pass attributes to the transition processor. The following fragment illustrates the use of the <param> element in the context of in-line transitions:

```
<transitionFilter type="colorBurst" subtype="orangeRose">
    <param name="numberOfPetals" value="5" />
</transitionFilter>
```

In this example, a new transition type named *colorBurst* has been implemented in a special-purpose SMIL player. It supports the *orangeRose* transition sub-type. This transition type accepts an argument that defines how many petals are included in the rose (in this case, 5).

The <param> element is described in detail in section *Initialization Attributes for Media Objects* on page 251 of Chapter 11: *Subsetting and Extending Media*.

10.3.6 Attributes for Integrating Inline Transitions

Inline transitions are not defined in a presentation's <head> section, but directly in the presentation <body>. The typical use of <transitionFilter> is as the child of a rendered media object. In this case, no additional integration attributes are necessary.

Since transition filters are based on the animation filter model, it is also possible to specify the <transitionFilter> element as a separate (peer-level) element in a presentation. In this case, a mechanism is required to determine the object in the presentation to which the transition effect is applied. The *Inline-Transitions* module provides the href and targetElement attributes.

Attribute: targetElement

This attribute identifies an object in the presentation to which the transition effect is to be applied. It is an XML ID reference.

Attribute: href

This attribute identifies an object to which the transition effect is to be applied. The value is an XLink locator. If both a targetElement attribute and an href attribute are present, the href attribute has precedence.

10.4 Modifying Basic and Inline Transitions

All the transitions defined in the SMIL *BasicTransitions* and SMIL *InlineTransitions* modules accept four addition attributes that can be used to control the visual appearance of the transitions.

10.4.1 Common Attributes for Modifying Transitions

The common attributes for modifying transitions are: `horzRepeat`, `vertRepeat`, `borderWidth`, and `borderColor`. Note that while these attributes can be specified for all transitions, they may not always produce visual effects.

Attribute: horzRepeat

The `horzRepeat` attribute specifies how often a given effect is to be repeated along the horizontal axis of the rendering region. The default is 1.

Attribute: vertRepeat

The `vertRepeat` attribute specifies how often a given effect is to be repeated along the vertical axis of the rendering region. The default is 1.

Attribute: borderColor

The `borderColor` attribute specifies the color of the border of wipe-based transition effects; it has no meaning for fade effects. The legal values are SMIL color definitions or the string "blend". The default is black.

Attribute: borderWidth

The `borderWidth` attribute specifies the width (in integer pixels) of the border of wipe-based transition effects; it has no meaning for fade effects. If the effective value is 0, then no border is shown. The default value is 0.

10.5 Examples Using SMIL Transition Effects

SMIL uses a transition effects model that is based on the animation filter model defined as part of the SMIL *Animation* module (see Chapter 15: *SMIL Animation*). While understanding the animation filter model can be useful for implementing SMIL transition effects, it is not necessary for using SMIL transitions.

10.5.1 Examples of Basic Transitions

The SMIL *BasicTransitions* module defines a mechanism to create transition templates as part of the <head> section of a document. These templates can then be instanced in the main body as input or output transitions on a media element. This is illustrated by the code fragment in Example 10-2.

```
1  <smil ...>
2  <head>
3    ...
4    <region id="v" backgroundColor="red" ... />
5    ...
6    <transition id="f2s" type="fade" dur="2s" />
7    ...
8  </head>
9  <body>
10   ...
11   <video id="X1" src="news1.mpg" transIn="f2s" region="v"/>
12   ...
13   <video id="X2" src="news2.mpg" transOut="f2s" region="v"/>
14   ...
15   <video id="X3" src="news3.mpg" transIn="f2s" transOut="f2s" region="v"/>
16   ...
17  </body>>
18 </smil>
```

Example 10-2. Using SMIL basic transitions.

In this example, a region named *v* is defined on line 4; this is the background area that will be used during the transition. A <transition> element on line 6 is used to define a 2-second fade transition template. The video object on line 11 applies this template as a *begin* transition: the video will fade up from the background color of the region (in this case, red) over a period of 2 seconds. Similarly, the video element on line 13 uses the same transition template to define an output transition: two seconds before the end of the element (whenever that is), a fade down to the background color will start. The video element on line 15 defines both an input and an output transition using the same template definition. In this case, the element fades up from the background and then fades down to the background at the end. This is SMIL's way of defining transitions similar to those shown in Figure 10-2, except that the media element itself is not changed. Note that, for purposes of this example, we assume that videos *news1* and *news2* are longer than two seconds and that *news3* is longer than four seconds. (This is not required, but it makes the example easier to understand.)

Defining Cross-Fades

In Example 10-2, each of the video elements fade from or to the background. While this can be very useful, it is often the case that a cross-fade is desired in which the last frames of the first object are blended into the first frames of the next element. This is easy to do in SMIL — although it does require using a fill attribute value that we'll discuss more fully later: fill="transition".

Example 10-3 shows how a cross-fade can be defined in a SMIL <seq>:

- The video *Y1* on line 12 defines a 2-second fade up from the background. (Note that this is typically very long for a fade-up operation.)
- The video *Y2* on line 13 will cross-fade from the end of video *Y1*. The last frame of video *Y1* will be held frozen while the transition associated with *Y2* takes place. (This is the meaning of the fill="transition" attribute on

```
1 <smil ...>
2   <head>
3     ...
4     <region id="v" backgroundColor="red" ... />
5     ...
6     <transition id="f2s" type="fade" dur="2s" />
7     ...
8   </head>
9   <body>
10    ...
11    <seq>
12      <video id="Y1" src="news1.mpg" transIn="f2s" fill="transition"/>
13      <video id="Y2" src="news2.mpg" transIn="f2s" fill="transition" .../>
14      <video id="Y3" src="news3.mpg" transIn="f2s" ... />
15    </seq>
16    ...
17  </body>>
18 </smil>
```

Example 10-3. Using SMIL Basic Transitions in a <seq>.

Y1: extend the rendered life of my object until it is no longer needed by the next transition to take place in my rendering space.)

- The video Y3 on line 14 cross-fades from the last frame of video Y2.

Note that since there is no transition that follows video Y3, it does not need a fill="transition" attribute.

Cross-Fading Continuous Media

The use of transitions in a <seq> always has the behavior that a new object is mixed with a background object that is in a frozen state. (The reason for this is explained in *Issues for Supporting Transition Effects* on page 226.) Sometimes you may want to create a transition effect in which the last active frames of an active video are included in the transition. This can be done (albeit with a bit more work) using the SMIL parallel container, as shown in Example 10-4. If we know that the *news1* object is 10 seconds long, we can schedule the start of *news2* to be at 8 seconds into the parallel element. (That is, two seconds before the end of *news1*.) It will then fade into the region *v* using the incremental back-

```
1 <smil ...>
2   <head>
3     ...
4     <region id="v" backgroundColor="red" ... />
5     ...
6     <transition id="f2s" type="fade" dur="2s" />
7     ...
8   </head>
9   <body>
10    ...
11    <par>
12      <video id="Z1" src="news1.mpg" region="v"/>
13      <video id="Z2" src="news2.mpg" region="v" begin="8s" transIn="f2s"/>
14    </par>
15    ...
16  </body>>
17 </smil>
```

Example 10-4. Using SMIL Basic Transitions in a <par>.

ground available: the last few seconds of *news1*. Now, what happens if the length of *news1* changes from 10 seconds to 18 seconds? Left unchanged, the object *news2* will still be started at 8 seconds into *news1*, since the start timing only depends on the attributes associated with *news2*.

You can avoid having to hard-wire the begin time of the second media object by changing the start time of object *Z2* on line 13 to be:

```
13   <video id="Z2" ... begin="Z1.end-2s" ... />
```

The SMIL scheduler is now told to figure out the end time of *Z1* and to schedule the start of *Z2* to be two seconds earlier. (The use of relative begin times is discussed in Chapter 13: *Advanced SMIL Timing Behavior and Control.*)

10.5.2 Examples of Inline Transitions

Where SMIL *BasicTransitions* provide a convenient means of specifying transitions as templates and instances, the SMIL *InlineTransitions* module defines more fined-grained timing and progress control over transitions.

The basic functionality provided by in-line transitions is illustrated in Example 10-5. In this example, which duplicates the functionality of the first two cases of Example 10-2, an input transition is attached as a child of the video object *A1* on line 2 and an output transition is attached as a child of object *A2* on line 6. The input transition on object *A1* is straight-forward: a transition filter is defined that identifies a type and a duration. By default (for this type of transition), the content of the background is combined with the video media object. The output transition is more complex. The reason for this is that transition filters were engineered to be input transitions; to make them behave like output transitions, the start time of the transition is set to two seconds before the end of the parent media and an 'inverse' transition is defined that runs from full visibility (a value of '1.0') to full invisibility (a value of '0.0'). Note that if the duration of the media object was known, the begin time could have been defined as a duration-based value rather than as the parent's relative end time.

As with basic transitions, transition filters can also be applied within a sequence. Example 10-6 illustrates the encoding of a sequence that is similar to that shown in Example 10-3. Note that, as with basic transitions, you must specify the `fill="transition"` attribute value on objects whose rendering duration needs to be extended into the transition of the successor object.

```
1   ...
2   <video id="A1" src="news1.mpg" >
3     <transitionFilter type="fade" dur="2s" />
4   </video>
5   ...
6   <video id="A2" src="news2.mpg" >
7     <transitionFilter type="fade" dur="2s" begin"A2.end-2s"
          from"1.0" to="0.0" />
8   </video>
9   ...
```

Example 10-5. Using SMIL Inline Transitions.

```
 1    . . .
 2    <seq>
 3      <video id="B1" src="news1.mpg" fill="transition">
 4        <transitionFilter type="fade" dur="2s" />
 5      </video>
 6      <video id="B2" src="news2.mpg" fill="transition" >
 7        <transitionFilter type="fade" dur="2s" />
 8      </video>
 9      <video id="B3" src="news3.mpg" >
10        <transitionFilter type="fade" dur="2s" />
11      </video>
12    </seq>
13    . . .
```

Example 10-6. Using SMIL transition filters within a <seq>.

Other than perhaps helping you sharpen your typing skills, the uses of the transition filter shown in Example 10-5 and Example 10-6 would seem to have no real advantage over the syntax and structure provided by SMIL's basic transitions. This is not really true, however. Since a transition filter is actually an animation object (in which the control of the animated parameter is specified indirectly via the transition type and sub-type definition), it is also possible to construct complex transition control definitions using animation-like syntax. An example of this is shown in Example 10-7. Here, a clock transition is defined that incrementally shows more of the video object on top of the background of the rendering space. The transition begins 0 seconds into the start of the video; successive parts of the video are revealed during the next twelve seconds.

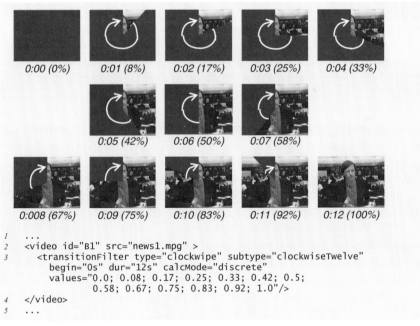

| 0:00 (0%) | 0:01 (8%) | 0:02 (17%) | 0:03 (25%) | 0:04 (33%) |

| 0:05 (42%) | 0:06 (50%) | 0:07 (58%) |

| 0:008 (67%) | 0:09 (75%) | 0:10 (83%) | 0:11 (92%) | 0:12 (100%) |

```
 1    . . .
 2    <video id="B1" src="news1.mpg" >
 3      <transitionFilter type="clockwipe" subtype="clockwiseTwelve"
          begin="0s" dur="12s" calcMode="discrete"
          values="0.0; 0.08; 0.17; 0.25; 0.33; 0.42; 0.5;
                  0.58; 0.67; 0.75; 0.83; 0.92; 1.0"/>
 4    </video>
 5    . . .
```

Example 10-7. Using SMIL transition filters for fine-grain control.
(The white arrows have been added to show transition direction.)

10.6 Issues for Supporting Transition Effects

The purpose of SMIL transition support is to provide a means of having the visual content in a target media object flow smoothly into a presentation. The transition can occur at the beginning or end of a media object — or, if inline transitions are supported, at some intermediate point — but in all cases, the transition itself is considered to be a non-required hint to the implementation environment. If the transition can't be supported, this is never an error.

There are several issues that arise when transitions are included in a presentation. This section discusses the timing and rendering implications of adding transition effects to a SMIL document.

10.6.1 SMIL Timing and Transitions

Every media element in a SMIL presentation has a duration. As we saw in Chapter 7: *Basic SMIL Timing*, there are several durations that apply to media:

- *Intrinsic duration*: this is the native duration of the object. Video objects have an intrinsic duration equal to their temporal length. Images have an intrinsic duration of 0 seconds.
- *Simple duration*: this is the intrinsic duration modified by the dur attribute.
- *Active duration*: this is the simple duration modified by a repeat.
- *Rendered duration*: this is the active duration modified by any fill behavior.

A transition effect will happen either at the beginning of the active duration or at the end of the rendered duration. (If the value of the fill attribute is *remove*, then the end of the rendered and the active durations are the same.)

Figure 10-6 illustrates six timing cases of incorporating transitions into a presentation. In each of these examples, we assume that a two second fade transition has been defined and that the target media object is 5 seconds long.

- *Case A*: a transition definition does not alter the active or rendered durations of a media object. A 5 second video object with a 2 second begin transition and a 2 second end transition still has a duration of five seconds.
- *Case B*: if a media object explicitly defines an active duration, then the output transition ends at the end of that active duration. A 5 second video object with a dur="15s" attribute will have its last frame frozen. At 13 seconds after the start, the output transition begins.
- *Case C:* the fill period control takes effect after the active duration; the fill="remove" attribute only takes effect after the 15 second duration period, so the transition still occurs at 13 seconds.
- *Case D*: the default fill behavior for visual media in a <par> is *default*; this will mean an effective value of *freeze* if no dur or end was defined. The out transition ends at the end of the freeze period. Thus the output transition begins at 13 seconds after the <par> started.

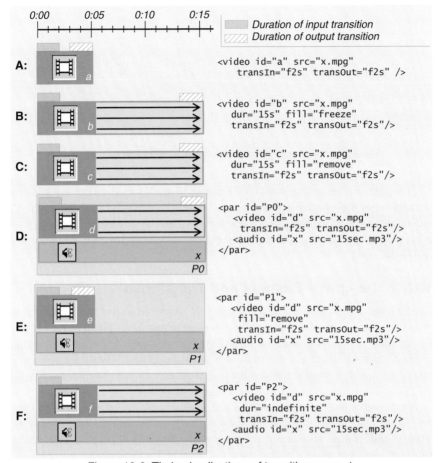

```
<video id="a" src="x.mpg"
     transIn="f2s" transOut="f2s" />
```

```
<video id="b" src="x.mpg"
     dur="15s" fill="freeze"
     transIn="f2s" transOut="f2s"/>
```

```
<video id="c" src="x.mpg"
     dur="15s" fill="remove"
     transIn="f2s" transOut="f2s"/>
```

```
<par id="P0">
  <video id="d" src="x.mpg"
     transIn="f2s" transOut="f2s"/>
  <audio id="x" src="15sec.mp3"/>
</par>
```

```
<par id="P1">
  <video id="d" src="x.mpg"
     fill="remove"
     transIn="f2s" transOut="f2s"/>
  <audio id="x" src="15sec.mp3"/>
</par>
```

```
<par id="P2">
  <video id="d" src="x.mpg"
     dur="indefinite"
     transIn="f2s" transOut="f2s"/>
  <audio id="x" src="15sec.mp3"/>
</par>
```

Figure 10-6. Timing implications of transition support.

- *Case E*: if an explicit fill="remove" has been set on the media without an explicit duration, the out transition begins at the end of the intrinsic duration. A 5 second video with fill="remove" that is played in parallel with a 15 second audio object will have its out transition start at 3 seconds.

- *Case F*: if an indefinite duration is defined, the out transition will never occur since the scheduler cannot determine the end of the object. If a 5 second video is given an explicit duration of *indefinite*, the last frame will be displayed and then cut off when the parent time container ends.

The SMIL scheduler is required to figure out when the end of the rendered period will be, and to then plan backwards to determine the start time of the presentation. For most common use cases, this is not a problem. For interactive ends of an object, however, this is a big problem!

```
 1  <smil ...>
 2   ...
 3   <body>
 4    ...
 5    <par>
 6     <video id="Z1" src="news2.mpg" fill="freeze" region="v"
          transOut="f2s" end="activateEvent"/>
 7      ...
 8    </par>
 9    ...
10   </body>>
11  </smil>
```

Example 10-8. Using SMIL transitions with interactive timing.

Consider the code fragment in Example 10-8. A video object with an out transition begins when the parent <par> begins. It ends on a mouse-click on the video. Since the scheduler cannot know when the object's end will occur, there is no way to plan the time to start the end transition. In this case, the transition will be ignored.

10.6.2 The <par> Element and Transitions

Content inside a single <par> container gets rendered in the context of a common time base. Consider the code fragment in Figure 10-7. The parallel element *P3* contains two videos, both rendered in the same region. Object *a*'s duration is 15 seconds and object *b*'s duration is 5 seconds. Object *b* will fade on top of object 5 starting 5 seconds into object *a*. At 8 seconds into the <par>, object *a* will fade out, revealing the last 5 seconds of object *b*.

It is possible to construct complex visual effects by having object with input and/or output transitions overlap other objects without transition effects, but from a SMIL timing and structural perspective, the transition always impacts a single media item and its background.

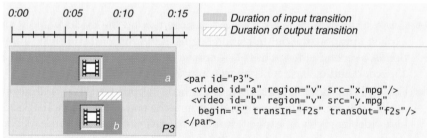

Figure 10-7. Embedding transitions in a <par>.

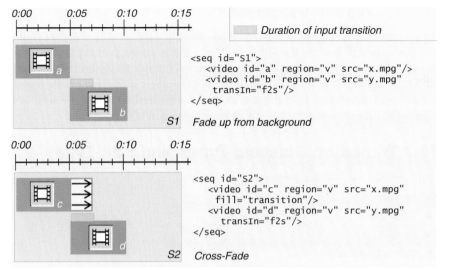

Figure 10-8. Embedding transitions in a <seq>.

10.6.3 The `<seq>` Element and Transitions

Content inside of a single <seq> container gets rendered in order of appearance in the <seq>. Once an object ends, it is removed from the display. As is illustrated in the *S1* sequence in the upper part of Figure 10-8, this means that subsequent objects will always transition in from the background.

In order to allow transitions to work within sequential time containers, a special value for the `fill` attribute was defined: `fill="transition"`. Any media object that has defined a `fill="transition"` attribute will have the final state of that content stay on the screen until the completion of the first following transition with content in the same rendering space. This is illustrated in the *S2* sequence in the lower part of Figure 10-8.

The transition value of the fill attribute can be considered to be a special case of the freeze value: the content is frozen until the end of the following transition — even if that transition only uses a small part of the frozen media item.

The rules for determining the end of the `fill="transition"` period state that the fill period does not end until the end of the first transition that overlaps any of the rendering space associated with the frozen object. Some implementations take this to mean the end of the first transition anywhere on the screen. You should experiment with various player to determine a uniform behavior.

10.6.4 The `<excl>` Element and Transitions

The `fill="transition"` attribute value can be used to extend the visual components of a de-selected media object in an <excl> element. When the object ends, the rendered version will stay on the screen until the next piece of content ends its input transition.

10.6.5 Audio and Transitions

If you fade in a video object that contains an audio soundtrack, only the visual components will have a transition applied — the audio portion will be rendered at 100% of its sound level. It is possible to combine audio and visual transitions, but this needs to be done as two operations: a transition on the visual content and an animation of the sound level for the audio portion. (Future versions of SMIL may provide more useful audio transition support.)

10.7 Transition Classes, Types and Sub-Types

SMIL defines five classes of transitions:

- *edge wipes,*
- *iris wipes,*
- *clock wipes,*
- *matrix wipes* and
- SMIL *transitions.*

This section reviews the set of transition sub-types available as part of the SMIL standard.

Both SMIL Basic Transitions and SMIL Inline Transitions use the same list of transition types and sub-types. This section summarizes the behavior of each of the transitions defined in the SMIL 2.0 specification. It is important to note that while the SMIL specification describes a wealth of transition effects, not all implementations are required to support all types and sub-types. Every implementation that supports transitions (either Basic or Inline) is required to support at least four distinct types (see Table 10-3), but this support is provided on a best-effort basis. If a transition can't be handled, it may be ignored by the implementation.

10.7.1 Required Types/Sub-Types

Of all of the transitions listed in this section, only four types are required to be supported by implementations that provide transitions support. The required transitions are shown in Table 10-3.

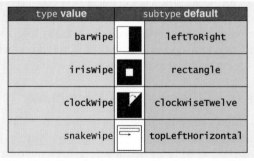

type **value**		subtype **default**
barWipe		leftToRight
irisWipe		rectangle
clockWipe		clockwiseTwelve
snakeWipe		topLeftHorizontal

Table 10-3. Required **type** and **subtype** attributes.

10.7.2 Edge Wipe Transition Types and Sub-Types

Edge wipes are a collection of transitions in which a well-defined edge is used to separate the existing content from the new content. During execution of the transition, the edge moves in a transition-specified direction to successively expose a part of the new image.

Table 10-4 lists the edge wipes provided in the SMIL specification.[1]

type **value**		subtype **default**	subtype **alternatives**
barWipe		leftToRight	topToBottom
zigZagWipe			
veeWipe		down	left up right
barnVeeWipe			
diagonalWipe		topLeft	topRight
boxWipe		topLeft	topRight bottomRight bottomLeft topCenter rightCenter bottomCenter leftCenter
barnZigZagWipe		vertical	horizontal
bowTieWipe			
barnDoorWipe		vertical	horizontal diagonalBottomLeft diagonalTopLeft
fourBoxWipe		cornersIn	cornersOut
miscDiagonalWipe		doubleBarnDoor	doubleDiamond

Table 10-4. Edge Wipe **type** and **subtype** attributes.

1 The transition icons in this section are: Copyright © 2001 World Wide Web Consortium, (Massachusetts Institute of Technology, European Research Consortium for Informatics and Mathematics, Keio University). All Rights Reserved.

10.7.3 Iris Wipe Transition Types and Sub-Types

Iris wipes are transitions that start at the center of a rendering area and then move outward as the transition progresses. The default shape for the center area is a square box.

Table 10-5 lists the iris wipes provided in the SMIL specification.

type **values**		subtype **defaults**	subtype **alternatives**
irisWipe	■	rectangle	diamond
pentagonWipe	⬠		down
arrowHeadWipe	▲	up	down right left
triangleWipe	▲		
hexagonWipe	⬡		
eyeWipe	◆	horizontal	vertical
roundRectWipe	▭		
ellipseWipe	●	circle	horizontal vertical
starWipe	✦	fourPoint	fivePoint sixPoint
miscShapeWipe	♥	heart	keyhole

Table 10-5. Iris Wipe **type** and **subtype** attributes

10.7.4 Clock Wipe Transition Types and Sub-Types

Clock wipes are transitions that start at the center of a rendering area and then move along the outside edge as the transition progresses. The default shape for the center area is a wedge shaped area that moves around the image.

Table 10-6 lists the eight types of clock wipes provided by SMIL.

type **values**		subtype **defaults**	subtype **alternatives**
clockWipe		clockwiseTwelve	clockwiseThree clockwiseSix clockwiseNine
saloonDoorWipe		top	left bottom right
windshieldWipe		right	up vertical horizontal
fanWipe		centerTop	centerRight top right bottom left
doubleFanWipe		fanOutVertical	fanOutHorizontal fanInVertical fanInHorizontal
singleSweepWipe		clockwiseTop	clockwiseRight clockwiseBottom clockwiseLeft clockwiseTopLeft counterClockwiseBottomLeft clockwiseBottomRight counterClockwiseTopRight
doubleSweepWipe		parallelVertical	parallelDiagonal oppositeVertical oppositeHorizontal parallelDiagonalTopLeft parallelDiagonalBottomLeft
pinwheelWipe		twoBladeVertical	twoBladeHorizontal fourBlade

Table 10-6. Clock Wipe **type** and **subtype** attributes.

10.7.5 Matrix Wipe Transition Types and Sub-Types

Matrix wipes expose a portion of the target as an image tile that extends along the rendering area. Table 10-7 illustrates the five types of matrix wipes.

type **values**		subtype **defaults**	subtype **alternatives**
snakeWipe		topLeftHorizontal	topLeftVertical topLeftDiagonal topRightDiagonal bottomRightDiagonal bottomLeftDiagonal
waterfallWipe		verticalLeft	verticalRight horizontalLeft horizontalRight
spiralWipe		topLeftClockwise	topRightClockwise bottomRightClockwise bottomLeftClockwise topLeftCounterClockwise topRightCounterClockwise bottomRightCounterClockwise bottomLeftCounterClockwise
parallelSnakesWipe		verticalTopSame	verticalBottomSame verticalTopLeftOpposite verticalBottomLeftOpposite horizontalLeftSame horizontalRightSame horizontalTopLeftOpposite horizontalTopRightOpposite diagonalBottomLeftOpposite diagonalTopLeftOpposite
boxSnakesWipe		twoBoxTop	twoBoxBottom twoBoxLeft twoBoxRight fourBoxVertical fourBoxHorizontal

Table 10-7. Matrix Wipe **type** and **subtype** attributes.

10.7.6 SMIL-Specific Transition Types and Sub-Types

Most of the transitions supported by SMIL are based on a transition suite defined by SMPTE. SMIL extends this set with three additional transition effects.

Table 10-8 lists the three extended types of transitions supported by SMIL.

type **values**		subtype **defaults**	subtype **alternatives**
fade		crossfade	fadeToColor fadeFromColor
slidewipe		fromLeft	fromTop fromRight fromBottom
pushwipe			

Table 10-8. Values for the **type** and **subtype** attributes.

10.8 Summary and Conclusion

With the introduction of transitions into SMIL, presentations can be made more fluid and more visually appealing. Transitions over a set of images can be considered to be a poor man's video: a feeling of motion is provided even when the media is static.

A primary advantage of transitions is that all operations are local. Transitions consume no extra network bandwidth and do not require fast(er) network connections. At the same time, the image processing requirements for transitions can result in a major performance drain on low-capability devices (such as mobile and hand-held computers). In these cases, implementations are allowed to ignore transitions if necessary.

In order to fully understand the transitions model, we recommend that you also study the implementation model for animation described in Chapter 15: *SMIL Animation*.

10.9 Further Resources

SMPTE Transitions

*Time and Control Codes for 24, 25 or 30 Frame-Per-Second Motion Picture Systems —
RP 136-1995*, Society of Motion Picture and Television Engineers.

Advanced SMIL Features

Part Three provides descriptions of the more advanced features of SMIL 2.0. This includes all of the advanced constructs from SMIL's media, layout, timing, animation, content control and meta-information modules.

Since this part takes a detailed look at individual constructs, it is less tutorial in nature than parts one and two. Still, every chapter shows how SMIL works by using examples from complete SMIL presentations. As with the earlier chapters, all of the presentations referenced in this section are available on the book's Web site.

Topics Covered

 Chapter 11 considers the sub-setting of media assets in a presentation. Where basic SMIL functionality includes facilities for referencing complete objects, this chapter looks at the various elements and attributes that support spatial, temporal and logical sub-division of media content and parameters.

 Chapter 12 describes the advanced facilities supported by the full SMIL 2.0 Language profile for hierarchical and multi-window layout. We consider facilities for logical media alignment in regions, sub-region position of media, hierarchical layout and the use of multiple top-level presentation windows.

 Chapter 13 provides a description of advanced SMIL timing behavior and control. This chapter focuses on SMIL support for event based timing and the selective composition of media elements. It also provides a detailed description of the SMIL timing model.

 Chapter 14 describes the advanced use of SMIL timing attributes. This chapter looks in detail at attributes that control fill behavior, repeat behavior and synchronization behavior. It also describes the facilities available for manipulating the order and pace of time within a SMIL presentation.

 Chapter 15 provides an overview of SMIL Animation. The chapter provides an introduction to the SMIL animation model and then describes the elements and attributes available for both SMIL Basic Animation and SMIL Spline Animation.

Chapter 16 considers advanced support for SMIL Content Control. We describe the facilities provided to pre-fetch content before it is needed in an application, the facilities for defining and using custom test attributes and the facilities available for creating future-proof SMIL presentations.

 Chapter 17 closes this part with a description of SMIL meta-data and media description facilities. While many of these constructs define basic functionality, they are included in this part because not all SMIL profiles provide complete meta-information support.

Goals

By the time you complete Part Three, you should have a thorough understanding of all of SMIL's elements and attributes. You will be able to not only read and write SMIL code for all of the SMIL profiles, but you have an in-depth understanding of why SMIL does things the way it does.

Prerequisites

In order to get the most out of this part, you should have read and understood the material in Part One and Part Two of this book. You should be familiar with the SMIL timing model and the general element and attribute architecture of the constructs in the various SMIL profiles. Perhaps the most important prerequisite is a willingness to dive into the details of the more esoteric aspects of the SMIL 2.0 specification.

11

Subsetting and Extending Media

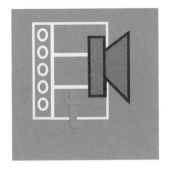

SMIL provides a host of options for limiting the scope of media objects used in presentations. Some of these options are purely visual — such as defining layout behavior for cropping, scaling or stretching media objects to fit a display area. Other facilities exist for restricting the active area of media objects or for limiting the amount of continuous media that gets transferred from the server to the player/browser. Still other facilities exist for extending the way that media objects get processed by providing a general purpose parameter-passing mechanism.

This chapter provides descriptions of most of the SMIL media subsetting and extension mechanisms. Facilities that deal purely with the rendering transformations on media objects were covered in Chapter 6: *SMIL Basic Layout* and Chapter 12: *Advanced Layout Topics*; these will not be repeated here. Facilities for restricting the active area of media objects were introduced in Chapter 8: *Basic Linking*, but they are defined more completely in the sections below.

We begin with a discussion of spatial cropping of a media object's active selection area. We then consider temporal clipping (both physical and logical) of continuous media objects. Next, we look at the subsetting of text media via fragments. We conclude with SMIL's support for passing initialization parameters to media objects and media renderers.

11.1 Cropping Media Spatially

The main mechanisms for defining spatial cropping of media objects are defined in the SMIL layout modules and the SMIL linking modules. Spatial cropping for layout in the SMIL 2.0 Language profile is done using the `fit` attribute of the `<region>` element. Spatial cropping that restricts the active area of links is done using the `coords` and `shape` attributes of the `<area>` element.

The use of the `fit` attribute is discussed completely in our section on *Stacking and Scaling Attributes* on page 114. The use of the `coords` and `shape` attributes of the `<area>` element was introduced on page 168. That introduction will be expanded upon in the following section.

11.1.1 Understanding Spatial Cropping for Linking

SMIL's linking support defines three elements that are used to identify the active area of a link anchor: `<a>`, `<area>` and `<anchor>`. Of these, the `<a>` element always uses the entire geometry of the media object with which it is associated for the link anchor. (The `<a>` element may have timing attributes that limit the active *period* of the anchor, but not the active *area*.) The `<area>` and `<anchor>` elements allow the active area to be restricted to a portion of the media's geometry. They also allow limiting the active period to a portion of the anchor's duration. The `<anchor>` is a SMIL 1.0 element that is, for all intents and purposes, functionally equivalent to `<area>`. We will not consider `<anchor>` separately in this chapter.

Figure 11-1 illustrates the typical use of the spatial cropping provided by the `coords` and `shape` attributes of the `<area>` element. Here we see an image that has 12 anchors defined as child content. Each `coords` attribute specifies the

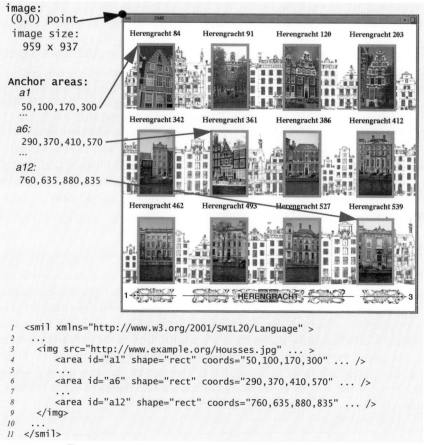

```
1   <smil xmlns="http://www.w3.org/2001/SMIL20/Language" >
2   ...
3     <img src="http://www.example.org/Housses.jpg" ... >
4       <area id="a1" shape="rect" coords="50,100,170,300" ... />
5       ...
6       <area id="a6" shape="rect" coords="290,370,410,570" ... />
7       ...
8       <area id="a12" shape="rect" coords="760,635,880,835" ... />
9     </img>
10  ...
11  </smil>
```

Figure 11-1. Defining anchors using the `coords` attribute.

extents of an anchor. (Our example uses the default rectangle shape.) In most use cases, each <area> element definition will also include linking and/or temporal scope attributes, but these are not important for our discussion and have been left out of the code fragment. The image used in this example is a screen-dump that is used within a presentation: the window system's borders and control areas are part of the image, not part of the player background.

The use of the coords attribute seems very straightforward: each coordinate pair is mapped to a part of the image. Unfortunately, the values given in the coords attribute have only an indirect association with the coordinates of the image because they represent *region space* coordinates instead of media space coordinates. (This was done to provide compatibility with HTML.)

Why is this a problem? First, consider that the image used in the example is not small: it is 959 x 937 pixels. It may be that a presentation that uses the image will apply the visual scaling properties available in SMIL layout to reduce the space needed to show the houses. If the image was scaled to fit an area that was 50% of the original image size, the coordinates used in the coords attribute would also need to be resized by the presentation author. (See Figure 11-2.) A second problem is that the image may be clipped if it does not fit inside the region provided by the layout system. As a result, (part of) an anchor may be placed outside the viewable space of the image. This is a problem for linking, since the unseen part of the anchor is not active. A third problem is that an image may be positioned at a point other than the upper left corner of the

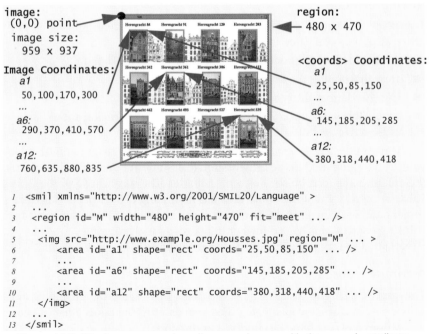

```
1   <smil xmlns="http://www.w3.org/2001/SMIL20/Language" >
2    ...
3    <region id="M" width="480" height="470" fit="meet" ... />
4    ...
5     <img src="http://www.example.org/Housses.jpg" region="M" ... >
6        <area id="a1" shape="rect" coords="25,50,85,150" ... />
7        ...
8        <area id="a6" shape="rect" coords="145,185,205,285" ... />
9        ...
10       <area id="a12" shape="rect" coords="380,318,440,418" ... />
11   </img>
12    ...
13  </smil>
```

Figure 11-2. Display-space and media-space issues with the coords attribute.

region. If this happens as a result of animating the image using sub-region placement (as discussed in Chapter 12), the coordinate values in the `coords` attribute also will need to be adjusted. Often, authoring software will handle these cases, but for documents edited by hand, the mis-match between media space and display space coordinates can lead to frustrations.

11.1.2 Elements for Spatial Cropping

This section defines the `<area>` element.

Element: `<area>`

The structure of the `<area>` element's cropping attributes is laid out in Table 11-1. The use of these attributes are similar to the use in HTML. In most cases, the `<area>` element is applied as a child of a media object to define an anchor's active area.

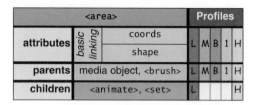

			<area>	Profiles				
attributes	basic	linking	coords	L	M	B	1	H
			shape					
parents			media object, `<brush>`	L	M	B	1	H
children			`<animate>`, `<set>`	L				H

Table 11-1. Structure of the `<area>` element's cropping attributes

11.1.3 Attributes for Spatial Cropping

This section defines the `coords` and `shape` attributes.

Attribute: `shape`

The `shape` attribute allows one of three shapes to be defined for use with the active area, plus one value that selects the entire area.

- *rect*: this defines the anchor as a rectangle. This is the default.
- *circle*: this defines the active area to be a circle.
- *poly*: this defines the active area as a (closed) polygon.
- *default*: this value specified that the entire rendering region should be used as the active area.

The use of the value *default* for shape can be useful for two reasons. First, the value can be animated in the presentation to assume another value; in this case, the default value can be seen as a placeholder. The second use of the default value is to specify that the entire area has no linking behavior. (This is done in conjunction with the `href="nohref"` attribute assignment.) While interesting in a linking content, this has no further utility for spatial cropping.

Note that the default value of the `shape` attribute is *rect*, not *default*.

Attribute: `coords`

The `coords` attribute contains a set of values that define the geometry of the active area in display coordinates. The `coords` attribute takes a list of coordinate values and/or shape modifiers as arguments.

The number of arguments in the list and their interpretation depends on the value of the shape attribute. When a geometry values is expected, it may be either a pixel value or a percentage value (including the % character).

- *rect*: the values list contains four values representing the left and top offsets of the upper corner of the anchor and the left and top corner of the bottom of the anchor.

- *circle*: three values are expected. The first two values are the left and top offsets of the center point of the circle. The third value is the radius.

- *poly*: a closed set of coordinate pairs are expected, each representing a left and top coordinate for a point in the polygon. If the polygon is not closed, the player is expected to provide a closing value pair.

- *default*: the list of values is ignored. The *default* value allows a coords attribute list to be specified when it is expected that this element will be changed using SMIL Animation: the (ignored) coordinate list is specified so that when the value of the shape attribute is changed via animation, a valid coords argument will be available to be animated.

Since the coordinates used by the coords attribute are resolved to region space, care should be taken when (automatic) scaling of media is used or when sub-region positioning is applied to the media object. See the discussion on page 240 for details.

11.2 Clipping Media in Time

SMIL 2.0 offers many options for specifying when a media element starts in a presentation and it offers many options for specifying how much of the media object will be played before it terminates. Most of the mechanisms available in SMIL allow subsetting of media to occur once the media has been fetched from the server. The *MediaClipping* module provides extra control that prevents unused portions of a media object to be transferred to the SMIL player.

11.2.1 Understanding Temporal Clipping of Media

Continuous media objects typically consist of a series of samples that, when combined, allow a video or audio object to be digitally defined. Audio objects can consist of anywhere between 4K and 88K samples per second, with each sample requiring 8, 16 or 32 bits. Video objects may contain anywhere from 5 to 30 samples per second, with each sample requiring between 0.5Kbits and nearly 6 Mbits. A *media clip* is a sequence of samples that occur over a defined period of time. That time may be measured in clock-based timestamp (that is, seconds 12-48 of an audio object) or in terms of a frame-based timestamp (frames 3,000-46,000).

The structure of a video-based media clip is illustrated in Figure 11-3. Here we see a clip that is defined with $t_{clipBegin}$ as a begin time and $t_{clipEnd}$ as an end time.

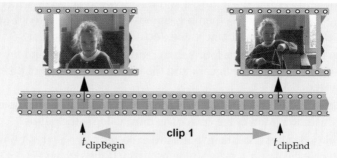

clip 1

$t_{\text{clipBegin}}$ t_{clipEnd}

Figure 11-3. Media clip structure based on timestamps.

There are two problems posed in defining a media clip. First, the notion of the begin and end times need to be specified in terms that are useful for the media encoding and the SMIL player. Since the SMIL player is media format agnostic, this time specification is non-trivial. A second, more challenging problem is that the source media object may be highly compressed or encoded. This means that, at the server, it may be difficult to translate a time value to a particular encoded sample/frame in the audio or video.

SMIL does not attempt to solve these problems directly. Instead, it defines two attributes for specifying the begin and end times and gives each the option of using SMIL's notion of playback time as a selection criteria for the clip or the ability of using a media standard timing structure. It is the media server's responsibility (via the object's API) to translate the time value to the appropriate sample or frame.

The efficiency with which media clips can be obtained will vary from format to format and from media server to media server. Some formats may not allow efficient media clipping because of compression or because of the lack of a seek command in the object's interface. In the worst case, the first 90% of a large media item may be required to be able to render the last 10%. Even if a format is amenable to subsetting, a media server or transport protocol may not be able to deliver a partial media object. In both cases, the SMIL player should simulate media clipping internally.

11.2.2 Attributes for Temporal Clipping

The SMIL *MediaClipping* module defines two attributes for defining a media clip: `clipBegin` and `clipEnd`. (The SMIL 1.0 versions were `clip-begin` and `clip-end`.) No SMIL elements are required to support temporal clipping.

Attribute: clipBegin

The `clipBegin` attribute specifies the start point of a media clip. It is an offset from the beginning of the media object. The default value for `clipBegin` is 0 (the start of the media object).

The `clipBegin` attribute takes a single timestamp value as an argument. This argument consists of a *media metric specifier* and a *time value*. The media metric specifier will determine the format of the time value. SMIL 2.0 allows the following media metric specifiers:

- *npt*: the normal playtime metric. The normal play time of an object is a SMIL clock value. The syntax is:

  ```
  clipBegin="npt=10s"
  ```

  The meaning of this specification is that the clip begins 10 seconds into its normal play time. This specification is coarse (that it, it does not correspond to a particular frame), but it is useful for many subsetting applications. Use of the 'npt=' prefix is optional in all profiles except SMIL 1.0.

- *smpte* (also specified as **smpte-30-drop**): a video-based timecode specifier that uses a frame selector based on the NTSC standard. The *smpte* time value consists of an hours:minutes:seconds:frames.subframes specification. (Sub-frames are expressed in hundredths of a frame; a sub-frame value of 0 many be left unspecified.) An example of the syntax is:

  ```
  clipBegin="smpte=00:00:10:24.97"
  ```

  for a video clip that starts just before the 25th frame in the 10th second of the video. The *smpte* specifier is used with an encoding that contains approximately 30 frames per second, except that the first two frames of every minute are dropped (but not in each 10th minute). One can consider this a reasonably fine-grained time specification.

- *smpte-25*: This is similar to the *smpte* value, except that a frame selector is used that is based on the PAL standard. Each second consists of 25 frames, with each frame being further divided into 100 sub-frames.

The `clipBegin` attribute does not have support for special audio time encoding. The `clipBegin` attribute also does not have support for specifying an index into a compressed media object. The `clipBegin` *does* allow times to be expressed indirectly using the media marker format defined on page 248.

If specified together with other SMIL attributes, the `clipBegin` time is applied first.

Attribute: clipEnd

The `clipEnd` attribute is similar to the `clipBegin` attribute, except that it defines an end time for the clip. It accepts timestamps in the same manner as `clipBegin`. If the time defined by `clipEnd` is greater than the duration of the media object, the `clipEnd` attribute is ignored. The default value is the intrinsic duration of the media object.

11.2.3 Examples of Temporal Clipping

The following fragment illustrates the specification of a media clip:

```
<video id="c1" src="rtsp://www.example.org/wb.mpg"
    clipBegin="9.25s" clipEnd="npt=6:42:25" />
```

The start of the clip is set to 9.25 seconds of normal play time. (The 'npt=' prefix is the default.) The end time is at 6 hours, 42 minutes and 25 seconds.

If either clipBegin or clipEnd is missing, the default values are assumed:

```
<audio id="c2" src="http://www.example.org/wb.mp3" clipBegin="npt=4"/>
```

```
<audio id="c3" src="http://www.example.org/triangle.wav" clipEnd="npt=58s"/>
```

The first audio object will start at 4 seconds into the object and will play to completion. The second audio object starts at the beginning and plays until the end of the intrinsic duration or 58 seconds, whichever comes first.

If special timing attributes accompany clipBegin or clipEnd, the clip is extracted first:

```
<video id="c4" src="http://www.example.org/wb.mpg" begin="3s"
    repeatCount="2" clipBegin="npt=4" clipEnd="npt=58s"/>
```

When processing this video, first the clip is extracted. Next, the clip is rendered starting at 3 seconds after the nominal begin time of the element. The video clip between the clipBegin and clipEnd is repeated twice.

The clipBegin and clipEnd attributes cannot be used on the <area> element. In order to specify a temporal subset for a linking operation, begin, dur and/or end timing attributes must be used on the <area> element. Examples are given in *Specifying the Activation Period of Source Anchors* on page 166.

11.3 Clipping Media Using Media Markers

The basic clipBegin and clipEnd attributes allow a media clip to be defined in terms of its begin and end times. This assumes, of course, that the author knows the begin and end times of the clip in the media object. If you don't know how long the video is (or if it changes daily), this could be a problem. Luckily, SMIL also supports mechanisms for the logical indexing into media using the media marker attribute values. Media markers are timestamp formats that can be used instead of normal play time (*npt*) and SMPTE timecode media metric specifiers in clipBegin or clipEnd.

In this section, we'll introduce the concepts of media marker use. Media markers are a new facility in SMIL and not all players provide uniform support for indirect media marker clip files. The Ambulant player supports logical markers using an open media marker format that is available on the book's Web site.

11.3.1 Understanding Media Clip Markers

Figure 11-3 on page 244 illustrated the use of time-based clip markers. Contrast that approach with the situation in Figure 11-4. Here we see two video clips, each representing the top food story in an evening newscast. The SMIL version of this newscast extracts a set of clips from a single 30-minute video object. The problem to be solved is that on Tuesday, the top food story starts at about 12 minutes into the source file, while on Friday the top food story starts nearly 17 minutes into the source. In order to provide the correct index using standard clipBegin/clipEnd parameters, two separate SMIL files would need to be constructed: one for Tuesday's newscast and one for Friday.

An alternative is to use logical markers that point indirectly at the appropriate story and the correct time. Figure 11-5 illustrates this approach. A general clip file (*newsClips*) points to the start and end of the top food story for that day. This file can be created fresh daily to contain the correct food index values.

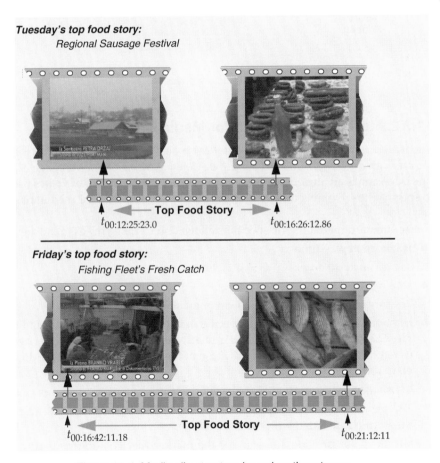

Figure 11-4. Media clip structure based on timestamps.

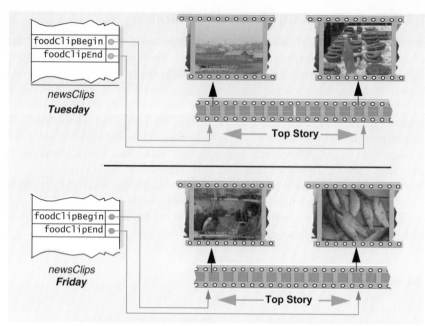

Figure 11-5. Media clip structure based on timestamps.

11.3.2 Attribute Extensions for Media Markers

The SMIL *MediaClipMarkers* module defines a single attribute value extension for use with clipBegin and clipEnd. (See *Clipping Media in Time* on page 243.) The extension is an attribute value substring that extends the set of values used to specify clips. No new elements and attributes are required for media markers.

The standard media metric specifiers allowed in clipBegin/clipEnd are:

- *npt*: normal play time
- *smpte (smpte-30-drop)*: NTSC SMPTE timestamp
- smpte-25: PAL SMPTE timestamp.

These are extended with the following media metric specifier:

- *marker*: a URI name string that specifies a marker file and a location in that file. The file pointed at by the URI is relative to the src attribute of the associated media item, not to the XML base of the SMIL document or the document root. An example of the syntax is:

```
clipBegin="marker=newsClips#foodClipBegin"
```

The player/browser is expected to open the marker file and to extract the timestamp associated with the named fragment.

SMIL does not provide a syntax for the marker file. This means that each player/browser will need to publish the syntax for marker files it supports.

11.3.3 Examples Using Media Markers

The following fragment illustrates the specification of a media clip using logical media markers:

```
<video id="c1" src="rtsp://www.example.org/todaysNews.mpg"
  clipBegin="marker=newsClips#foodClipBegin"
  clipEnd="marker=newsClips#foodClipEnd"/>
```

The start and end of the clips are set to the time found at the referenced begin and end markers. The markers are stored in a marker file that is located relative to the named media object. If the media object *todaysNews* changes and the associated *newsClips* media file is updated, the SMIL fragment will always point to the correct clip.

Logical media marker metric specifiers may be mixed with other forms. The following fragment illustrates this:

```
<video id="c1" src="rtsp://www.example.org/todaysNews.mpg"
  clipBegin="npt=29.4s" clipEnd="marker=newsClips#foodClipEnd"/>
```

While this syntax is allowed, it will rarely be useful. The importance of mixing clock times with media markers is that if only one marker is specified, default timing semantics make sense. As with other uses of `clipBegin` and `clipEnd`, a non-specified begin time defaults to the beginning of the clip and a non-specified end time defaults to the end of the clip. If the value resolved through the marker file is invalid, the attribute is ignored.

11.4 Subsetting Media Via Fragment Identifiers

The media markers discussed on page 246 provide one example of the use of URI fragment identifiers to locate portions, or fragments, of files. Fragments of media objects will most often be specified for text media types. (They are also used within SVG files and within SMIL itself.) Individual media types can specify if fragment identifiers are allowed for their files and how fragmented displays are evaluated and rendered. The fragment identifier after a URI starts with a '#' character.

11.4.1 Understanding Fragment Identifiers

A fragment identifier points to a particular point in a target document. The target document may contain text or it may contain media. The renderer for the target document is expected to be able to interpret the fragment name and resolve it to a location within the file.

Naked Fragment Identifiers

The vast majority of fragment identifiers in use on the Web are *naked* — that is, they each consist of a single name, rather than having a multi-component structure. Typically, naked fragment identifiers are unique identifier references to particular elements in XML-defined media.

XLink, XPointer and XPath

In addition to naked fragment identifiers, SMIL also supports *XLink*-like elements and attributes for linking. *XPointer* and *XPath* fragment specification may also be supported, depending on the SMIL player.

XLink. XLink provides a generalized XML structure of elements and attributes for referencing external fragments. SMIL does not use Xlink because of its complexity. Instead, SMIL uses constructs similar to XLink for equivalent features and behaviors.

XPointer. XPointer provides attributes that can be used to define location syntax in URI attribute values. One such syntax is XPath.

XPath. Xpath allows fragments to be specified in terms of their structural placement in an XML document rather than by using an explicit XML ID. In this way, document content can be referenced without having to edit the target document source. The SMIL 2.0 specification allows the use of XPath syntax in a URI, but support is not required.

Passing Attributes via Fragments

In early Web documents — and in early versions of SMIL — parameters containing media-specific arguments and values were often passed to a media renderer via private extensions to fragment names using the form:

```
<video id="c1"
   src="rtsp://www.example.org/todaysNews.mpg?action=registered#story1/>
```

With the introduction of the <param> element and other forms of media parameter passing mechanisms in SMIL (see page 251), the use of fragments to pass arguments is discouraged.

11.4.2 Language Support for Fragment Identifiers

SMIL does not provide any elements or attributes to support fragment identification. General URI syntax is supported by SMIL; XPointer and XLink extensions may be available in some SMIL players.

11.4.3 Examples Using Fragment Identifiers

The following example illustrates the use of a naked fragment identifier:

```
<text id="Z1" src="http://www.example.org/text.html#chapter3" ... />
```

The media renderer is expected to locate the named fragment. Scrolling behavior (that is, showing the fragment identified at the top of the display area) is managed by the media renderer.

Naked fragment identifiers may also be used with media markers:

```
<video id="c1" src="rtsp://www.example.org/todaysNews.mpg"
   clipBegin="marker=newsClips#foodClipBegin" ... />
```

See page page 247 for a description of the use of media markers.

SMIL files may also refer to locations within the file using fragment identifiers, as in the destination anchor named *Credits*:

```
<img id="HHbkg" region="SkinHH" fill="freeze" syncBehavior="independent"
     src="Assets/SkinHH.gif" customTest="HandHeld">
  <area id="ExitHH" href="#Credits" coords="6,290,28,323"/>
</img>
```

The following fragment illustrates a non-standard extension use of XPath syntax to identify a fragment in GR*i*NS (only!). An exclusive element has 5 10-minute children. Each follows the next at 10 minute intervals unless the second child of its parent's first preceding sibling catches a mouse click event:

```
<excl>
<par begin="0">
  <audio src="longAudio1" />
  <img ... />
</par>
<par begin="10:00; xpath(../preceding-sibling::*[1]/*[2].activateEvent)">
  <audio ... />
  <img ... />
</par>
...
<par begin="40:00; xpath(../preceding-sibling::*[1]/*[2].activateEvent)">
  <audio ... />
  <img ... />
</par>
</excl>
```

Readers interested in learning more about XPath, XPointer and XLink are encouraged to read the references suggested at the end of this chapter.

11.5 Initialization Attributes for Media Objects

The SMIL *MediaParam* module defines the <param> element for media initialization. The <param> is a child of a media object or the <brush> element. In addition, the SMIL *MediaParam* module defines three attributes that can be used to initialize media renderers: the erase, mediaRepeat and sensitivity attributes. The erase and sensitivity attributes may be used with media object references or the <brush> element. The mediaRepeat attribute is only available for use with media object references.

11.5.1 Understanding the Use of Media Parameters

The SMIL media parameter facilities allow initialization and other media control attributes to be defined and managed in a common manner. The provision of these elements and attributes obsolete the need to define custom extensions to media fragment identifiers.

The <param> element provides a media and transfer protocol agnostic means of specifying fetching, transfer and rendering initialization parameters. It allows a parameter to be named, a value to be passed and a value type to be specified. Multiple <param> elements may exist as children of a media object reference or of a <brush> element.

The `mediaRepeat` attribute allows any repeat behavior that is specified within the media object to be ignored during presentation. The attribute will only have effect with media objects that have a notion of repeat behavior. It assumes that the media renderer will be able to disable repeat behavior.

The `erase` attribute controls the visual persistence of media objects after their active duration and fill period ends. It can be used to supplement `fill` behavior and to preserve media content after the timing context of an object is completed. A typical use is to make sure that a piece of media remains visible until the end of a presentation (unless the display bits are explicitly used for other objects).

The `sensitivity` attribute controls a media object's response to SMIL events. If an object is sensitive to an event such as a mouse click, it will catch the event. If it is declared as being transparent to events, the SMIL engine will pass the event to another media object at a (lower) rendering order.

11.5.2 Elements for Media Initialization

This section defines the `<param>` element.

Element: `<param>`

The `<param>` element provides a general-purpose parameter passing mechanism for use with media objects or the `<brush>` element. The structure of the element is shown in Table 11-2.

The `<param>` element accepts the core SMIL 2.0 element and the system, custom and skip-content control attributes. It makes use of the `name`, `value`, `type` and `valuetype` attributes.

The `<param>` element is empty (it has no children). The parents for `<param>` are media objects and the `<brush>` element.

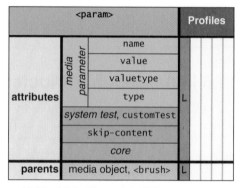

`<param>`			Profiles
attributes	media parameter	name	
		value	
		valuetype	
		type	L
	system test, customTest		
	skip-content		
	core		
parents	media object, `<brush>`		L

Table 11-2. Structure of the `<param>` element.

11.5.3 Attributes for Media Initialization via `<param>`

The following attributes are used to control and initialize media object content.

Attribute: name

The name attribute identifies the parameter to be initialized. It is assumed to be supported by the associated media renderer. If the name is unrecognized or unsupported, the `<param>` element instance is ignored.

Attribute: value

The value attribute defines an argument to be sent to the media renderer. The processing of the value is not performed in the SMIL engine.

Attribute: valuetype

The valuetype argument is used to specify the type of value provided by the value attribute. Legal values for valuetype are:

- *data*: pass the data specified in the value attribute to the object renderer as a string. This is the default.
- *ref*: pass the data specified in the value attribute to the object renderer as a string that should be interpreted as a URI. This informs the renderer that the location specified in the URI contains further initialization information.
- *object*: pass the data specified in the value attribute to the object renderer as a string that should be resolved as the name of a media object within the same source document. The media object specified by this element is then passed as this parameter's value to the rendering process.
- *type*: inform the user agent that the media referenced identified by the value attribute is of the type defined by this attribute. Note that the type attribute is only legal if the value of the valuetype attribute is *ref*.

The set of parameter names and the acceptable values are determined by the rendering engine, not the SMIL player (or the SMIL standard).

11.5.4 Attributes for Player Media Initialization

This section defines the mediaRepeat, erase and sensitivity attributes.

Attribute: mediaRepeat

The mediaRepeat attribute is used as a short-hand control attribute that informs the media renderer whether or not to observe any repeat behavior inside the media object.

The legal values for mediaRepeat are:

- *strip*: the repeat behavior inside the media object should be ignored; the media object should not repeat.
- *preserve*: the repeat behavior inside the media object should be respected. This is the default.

The use of mediaRepeat assumes that the renderer is able to detect repeat behavior and it is able to strip this behavior on request. If the media renderer cannot process the mediaRepeat attribute, the attribute value is ignored. (The SMIL renderer will not simulate mediaRepeat behavior.)

Attribute: erase

The erase attribute is used to control rendering persistence after the termination of the timing context of the associated media object.

The legal values for the `erase` attribute are:

- *whenDone*: remove the media object after the application of all SMIL timing and rendering attributes (such as fill). This is the default.

- *never*: do not remove the media object from the screen after its timing content has completed. For discrete media, the image or text will stay on the screen. For continuous media, the final frame will remain visible.

A value of *never* does not mean that the media is always visible. If, for example, another media object is rendered in the same region as the media containing erase="never", the temporal order will determine which object is visible.

An important side-effect of this attribute is that any link source anchors associated with the media object on which the `erase` attribute is placed remain active until the object is not longer visible.

Attribute: sensitivity

The `sensitivity` attribute allows the event sensitivity of an associated media object to be set. This is used to determine if the media object will respond to UI events such as mouse clicks.

The legal values for this attribute are:

- *opaque*: the object is sensitive to events over the entire area specified with the object. This is the default.

- *transparent*: the object is not sensitive to events. Any event active areas of media objects at a lower rendering priority will be exposed as if the object containing the `sensitivity` attribute was transparent.

- *percentage-value*: the non-negative CSS percentage value provided is compared with the opacity defined for the associated media object's alpha channel value. If the opacity value is defined in the alpha channel is less than the value provided as an argument to the `sensitivity` attribute, the object will be treated as *transparent*. Otherwise, it will be treated as *opaque*.

If a percentage value is provided for a media object that does not have alpha channel support, the default value of *opaque* will be used.

11.5.5 Examples of Media Initialization

The section gives examples of using the `<param>` element and the `erase`, `mediaRepeat` and `sensitivity` attributes.

Using `<param>`

The following example illustrates the use of the `<param>` element:

```
<text id="TX1" region="Text" fill="freeze" src="Assets/text.myFormat" >
  <param name="settings" value"http://www.example.org/text/salesSetup.css"
    valuetype="ref" />
  <param name="font" value="palatino" valuetype="data"/>
  <param name="contents" value="missionStatement" valuetype="object" />
</text>
```

This fragment shows a text object that takes three initialization parameters. First, a pointer to a collection of settings that are saved at the specified URI are passed to the object. The settings file is opened and processed by the media renderer. Next, an explicit font setting is passed as a character string value. Whether this overrides the value provided in the settings file is determined by the media object renderer. Finally, a collection of content defined at the object named *missionStatement* is passed to the renderer. Whether this content will be integrated with or will replace the contents in the *text.myFormat* file is up to the renderer. The SMIL player will render the result of the processed file.

Using mediaRepeat

The following example illustrates the use of the mediaRepeat attribute:

```
<img id="GX1" region="M" fill="freeze" src="Assets/face.gif"
    mediaRepeat="strip" repeatDur="20s"/>
```

The media object referenced in this element is presumed to be an animated GIF image, which by default will repeat indefinitely. Instead, the mediaRepeat attribute will specify that the media renderer will not repeat the animation, but that the SMIL file will be used to explicit bound the duration of the repeat.

Using erase

The following example illustrates the use of the erase attribute:

```
<seq id="SX1">
  <par id="PX1">
    <img src="static.jpg" region="background" fill="freeze" erase="never"/>
    <audio src="tune.mp3" region="audio" dur="10s" />
  </par>
  <img ... />
  ...
  <img ... />
</seq>
```

In this sequence, the image *static.jpg* is displayed in a background region together with the music object *tune.mp3*. At the end of *tune*'s active duration, the timing context of *PX1* ends and the following image in the sequence is displayed. Ordinarily, the background image *static.jpg* would be erased at the conclusion of *PX1*, but because the erase attribute has been set to never, it will remain on the screen. Note that the use of the erase attribute is a brute force method of providing visual persistence. Often, the use of a clean SMIL structure is preferred.

Using sensitivity

The following code fragment illustrates the use of sensitivity:

```
...
<region id="a" height="100" width="100" z-index="1">
<region id="b" height="100" width="100" z-index="2">
...
<par>
   ...
   <img id="bottom" src="productList.png" dur="1:00:00" region="a">
      <area id="a1" href="http://www.example.org/buyNow.html"
      coords="10,10,90,90"/>
   </img>
   <img id="top" src="pitchImage.png" fill="freeze"
      sensitivity="transparent" region="b" >
      <area id="b1" href="http://www.example.org/sellNow.html"
      coords="10,10,90,90" />
   ...
</par>
   ...
   <animate targetElement="top" attributeName="sensitivity"
      value="opaque" ... />
```

Here, two regions are defined that cover the same screen space but at different stacking values. In the body of the presentation, two images are displayed. The image *bottom* is displayed logically under image *top*. In order to allow any events associated with *top* to be ignored, the sensitivity attribute has been set to *transparent*. Any mouse clicks on *top* will be passed on to *bottom*. At some point later in the presentation, the sensitivity value is animated to *opaque*. Now, any link events are processed as if they occurred on *top* instead of *bottom*. (For a detailed discussion of the animation facilities in SMIL, see Chapter 15: *SMIL Animation*.)

11.6 Summary and Conclusion

SMIL provides a host of facilities for controlling the active area or the temporal duration of media items. Spatial cropping is provided via the coords attribute of the <area> element. Temporal cropping is provided by the clipBegin and clipEnd attributes. Fragments within objects can be identified by simple or complex fragment identification syntax. Finally, the initialization and control of the rendering of media can be performed using the <param> element and the various media control attributes.

Media subsetting is an activity that is supported in several SMIL profiles. The SMIL Language profile supports all of the constructs defined in this chapter. The XHTML+SMIL profile supports spatial cropping, but the Microsoft HTML+Time implementation has no support for timed links; this makes the spatial cropping support of marginal utility from a SMIL perspective.

Most of the media processing elements are supported only in the SMIL 2.0 Language profile. (This is because media processing is often tightly coupled with the nature of the host language document.) Readers should be aware that support for the advanced temporal subsetting settings of clipBegin and clipEnd require support from the media rendering and transport engines. Check the capabilities of your media server carefully to make sure that the requested clipping activities will actually be supported.

11.7 Further Resources

XPointer

XML Pointer Language (XPointer) Version 1.0, Steven DeRose, Eve Maler and Ron Daniel Jr. (eds.), W3C Candidate Recommendation, 11 September 2001. `http://www.w3.org/TR/xptr`.

XLink

XML Linking Language (XLink) Version 1.0, Steven DeRose, Eve Maler and Ron Daniel Jr. (eds), W3C Recommendation, 27 June 2001. `http://www.w3.org/TR/xlink`.

URI

RFC 2396: Uniform Resource Identifiers (URI): Generic Syntax, Tim Berners-Lee, Roy Fielding, Larry Masinter, IETF (Internet Engineering Task Force), 1998, `http://www.ietf.org/rfc/rfc2396.txt`.

12

Advanced Layout Topics

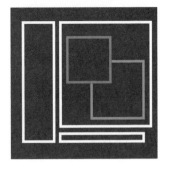

Most of the constructs you will initially need to build presentations in the SMIL Basic and SMIL Language profiles were covered in Chapter 6: *SMIL Basic Layout*. The elements and attributes described in that chapter provide the basic mechanisms to define the outer player window and to define regions within that window. Nearly all of these facilities were also available in SMIL 1.0.

SMIL 2.0 extends the facilities available for layout in a number of dimensions. The SMIL *HierarchicalLayout* module provides a range of media positioning features that simplify presentation authoring and which reduce the size of more complex SMIL 2.0 documents. The SMIL *MultiWindowLayout* module allows multiple top-level windows to be created. It also provides an alternative to the <root-layout> element for creating an outer display region.

The *HierarchicalLayout* module provides elements and attributes to support the following groups of activities:

- *Logical media alignment points*: the ability to define alignment points within a region, allowing media of different sizes to be easily centered or aligned on points other than the top-left corner of a region;

- *Dynamic sub-region positioning*: the ability to create nested regions from within the presentation body instead of within the layout section;

- *Hierarchical region definition*: the ability to define hierarchies of regions, with local z-index stacking levels and relative region positioning; and

- *Media element extensions for layout adjustment*: the ability to modify the backgroundColor, fit and z-index attributes dynamically from media object references.

The features provided by this module can be considered to be authoring convenience extensions to SMIL. All of the functionality can be duplicated by creating (many) special-purpose regions within the layout section, but by providing these features as part of the SMIL language, the efficiency of creating and maintaining SMIL documents is increased.

The *MultiWindowLayout* module provides elements and attributes to support the following groups of activities:

- *Refined top-level window definition*: the ability to create a top level (root) window with more sophisticated rendering control; and

- *Multiple top-level windows*: the ability to segment a presentation into multiple top-level windows, each with special controls for opening and closing the window and its contents.

The functionality in both of these modules is described in this section. At present, this functionality is only supported by players conforming to the full SMIL 2.0 Language profile.

12.1 Logical Media Object Alignment in Regions

A limitation of SMIL 1.0 layout was that media positioning was inflexible. All media elements were anchored at the (0,0) position of a region, which was inconvenient in a <seq> when each of the objects for the region were of a different size. The logical media alignment elements and attributes of SMIL 2.0's *HierarchicalLayout* module address this problem with the definition of new elements and attributes to control logical media positioning.

12.1.1 Understanding Registration and Alignment Points

One of the most requested features from authors of SMIL 1.0 content was to have a way of centering a series of dissimilarly sized media objects inside a region. For example, consider the five images in Figure 12-1. If we wanted to construct a simple slide show that has all of these images centered in the display window, either separate regions would need to be defined for each media object and placed so that a common mid-point is achieved (see Example 12-1) or each of the source media objects would need to be edited so that they all had the same size. Neither approach is particularly handy for our collection of 5 images, and neither are acceptable if we have 500 images!

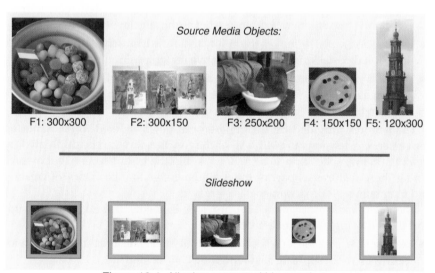

Figure 12-1. Aligning content within a region.

```
1 <smil >
2  <head>
3   <layout>
4    <root-layout height="400" width="400" backgroundColor="blue" />
5    <region id="R1" top="50" left="50" height="300" width="300" />
6    <region id="R2" top="75" left="50" height="150" width="300" />
7    <region id="R3" top="100" left="75" height="200" width="250" />
8    <region id="R4" top="100" left="100" height="200" width="200" />
9    <region id="R5" top="50" left="140" height="300" width="120" />
10   </layout>
11  </head>
12  <body>
13   <seq>
14    <img src="F1.jpg" region="R1" dur="5s" />
15    <img src="F2.jpg" region="R2" dur="5s" />
16    <img src="F3.jpg" region="R3" dur="5s" />
17    <img src="F4.jpg" region="R4" dur="5s" />
18    <img src="F5.jpg" region="R5" dur="5s" />
19   <seq>
20  </body>
21 </smil>
```

Example 12-1. Constructing separate layout regions for dissimilar media sizes.

SMIL 2.0 addresses this issue with *registration points* and *alignment points*. A *registration point* defines a position in a region. Each registration point is defined by a <regPoint> element and referenced by a media object via the regPoint attribute. An alignment point defines a position on a media object that is used to anchor that media to the registration point. A media object references the alignment point using the regAlign attribute.

Example 12-2 gives an overview of the use of registration and alignment points. The <regPoint> element is placed in the layout section in the document <head>. It defines one registration point named *middle*, with the registration coordinates at the center of the region. It also contains a regAlign attribute which says that default alignment behavior for media is in the center of the media object.

```
1 <smil >
2  <head>
3   <layout>
4    <regPoint id="middle" top="50%" left="50%" regAlign="center" />
5    <root-layout height="400" width="400" backgroundColor="blue" />
6    <region id="R1" top="50" left="50" height="300" width="300" />
7   </layout>
8  </head>
9  <body>
10   <seq>
11    <img src="F1.jpg" region="R1" dur="5s" regPoint="middle"/>
12    <img src="F2.jpg" region="R1" dur="5s" regPoint="middle"/>
13    <img src="F3.jpg" region="R1" dur="5s" regPoint="middle"/>
14    <img src="F4.jpg" region="R1" dur="5s" regPoint="middle"/>
15    <img src="F5.jpg" region="R1" dur="5s" regPoint="middle"/>
16   <seq>
17  </body>
18 </smil>
```

Example 12-2. Placing dissimilar media with registration and alignment points.

SMIL's model for aligning images in their regions is much like tacking post-cards on a bulletin board. The alignment point defines a place on the postcard where a pin can be pushed, and the registration point defines a place on a bulletin board when the pin is placed. If you substitute the words "media" for "postcard" and "region" for "bulletin board", the analogy is complete.

As an authoring convenience, SMIL defines nine locations that may be used as alignment points on media objects or registration points on regions. These points, shown in Figure 12-2, are:

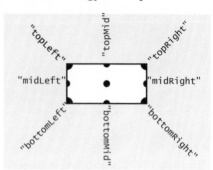

Figure 12-2. The Pre-defined Alignment Points

- *topLeft*: use the top, left point as a reference for alignment.

- *topMid*: use the top, middle point as a reference for alignment.

- *topRight*: use the top, right point as a reference for alignment.

- *midLeft*: use the middle, left point as a reference for alignment.

- *center*: use the center point as a reference for alignment.

- *midRight*: use the middle, right point as a reference for alignment.

- *bottomLeft*: use the bottom, left point as a reference for alignment

- *bottomMid*: use the bottom, middle point as a reference for alignment.

- *bottomLeft*: use the bottom, left point as a reference for alignment.

These nine points may apply to either the registration point (the point in the region at which the alignment should take place) or the alignment point on the media (the point around which the media is aligned). Custom alignment points may be defined and applied to object placement in SMIL regions.

A key aspect of the registration and alignment point architecture is that each point is not defined for a particular region, but may be applied to any region associated with the media object on which the regPoint attribute exists.

The default alignment behavior is a registration point of *topLeft* for all regions and a regAlign point of *topLeft* on all media. In this way, standard SMIL (and CSS) behavior is supported as default alignment.

12.1.2 Elements for Layout Alignment

The SMIL *HierarchicalLayout* module defines the <regPoint> element for defining registration points.

Element: <regPoint>

The structure of the <regPoint> element is shown in Table 12-1. The element accepts the four positioning attributes top, left, bottom and right. These attributes take the same values (pixels and percentages) and function in the same way as in the <region> element. The regAlign attribute specifies default placement point on the media object using the registration point. The element's id attribute value defines a name that is used by media object elements to reference this definition.

The <regPoint> element is placed within the <layout> section of the document. Since the definition can be used with any region, care should be taken when using pixel-based positioning rather than percentage-based positioning, since a pixel offset beyond the bounds of some regions may be specified.

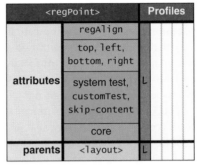

<regPoint>		Profiles
attributes	regAlign	
	top, left, bottom, right	
	system test, customTest, skip-content	L
	core	
parents	<layout>	L

Table 12-1. Structure of the <regPoint> element

In addition to the positioning and default media alignment point, the <regPoint> element also accepts the system and custom test attributes defined by SMIL content control. It also accepts the core attributes.

The parent of the <regPoint> element must be the <layout> element. Although registration point definition may be mixed with <region> definition, it is considered good style to define all registration points in a separate part of the layout section. The <regPoint> element has no children.

12.1.3 Attributes for Layout Alignment

The SMIL *HierarchicalLayout* module defines the regAlign attribute for creating custom registration points for visual media alignment and the regPoint and regAlign attributes for use with media object references for specifying alignment behavior.

Attribute: regAlign

When used with the <regPoint> element or on a media object reference, the regAlign attribute defines the point on the media object that is to be aligned with an associated registration point. It always takes the pre-defined registration points as its allowed values, with *topLeft* as the default. If a non-existent or incorrect alignment policy is defined, the default *topLeft* policy is used.

Attribute: regPoint

The regPoint attribute may only be used on a media object reference. It is used to reference either a pre-defined or a custom-defined registration point to define where in the target region the media will be aligned. The use of a particular regPoint will imply the use of a default regAlign point (either defined by the custom <regPoint> element or by the system default *topLeft*). The regAlign attribute will determine where the media object is aligned with the registration point. The default regPoint value is *topLeft*. If a non-existent or incorrect registration point is defined, the default *topLeft* value is used.

12.1.4 Other Aspects of Registration Point Alignment

The registration point alignment architecture provides a set of convenience alignment facilities that fit nicely into SMIL's layout mechanism. While the system of alignment and registrations points is simple to use, there are two aspects of the approach that are important to consider: the impact of layout's scaling and clipping provided by the fit attribute and the interaction of registration points and sub-region alignment. (We consider this second point on page 268.)

The fit attribute determines how a media element is scaled to fit a region. For a complete discussion, see *Stacking and Scaling Attributes* on page 114. The default fit attribute value is *hidden*: the media object is shown at full size and any parts that fall outside of the geometry of the region are clipped. When various forms of fit are used with registration and alignment points, the location of the registration point is always respected.

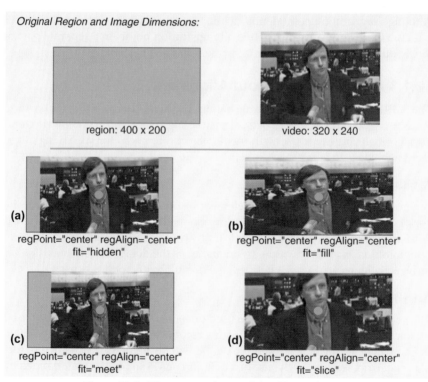

Original Region and Image Dimensions:

region: 400 x 200

video: 320 x 240

(a)
regPoint="center" regAlign="center"
fit="hidden"

(b)
regPoint="center" regAlign="center"
fit="fill"

(c)
regPoint="center" regAlign="center"
fit="meet"

(d)
regPoint="center" regAlign="center"
fit="slice"

Figure 12-3. Alignment points and the fit attribute.

Figure 12-3 illustrates the consequences of applying various fit values on a media object for which the region registration point and the media alignment point are both set to *center*.

- fit="hidden" *(the default)*: The alignment point of the media object is placed over the registration point in the region. Any excess media is clipped.
- fit="fill": the media object is placed at the center of the region; the height and width are scaled independently to fill the region.
- fit="meet": the media object is scaled a size that requires the smallest change to fit the object to the region and is then aligned.
- fit="slice": the media object is scaled a size that requires the largest change to fit the media to the region and is then aligned. The remainder is clipped.

Alignment behavior can be complex when various non-centered combinations are used. Three examples are given in Figure 12-4, all of which use a regPoint value of *center*.

- fit="fill" *and* regAlign="topLeft": the upper left corner of the image is anchored at the center registration point. The image is scaled so that the region's lower right area is filled with content.
- fit="meet" *and* regAlign="topMid": the upper middle corner of the image is anchored at the center registration point. The image's aspect ratio is maintained and the image is scaled so that the lower boundary is filled with content.
- fit="slice" *and* regAlign="bottomMid": the lower edge of the image is anchored at the center registration point. The image's aspect ratio is maintained and the image is scaled so that the upper area is filled with content.

Clearly, not all combinations will make sense in normal use cases.

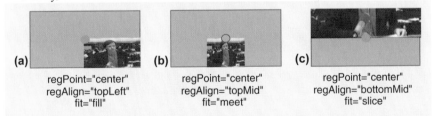

(a) regPoint="center" regAlign="topLeft" fit="fill"

(b) regPoint="center" regAlign="topMid" fit="meet"

(c) regPoint="center" regAlign="bottomMid" fit="slice"

Figure 12-4. More alignment points and the fit attribute.

12.1.5 Examples of Registration Point Alignment

Figure 12-5 illustrates several combinations of region registration points and media alignment points. (In these examples, the default fit behavior of *hidden* is used.) Most of the behavior is self-explanatory. Note that in Figure 12-5(d), the upper left portion of the media object is clipped because the center of the image is aligned with the upper left corner of the region. Note also that the reg-

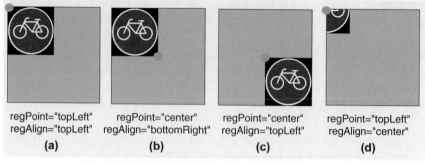

regPoint="topLeft"	regPoint="center"	regPoint="center"	regPoint="topLeft"
regAlign="topLeft"	regAlign="bottomRight"	regAlign="topLeft"	regAlign="center"
(a)	**(b)**	**(c)**	**(d)**

Figure 12-5. Registration point alignment examples.

istration point and alignment point behavior can be explicitly specified or implied.

If only the default nine placement points are used, no <regPoint> element is required. The advantage of defining a custom <regPoint> is that both a region registration point and a media alignment point can be specified. This is illustrated in Figure 12-6. A custom registration point named *Ajax* is defined that creates a region registration point at *midLeft* and a default media alignment location of *midLeft*. Element *W1* uses the custom registration point to place the middle left point on the media at the middle left part of the region. Element *W2* is similar to *W1*, except that it overrides the default media alignment point to be the center of the image. Element *W3* uses the standard placement point *midLeft* for the region and, since no regAlign is given, *topLeft* is used on the image. Finally, *W4* specified both the region registration point to be *midLeft* and the media alignment point to be *midLeft* — this is the long-hand form of the *Ajax* custom specification.

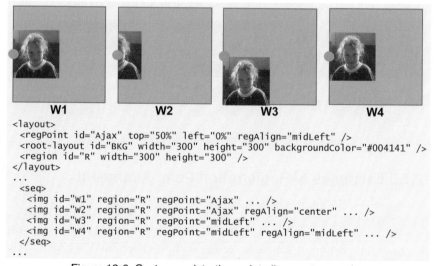

```
<layout>
  <regPoint id="Ajax" top="50%" left="0%" regAlign="midLeft" />
  <root-layout id="BKG" width="300" height="300" backgroundColor="#004141" />
  <region id="R" width="300" height="300" />
</layout>
...
  <seq>
    <img id="W1" region="R" regPoint="Ajax" ... />
    <img id="W2" region="R" regPoint="Ajax" regAlign="center" ... />
    <img id="W3" region="R" regPoint="midLeft" ... />
    <img id="W4" region="R" regPoint="midLeft" regAlign="midLeft" ... />
  </seq>
...
```

Figure 12-6. Custom registration point alignment examples.

12.2 Sub-Region Positioning

The <region> element provides specification efficiency by allowing a region to be used by many media objects. This is especially convenient if all of the objects intended for a region have the same dimensions, such as in a fixed-size slide show. If some of the media objects are of unusual sizes, or if smaller images must be placed within the screen extents of a larger region, extra regions must be created to hold the off-size content. One solution to the positioning problem is the definition of media alignment and region registration points discussed on page 260. This solution is good for using standard positioning, but it is less convenient for the fine-tuned placement of objects relative to others on the display.

SMIL 2.0 addresses this issue by providing a facility for offsetting the base position of media objects within existing regions: this is called *sub-region positioning*. Rather than being defined as part of the layout section, sub-region positioning is specified using positioning attributes on media object elements.

12.2.1 Understanding Sub-Region Positioning

Figure 12-7 illustrates the use of sub-region positioning. A 640x480 region is defined with a fit="hidden" attribute, meaning that all images will be shown at full size in the region (even if this results in clipping). The region is referenced by three images in a sequence.

The first image (*SA*) uses default layout: the 480x320 image is anchored at the upper left corner of the region.

The second image in the sequence (*SB*) uses sub-region positioning to define a drawing area that is anchored at 35 pixels from the top and 60 pixels to the left of region A. Since no bottom or right coordinates are given, the sub-region fills the rest of *A*'s extent. (This is shown by the blue background color.) This

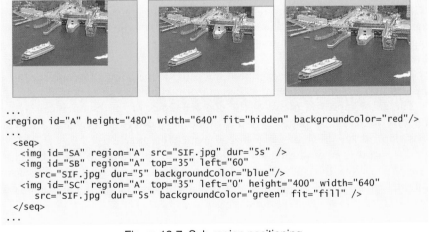

```
...
<region id="A" height="480" width="640" fit="hidden" backgroundColor="red"/>
...
<seq>
  <img id="SA" region="A" src="SIF.jpg" dur="5s" />
  <img id="SB" region="A" top="35" left="60"
      src="SIF.jpg" dur="5" backgroundColor="blue"/>
  <img id="SC" region="A" top="35" left="0" height="400" width="640"
      src="SIF.jpg" dur="5s" backgroundColor="green" fit="fill" />
</seq>
...
```

Figure 12-7. Sub-region positioning.

region is inside of region *A*; it is not a separate region with a separate name. The sub-region is a dynamic, single use region. Since the scaling policy is the same as for region *A*, the image is placed at the top, left corner of the new sub-region.

The third image in the sequence (*SC*) defines a new sub-region; it has no relationship to the sub-region defined with image *SB*. The element defines the total extent of the sub-region explicitly, plus a new `fit="fill"` scaling policy. The image is now stretched to include the entire area. Note that although the background color has been redefined to green, none of the background is shown because the image fills the entire sub-region.

Normally, all of the attributes of the containing region are transferred to the sub-region, including `top`, `left`, `height`, `width`, `z-index`, `fit`, `backgroundColor`, etc. Unless these attributes are overridden on the media object element, the values from the containing region will influence the rendering of the image modified by sub-region positioning.

In normal use, the sub-region should be defined to be the same size as the media object — with explicit height and width — so that the impact of the `fit` attribute will be minimal.

12.2.2 Sub-Region Positioning Elements

No new elements are required to support sub-region positioning.

12.2.3 Sub-Region Positioning Attributes

The *HierarchicalLayout* module does not define new attributes for use with sub-region positioning, but it does make a set of attributes available that were only contained on the `<region>` element. For example, in the SMIL 2.0 Language profile, the region positioning attributes `top`, `left`, `width`, `height`, `bottom` and `right` can be assigned to media object elements. When assigned, they define a new (temporary) region for that media object — a sub-region within the `<region>` element region indicated by the `region` attribute. The referenced region defines the containing block in which the sub-region positioning attributes are applied in determining the sub-region's position and size on the visual display.

If used together with registration and alignment points, the sub-region is created first and the alignment is then performed on the sub-region.

The sub-region has many of the characteristics of the hierarchical layout regions discussed on page 271, except that the sub-region is dynamic: it only exists during the lifetime of the object to which it is attached.

For purposes of rendering sub-region content, the z-index of the sub-region is set to be above the containing region. As with hierarchical regions, this is an internal z-indexing; content in other regions will treat the sub-region as having the same z-index as its containing region.

12.2.4 Examples of Sub-Region Positioning

Figure 12-7 provides an overview of the general use of sub-region positioning. In this section, we'll look at some more unusual uses of sub-region positioning to help build a broader understanding of the details of layout implementation.

Consider the short presentation illustrated in Figure 12-8. A single region *A* has been defined with a red background. In the <par>, two images are displayed. The first image is displayed at the default top, left position. Two seconds into the <par> a second image is displayed in the same container region, but it uses a sub-region anchored at the center of the parent. Since the sub-region displays at the same z-index as the parent, it will be rendered on top of the first image. (Note that the image is stretched to fill the sub-region.) After 5 seconds, the first image is removed and only the sub-region is presented.

Original Images: 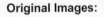 SIF1  SIF2

Presentation Rendering:

| After 1 second | After 3 seconds | After 6 seconds |

```xml
<?xml version="1.0"?>
<smil xmlns="http://www.w3.org/2001/SMIL20/Language">
  <head>
    <layout>
      <root-layout title="SubRegions" width="640" height="480" />
      <region id="A" fit="hidden" width="640" height="480" z-index="1"
        backgroundColor="red"/>
    </layout>
  </head>
  <body>
    <par>
      <img region="A" src="SIF1.jpg" dur="5s" />
      <img region="A" src="SIF2.jpg" dur="5s" begin="2s"
        fit="fill" top="50%" left="50%" />
    </par>
  </body>
</smil>
```

Figure 12-8. Sub-region positioning and the <par> element (part 1).

Presentation Rendering:

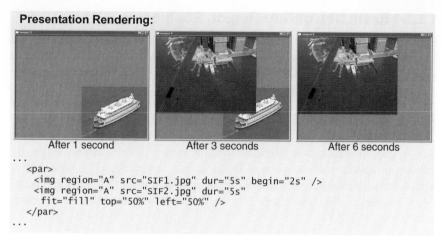

| After 1 second | After 3 seconds | After 6 seconds |

```
...
  <par>
    <img region="A" src="SIF1.jpg" dur="5s" begin="2s" />
    <img region="A" src="SIF2.jpg" dur="5s"
     fit="fill" top="50%" left="50%" />
  </par>
...
```

Figure 12-9. Sub-region positioning and the <par> element (part 2).

Figure 12-9 shows the result of changing the display order of the sub-region. Now, the content in the sub-region is shown first, thus it is rendered under the larger image. (All other aspects of the presentation are the same.)

In Figure 12-10, a second region (*B*) is added at a z-index of *2*. Since it has a background color defined, it will be rendered throughout the presentation, even if it has no content. The z-index of the sub-region is *3*. (The z-index of the original region *A* was *1*.) The interesting thing about this example is that although the sub-region has a z-index of *3*, it is rendered below a region with a z-index of *2*. This is because a sub-region defines a local stacking order.

Presentation Rendering:

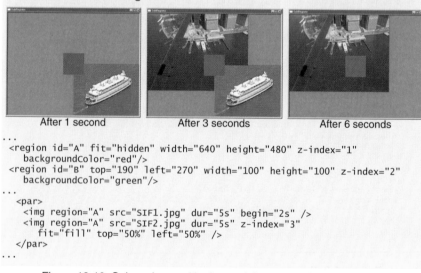

| After 1 second | After 3 seconds | After 6 seconds |

```
...
<region id="A" fit="hidden" width="640" height="480" z-index="1"
    backgroundColor="red"/>
<region id="B" top="190" left="270" width="100" height="100" z-index="2"
    backgroundColor="green"/>
...
  <par>
    <img region="A" src="SIF1.jpg" dur="5s" begin="2s" />
    <img region="A" src="SIF2.jpg" dur="5s" z-index="3"
     fit="fill" top="50%" left="50%" />
  </par>
...
```

Figure 12-10. Sub-region positioning and the <par> element (part 3).

12.3 HierarchicalLayout

SMIL's hierarchical layout facilities allow regions to be defined inside other regions. They provide the foundation for supporting sub-region positioning (see page 267) and they are also used to implement logical media positioning (see page 260.) Although they share many of the facilities and features of these other two layout extensions, the SMIL hierarchical layout support provides a separate set of features that make presentation authoring and maintenance more convenient. They also provide a mechanism for high-level animation of a collection of related regions.

12.3.1 Understanding Hierarchical Layout

The *BasicLayout* module defines visual regions as collections of pixels within a top-level window container. There is no structuring of region definitions and the semantic and spatial relationships *among* groups of regions is not exposed. This is illustrated in the simple presentation layout shown in Figure 12-11. The captions in this presentation are related to the video content, but this relationship is not expressed anywhere in the spatial design.

Figure 12-3 shows the same presentation with its regions defined as a hierarchy. We see that one extra parent region has been defined (named *VC*) that contains video and captions regions as children. All of the attributes of the parent region are inherited by the children — in this case, the base position, the `fit` type and the `backgroundColor`. These attributes may be overridden or augmented by the children.

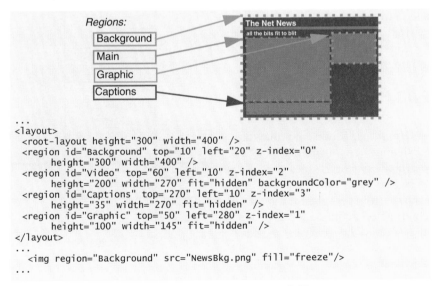

```
...
<layout>
  <root-layout height="300" width="400" />
  <region id="Background" top="10" left="20" z-index="0"
       height="300" width="400" />
  <region id="Video" top="60" left="10" z-index="2"
       height="200" width="270" fit="hidden" backgroundColor="grey" />
  <region id="Captions" top="270" left="10" z-index="3"
       height="35" width="270" fit="hidden" />
  <region id="Graphic" top="50" left="280" z-index="1"
       height="100" width="145" fit="hidden" />
</layout>
...
  <img region="Background" src="NewsBkg.png" fill="freeze"/>
...
```

Figure 12-11. Standard region definitions

```
<layout>
  <root-layout height="300" width="400" />
  <region id="VC" backgroundColor="red" fit="hidden"
      top="5" left="55" height="270" width="280" z-index="0" >
    <region id="Video" top="5" left="5" height="480" width="640" z-index="2"/>
    <region id="Captions" top="210" left="5" height="35" z-index="3"/>
  </region>
  <region id="Graphic" top="50" left="280"height="100" width="145" ... />
  <region id="Background" top="10" left="20"height="300" width="400" ... />
</layout>
```

Example 12-3. Hierarchical region definitions of Figure 12-11.

One advantage of hierarchical layout is the clarity of the relationships among the layout regions: if you were given this layout section to maintain, the relationship between the video area and the captions would be immediately clear. This relationship is less clear with conventional SMIL layout.

Other than for authoring convenience and maintenance, the use of hierarchical regions also has a benefit when combined with animation functionality (see Chapter 15: *SMIL Animation*): if the position of the containing region is animated — such as moving it from left to right during the video — then all of the containing regions are moved automatically.

12.3.2 Hierarchical Layout Elements

This section reviews the extensions required to support Hierarchical Layout.

Element: <region>

The *HierarchicalLayout* module extends the <region> element to define regions as children. The complete structure of the extended <region> element is shown in Table 12-2 when all of the available layout modules have been applied.

12.3.3 Hierarchical Layout Attributes

The *HierarchicalLayout* module does not define new attributes for the <region> element. It does provide a qualification on the use of the z-index attribute: a z-index value on a child region defines a local stacking order within the parent's z-index. The internal stacking order is not made visible outside the hierarchical region: from outside the hierarchy, all regions have the z-index of the parent.

<region>		Profiles			
attributes	regionName				
	top, left, width, height, bottom, right	M	B	1	
	z-index, fit				
	soundLevel	L			
	showBackground				
	backgroundColor				
	system test, customTest, skip-content	M	B	1	
	core				
parents	<layout>	M	B	1
	<topLayout>	L			
parents & children	<region>	L			

Table 12-2. The <region> element's place in SMIL structure

12.3.4 Examples of Hierarchical Layout

In Figure 12-12, the region structure defined in Example 12-3 is used in a presentation. For rendering purposes, the use of hierarchical regions is transparent: if we had used a non-hierarchical approach, the visual look of the presentation would be the same. To see the use of hierarchical regions, consider the following example. Assume that in the news presentation, the main video window and the captions were to be moved towards the center of the screen. (This is done to make room for new content at the left size, or to simply add variety in the presentation. In order to perform the animation, the following fragment could be used:

```
...
    <animate targetElement="VC" attributeName="left"
        from="55" to="85" dur="5s" begin="23s" />
...
```

The parent region of the video and captions (*VC*) has a `z-index` of 0 and the child regions (*Video* and *Captions*) have z-indexes of 2 and 3, respectively. In case of any pixel overlap conflicts, these z-indexes are treated as if they were sub-indexes of the parent: *Video* would have a z-index of 0:2 and *Captions* would have a z-index of 0:3. The right part of Figure 12-12 shows that after the animation, the content in the *VC* hierarchy is rendered below the content in the *Graphic* region, even though the z-index of *Graphic* is lower than that of *Video*. The reason for this is that *Graphic* has an effective z-index of 1:0 while *Video* has an effective index of 0:2.

Although not shown, it is important to realize that the stacking order within a hierarchical region is private. If another hierarchical region with an effective stacking order of, say, 0:6 were to be positioned on top of the *Video* region (with an effective stacking order of 0:2), it would not necessarily be visible — the ordering would depend on the temporal relationship between the objects.

Declared z-index values:	Effective z-index values:
VC: z-index="0"	VC: z-index="0"
Video: z-index="2"	Video: z-index="0:2"
Captions: z-index="3"	Captions: z-index="0:3"
Graphic: z-index="1"	Graphic: z-index="1"

Figure 12-12. Evaluating z-index with hierarchical regions.

12.4 Media Object Overrides of Layout Positioning

In addition to defining the facilities for hierarchical layout, sub-region positioning and media alignment, the *HierarchicalLayout* module also allows a number of layout attributes to be exported to other modules. These are:

- *positioning attributes*: As we discussed, sub-region positioning allows the `top`, `left`, `height`, `width`, `right` and `bottom` attributes to be referenced on the media object element.

- *scaling attributes*: The *HierarchicalLayout* module also allows the `fit` attribute to be (temporarily) modified on the media object element.

- *other attributes*: the *HierarchicalLayout* module allows the attributes `backgroundColor` and `z-index` to be modified on the media object element.

When used with sub-region positioning, the specification of positioning attributes behaves as if a dynamic hierarchical region is created. In the case of scaling and other attributes, the values defined in the sub-region temporarily modify the associated region values for the duration of the media object's active duration and associated fill period.

12.5 Defining Multiple Top-Level Windows

SMIL's *MultiWindowLayout* module defines a new model for partitioning regions into groups of top-level container windows (which SMIL 1.0 defined using the `<root-layout>` element, defined on page 107), and new facilities for controlling when each top-level collection of regions is visible during a presentation.

The *MultiWindowLayout* module introduces one new element, named `<topLayout>`, and several new attributes for use in the layout section. These new attributes are also made available to other modules. While `<topLayout>` is required for supporting multiple top level windows, it is also useful as a replacement for `<root-layout>` in single-window applications: it gives extra window control and it provides a cleaner organization of rendering regions.

12.5.1 Understanding Multiple Top-Level Windows

Figure 12-13 illustrates the use of multiple windows in a complex presentation. The presentation contains a number of logical section, each of which are identified on a menu page. Figure 12-13(a) shows the main link page for the presentation. When a link is followed, the presentation starts the new section by opening an extra top-level window containing a viewer's guide. Figure 12-13(b) shows that a *Viewer's Guide* opens in addition to the *Main Window* after the *What do they think of it?* link is followed. After reading the background information in the guide, the user can activate the selected content in the presentation. This is shown in Figure 12-13(c), where after selecting the *Push HERE to Activate* button, the content in the *Main Window* becomes active and the acti-

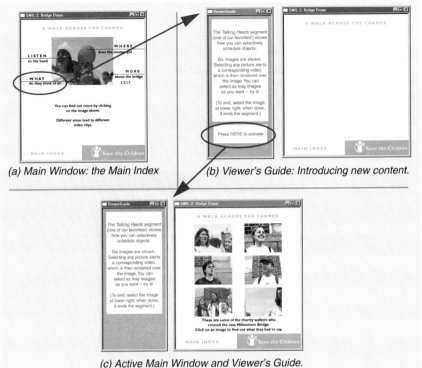

(a) Main Window: the Main Index

(b) Viewer's Guide: Introducing new content.

(c) Active Main Window and Viewer's Guide.

Figure 12-13. An application of multi-window layout.

vation button is removed from the *Viewer's Guide*. If either of the *MAIN INDEX* or the *Save the Children* links are followed, the supplemental *Viewer's Guide* window is closed and only the main window is left open.

The use of multiple top-level windows has a number of practical advantages during presentation design and maintenance:

- *related regions are grouped together*: if you design complex presentations that contain multiple classes of content, it is often useful to group collections of regions together into separate layout windows. This can help organize the information presentation, and it localizes the maintenance of a larger presentation by having all of the layout regions that logically belong together also being defined together.

- *Layout substitution is simplified*: the use of multiple top-level windows allows entire sets of regions to be easily replaced (in conjunction with the SMIL content control elements) by a totally different layout if multiple display geometries are being targeted: one top-level window per screen.

- *On-demand activation of windows allows focused attention to content*: since top-layouts can be turned on and off as a group, you can focus attention to particular types of content based on temporal or topical needs of the application — pop-up windows can be displayed for well-defined intervals during your presentation.

It is beyond the scope of this book to provide examples of all of these advantages, but we will discuss all of the elements and attributes that SMIL makes available for controlling multi-window layout.

12.5.2 Multi-Window Elements

The SMIL *MultiWindowLayout* module defines the `<topLayout>` element.

Element: `<topLayout>`

The *MultiWindowLayout* module extends the *BasicLayout* module's `<layout>` element with one new child element: `<topLayout>`. The resulting structure of the `<layout>` element is shown in Table 12-3.

The nature of the `<topLayout>` element is very similar to the `<root-layout>` element, with the following exceptions:

<layout>		Profiles
attributes	type	
	system test, customTest	L M B 1
	core	
parents	<head>	
	<switch>	L M B 1
children	<region>	
	<root-layout>	M B 1 / L
	<topLayout>	

Table 12-3. Structure of the revised `<layout>` element

- a single `<layout>` section may have multiple `<topLayout>` elements, but at most one `<root-layout>`.

- each `<topLayout>` section defines its contained `<region>` elements as children, not as the siblings used by `<root-layout>`.

- each `<topLayout>` section contains control attributes (open and close) that determine when the top-level window is opened and closed during a presentation, and it determines whether that window should remain open even if there is no content active in any of its contained regions.

- the integration of `<topLayout>` functionality provides two *events* for use by other modules that signal when a given `<topLayout>` opens or closes. In contrast, `<root-layout>` does not define any window-related *events*.

Since `<topLayout>` provides a superset of window containment features, it may be used as a complete replacement for `<root-layout>` in all documents.

For *MultiWindowLayout* to be available, the type attribute of the `<layout>` element must be (or default to) text/smil-basic-layout, or to another layout model that explicitly supports this module.

Table 12-4 shows the structure of the `<root-layout>` element and Table 12-5 shows the structure of the `<topLayout>`. The `<topLayout>` element is only supported in the SMIL 2.0 Language profile.

The `<topLayout>` element accepts all of the attributes of the older `<root-layout>` element, and adds two new ones: `open` and `close`. These attributes provide a means of controlling the visibility of all of the regions inside each `<topLayout>`. Note that although `<topLayout>` allows region elements to be defined as children, this is not the same as using hierarchical layout: hierarchical layout allows the `<region>` element to accept other `<region>` elements as children; `<topLayout>` accepts regions as children as a way of organizing the top-level set of layout `<regions>`. In most cases, `<topLayout>` can be used as a full replacement for `<root-layout>`.

`<root-layout>`		Profiles			
attributes	backgroundColor		M	B	1
	width, height		M	B	1
	system test, skip-content	L			
	customTest				
	core		M	B	1
parents	`<layout>`	L	M	B	1
children	none	L	M	B	1

Table 12-4. Structure of the revised `<root-layout>` element.

The fact that a presentation has multiple top-level windows does *not* mean that it has multiple top-level timebases or timelines (one per window). Since SMIL layout is defined in the `<head>` element and not within the `<body>`, all of layout is defined outside the temporal scope of the document. This is a useful feature for coordinating content in multiple windows, since multi-window architecture is *temporally transparent*: it is separated from its timing and synchronization structure of the document. An event processed by an action in one top-level window can be associated with content in another top-level window. (This was illustrated in Figure 12-13.)

`<topLayout>`		Profiles			
attributes	backgroundColor				
	width, height				
	open, close				
	system test, skip-content	L			
	customTest				
	core				
parents	`<layout>`	L			
children	`<region>`	L			

Table 12-5. Structure of the `<topLayout>` element.

In terms of functionality for the outer-most layout windows, the main timing-based control that can be exercised on a collection of regions is their visibility. For presentations that use SMIL 1.0's single window model, there was no need to close the `<root-layout>` dynamically, since closing the window was essentially the same as ending the presentation. With multiple top-level windows, it becomes useful to allow authors to group collections of regions into fixed and optional portions of the presentation and to then provide extra support for opening and closing the optional parts on demand.

12.5.3 Multi-Window Attributes

The SMIL *MultiWindowLayout* module defines the open and close attributes. Used in the `<topLayout>` element, these attributes define the default policies for a top-level window's visibility. They may only be used in the `<head>` section of the presentation, without overrides on the media object.

Attribute: open

The open attribute of the `<topLayout>` element specifies when the top-level window opens. It either opens once at the start of the presentation or it (re)opens at various moments during the presentation. The legal values for open are:

- *onStart*: The default value of open is *onStart*, which declares that the window opens when the presentation starts — even if no content is placed in any of the regions within the `<topLayout>`. With *onStart*, if the window is closed by a user at some point during the presentation, the closing is permanent — the window will not automatically reopen later in the presentation, even if regions within become active. (This assumes that a user interface facility is provided so that a user can perform the closing action.)

- *whenActive*: The *whenActive* value states that the regions within the `<topLayout>` will only become visible when one or more of the regions have active content. (Once opened, all regions will be shown, even if only some are active.) With *whenActive*, a `<topLayout>` will not open at the start of the presentation unless its contains media that is active at the start. If a top-level window defined with a *whenActive* value is closed during the presentation (either by user interaction or as a result of the close attribute), it will open again when any of its contained regions become active.

Note that the showBackground attribute for `<topLayout>` (see page 276) also supports a *whenActive* value, but this controls whether the background fill color is visible, not whether the element with the showBackground is visible.

Attribute: close

The close attribute specifies when the window closes. It either closes directly upon user request (assuming the user *can* request it), or indirectly whenever none of the regions in the top-level window are active. To the potential disappointment of the on-line advertising community, SMIL 2.0 does not provide a facility that guarantees that a window will never close, even if a user requests it! The legal values for close are:

- *onRequest*: The default value of *onRequest* declares that the `<topLayout>` only closes when the user requests it though the SMIL player's user interface. If the player does not support this facility, the `<topLayout>` never closes.

- *whenNotActive*: The *whenNotActive* value directs a `<topLayout>` to close when none of its regions are active. According to SMIL's Timing and Synchronization behavior, a <topLayout> is active when any media object element assigned to it is in its *active duration* or *freeze* period. A region is also active if it has any <region> element children, or further descendants, that are active.

For a given top-level window with many regions in documents with complex timing, it may be hard for the author to control when a <topLayout> closes, since this involves eliminating any possibility of media playing anywhere in one of the contained regions. Careful layout design can minimize these difficulties.

12.5.4 Aspects of Multi-Window Layout

This section discusses some of the timing and layout consequences of using multiple top-level windows in a presentation.

Events from Opening and Closing Top-Level Layouts

Authors can synchronize content in a SMIL presentation with the opening and closing of top-level windows by scheduling their begin or end with one of SMIL's two layout-related events. These events are topLayoutOpenEvent, which is triggered when a <topLayout> opens, and topLayoutCloseEvent, which is triggered when a <topLayout> closes.

Timing Implications of Multiple Top-Level Windows

SMIL Layout provides a set of facilities to help you arrange content during a presentation, but it does not define separate temporal containers or semantics for each top-level window. The layout structure (the number of regions and the grouping of regions) is time-transparent: there is one temporal structure for the entire presentation, not one temporal tree per top-level window. This is a very key layout concept.

Using Both <root-layout> and <topLayout> in One Presentation

SMIL 2.0 allows the use of both <root-layout> and <topLayout> in one presentation. The regions associated with the <topLayout> windows are grouped as children of that top-level window and any remaining regions are associated with the root-layout window. Since the functionality of <root-layout> can be obtained by setting open="always" and close="onRequest", and since having regions defined as children rather than siblings is more in line with the use of other SMIL elements, there is no reason to use <root-layout> within a presentation other than for compatibility with SMIL 1.0.

```
1  <smil xmlns="http://www.w3.org/2001/SMIL20/Language">
2  <head>
3   <layout>
4    <topLayout id="BridgeDemo" title="SMIL-2: Bridge Demo"
        backgroundColor="white" open="onStart"
        width="400" height="440">
5     <region id="audio"/>
6     <region id="BigLinkPicture" title="Big Link Picture"
         width="400" top="40" height="190" z-index="3"/>
7      ...
8     <region id="BottomLinksTitle" title="Bottom Links Title"
         width="400" top="394" height="46" z-index="1"/>
9    </topLayout>
10   <topLayout id="ViewerGuide" backgroundColor="#e7ac44"
        open="whenActive" close="whenNotActive" width="200" height="440">
11    <region id="Help" title="Viewer's Guide" left="10"
         width="180" top="10" height="320"/>
12    <region id="button" title="Start Button"
         left="14" top="340" height="58"/>
13   </topLayout>
14  </layout>
15 </head>
16 <body>
17   ...
18 </body>
19 </smil>
```

Example 12-4. Defining the multiple top-level windows of Figure 12-13.

12.5.5 Examples of Multi-Window Layout

Example 12-4 shows the layout section code for defining the two top-level windows in Figure 12-13. Note that in this example, there is no <root-layout> element. Note also the use of the open and close attributes.

The main presentation window is defined on line 4. It contains an open attribute that instructs the player to always keep the top-level window open, even if it is not rendering content. (This usually provides a less chaotic presentation environment.) This top level window contains a host of regions, all of which are defined as children of the top-level window. The closing bracket for the main top-level window is given on line 9.

The viewer's guide window is defined on line 10. It has an open attribute value of *whenActive* and a close attribute value of *whenNotActive*: these allow the window to act as a pop-up window when additional content is to be presented. The window can also be closed by explicit author request from within the body section of the SMIL code; once closed, the window will re-open the next time it is active. The top-level window contains two regions as children: one area to display window content and one area that is used as a link activation button.

The definition of the <topLayout> element tries to balance the facilities that all conforming players should be able to support, without dictating exactly how a SMIL player needs to implement its windowing facility. SMIL allows all of the presentation's windows to be placed in one (player-defined) master window, or to 'float' independently on the presentation surface. SMIL does not dictate how a user can manually close a window, or even if this user interface facility is available. Finally — and perhaps somewhat surprisingly — SMIL does not define where on the desktop (or rendering surface) each of the top-level layouts are placed: this, too, is the responsibility of the player. (Note that some players may provide extensions to handle each of these concerns.)

12.6 SMIL Layout and CSS

SMIL basic layout performs functions similar to that of CSS, such as the positioning of media content on the screen, and the establishing of background colors. The two formats have their differences as well, stemming primarily from CSS's orientation toward the display of text, and SMIL's introduction of scheduling to Web formats. In the interest of exploiting and enforcing the similarities, SMIL basic layout constructs were designed to be isomorphic with CSS constructs. Furthermore, CSS can be used as an alternative layout-defining syntax in SMIL itself. In this section we discuss the relationship between CSS and SMIL, and how CSS can be used in SMIL.

12.6.1 CSS Attributes for SMIL Layout

CSS can be used to define the layout of a SMIL presentation. It must, however, be an alternative layout: if CSS layout is not recognized, SMIL default layout will be applied. (This is almost never useful.) CSS-defined layout is placed in a `<layout>` element with an attribute assignment of `type="text/css"`. The player will decide which style format to use if CSS is available based on `<switch>` evaluation. The primary drawback of CSS-defined layout for SMIL is that, as of this writing, no one has implemented it — though this, of course, may change.

For the most part, CSS can be used with SMIL in the same manner as it is with any HTML or XML document. CSS declarations have placement-defining rules with equivalents in SMIL basic layout attributes. CSS selectors can be used for assigning these declarations to SMIL media object elements just as they would for elements in any XML document. For example, to display all image elements in the main window with a five-pixel border, the following CSS code could be used:

```
img { top:5px; left:5px; bottom:5px; right:5px }
```

SMIL body code used with SMIL basic layout often refers to region specifications by name. Such body code could be used with a CSS equivalent for the SMIL basic layout that uses `region` attributes in its selectors, as follows:

```
[region="border5px"] { top:5px; left:5px; bottom:5px; right:5px }
```

The isomorphism of SMIL basic layout constructs with CSS facilitates translation between the two layout formats. The next section discusses SMIL's `class` attribute, which works specifically with CSS-defined layout.

Attribute: class

The `class` attribute lets you assign style to individual elements using CSS's primary style assignment mechanism: class selectors. This attribute is recognized by CSS processors as the attribute in SMIL to use with CSS class selectors. Its value is a comma-separated list of class names. As a core attribute, `class` can be assigned to any SMIL element. The `class` attribute provides no new utility, however, since the `region` attribute performs the same service (though with different CSS syntax). While the `region` attribute can assign layout to elements for both SMIL basic layout and CSS-defined layout, the use of the `class` attribute has the disadvantage of only being recognized by CSS processing, not by SMIL basic layout.

12.6.2 CSS and SMIL Layout Comparison

To help those already familiar with CSS to better understand SMIL and to help those who want to make CSS style sheets for SMIL presentation, Table 12-6 provides a comparison between the constructs in CSS and SMIL. SMIL and CSS have very similar positioning mechanisms, with the primary constructs having identical names. Both formats resolve image and containing block size mismatches similarly, though sometimes with quite different means. The primary distinction between SMIL basic layout and CSS is that, as a media-independent format, SMIL does not handle text directly, whereas CSS has very many constructs for styling text display. CSS selectors have many means of locating body elements that are unavailable to SMIL basic layout. CSS's inheritance of properties through the body hierarchy also provides additional expressive power. On the other hand, SMIL handles multiple windows, and the opening and closing of display spaces over time, both of which CSS lacks.

12.7 Summary and Conclusion

The facilities provided by *MultiWindowLayout* and *HierarchicalLayout* modules provide useful extensions to SMIL that make document authoring and document maintenance easier. These facilities will typically not be available with SMIL Basic players because they require a degree of processing overhead that may exceed the capabilities of the runtime platform — in these cases, the burden is shifted to authors, who must solve the same processing problems during presentation authoring.

Other than making authoring and maintenance easier, and reducing the size of the SMIL source document, the facilities described in this chapter provide a powerful encapsulation mechanism for layout constructs. This is especially useful when combined with functionality from SMIL animation.

	SMIL Constructs	CSS Constructs
Display Window	`<root-layout>` and `<toplayout>` elements	only one window (the viewport) no CSS control over window size
Back-Ground	`backgroundColor` attribute	`background-color` property
	no equivalent	remaining background properties
Window References	`<region>` elements	declarations
	`id`, `regionName` and `region` attributes	selectors
Positioning	`top`, `left`, `bottom`, `right`, `width`, `height` and `z-index` attributes	`top`, `left`, `bottom`, `right`, `width`, `height` and `z-index` properties
	hierarchical regions (in head)	inheritance (in body)
	sub-regions	relative positioning
	units of measure: pixels, percentage	units of measure: pixels, percentage
	no equivalent	absolute length units: points, centimeters, etc.
	no equivalent — SMIL defines no text	font size as length unit
Overflow and Fit	`fit="hidden"` (default)	`overflow:hidden` (not default)
	`fit="scroll"` (not default)	`overflow:scroll` (default)
	`fit="fill"`	define both `width` and `height` properties
	`fit="meet"`	define only one of `width` and `height` properties
	`fit="slice"`	no equivalent
	no equivalent	`overflow:visible`
Sound	`soundLevel` attribute (applies to all audio)	`volume` property (applies to synthesized speech)
	no equivalent	remaining synthesized speech properties
Other	`showBackground`, `open` and `close` attributes	no equivalent (CSS has no timing)
	no equivalent (SMIL defines no text)	text-related properties

Table 12-6. Comparing CSS and SMIL Constructs

12.8 Further Resources

CSS

Cascading Style Sheets, Level 2, Bert Bos, Håkon Wium Lie, Chris Lilley and Ian Jacobs (eds), W3C Recommendation, 12 May 1998.
`http://www.w3.org/TR/CSS2`.

HTML

XHTML 1.0: The Extensible HyperText Markup Language (Second Edition), Steven Pemberton, (ed. chair), W3C Recommendation, 1 August 2002,
`http://www.w3.org/TR/xhtml1` .

13

Advanced SMIL Timing Behavior and Control

In the normal course of processing, the temporal activation hierarchy of a SMIL 2.0 document determines the rendering of document elements. The user can influence the elements selected by using SMIL 2.0 *events*. The event architecture allows document components that are waiting to be activated or terminated to actually start or stop. There are several uses of events allowed in SMIL 2.0, but perhaps the most important new semantic in the language is the combination of events and the `begin` and `end` attributes. In further combination with the `<excl>` element, events provide a very powerful mechanism for conditional content activation.

SMIL 2.0 also supports a rich hyperlinking architecture. Unlike links in HTML, the fundamental concept of the SMIL link is that it models a *temporal seek* in a presentation. Rather than simply activating a destination element, the destination play state that is activated is identical to the state that the presentation would have been in if the destination had been arrived at "naturally". (One exception is that all event-based activation is ignored.) This means that all nodes temporally between the source and destination of the link need to be evaluated to see if they would have contributed to the final destination play state. The temporal seeking and activation facility allows very polished presentation construction — but its implementation in the player is not for the faint-hearted!

This chapter provides a comprehensive summary of SMIL 2.0 interactive and event behavior. We start with background information on SMIL's event processing and the interaction facilities available to users. We then contrast event behavior with link-based interaction. We then discuss how scheduled and interactive timing is used in selective content activation using the exclusive (or `<excl>`). We next revisit the SMIL 2.0 timing model and look in detail on how objects are timed and scheduled. The chapter concludes with special elements that allow SMIL's temporal behavior to be integrated into other XML languages.

Our discussion in this chapter is largely example driven. This should benefit authors of complex SMIL presentations. The material in this chapter will also provide extensive background information for readers who wish to implement or maintain their own SMIL player engines.

13.1 Event Based Timing

In SMIL 1.0, all of the begin and end times in a document could be determined (in theory!) by inspecting the document structure and the various temporal elements and attributes defined for a presentation. The only uncertainty provided by SMIL 1.0 was its support for temporal linking: following a link not only brought the focus of a presentation to another place in the structure of a document, it also required that the temporal consequences of beginning within a nested set of timelines be addressed explicitly.

SMIL 2.0 provides a set of rich enhancements to the SMIL 1.0 model. From a temporal perspective, the major enhancement to SMIL 1.0 was the introduction of event behavior in a document. An *event* is a signal provided to the player that some condition has occurred. The event may be related to an external condition, such as that a mouse click has occurred on some element in the document, or it may be related to an internal condition, such as that a particular other element in the presentation has begun or ended. For implementations that support a document object model (DOM) processor, events may also come from DOM method calls that target some element in the presentation.

13.1.1 Understanding Events, Links and Interaction

This section looks at various aspects of event processing in SMIL 2.0 and contrasts it with the link based processing that was provided in SMIL 1.0 (and continues to exist in SMIL 2.0).

Events and Interaction

In order to understand the structure of event timing, we review some basic timing concepts. Consider the following code fragment:

```
...
<par id="P1">
  <img id="I1" begin="0s" src="backgroundIntro.png" fill="freeze" ... />
  <video id="V1" begin="3s" src="story.mpg" ... />
</par>
...
```

A <par> time container *P1* contains two child elements: a background image *I1* and a video *V1*. I1 is defined to start 0 seconds after the beginning of *P1* — this is the default behavior of the image, but we include it here for clarity. The video *V1* is defined to start 3 seconds after *P1* (and thus, 3 seconds after the start of the image). This code fragment illustrates aspects of SMIL scheduled behavior semantics.

We can replace the begin time of the *V1* video to reference a *syncbase* value: a syncbase is the name of an element in the presentation that will act as the timing reference for another element. The SMIL syntax for the updated video object is:

```
<video id="V1" begin="I1.begin+3s" src="story.mpg" ... />
```

The begin of *V1* is now de-coupled from the beginning of its parent *P1* and associated with the start of peer element *I1*. (This relationship is called a *sync arc*; the name comes from the graphical synchronization relationships defined in the CMIF language). From a scheduler's perspective, nothing particularly complex has happened by moving from parent-relative timing to syncbase timing: the begin time of *V1* can still be resolved easily by working through the activation chain. The only extra check that the scheduler must make is that the temporal constraint imposed by the *P1* parent time container is respected: the video may not begin rendering before the parent <par> is active.

We can dramatically change the scheduling within this time container by introducing event-based timing. The following fragment gives an example:

```
...
<par id="P0">
  ...
  <par id="P1">
    <img id="I1" begin="X.activateEvent" src="backgroundIntro.png"
      fill="freeze" ... />
    <video id="V1" begin="I1.begin+3s" src="story.mpg" ... />
  </par>
  ...
  <img id="X" src="button.png" dur="20s" ... />
</par>
...
```

Here, an outer parallel element *P0* is defined. It has *P1* as a child, as well as an image *X* that contains a button. The begin condition of *I1* has been changed to become relative to an *eventbase*: *I1* starts when the viewer clicks on the button image — assuming, of course, that the mouse click occurs within the first 20 seconds of this presentation fragment.

From the perspective of the SMIL scheduler, a fundamental new concept has now been introduced into the language. The actual begin time of *I1* cannot be resolved based on document structure and (syncbase) timing. The exact begin time of *I1* has become unpredictable; as a result, the begin time of *V1* has become equally unpredictable.[1]

The SMIL 2.0 scheduler needs to take many aspects of the presentation above into account when defining an activation sequence. We will return to these in *SMIL 2.0 Timing Model, Revisited* on page 310. For now, we'll continue to look at how to specify event-based behavior without worrying about how it gets implemented.

---

1 There is another unpredictably: will the image I1 *ever* start? The RealOne player and HTML+Time think so: they start the object I1 after the image X receives a mouse click. The GRiNS and Ambulant players disagree: they do not start I1 because the parent P1 will end right after the start of the P0. (It ends because children with unresolved begin times do not contribute to the duration of the P1 container, thus the container ends right after it begins.) We determine who is right in *Mixing Syncbase and Eventbase Activation* on page 317.

Interactive and Non-Interactive Events

In the previous example, we used an interactive event to start part of the presentation. An interactive link gets triggered in response to some form of user interaction. A mouse click is one common form, but not the only type of user interaction. Each SMIL profile that supports events is required to provide a list of interactive events that it supports. (We list the various types in *Event Support in SMIL Profiles* on page 292.)

In addition to interactive events, SMIL also supports non-interactive events. These are events that are generated by the SMIL player itself in response to behavior within the presentation. The following fragment illustrates the use of non-interactive events:

```
...
<par id="P3">
  <img id="I3" src="backgroundIntro.png" fill="freeze" ... />
  <video id="V3" begin="I3.begin+3s" src="story1.mpg" repeatCount="2" ... />
  <video id="V4" begin="V3.endEvent" src="story2.mpg" ... />
</par>
...
```

We see a `<par>` element *P3* that contains two videos (*V3* and *V4*) and one image (*I3*). The image *I3* starts when *P3* starts. Video *V3* starts 3 seconds after the start of *I3*. Both the start of the image and that of the first video are examples of syncbase timing. The video *V4* starts when the *endEvent* event has been triggered. This occurs at the end of the active duration of *V3*: that is, after it has repeated twice. The start of *V4* is an example of eventbase timing.

Syncbase and Eventbase Timing

Consider the following fragment:

```
...
<par id="P4">
  <img id="I4" src="backgroundIntro.png" fill="freeze" ... />
  <video id="V5" begin="I4.begin+3s" src="story1.mpg" repeatCount="2" ... />
  <video id="V6" begin="V5.endEvent" src="story2.mpg" repeatCount="2" ... />
  <img id="I5" begin="V6.end" src="advert.png" dur="3s" ... />
</par>
...
```

In this example, which is similar but not the same as the one above, the `<par>` P4 contains two videos (V5 and V6) and two images (I4 and I5). Image I4 starts when P4 begins, video V5 starts 3 seconds after I4 begins and video V6 begins at the end of the active duration of V5. (This is behavior we have already discussed.) The image I5 begins when the *end* syncbase condition occurs; this happens at the end of V6's active duration. Note that both the begin condition on V6 and I5 trigger at the end of the active duration of the associated element. The only difference is that the begin of V6 depends on a eventbase relationship while the begin of I4 depends on an syncbase relationship.

In many cases, the use of a syncbase *begin* or *end* condition will be functionally equivalent to the use of an eventbase *beginEvent* or *endEvent*. There are two aspects of syncbase and eventbase timing that are potentially different:

- A syncbase relationship is resolved based on computations made by the scheduler, not events sensed by the scheduler. As soon as image *V6* begins, the scheduler can compute the desired begin time of image *I5* based on information it has about *V6*'s duration and the repeat count. The begin time of *V6* is not pre-computed: the scheduler will wait with determining the actual begin time of *V6* until it gets a notification that *V5* has ended. This can have performance implications within the player: in most cases, syncbase timing will be more efficient than eventbase timing, although the differences may in practice be marginal on desktop players.

- SMIL allows syncbase values to be resolved to points before the begin time or after the end time of a parent element has terminated. While the actual begin of rendering starts when the parent is active, the scheduled element begin time is the time that it would have started rendering if the parent were active. The Eventbase timestamp will always correspond to the moment that things actually begin or end to render — thus, the start of the parent's active duration. In pathological cases, this can make a difference in the behavior of eventbase and syncbase timing.

In general, you should use syncbase timing whenever possible. Eventbase timing should be reserved for dealing with interactive events (such as mouse clicks).

Linking and Interaction

The eventbase timing of SMIL 2.0 was not available in SMIL 1.0. In SMIL 1.0, all forms of interaction were expressed using the link constructs discussed in Chapter 8: *Basic Linking*. From a user's perspective, presentations using linking can often appear to be identical to presentations that base interaction on events. From the perspective of the player, there are major differences.

The following example illustrates interaction via links:

```
...
<par id="P5">
  ...
  <par id="P6">
    <img id="I6" begin="indefinite" src="backgroundIntro.png"
        fill="freeze" ... />
    <video id="V7" begin="I1.begin+3s" src="story.mpg" ... />
  </par>
  ...
  <img id="Y" src="button.png" dur="20s" ... >
    <area href="#I1" />
  </img>
</par>
...
```

Here, the <par> *P5* contains a child <par> *P6* and an image (*Y*). The image will start and be active for 20 seconds. If during this period the user clicks on the image, the begin time of the *I6* element will be resolved. This also activates *V7*. (You should compare this example with the fragment on page 288.)

The main difference between event-based and link-based interaction is that the element that serves as the link target does not need to be active in order for the link to be followed, but the element that depends on an eventbase must be active in order for the event to be sensed.

Note that in the fragment above, the link target was placed in the temporal scope of the link source anchor. This is not necessary. When a link is followed, the presentation time is adjusted so that the temporal moment in the presentation is set to be identical to the moment at which the link target would otherwise have occurred. This seek behavior (either forward or backward) is impossible with events.

Linking, Events and SMIL Timing

As we read in *The Temporal Moment of the Destination Anchor* on page 166, the rules for determining the temporal behavior after a link is activated can be summarized as follows:

- *Destination is already active*: If the destination of the link is already active, the element is effectively restarted. The temporal moments of all of its peer and ancestral elements are also effectively reset based on the begin time of the link destination.

- *Destination is inactive, begin time is resolved*: If the begin time of the destination is resolved (that is, if it has a defined begin time because of explicit or implied timing semantics or if the begin time was resolved based on an earlier traversal of the link), then the presentation seeks to that temporal moment. The temporal state of the peers and ancestors is also realigned to match the temporal moment of the link destination.

- *Destination is inactive, begin time is unresolved*: This is the most complex case. If the destination is not active and if it has an unresolved begin time (it is waiting on an event or it has begin="indefininte" defined), the scheduler has to recurse up the document tree to find the first resolved parent. This time is applied to each of the children until the link destination is reached. The resolved begin time is applied to the link destination and it is saved by the scheduler for potential resuse in resolving this link (or any link that targets a child of the destination) in the future. The pseudo-resolved begin time for the link may be reset if a parent restarts or if some other condition exists that causes a new effective begin time to be defined.

Example 13-1 provides an example of how link timing is processed in SMIL. It shows an outer <par> *X* containing images *button1* and *button2* (these are used as link sources) and an interior <par> *Y*. *Y* contains four media objects: images *I1* and *I2*, a 15-second audio object *A* and a 30-second video object *V*. The <par> *Y* ends when the video *V* ends. We will look at several separate execution paths through this document to highlight linking behavior.

1) The presentation starts. Both images *button1* and *button2* (lines 9 and 12) are started, and both have source anchors activated. The user does not activate either link. At 10 seconds into the presentation, the <par> *Y* on line 2 begins. The video *V* on line 3 starts 5 seconds later, and 7 seconds after *V*

```
1   <par id="X" begin="0">
2     <par id="Y" begin="10s" endsync="V" />
3       <video id="V" begin="5s" src="30sVideo.mpg" ... />
4       <img id="I1" begin="V.begin+7s" ... >
5       <img id="I2" begin="I1.click" .../>
6       <audio id="A" begin="I2.begin+5s" src="15sAudio" .../>
7     </par>
8     <a href="#I1">
9       <img id="button1" dur="90s" ... />
10    </a>
11    <a href="#A">
12      <img id="button2" dur="90s" />
13    </a>
14  </par>
```

Example 13-1. Determining the temporal moment of a link destination.

starts, the image *I1* on line 4 begins. (We are now 0+10+5+7=22 seconds into the presentation.) If the viewer does not click on *I1*, the <par> on line 2 ends when *V* ends without ever seeing image *I2* or hearing audio *A*. The presentation ends after 90 seconds.

2) The presentation starts and executes as in (1). At 25 seconds into the presentation (3 seconds after image *I1* has started), the user click on *I1*. This starts image *I2* on line 5. After 5 seconds (at 30 seconds into the presentation and 20 seconds into video *V*), the audio *A* begins. Since the <par> ends when *V* ends, only 10 seconds of *A* will be heard.

3) The presentation starts. After 5 seconds, the user clicks on *button1* on line 9. This causes a link to be followed that starts the image *I1* on line 4. Since *I1* has a resolved begin time (it is 12 seconds after the start of <par> *Y*), the temporal moment of the presentation is set to the effective begin time of *I1*. This means that the video *V* starts being rendered in its 7th second (because of the start offset of *I1*), and the <par> *X* has its temporal moment set to 22 seconds into its effective 90 second duration. If, 5 seconds later, the user re-clicks *button1*, the time of *X* is reset to 22 seconds (and the times of *I1*, *V* and *Y* are also reset to reflect the start of *I1*).

4) The presentation starts. After 5 seconds, the user clicks on *button2* on line 12. This causes a link to be followed to audio *A*. *A* has an unresolved begin time, so the scheduler will look for the first ancestor with a resolved begin time: this is the <par> *Y*, with a resolved begin of 10 seconds into the presentation. The effective begin time for *A* is set to the beginning of <par> *Y*, which now start together. After 5 seconds of audio *A*, the video *V* begins, and 7 seconds later image *I1*. The start of audio *A* does not cause an inverse event to start *I2* — *I2* will only start if *I1* is selected when it becomes active. The effective begin time of audio *A* is *sticky*: if the user clicks on *button2* again, the most recently-determined begin time for *A* will be used. Note that if the user clicks on *button1* after selecting *button2*, the pseudo-resolved begin time of *A* will no longer be used, since the presentation will now act as though it the link to audio *A* had never been followed.

The implementation of linking behavior is very interesting — and very complex. This complexity does not only need to be managed when the scheduler is implemented, but each time a link is followed. For this reason, it is usually better to use pure events or events combined with the `<excl>` element to define interactive presentations.

13.1.2 Event Support in SMIL Profiles

SMIL 2.0 allows events to be used as values in the `begin` and `end` attribute of timed objects. The event is used in conjunction with eventbase syntax:

```
{eventbase-element.}event-symbol{clock-value-offset}
```

The eventbase reference has the following components:

- *eventbase-element*: this is an element on which the event identified by the event-symbol will take place. The specification of an eventbase element is optional. If an eventbase element is specified, it must be followed by the literal ".".

- *event-symbol*: this is the name of the event to be waited on. If an eventbase element was defined, the event will occur on the named element and the waiting element will be notified via event propagation. If no eventbase element was specified, then the behavior depends on the event. Some events are global (such as *keyEvent*), but most use the element itself as the default syncbase (such as *activateEvent*).

- *clock-value-offset*: This is a SMIL clock value, preceded by a "+" or "-" literal. The clock value specified an offset in time that is used in determining an actual begin or end time relative to the timestamp of the event.

The following list illustrates several forms of eventbase syntax:

```
begin="activateEvent"
begin="X.activateEvent"
begin="X.activateEvent+10s"
begin="X.activateEvent-2s"
```

The first `begin` will resolve once a mouse click occurs in the timing context of the object using the `begin` attribute. The second `begin` resolves when a mouse click is sensed on object X. The third `begin` resolves to 10 seconds after the a mouse click was sensed on object X. The fourth form of `begin` resolves to a time that is two seconds before a mouse click was sensed on object X. Note that actual begin times may be constrained by the parent.

Note that this fourth form is perfectly legal, although it may not always be useful. Consider the following fragment:

```
<video begin="startButton.activateEvent-5s" src="tenSecVideo.mpg" ... />
```

The 10 second video will be considered to have begun 5 seconds before a mouse click on the object *startButton*. We do not know in advance when this will be, but we do know that at the moment the start button was clicked, five seconds of the video should have elapsed. As a result, only the last five seconds of the video will be shown. (This makes some assumptions about the active period of the parent time container, but these are not critical to the example.)

All of our examples use the `begin` attribute; when the `begin` is resolved, the active duration begins with (the first) instance of simple duration. When used with end, the resolved time specifies the end of the object's active duration.

Non-Interactive Event Symbols Supported

Various SMIL profiles support a partially-overlapping set of non-interactive event symbols. While the names of the event symbols for a given event are often the same, this is not always so because of historical reasons.

Table 13-1 identifies events and the associated event symbols. The profiles supporting each event symbol are also specified. For columns with a **M** indication, this means that some mainstream mobile implementations — such as the 3GPP PSS5 (and later) profiles — support these events.

Of the set of support events, the *beginEvent* and *endEvent* trigger at the beginning or end of the actual active duration of an element, while the *repeatEvent/ repeat* event triggers when a element begins the second or higher iteration of its simple duration. The media-related events of XHTML+SMIL may all be triggered by DOM method calls. The *topLayoutOpenEvent* and *topLayoutCloseEvent* events presume support for SMIL's multi-window layout mechanisms.

In case of event conflicts, each profile specifies a priority order for processing events. Interested readers are encouraged to consult the profile definitions.

Event	Event Symbol	Profile		
Actual begin of active duration	beginEvent			H
Actual end of active duration	endEvent	L	M	
Start of repeat of simple duration	repeatEvent			
	repeat			H
A top-level window closes	topLayoutCloseEvent	L		
A top-level window opens	topLayoutOpenEvent			
A media element finishes loading	mediacomplete			
An element loses sync with its timeline	outofsync			
An element regains sync with its timeline	syncrestored			
An element is paused	pause			
A paused element resumes	resume			H
An element reverses temporal direction	reverse			
A seek operation is performed	seek			
An element's timeline is reset	reset			
An invalid SMIL time attribute value is set	timeerror			

Table 13-1. Non-interactive event symbols and profile support.

Interactive Events

Various SMIL profiles support a partially-overlapping set of interactive event symbols. While the names of the event symbols for a given event are often the same, this is not always so because of historical reasons.

Table 13-2 identifies events and the associated event symbols. The profiles supporting each event symbol are also specified.

For the XHTML+SMIL profile, most of the mouse interaction events come from the DOM-2 set of dynamic events. More events are supported than are shown, but we have focused on the overlapping set of event types.

The main authoring constraint for various profiles is the use of the name *click* for XHTML+SMIL events and the *activateEvent* name for the SMIL Language profile and derivatives.

Note that for mobile profiles, the presence of mouse events presupposes the availability of a pointing device or a keyboard.

Event	Event Symbol	Profile		
A mouse click occurs over an element	activateEvent	L	M	
	click			H
The mouse is over an element	inBoundsEvent	L	M	
	mouseover			H
The mouse is moved away from an element	outOfBoundsEvent	L	M	
	mouseout			
A mouse button is pushed down	mousedown			
A mouse button is released	mouseup			H
A mouse moves over the element	mousemove			
Keyboard focus is obtained	focusInEvent	L		
Keyboard focus is lost	focusOutEvent			

Table 13-2. Interactive event symbols and profile support.

13.1.3 Examples of Event Syntax and Semantics

Eventbase syntax can be applied to define the beginning or end of an element's active duration. It cannot be used to define the duration itself or to define other characteristics of the media object.

The following fragment illustrates the use of eventbase syntax as a value for a begin attribute:

```
<video begin="startButton.activateEvent" src="Video1.mpg" ... />
```

The video will start when the user clicks on the media associated with the element whose ID is *startButton*. In order for the element to start, its time container must be active.

Events and the Temporal Scope of Elements

The following fragment illustrates the implications of the temporal scope of the parent on the child element waiting to start:

```
...
<par dur="10s">
  <video begin="startButton.activateEvent" src="Video2.mpg" ... />
</par>
...
```

If the user does not click on the *startButton* element within 10 seconds after the start of the <par>, the element will not be activated. In addition, *startButton* must also be active in order for it to receive a mouse event. Once the video starts, it will not extend the duration of its parent: in the example above, if a video is started 9 seconds after the parent <par> started, only one second of the video will be shown.

Specifying Eventbase Start and End Behavior

Both the start and end of an element may be determined using eventbase timing. Consider the following fragment:

```
...
<par dur="10s">
  <video begin="startButton.activateEvent" end="startButton.activateEvent"
    src="Video2.mpg" ... fill="freeze" />
</par>
...
```

This fragment defines a begin and end condition that use the same event. As specified, the video starts the first time that the start button is clicked. (The event is passed to the begin attribute whenever an element is inactive or when it is running and able to accept restarts; in these cases, the end attribute is ignored.) The next time that the *startButton* element is clicked, the video will not end — this is not because of the multiple instances of *activateEvent*, but because of the restart characteristics of the video element: since restart behavior is set to the default of always, the second mouse click will restart the video.

In order to avoid unwanted restart behavior, the toggle function should be implemented as follows:

```
...
<par dur="10s">
  <video begin="startButton.activateEvent" end="startButton.activateEvent"
    src="Video2.mpg" restart="whenNotActive" fill="freeze" ... />
</par>
...
```

Now, the first occurrence of the event will be used by the begin attribute. The second instance will go to the end attribute because the begin attribute is not waiting for events when its media is already active. (For more on restart behavior, please see *Restart Behavior* on page 341 of Chapter 14: *Advanced SMIL Timing Attributes*.)

Continuing with the toggle example, assume that we had written the fragment as follows:

```
...
<par dur="10s">
  <video begin="activateEvent" end="activateEvent"
    src="Video2.mpg" restart="whenNotActive" fill="freeze" ... />
</par>
...
```

Here, the eventbase no longer references an external element but the video itself. In the SMIL 2.0 Language profile, it is not possible to click on an element that has not started yet. As a result, the video will never start, since it will never receive a mouse event. This problem can be avoided by defining multiple begin conditions on an element.

Quick Tip

The SMIL timing model explicit states that the same event (such as a mouse click) will never be used to satisfy both a begin and end condition on the same element.

Mixing Eventbase and Scheduled Timing

Consider the following fragment, which further refines our on-going example:

```
...
<par dur="10s">
  <video begin="0; activateEvent" end="activateEvent"
    src="Video2.mpg" restart="whenNotActive" fill="freeze" ... />
</par>
...
```

When the <par> begins, the video element starts because it explicitly defines that a start at 0 seconds should occur. Once the video is active, it can receive mouse clicks. The first mouse click will terminate the element. Any following mouse click will restart the element.

Note that in all of these examples, the video remains visible after it is stopped because of the fill="freeze" behavior. The freeze behavior may be the default behavior or it may need to be defined explicitly, depending on other attributes on the element. For more information on fill behavior semantics, please see *Fill Behavior Control* on page 328 of Chapter 14: *Advanced SMIL Timing Attributes*.

Using Eventbase Timing to End the Active Duration

Eventbase timing, when applied to the end attribute, ends the active duration of an element, not its simple duration. As one final example, consider the fragment at the end of this paragraph. When the end attribute is triggered by the mouse click, the active duration of the entire element ends. This does not start a new repeat cycle, all repeat cycles end. If it is restarted by a mouse click, the entire repeat cycle starts as if this were the first time it was played. (The `<par>` timing will still dominate.)

```
...
<par dur="60s">
  <video repeatCount="3" begin="0s;activateEvent" end="activateEvent"
    src="Video2.mpg" restart="whenNotActive" fill="freeze" ... />
</par>
...
```

13.2 Selective Time Composition

The introduction of eventbase timing not only has implications for the begin and end times of media objects and time containers, it also provides a framework for the introduction of new, interaction-based time containers into the SMIL 2.0 specification. SMIL supports two new elements for what is technically called *a-temporal object composition*: compositing objects based on interaction rather than on scheduled timing. The two elements are the `<excl>` or exclusive time container, and the `<priorityClass>` element for supporting preemptive scheduling of alternative content.

This section describes both new elements and their associated attributes. We start with a general section on integrating event-based timing into SMIL temporal framework and then consider the composition and structure of the elements and attributes. We close this section with a series of examples.

13.2.1 Understanding Selective Composition

The standard SMIL 2.0 time containers are `<seq>` and `<par>`. Children of a `<seq>` have the property that they are evaluated sequentially based on simple begin time constraints. Children of the `<par>` have the property that they are all evaluated based on a common timeline. For many applications, these two containers provide a comprehensive foundation for structuring media presentations. For some applications, where selectivity in content is important, these two containers require careful authoring and structuring to meet all presentation needs. In SMIL 2.0, interaction-based timing is made significantly easier by the introduction of the `<excl>` container.

The `<excl>` is an advanced time composition container that has the property that at most one of its children is active at any time. If a child is active and a sibling becomes active, it causes the original element to either *terminate* or *pause*; the terminate/pause choice depends on the setting of various attributes on the `<priorityClass>`.

The use of the `<excl>` element is illustrated in Figure 13-1. Figure 13-1(a) shows the main frame of a presentation. Selecting any of the small images in the sidebar will cause a media object to play in the main window. Two options are shown: if the young girl is selected, a collection of objects about her is presented in the main window, as shown in Figure 13-1(b); if the young boy is

| (a) | (b) | (c) |

Figure 13-1. Interaction-based structuring of a presentation.

selected, a collection of assets associated with him are presented in the main window, as shown in Figure 13-1(c).

As shown in Example 13-2, the presentation in Figure 13-1 is structured as a background image played in parallel with four thumbnail images and an <excl> container. The <excl> contains four simple video objects and an interior <par> that contains a sequence of images and videos that are shown together with some background audio. The begin times of each of the simple videos on lines 25-27 and the <par> are tied to mouse click events on the image thumbnails; when any of them are selected, the associated content plays. If con-

```
1  <smil xmlns="http://www.w3.org/2001/SMIL20/Language">
2   <head>
3    <layout>
4     ...
5    </layout>
6   </head>
7   <body>
8    <par id="Birthday">
9     <par id="MenuImages" dur="indefinite">
10      <img id="Fls" region="Menu" src="Fls.jpg" ... />
11      <img id="Wls" region="Menu" src="Wls.jpg" ... />
12      <img id="Als" region="Menu" src="Als.jpg" ... />
13      <img id="FBTs" region="Menu" src="FBTs.jpg" ... />
14      <excl id="Videos" dur="indefinite" fillDefault="freeze">
15       <video begin="Fls.activateEvent" region="Video" src="Fz3.avi"/>
16       <video begin="Wls.activateEvent" region="Video" src="Wz3.avi"/>
17       <video begin="Wls.activateEvent" region="Video" src="Az3.avi"/>
18       <par begin="FBTs.activateEvent">
19        <seq>
20         <img id="FBT" region="Video" dur="6s" src="FBT.jpg"/>
21         <video id="BTz3" region="Video" src="BTz3.avi" />
22         <img id="FBP" region="Video" dur="10s" src="FBP.jpg"/>
23         <video id="BPz3" region="Video" src="BPz3.avi"/>
24        </seq>
25        <audio id="Music" region="audio" src="Ballgame.mp3"/>
26       </par>
27      </excl>
28     </par>
29     <img id="BkgdImg" region="bkgd_image" fill="freeze" src="Back3s.jpg"/>
30    </par>
31   </body>
32  </smil>
```

Example 13-2. Using the <excl> in a presentation.

tent was already active, it is replaced with new content. This is an example of (video) jukebox interactivity.

We would like the outer structure of this presentation to be static: whenever nothing is played, the thumbnails and the background image is shown. We also want the <excl> to be active indefinitely, since the user should have the opportunity of selecting all of the content available in whatever order the viewer chooses. In order to facilitate this, both the duration of the *MenuImages* <par> on line 9 and the *Videos* <excl> have *indefinite* durations defined. The most important initial thing to notice about this presentation is that the children of a <par> may be media content or other SMIL timing or content control elements.

In the *Birthday* presentation, the viewer is given the opportunity to select one of the four content groups, but no default content is activated at the start of the presentation. We can change this by re-coding the begin condition on line 15:

```
15    <video begin="0s; F1s.activateEvent" region="Video" src="Fz3.avi"/>
```

By mixing scheduled and eventbase timing, the author can define that this video element will start at a particular scheduled time in addition to any event-related begin time.

The scheduled timing does not need to be at the beginning of the exclusive element. In the following fragment, an <excl> contains three children, all of whom start at scheduled periods and some of whom also start based on interactive or non-interactive events:

```
<smil xmlns="http://www.w3.org/2001/SMIL20/Language">
  ...
    <par id="MenuImages" dur="indefinite">
      <img id="F1s" region="Menu" src="F1s.jpg" ... />
      <excl id="mixedBag" dur="indefinite" fillDefault="freeze">
        <video id="Va" begin="12s" src="Fz3.avi" ... />
        <video id="Vb" begin="5s; F1s.activateEvent" src="Wz3.avi" ... />
        <video id="Vc" begin="20s; Va.endEvent" src="Az3.avi" ... />
      </excl>
    </par>
  ...
</smil>
```

When the <excl> starts, nothing happens for the first 5 seconds. At this point, unless there has been a mouse click on the image *F1s*, the video *Vb* begins. Next, at 12s into the active duration of the <excl>, the video *Va* begins. At the conclusion of *Va*, *Vc* starts — unless *Va* lasts longer than 8 seconds; if so, it is cut off by the start of *Vc*. At any point, a user may initiate the start of *Vb*. Once *Vb* ends, none of the other elements will be able to be played, since all have begin times that are not related to user activity. Note that the order of elements within the <excl> is not important (except when a timing conflict occurs, in which the order in the <excl> determines the play order).

In all of the examples of the <excl> shown above, the content is started by scheduled or eventbase timing. The <excl> also allows its contents to be started by syncbase timing or by containing the target link. The main semantic contribution of the <excl> is that only one of its children can be active at any moment. The way in which content gets activated is less important than this temporal property.

The default behavior of an `<excl>` is that the activation of new content will terminate any existing content. The existing content may also be paused instead of terminated by wrapping the content in a priority class and then defining pause semantics for members of that class:

```
<excl id="mixedBag" dur="indefinite" fillDefault="freeze">
  <priorityClass peers="pause">
    <video id="Va" ... />
    <video id="Vb" ... />
    <video id="Vc" ... />
  </priorityClass>
</excl>
```

Whenever a peer within the priority class starts, it will now pause the content being displayed. When the new content completes, the paused material is resumed. A pause stack is defined, so that multiple levels of interrupts can be defined without any loss of presentation context.

Multiple priority classes may be defined, each grouping a logical collection of one or more children. Each priority class may define not only how its peers react to new content, but also to the way that content in higher or lower classes impact the rendering behavior of the content. (We will give examples when describing the `pauseDisplay` attribute on page 304.)

It is important to realize that the priority class elements are time transparent. This means that they define a logical collection of content, but not a temporal collection of content. In other words, a priority class is never scheduled, but only the children of priority classes are scheduled. The only impact that the priority class has is an ability to define a relative priority of content — such as defining if lower priority content can interrupt higher priority content — and the stop or pause behavior of its peers.

The `<excl>` element may be nested. The `<excl>` is not time transparent; it accepts all standard SMIL timing elements.

One of the most important side-effects of using the `<excl>` container is that it makes timeline-based authoring systems obsolete. It is impossible to draw the temporal relationships among the elements in Example 13-2 using a conventional timeline. Only a combination of structure-based authoring and flexible timing representation can express the functionality of presentations that use eventbase timing and the `<excl>` container. Figure 13-2 shows how the GRiNS Editor uses structure to identify how an exclusive element can be modelled. The purple boxes represent the `<excl>` element; each of the children are shown as timed element, but the timing of the entire `<excl>` is a-temporal.

13.2.2 Elements for Selective Composition

The SMIL 2.0 *ExclTimeContainers* module defines two elements for the selective presentation on one of their children during a presentation: `<excl>` and `<priorityClass>`. The `<excl>` element (pronounced *exclusive*) is a full SMIL

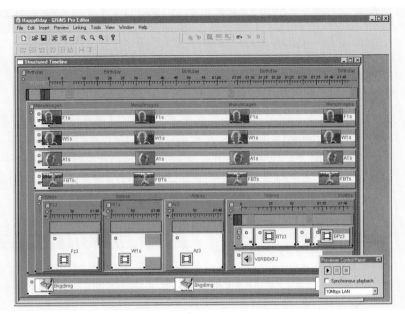

Figure 13-2. Structured timeline used with the `<excl>` element.

2.0 time container when supported by a profile. It supports all of the attributes of other SMIL 2.0 time containers. The `<priorityClass>` element is a content priority structuring element; it may only be used inside an `<excl>` element.

Element: `<excl>`

The structure of the `<excl>` element is given in Table 13-3. The `<excl>` is a full SMIL 2.0 time container that is similar in structure to the `<par>` element with the exception that is has the additional semantic that at most one of its children may be active at any time. (It is not an error condition if none of the children are active.)

The `<excl>` does not require any special-purpose attributes. It accepts all of the general timing, endsync, media description content control and core attributes associated with other SMIL time containers.

The parent of an `<excl>` may be another `<excl>` — that is, `<excl>` containers may be fully nested — or other SMIL 2.0 time containers. The `<excl>` may be wrapped in a link anchor via the `<a>` element and it may be one of the children of a `<switch>` construct. The parent of an embedded `<excl>` may also be an ancestor `<excl>`'s `<priorityClass>` element.

The children of an `<excl>` may be SMIL time containers (except for `<body>`), media objects or animation elements. The children may also be `<switch>` elements or `<a>` link anchors. The `<priorityClass>` element may also be a child of the `<excl>`, but in this case *all* children must be `<priorityClass>` elements.

When an `<excl>` starts, it provides a default syncbase for all of its children. That is, all children have their timing defined by default to be relative to the start of the `<excl>` element. Unlike a `<par>` or `<seq>` container, the default begin time of the children of an `<excl>` is not *0* but *indefininte*. This has implications for the duration of an `<excl>` object: since all of the children have unresolved active durations at the start (because of their indefinite begin times), an `<excl>` without an explicit duration will end as soon as it begins (unless endsync="all"). For this reason, make sure that at least one of the children has a scheduled begin or that the `<excl>` itself has either an explicit duration or that it has a duration of indefinite. (See the examples on page 305 for more details.)

The primary uses for the `<excl>` element are to support random-access jukebox functionality or to serve as an aid in providing audio or text captions.

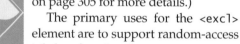

`<excl>`		Profiles
attributes	general timing	
	endsync	
	media description	
	region	L H
	test	
	core	
parents	`<body>`	L H
parents & children	`<priorityClass>`	
	`<seq>`, `<par>`	
	`<excl>`	L H
	`<switch>`	
	`<a>`	
children	media object	
	animation	L H

Table 13-3. Structure of the `<excl>` element

By default, when any child of an `<excl>` is activated, it causes any other active child to stop playing. This default behavior can be modified with the `<priorityClass>` element, described next.

Element: `<priorityClass>`

The structure of the `<priorityClass>` element is given in Table 13-4. An author can use the `<priorityClass>` to group children of an `<excl>` into content collections; these collections may then have a behavior defined that is applied to the children when they are preempted by other content.

The `<priorityClass>` accepts the media description, content control and core SMIL attributes. They also accept four new attributes: pauseDisplay, peers, higher, and lower. These new attributes are described below.

The only legal parent element for the `<priorityClass>` element is `<excl>`.

The legal children for `<priorityClass>` are other SMIL time containers (including an embedded `<excl>`), plus media, animation, linking and content control elements.

The `<priorityClass>` element does not define an explicit priority for its child elements. The priority is determined by its placement in the source file relative to the parent `<excl>`. Therefore, priorities cannot be animated or changed at runtime.

The `<priorityClass>` is *time transparent*. It simply defines child behavior if and when they are preempted. It does not have any begin, duration or end timing semantics: only the children of the priority class have temporal attributes.

The `<priorityClass>` element uses three attributes to assign behavior to its children when they are preempted by other content in the `<excl>`: `peers`, which determines the behavior among children in the same priority class; `higher`, which determines the behavior of children in the priority class when they are preempted by content in a higher priority class; and `lower`, which determines the behavior of children in the priority class when they are preempted by content in a lower priority class. In all cases, the behavior for the element active at the time the preempt takes place determines the pause/stop behavior and not the newly scheduled element.

`<priorityClass>`		Profiles	
attributes	peers		
	lower		
	higher		
	pauseDisplay	L L	H
	media description		
	test		
	core		
parents & children	`<excl>`	L	H
children	`<seq>`, `<par>`		
	`<switch>`		
	`<a>`	L	H
	media object		
	animation		

Table 13-4. Structure of the `<priorityClass>` element

If a child within a priority class is paused, one additional attribute can be used to control when the paused element is visible: `pauseDisplay` can be used to remove an item from view. (In practice, newly started elements will often overlay the paused element, but this is not always the case; this is especially true if SMIL Layout is not used.)

13.2.3 Attributes for Selective Composition

The `<priorityClass>` element defines several new attributes: `peers`, `higher`, `lower` and `pauseDisplay`.

Attribute: peers

The `peers` attribute is used within a `<priorityClass>` element to define how an active object will respond when it is preempted by another member of the same priority class. The legal values are:

- *stop*: The active element will stop (terminate) if another child in the same priority class begins. This is the default behavior for the priority class.
- *pause*: The active element will pause if another child in the same priority class begins. The paused element is placed on a pause stack; it will resume when no other child of higher priority is active.

- *defer*: The active element will continue to play and the to-be-started element will wait until it completes. In effect, the new element is placed on the pause stack at the beginning of its active duration.

- *never*: The active element will continue to play and the to-be-started element is ignored.

When an element is blocked because of the *never* value, it is not considered to have started or ended. No *beginEvent* or *endEvent* will be propogated.

Attribute: higher

The higher attribute is used within a <priorityClass> element to define how an active object will respond when it is preempted by a member of a higher priority class. The legal values are:

- *stop*: The active element will stop (terminate) if another child in a higher priority class begins.

- *pause*: The active element will pause if another child in a higher priority class begins. The paused element is placed on a pause stack; it will resume when no other child of higher priority is active. This is the default behavior for the children within a lower priority class.

Note that the default value for higher is different from the default value for peers. This is done to provide convenient defaults that match typical use cases.

Attribute: lower

The lower attribute is used within a <priorityClass> element to define how an active object will respond when a child of a lower priority class attempts to start. The legal values are:

- *defer*: The active element will continue to play and the to-be-started element will wait until it completes. In effect, the new element is placed on the pause stack at the beginning of its active duration. This is the default for the lower attribute.

- *never*: The active element will continue to play and the to-be-started element is ignored.

Children that exhibit defer behavior do not propagate a *beginEvent* until they actually start.

Attribute: pauseDisplay

The pauseDisplay attribute lets an author define whether a paused child is visible while it is paused and it defines how paused elements that remain visible respond to mouse events. The legal values are:

- *hide*: Do not display the element while it is paused.

- *show*: Display the element while it is paused and allow it to respond to mouse events from within its paused state. This is the default value for the pauseDisplay attribute.

- *disable*: Display the element while it is paused but disable any response to mouse events.

The pauseDisplay attribute only applies to priority classes that have a peer value of *paused* or a higher value of *paused* and then only to those elements within the priority class that actually exhibit pause behavior. It does not apply to elements that are paused for some other reason within a SMIL document.

13.2.4 Examples of Selective Temporal Composition

This section provides examples of <excl> and <priorityClass> behavior. The examples are organized by general use cases of the <excl> element.

Supporting Simple Jukebox Behavior Using Events

The fragment in Example 13-3 illustrates a simple event-based jukebox. Three

```
<smil xmlns="http://www.w3.org/2001/SMIL20/Language">
   ...
     <par id="MenuImages" dur="indefinite">
       <img id="btn1" ... />
       <img id="btn2" ... />
       <img id="btn3" ... />
       <excl id="selectMe" dur="indefinite" fillDefault="freeze">
         <video id="V1" begin="btn1.activateEvent" ... />
         <video id="V2" begin="btn2.activateEvent" ... />
         <video id="V3" begin="btn3.activateEvent" ... />
       </excl>
     </par>
   ...
</smil>
```

Example 13-3. An event-based jukebox.

images are used as buttons and three videos are placed in an <excl>. When a viewer selects one of the button images, the associated content element starts. If during play another button is selected, the new content will replace the earlier started video.

Since this example illustrates the basic functionality of the <excl> container, we can also use it to explain some of the consequences of using <excl>'s in a presentation. First, consider what would happen if we replace the <excl> container with a <par> element:

```
   ...
     <par id="selectMe" dur="indefinite" fillDefault="freeze">
       <video id="V1" begin="btn1.activateEvent" ... />
       <video id="V2" begin="btn2.activateEvent" ... />
       <video id="V3" begin="btn3.activateEvent" ... />
     </par>
   ...
```

(Everything else in the presentation is the same as in Example 13-3.) When the <par> is encountered, it is started and, because of the indefinite duration, it remains active even though none it its content is active. When a user clicks on a button, the associated video content will start. This is similar to the <excl>. When the video ends, the <par> continues to be active; this is also similar to the

<excl>. The difference between the <par> and the <excl> comes when a user selects an image button while another video is active; the new video will start and will play in addition to the first video started. This situation can be avoided by attaching explicit end conditions to the children of the <par>:

```
    ...
    <par id="selectMe" dur="indefinite" fillDefault="freeze">
      <video id="V1" begin="btn1.activateEvent"
        end="V2.beginEvent; V3.beginEvent" ... />
      <video id="V2" begin="btn2.activateEvent"
        end="V1.beginEvent; V3.beginEvent" ... />
      <video id="V3" begin="btn3.activateEvent"
        end="V1.beginEvent; V2.beginEvent" ... />
    </par>
    ...
```

Now, each child begins on a mouse click for the associated button and ends when another element starts. Thus, a <par> can model the default behavior of <excl>. For non-default behavior (that is, when we want to have the <excl>'s pause and continue semantics), a <par> cannot be used.

Supporting Simple Jukebox Behavior Using Events

Before moving to other aspects of <excl> behavior, we first re-code Example 13-3 so that it uses link behavior instead of event behavior to start the child elements. This is illustrated in Example 13-4. While most of the structure of the elements is the same, there are two important differences. First, the <excl> is no longer a child of the image parent time container. When using link based activation, the <excl> may be placed anywhere in the presentation. It does not need to be active when the source anchor is selected. Second, the children of the <excl> have no explicit begin attribute. As a result, they exhibit the default begin="indefinite" behavior.

For equivalent behavior, an <excl> that uses event-based behavior often provides an easier authoring interface than an <excl> that is based on link

```
<smil xmlns="http://www.w3.org/2001/SMIL20/Language">
    ...
    <par id="MenuImages" dur="indefinite">
      <a href="#V1">
        <img id="btn1" ... />
      </a>
      <a href="#V2">
        <img id="btn2" ... />
      </a>
      <a href="#V2">
        <img id="btn3" ... />
      </a>
    </par>
    ...
    <excl id="selectMe" dur="indefinite" fillDefault="freeze">
      <video id="V1" ... />
      <video id="V2" ... />
      <video id="V3" ... />
    </excl>
</smil>
```

Example 13-4. A link-based jukebox.

behavior. Note that both link-based and event-based activation can be combined in the same <excl>; this is also true for syncbase timing.

Determining the Duration of an <excl>

The active duration of an <excl> is determined in the same way as is done for a <par>: if an explicit dur is defined, this is used, otherwise the duration is set to the active duration of its longest child. (In other words, the default value for endsync is last.) As with a <par>, children that have unresolved durations do not contribute to the active duration of the <excl>. Consider this fragment:

```
<excl>
   <video id="V1" begin="btn1.activateEvent" ... />
   ...
   <video id="Vn" begin="btnn.activateEvent" ... />
</excl>
```

A set of videos is defined in an <excl>. The start times of the videos are all based on events. As a result, all of the timing is unresolved. This means that the effective duration of the <excl> is 0 seconds, which in turn means that the <excl> will end as soon as it begins. Unless someone can click the mouse very quickly, no video will be shown!

The situation can be avoided by explicitly adding a duration to the <excl>. If an appropriate duration exists, it can be used. If you don't know (or don't care) how long the <excl> should last, you can always use dur="indefinite". A potential problem with using indefinite is that the <excl> will remain active for a period that cannot be determined by the author. It is often useful to identify a child as the explicit end of the <excl> by using the endsync attribute:

```
<excl dur="indefinite" endsync="Vn">
   <video id="V1" begin="btn1.activateEvent" ... />
   ...
   <video id="Vn" begin="btnn.activateEvent" ... />
</excl>
```

In this example, the duration is set to *indefinite* and an element is identified as an explicit end. Any child may be used as the endsync target.

Using Scheduled Begin Times in an <excl>

One of the motivating cases for the <excl> was as a container that could integrate audio captions to video material. In this use, a video is played with its audio component, but when complex concepts are discussed — or when visual material in the video is displayed but not described in the video's audio track — an additional bit of audio commentary could be enabled.

The use of the <excl> for audio captions is given in Figure 13-3. This figure combines a number of timing constructs to provide an adaptive presentation. When the presentation begins, a video element is started on line 9 *if* audio descriptions have been turned off. (Thus, no audio descriptions are wanted.) In parallel, an <excl> is evaluated. The <excl> contains one priority class with four children: one <par> on line 12 and three audio objects on lines 16-18. The

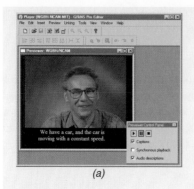 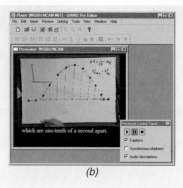

(a)   (b)

```
1  <smil xmlns="http://www.w3.org/2001/SMIL20/Language">
2   <head>
3    <layout>
4     ...
5    </layout>
6   </head>
7   <body>
8    <par>
9     <video src="lewin.rm" systemAudioDesc="off" .../>
10    <excl dur="indefinite">
11     <priorityClass peers="pause">
12      <par begin="0">
13       <video src="lewin.rm" systemAudioDesc="on" .../>
14       <video src="lewinCaps.rt" systemCaptions="on" .../>
15      </par>
16      <audio begin="34.5s" src="mrkr.wav" systemAudioDesc="on" .../>
17      <audio begin="50s" src="slashes.wav" systemAudioDesc="on" .../>
18      <audio begin="61s" src="deltat.wav" systemAudioDesc="on" .../>
19     </priorityClass>
20    </excl>
21   </par>
22  </body>
23 </smil>
```

Figure 13-3. Defining audio captions using the <excl> element.
(Media assets © 1998 M.I.T.)

<par> on line 12 has a scheduled begin that starts the child at 0 seconds after the <excl> starts. The children of the <par> each start at time 0 as well. If the audio descriptions and captions were both requested, these two elements will play. Note that here, two media objects are active in the <excl>, but since these are both the children of a single top-level element in the <excl>, this is not a violation of the single-active-child rule. If audio descriptions were not wanted but captions were requested, then only the captions element would be active. If neither captions nor audio descriptions were requested, nothing would be played in this <par>. Figure 13-3(a) shows both captions and the video being active.

At 34.5 seconds after the <excl> starts, the audio component on line 16 will interrupt the <par> on line 12. Since the priority class defines peers to pause other peers, the video and captions will freeze while the audio description

takes place. This audio description gives extra information about the diagram, as shown in Figure 13-3(b), and when it ends the paused video reactivates.

The example is constructed in such a way that any combination of system description and captions setting will yield a useful combination.

Setting the Pause Behavior

As noted, the default behavior within an exclusive is to terminate the active child when a new child starts. This is because the default value for the priority class settings is stop. An <excl> with a priority class defined that exhibits this behavior is shown in the following fragment:

```
<excl dur="indefinite" >
  <priorityClass peers="stop" >
   ...
  </priorityClass>
</excl>
```

The peers in the priority class will stop each other when a new peer starts. The <excl> element takes this as the default because it is assumed that this will be the typical use case.

The default behavior can be changed to other values for peers. For example, if we want to pause an active child when a successor is started, we can use:

```
<excl dur="indefinite" >
  <priorityClass peers="pause" >
   ...
  </priorityClass>
</excl>
```

If several priority classes are defined, then the relative behavior of active elements can be defined as follows:

```
<excl dur="indefinite" >
  <priorityClass peers="pause" lower="defer">
   ...
  </priorityClass>
  <priorityClass peers="stop" higher="pause">
   ...
  </priorityClass>
</excl>
```

In this fragment, any peers of the higher level priority class are paused when a new element starts and any request by a lower-level element are deferred until the higher-level element completes. Peers in the lower-level priority are stopped when new elements begin, but these peers are paused when higher level content starts.

Using pauseDisplay to Disable Interaction

Figure 13-4 illustrates a fragment containing two peer videos that are placed in one priority class. The peers attribute has been set to *pause*. The video objects render into non-overlapping regions. Each video starts when an associated button has been pushed. Since each video has a link anchor defined, we want to make sure that only the link associated with the active video is enabled. The

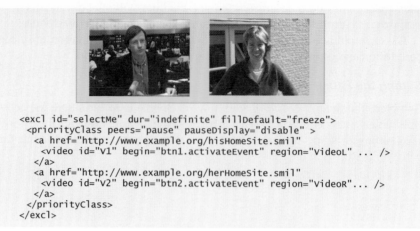

```
<excl id="selectMe" dur="indefinite" fillDefault="freeze">
  <priorityClass peers="pause" pauseDisplay="disable" >
   <a href="http://www.example.org/hisHomeSite.smil"
     <video id="V1" begin="btn1.activateEvent" region="VideoL" ... />
   </a>
   <a href="http://www.example.org/herHomeSite.smil"
     <video id="V2" begin="btn2.activateEvent" region="VideoR"... />
   </a>
  </priorityClass>
</excl>
```

Figure 13-4. Using the pauseDisplay attribute.

pauseDisplay attribute allows the paused video to remain visible without keeping its link active.

13.3 SMIL 2.0 Timing Model, Revisited

In this and the previous chapters we have introduced many of the advanced concepts used in defining the SMIL 2.0 element activation. In order to put all of these concepts into a common framework, this section provides a comprehensive overview of the SMIL timing model. It concludes with a number of interesting examples.

13.3.1 Element Activation, Duration and Termination

In many ways, there are only three topics of interest when it comes to timed elements: determining when they start, determining how long they last and determining when they end. This section considers all three of these aspects.

Timed Element Activation

A timed element starts its active duration when any one of a number of begin conditions have been met. These conditions can be explicitly defined or they can be inferred from the timing values of the element's parents or other ancestors.

The cardinal rule for determining when and *if* an element gets activated is that no element can become active if its parent is inactive. (And no element can remain active after is parent becomes inactive.) This applies to all SMIL timing behavior: event-based and schedule-based.

The default rules for determining when elements begin depend on the type of element and the type of the parent time container. In order to clarify SMIL behavior, we discuss how each container element is processed separately.

Media objects. A media element gets activated based on the characteristics of the parent time container unless modified by an explicit begin attribute. The begin attribute may specify that a media object will begin based on syncbase, eventbase of linking behavior. Continuous media items, such as audio and video, start by default at the beginning of the object unless modified by a clip-Begin or media marker attribute (if allowed).

The <seq> container. A `<seq>` container will start at the temporal moment defined by its parent time container, modified by the value of the begin attribute. The `<seq>` may begin based on scheduled or event timing. The sequential nature of the `<seq>` container may never be violated by other SMIL timing constructs, by interactive behavior (either link based or event based) or media timing on a begin condition.

Of all of SMIL's time containers, the `<seq>` provides the most restrictive set of begin rules for its children:

- The implicit start time for each of the children of a `<seq>` is the end of its predecessor element in the `<seq>`. For the first element, the implicit start time is the beginning of the `<seq>`.

- Children of a `<seq>` may use only a restricted set of values in their begin attribute: only a single, non-negative temporal offset is allowed. This means that a list of (multiple) start times, event timing, syncbase offsets, media marker offsets, accesskey values and wall-clock times are not allowed. The begin time may not be set to *indefinite* and the element may not contain a repeat value. Disallowing media marker offsets is probably an error in the SMIL specification, since media markers provide indexes into the media object rather than the SMIL schedule, but given the limited use of media marker timing, this is probably not a major issue.

The advantage of the `<seq>` (from a time model perspective) is that it is relatively easy to calculate the effective begin moments of the children. The effective begin of the `<seq>` itself is as complex as any other SMIL time container.

The <par> container. A `<par>` container will start at the temporal moment defined by its parent time container, modified by the value of the begin attribute. The `<par>` may begin based on scheduled or event timing. The begin time may be a wall-clock value or expressed via a syncbase relationship. The begin time may also have the value indefinite. The parallel nature of the `<par>` container does not mean that all of the elements are active at the same time, but that all of its children are bounded by the scope of the `<par>`'s active duration.

The children of a `<par>` all have a default start time that is equal to the syncbase (the beginning) of the `<par>`. The children of a `<par>` may further make unrestricted use of SMIL temporal semantics to define their begin times. The only operational restriction is that no content may be rendered before the start or after the end of the active duration of the `<par>`. If a continuous media element is scheduled to begin before the start of the parent `<par>`, only that portion that falls within the temporal scope of the `<par>`'s active duration will be rendered.

The **<excl> *container*.** An <excl> container will start at the temporal moment defined by its parent time container, modified by the value of the begin attribute. The begin time determination for the <excl> is identical to that of the <par>. The critical difference between a <par> and an <excl> is that at most one child of an <excl> may be active at any one time. Nothing may violate this condition. Under certain circumstances, inactive children of an <excl> may be in a paused state and may respond to certain UI events. For a temporal perspective, they are not active during these periods.

Unlike the children of a <par>, the children have a default begin time of *indefinite*. This means that, unless the time gets resolved during the active duration of the <excl>, they will never begin. The children of an <excl> may make unrestricted SMIL temporal semantics to define their begin times. As with the <par>, no content may be rendered before the start of the active duration of the <excl>. If a continuous media element is scheduled to begin before the start of the parent <excl>, only that portion that falls within the temporal scope of the <excl>'s active duration will be rendered.

Dealing with cycles and unknown begin times. It is possible to define a cycle by having the begin times of a collection of objects depend entirely on the begin or end of each other. In these cases, it will be impossible to ever define a resolved begin time. Usually, none of the elements in the cycle will be activated; a SMIL player may reject to start a presentation if a cycle is detected.

If begin times are unresolved, they cannot be used to build a timing instance for the object. Elements may become resolved during the active duration of their parent, but if they are not resolved, they are ignored for timing purposes.

Timed Element Duration

The duration of timed objects depends on several factors: the media-defined duration of an object, the explicit duration given to an object by SMIL's timing attributes and the number of times (or length of time) that an object repeats. Throughout the book we have used the terms *intrinsic duration, simple duration* and *active duration* for these concepts.

Under certain circumstances, elements will not have a known duration. This can be because they have end conditions that potentially extend or limit a duration which cannot be resolved when timing calculations are made. Other objects will have unknown begin times; if you don't know when an object will begin, you will not know how long it will last. (You may know how long it will last if it ever gets the chance to start, but this is useless information for a scheduler — it is rather like knowing exactly what you would do with a large sum of money that may never actually arrive.)

In order to create a runtime schedule, SMIL needs to define an *implicit duration* of an object. Each time container has a set of rules for determining its implicit duration.

Media objects. The implicit duration of a media object is equal to the intrinsic duration, modified by any clipBegin/clipEnd interval or media marker timing. The implicit duration of discrete media is 0 seconds. The default implicit duration of a continuous media object is the intrinsic duration of that object.

The <seq> container. The implicit duration of a <seq> container is the sum of the active durations of its children. If any of the children of a <seq> has a duration of indefinite, the implicit duration of the <seq> is indefinite.

The <par> container. The implicit duration of a <par> depends on the setting of the endsync attribute. By default, the implicit duration of a <par> is the active duration of its longest child plus any resolved begin timing offsets.

The <excl> container. The implicit duration of an <excl> is the same as a <par>, with this difference: the default begin time of the children of the <excl> is *indefinite*, which means that none of them (by default) contribute to the <excl>'s timing. Thus the effective implicit duration is 0. If a resolved begin time exists for any children, this time is used to determine the implicit duration. Since the <excl> supports the endsync attribute, the default implicit duration is the duration of the longest element plus any resolved begin time offset.

Timed Element Termination

For timing purposes, an element will end at the end of its active duration. An element may persist beyond the end of its active duration if it has an effective fill period behavior defined other than remove. During this period it is not active for purposes of the SMIL timing model, but it may be perceived as being active because of it response to UI events.

The end time of an element may be resolved or unresolved. Unresolved end times result from event-based end specifications that have not yet occurred. The end of an element may also be specified to be indefinite. While it is convenient to associate indefinite with forever, a more correct definition of indefinite is a time that will be determined by another context. In terms of timing calculations, a value of indefinite is considered to be greater than any resolved value, and a value of unresolved is considered to be greater than indefinite.

13.3.2 Determining Schedules

The primary role of the scheduler is to determine the active duration of an object and to use that active duration to influence the active duration of any parents and children. There are two cardinal rules that must be taken into account in determining schedules:

1) An element without a resolved begin time cannot be scheduled, even if its duration is resolved. Elements without resolved begin times either do not participate in the scheduling computation or they may keep their parent active until their begin times are resolved.

2) An element with an end time of *indefinite* will result in an active duration of *indefinite*.

Explicit Value of dur Attribute	Implicit Element Duration	Explicit end Attribute	Simple Duration
unspecified	(not used)	specified (and no repeats specified)	indefinite
dur="clock-value"	(not used)	(not used)	clock value
dur="indefinite"	(not used)	(not used)	indefinite
unspecified	resolved	(not used)	implicit element duration
unspecified	unresolved	(not used)	unresolved
dur="media"	resolved or unresolved	(not used)	implicit element duration

Table 13-5. Computing the simple duration.

In addition to the these rules, the SMIL 2.0 specification provides a table that can be used to determine the active duration of an object. Table 13-5 is based on the information in the SMIL specification.[2]

We will now consider computing the active duration in two cases: when no repeat behavior is defined and when repeat behavior is defined. (This distinction is made to simplify the discussion for the easy cases.)

Computing an Active Duration Ignoring Repeat Behavior

We can now determine the active duration for elements, using the following steps:

1) If a begin or end time for an element (including the children) is unresolved, the active duration is considered to be *indefinite*. Note that only elements that have unresolved eventbase start/end times or elements with cyclic behavior timing dependencies will have unresolved begin or end times.

2) Otherwise, if an explicit and resolved end time other than *indefinite* is specified but no dur attribute was specified, then the active duration is the time value obtained by subtracting the begin time from the end time.

3) Otherwise, if an explicit end value of *indefinite* is given and a dur attribute was not specified, the active duration is set to *indefinite*.

4) Otherwise, if no end attribute was specified and either no dur attribute was specified or a dur attribute was specified with values of *indefinite* or *media*, the active duration is the same as the simple duration as defined in Table 13-5. In general, this will result in an active duration of 0 seconds for discrete media objects or a the intrinsic duration of continuous media objects. It may also result in a value of *indefinite*.

---

2 This table is used to compute the simple duration. If a value is listed as not used, this does not mean it is not used in the computation of the active duration, but simply that the value is not important for determining the (intermediate) simple duration.

5) Otherwise, if an end value other than *indefinite* is specified and a dur attribute is provided, the active duration is the smaller of the dur attribute value and the value obtained by subtracting the begin from the end time.

While this all is very complex because of strange cases (such as when various attribute values conflict), the active duration will always be either:

- 0 seconds, for discrete media and objects with unresolved times;
- a duration determined by the dur attribute, the intrinsic duration of continuous media or child elements, or a value derived from subtracting an explicit end time from the effective begin time; or
- the special value *indefinite*.

Note that the implicit duration of the time containers <par>, <seq> and <excl> is determined by evaluating the children of those containers, as discussed on page 312.

Computing an Active Duration Including Repeat Behavior

Once you understand the process of obtaining an active duration without considering repeats, the extra work needed when the repeatCount or repeatDur attribute is present is minimal. While there are a few special cases (that are beyond the scope of this book), the main extra step is:

- The active duration will be the minimum of the following three values:
  a) the repeatCount times the computed simple duration (from the table),
  b) the repeatDur as specified on the element, and
  c) the value obtained by subtracting the begin time from the end.

  If any of these values are unknown, substitute *indefinite*; this will only result in an *indefinite* final result if all three values are *indefinite*.

The active duration is nearly always the repeat count times either the intrinsic object duration or a repeat duration.

Applying min and max to the Active Duration

Once the initial active duration has been computed, one final step is required: the value must be compared with the value of the min and max attributes. The final active duration is the greater of the min attribute value (or 0 if min is unspecified) and the initial active duration, but it may not exceed the max attribute value (or *indefinite*, if no max was specified).

Computing the Final Schedules

Once the active durations for all elements in the presentation are known, a schedule can be determined. This schedule is usually not static: if events are used, the schedule must be recomputed for the dependent sub-tree every time an event condition becomes resolved or unresolved. The schedule may also need to be recomputed when the system or custom test elements provided by SMIL's content control facilities change the set of elements included in a presentation. For presentations with internal links, the schedule will need to be recomputed when a link is followed.

The SMIL 2.0 specification allows multiple begin times to be specified for objects. A separate schedule needs to be computed for each possible resolved begin value. SMIL also allows repeat and restart behavior; this will also influence the schedule, since a significant part of the schedule may need to be recalculated each repeat or restart interval. Good schedulers can optimize this process, but it still all takes time.

13.3.3 Pathological Examples

Most of the interesting scheduling examples are the ones that yield useful active duration results that can then be used to build (efficient) schedules. We have given examples of such usable cases throughout the book. In this section, we look at some strange scheduling cases; these are used to illustrate the complexities of SMIL.

Cycles in Begin and End Lists

The first short example illustrates a simple case of cycles within a document.

```
<par id="P">
  <video id="A" begin="B.begin" ... >
  <image id="B" begin="A.begin" ... >
</par>
```

The <par> P will have an effective active duration of 0 because neither of its children have a resolved begin time. If we give P a dur="10s" attribute, P will start and be active for 10 seconds, but neither A nor B will be scheduled.

This cycle is obvious, but sometimes the cycles are hidden in chains of activations. A good scheduler will detect the chain and then refuse to play the document.

Invalid Begin Times

Consider the following simple fragment:

```
<seq id="S">
  <video id="A" begin="0" ... >
  <image id="B" begin="A.end" ... >
</seq>
```

While this example looks harmless, it will also result in a scheduling problem. The reason is that chidren of a <seq> element may only have begin offsets that consist of non-negative numbers. Syncbase, eventbase and other forms of begin conditions are not allowed.

An <excl> Without Explicit Durations

The following example illustrates the most common problem with <excl> timing. (The *btn1*, *btn2* and *btn3* objects are defined elsewhere in the presentation.) Here, even though the simple durations of each of the objects are defined, the begin times are unresolved. (They are not *indefinite*.) As a result, none of the objects participate in contributing to *nonStarter*'s active duration. Since it also has no explicit duration declared, it resolves to a duration of 0: the element will be skipped.

```
<excl id="nonStarter" fillDefault="freeze">
    <video id="Va" begin="btn1.activateEvent" dur="10s" ... />
    <video id="Vb" begin="btn2.activateEvent" dur="10s" ... />
    <video id="Vc" begin="btn3.activateEvent" dur="10s" ... />
</excl>
```

Combining dur and end in an Element

SMIL allows the specification of a simple duration on an element and an active duration via the end attribute. This is illustrated in the following fragment. Each of the images will be scheduled based on their implicit begin time and the expected duration of 10 seconds per image. If a mouse event occurs, the schedule will be recomputed and the minimum of the mouse time and the scheduled end time will be used for the object. (The mouse always wins.)

```
<seq>
    <image id="Ia" end="activateEvent" dur="10s" ... />
    <image id="Ib" end="activateEvent" dur="10s" ... />
    <image id="Ic" end="activateEvent" dur="10s" ... />
</excl>
```

Mixing Syncbase and Eventbase Activation

At the beginning of this chapter, we provided a short example that combined eventbase timing with syncbase timing. (See page 288.) On that same page, we provided a footnote saying that various SMIL players interpreted the timing in this example differently. We close this discussion of the SMIL Timing Model by revisiting this example.

Consider the following SMIL fragment:

```
...
<par id="P0">
  <par id="P1">
    <img id="I1" begin="X.activateEvent" src="backgroundIntro.png"
        fill="freeze" ... />
    <video id="V1" begin="I1.begin+3s" src="story.mpg" ... />
  </par>
  <img id="X" src="button.png" dur="20s" ... />
</par>
...
```

In building a schedule for this code, the following steps are taken:

- The children *P1* and *X* of <par> *P0* start at 0 seconds after the beginning of *P0*. The active duration of *X* is 20 seconds; this defines one of the bounds for the active duration of *P0*.

- The active duration of *P1* depends on the durations of the children. Image *I1* has no explicit duration declared, but an it an intrinsic duration of 0 seconds. The video *V1* also has no explicit duration declared, but assume it has an intrinsic duration of 10s. Although resolved durations exist for *I1* and *V1*, neither has a resolved begin time. As such, neither will contribute to the active duration of *P1*. *P1* is determined to have an active duration of 0 seconds.

- P1 will start and then immediately stop. *X* will remain active for 20 seconds, but clicking on it will have no effect because *I1* and *V1* cannot be started outside of the active duration of *P1*.
- After 20 seconds, *X* ends and *P0* terminates.

The key to understanding this example is that elements that have no resolved begin time will have an effective active duration of 0. (Actually, they will simply be ignored for purposes of computing a parent's active duration.) As a result, what looks to be a reasonably simple example turns out to be a complex scheduler problem.

The complexity of this problem is illustrated by the fact that both the Real-One player and HTML+TIME in IE-6 get it wrong. For many users, keeping track of SMIL's complex timing relationships without the support of a sophisticated presentation authoring system can lead to a range of scheduling problems that are difficult to debug.

The SMIL 2.0 specification's discussion on timing is comprehensive but the material remains very complex. In trying to understand the details of timing, dare to trust your own judgements and try your presentation on a range of SMIL players. This will lead to maintainable, future-proof SMIL documents.

13.4 Integrating SMIL Timing in Other Languages

We close this chapter with one last timing topic: how do you integrate SMIL timing into XML languages that are not based directly on the SMIL 2.0 Language profile? When used in a native SMIL 2.0 document (one in which the outer XML tag is <smil>), the nature and meaning of various timing elements is clear. When integrating SMIL timing into other XML languages, a mechanism is required to identify timing containers with the target language.

The SMIL 2.0 specification supports host language integration using two attributes: timeContainer and timeAction.

13.4.1 Time Container Integration Issues

One of the advantages of the SMIL 2.0 specification is that it provides a modularized architecture. This allows designers of other XML languages to take SMIL modules and integrate the associated functionality into their languages. This has been done successfully for SVG and XHTML.

One of the problems of the integration of SMIL functionality is to determine how SMIL's time containers can be modelled in the target language. There are essentially two choices: a set of namespace extensions can be defined for a language to add new elements and attributes, or a set of extra attributes can be integrated into the target language that allow special behavior to be associated with any element using those attributes.

While the namespace approach is useful in integrating large numbers of constructs into a language, the use of integration attributes provides a clean method of being able to add limited functionality to existing elements without having to redefine them via a namespace.

A simple example of integrating attribute-based extension functionality is given in the following HTML fragment:

```
<html>
  <P timeContainer="seq">
    <img id="H1" dur="5s" ... />
    <img id="H2" dur="7s" ... />
  </P>
</html>
```

Here, the `<P>` container is defined to have behavior of a SMIL `<seq>`. The children of the container are each given SMIL-like attributes to control their temporal behavior.

Note that it is up to language designers and browser suppliers to create an infrastructure that allows use of time container semantics. As with namespaces and other extension technology, these changes can only be integrated into the presentation environment if they are both supported in the language and in the implementation.

13.4.2 Time Container Integration Attributes

The SMIL *TimeContainerAttributes* module defines two attributes that facilitate integration of SMIL time containers into non-SMIL languages. These are `timeContainer` and `timeAction`. The module also makes the `fill` and the `endsync` attributes available to XML languages that are do use SMIL as the host level language.

This section discusses only `timeContainer` and `timeAction`. The `fill` attribute is covered in detail in Chapter 13: *Advanced SMIL Timing Behavior and Control* (see *Fill Behavior Control* on page 328) and the `endsync` attribute is described in Chapter 7: *Basic SMIL Timing* (see *endsync* on page 150).

Attribute: timeContainer

The three time containers available in SMIL are `<par>`, `<seq>` and `<excl>`. They define behavior that is used to manage the temporal hierarchy of a SMIL document. In XML languages that have no notion of time or which do not manage time as a structure container, SMIL provides the `timeContainer` attribute. It allows an author to assert that an element in the non-SMIL language should assume SMIL time container semantics.

The legal values for this attribute are:

- *par*: defines a SMIL parallel time container;
- *seq*: defines a SMIL sequential time container;
- *excl*: defines a SMIL sequential time container; and
- *none*: states explicitly that the element *does not* implement a SMIL time container. This is the default value of `timeContainer`.

The `timeContainer` attribute cannot be applied to existing SMIL `<par>`, `<seq>` and `<excl>` containers. (They would either be redundant or cause havoc.) They may, in principle, be applied to any element in a target host language, but such a language may limit the elements to which this attribute may be applied. The intrinsic duration of an element using `timeContainer` is defined to be equivalent to media object timing. Language designers using `timeContainer` must define how the intrinsic duration is defined.

Note that it is theoretically possible to apply `timeContainer` to a SMIL media object; this allows media objects with children to exhibit time container functionality. While this is useful for direct insertion of media in a presentation (such as supporting in-line text), this is currently not supported in the SMIL Language profile. None of the mainstream SMIL players (RealOne, GRiNS and Ambulant) support the *TimeContainerAttributes* module. It is supported in the HTML+TIME implementation of XHTML+SMIL.

Attribute: timeAction

Where the `timeContainer` attribute enables a 'foreign' element to assume SMIL time container semantics, the `timeAction` attribute allows an author to define how those semantics should apply to the associated element. The `timeAction` attribute does not define timing semantics, but it defines which semantics apply to the definitions in the current element.

Language designers may define the values for `timeAction`. The legal values defined in the SMIL specification are:

- *intrinsic*: specifies that the intrinsic timing behavior is controlled;
- *display*: specifies that timing behavior of the display is controlled, as defined by CSS (which can impact the layout of the presentation);
- *visibility*: specifies that timing behavior of the element's visibility is controlled, as defined by CSS;
- *style*: specifies that timing behavior of any in-line style is controlled, as defined by CSS;
- *class:classname*: specifies behavior of the inclusion of the given *classname* is controlled; and
- *none*: specifies that timing behavior does not control any actions.

The default behavior for `timeAction` is *intrinsic*.

SMIL time containers provide scheduling control over their children. Other control is exercised by attributes on the child elements. When using time containers, a scheduling-only behavior is obtained by the use of the *intrinsic* behavior. If the value of *intrinsic* is not selected, then the control of any other scheduling will be done in addition to *intrinsic*. This does not apply to the value of *none*.

For the use and restrictions on `timeAction`, please see the following examples section.

13.4.3 Examples of Time Container Integration

This section give several examples of the syntax and semantics of the time container integration attributes. Note that the application of these examples requires a language implementation that supports time container integration.

The timeContainer *Attribute*

The use and utility of the `timeContainer` element is strongly dependent on the implementation of the playback browser. In the HTML+TIME implementation of the XHTML+SMIL profile, the use of a `timeContainer` semantic is typically not required, since the language has namespace extensions that recognize basic SMIL containers. This is shown in the following fragment:

```
 1 <html xmlns:t="urn:schemas-microsoft-com:time">
 2  <head>
 3 <style>
 4    .time { behavior: url(#default#time2) }
 5    .FatFirst:first-letter { font-size:200%; color:blue; float:left; }
 6    .FatFirst:first-line   { color:red; font-size:24pt; }
 7  </style>
 8  <?IMPORT namespace="t" implementation="#default#time2">
 9  <TITLE>timeContainer and timeAction</TITLE>
10  </head>
11  <body bgcolor="gold">
12   <t:par id="BasicVideoshow">
13    <div class="time" timeContainer="seq" ... >
14     ...
15    </div>
16    <t:excl ... >
17     ...
18    </t:excl>
19   </t:par>
20  </body>
21 </html>
```

This example relies on the inclusion of the *time2* behavior of Internet Explorer 6. On line 9, we see a declaration of a SMIL <par> container, qualified with the HTML+TIME *t* namespace identifier. On line 10, we see the declaration of a SMIL sequential container using the `timeContainer` attribute. Line 13 shows the use of namespace extensions to define a SMIL <excl>.

In theory, the namespace extended version of a SMIL element can be used as a wrapper around child elements and the `timeContainer` attribute can be used inside of an existing host-language construct. In practice, some situations in HTML+TIME require the use of `timeContainer`, while others require the use of namespace qualified elements. Often, the distinction needs to be found by using trial and error.

Note that in the current implementation, the *time* style, which is linked to the *time2* behavior, needs to be included when `timeContainer` is used. Note also that the <head> section contains not only the HTML+TIME behavior declaration, but it also contains an extra style definition used in some of the examples below. We include it here for general reference.

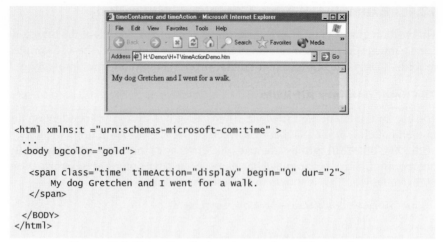

```
<html xmlns:t ="urn:schemas-microsoft-com:time" >
...
  <body bgcolor="gold">

    <span class="time" timeAction="display" begin="0" dur="2">
        My dog Gretchen and I went for a walk.
    </span>

  </BODY>
</html>
```

Figure 13-5. Using the *display* timeAction attribute value.

The timeAction *Attribute*

The use of the timeAction attribute in conjunction with the *time2* behavior can often lead to interesting presentations. In this section we develop a multi-step example that illustrates several aspects of timeAction behavior.

The presentation fragment in Figure 13-5 takes a single line of text and changes the visibility attribute to display it for two seconds.[3] An HTML <span> element is used to encode a time action that begins at the start of the presentation and lasts 2 seconds. After the 2 seconds pass, the text will be removed.

We illustrate the *class:classname* attribute value for timeAction in Figure 13-6. This line is defined to be visible starting at 2 seconds into the presentation and will last for 4 seconds. It has an embedded effect that changes the text styl-

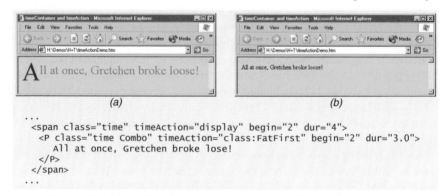

```
...
  <span class="time" timeAction="display" begin="2" dur="4">
   <P class="time Combo" timeAction="class:FatFirst" begin="2" dur="3.0">
     All at once, Gretchen broke lose!
   </P>
  </span>
...
```

Figure 13-6. Using the *class:classname* timeAction attribute value.

---

3 Note that to save space, the HTML+TIME *time2* behavior declaration is not repeated. All of the examples use the <head> section illustrated in the fragment on page 321.

ing (Figure 13-6(a)). Since the embedded effect only has a duration of 3 seconds, the text is un-styled at the end of its display time (Figure 13-6(a)). Note that the timing in the embedded <P> is relative to the start of the document, not the parent <span>. This is because the <span> is not a time container. (See page 321 for the *FatFirst* class definition.)

Figure 13-7 illustrates the behavior of the presentation if we give the <span> the time container semantics of a SMIL <seq> and then define three children that each color in part of a line of text. The <span> begins at 6 seconds into the presentation and lasts 6 seconds. Each of the children last 2 seconds. There is one image for each child's active period (Figure 13-7(a), (b) and (c)).

There are two important things going on here. First, the `timeAction` attribute defines both a display setting and the intrinsic timing of the <seq> container. Second, each of the *effects* of the `timeAction="style"` attribute on the children are scheduled in sequential order but the combined *content* of the children is visible for the entire 6 second duration of the <seq>. (The content is the text string: *This was -- of course -- very sad.*)

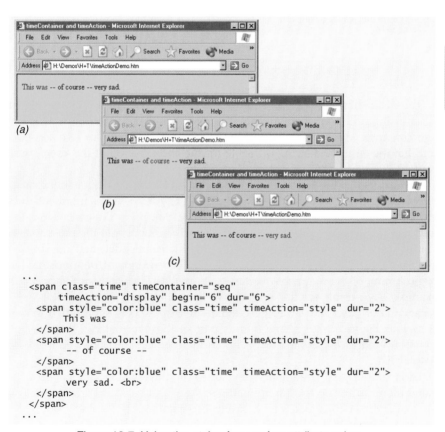

```
...
<span class="time" timeContainer="seq"
      timeAction="display" begin="6" dur="6">
  <span style="color:blue" class="time" timeAction="style" dur="2">
      This was
  </span>
  <span style="color:blue" class="time" timeAction="style" dur="2">
      -- of course --
  </span>
  <span style="color:blue" class="time" timeAction="style" dur="2">
      very sad. <br>
  </span>
</span>
...
```

Figure 13-7. Using the *style* `timeAction` attribute value.

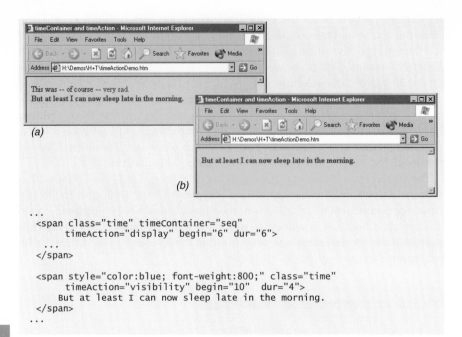

(a)

(b)

```
...
<span class="time" timeContainer="seq"
      timeAction="display" begin="6" dur="6">
   ...
</span>

<span style="color:blue; font-weight:800;" class="time"
      timeAction="visibility" begin="10"  dur="4">
   But at least I can now sleep late in the morning.
</span>
...
```

Figure 13-8. Using the *visibility* timeAction attribute value.

The distinction between timed effects and timed content is very important when using time containers and time actions. You should study this example and convince yourself that each of the text blocks turn blue for two seconds, but that the entire text string is visible for the entire period of the <seq> time container.

The last step in this example is to add a visibility attribute value to the set of effects in the presentation. This is illustrated in Figure 13-8. This fragment adds a final sentence to our man-and-his-dog story. Since it is the conclusion, the author puts it in bold. The fragment starts at 10 seconds into the presentation and ends 4 seconds later. The author had initially intended that the display shown in Figure 13-8(b) would result from the code fragment, but note that the begin timing of the fragment overlaps with the last 2 seconds of the previous example. As a result, we first see the two lines shown on Figure 13-8(a) and 2 seconds later (after the earlier part ends), the display gets reformatted to that shown in Figure 13-8(b). Note that as part of the reformatting, the text line moves up in the display: the text is not hidden but actually removed from the display list.

Each of the code fragments developed in this section can be used as stand-alone effects on text (or animations or any other content). They can also all be combined together into a single presentation. The entire example is shown in Figure 13-9.

```
<html xmlns:t ="urn:schemas-microsoft-com:time" >
 <head>
  <style>
   .time { behavior: url(#default#time2) }
   .FatFirst:first-letter { font-size:200%; color:blue; float:left; }
   .FatFirst:first-line  { color:red; font-size:24pt; }
  </style>
  <?IMPORT namespace="t" implementation="#default#time2">
  <TITLE>timeContainer and timeAction</TITLE>
  </head>
<body bgcolor="gold">

  <span class="time" timeAction="display" begin="0" dur="2">
     My dog Gretchen and I went for a walk.
  </span>

  <span class="time" timeAction="display" begin="2" dur="4">
   <P class="time Combo" timeAction="class:FatFirst" begin="2" dur="3.0">
     All at once, Gretchen broke lose!
   </P>
  </span>

  <span class="time" timeContainer="seq"
       timeAction="display" begin="6" dur="6">
   <span style="color:blue" class="time" timeAction="style" dur="2">
      This was
   </span>
   <span style="color:blue" class="time" timeAction="style" dur="2">
      -- of course --
   </span>
   <span style="color:blue" class="time" timeAction="style" dur="2">
      very sad. <br>
   </span>
  </span>

  <span style="color:blue; font-weight:800;" class="time"
       timeAction="visibility" begin="10"  dur="4">
    But at least I can now sleep late in the morning.
  </span>

 </body>
</html>
```

Figure 13-9. The complete example, ready for testing.

It might have been wise for the author to wrap the entire presentation into an outer sequential container and to then use relative timing at the beginning of each of the elements. This seemingly trivial task is left as an exercise to the reader.

13.5 Summary and Conclusion

This chapter has provided a broad review of advanced timing features in SMIL 2.0. We began with a discussion of how event timing has been integrated into the language, and how event processing can be used to control the beginning and end of attribute activation. We then provided a summary of how SMIL's <excl> and <priorityClass> elements can be used to support selective activation of one out of a set of elements. We then considered the scheduling and active duration calculations that are required to support general SMIL timing. We closed with a discussion of how time functionality can be integrated by language designers into other XML languages.

The material in this chapter is advanced. If you are new to SMIL or have only a superficial understanding of how SMIL's elements and attributes work, we encourage you to spend time building examples rather than building execution instance lists. At the same time, it is good to understand the intricacies of how event timing and syncbase activation can lead to more interesting and interactive content.

We encourage you to visit the book's Web site to obtain copies of sample presentations that make use of these features. As you become comfortable with our examples, you can start building your own. Ultimately, this should help spice up content on the Web!

13.6 Further Resources

CSS

Cascading Style Sheets, Level 2, Bert Bos, Håkon Wium Lie, Chris Lilley and Ian Jacobs (eds), W3C Recommendation, 12 May 1998.
`http://www.w3.org/TR/CSS2`.

IE-6's HTML+TIME

For information on the SMIL 2.0 XHTML+SMIL compatible HTML+TIME player in Microsoft's IE-6 browser, see:
`http://msdn.microsoft.com/library/default.asp?url=/workshop/author/behaviors/reference/time2/htime_node_entry.asp`.

DOM events

Document Object Model Events, Tom Pixley (ed.), W3C Recommendation, 13 November 2000,
`http://www.w3.org/TR/DOM-Level-2-Events/events.html`.

14

Advanced SMIL Timing Attributes

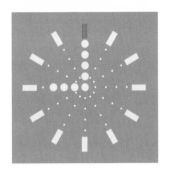

As explained in previous chapters, SMIL has four time containers that are used to schedule media and SMIL element content: <par>, <seq>, <excl> and <body>[1]. All of the time containers take a wide range of SMIL timing attributes, plus attributes to control rendering and animation.

In addition to the standard SMIL timing and control attributes, three classes of attributes also exist to control generic aspects of time container processing: *fill behavior*, *restart behavior*, and internal multi-object *synchronization behavior*. SMIL also provides a set of attributes to control how the SMIL is to interpret the pace and direction of rendering: the *time manipulation attributes*. Table 14-1 provides an overview of these attributes and indicates the elements to which they apply.

The fill behavior attributes control rendering behavior of an object after its active duration has ended; this is useful to have object visibility match the duration of other objects in a container or to allow special effects for transitions

attributes		elements		Profiles		
Fill Behavior	fill	*animation*		M	B	1
	fillDefault	<prefetch>	L			
Restart Behavior	restart			L		H
	restartDefault					
Synchronization Behavior	syncBehavior	*media object*, <brush>				H
	syncBehaviorDefault		L			
	syncTolerance					H
	syncToleranceDefault	<body>,<seq>, <par>,<excl>				
	syncMaster					H
Time Manipulation	autoReverse	*animation*	<transition-Filter>			
	speed					H
	accelerate, decelerate					

Table 14-1. Structure of this chapter's attributes

---

1 The <body> element is only a time container in profiles that use SMIL as the host language; profiles based on XHTML+SMIL or SVG do not use <body> as a time container.

that are difficult to describe using standard timing. The restart behavior attributes allow an author to control how and when an element restarts with respect to external events or internal SMIL syncbases; this can be used to provide predictable behavior in interactive or event-driven application. The synchronization behavior attributes allow an author to determine which object or element should serve as the master media object for timing control purposes; this allows, for example, the timing of an audio element to pace the rendering of other objects in a presentation. Finally, the time manipulation attributes allow the speed and direction of the SMIL clock to be manipulated in many interesting ways — such as reversing the order of presentation of a media object; these are especially useful for controlling local animations on media objects.

This chapter discusses these advanced timing attributes in detail. Some attributes were introduced in earlier chapters, but all of the behavior aspects of element fill, restart, synchronization and time manipulation attributes are covered below.

14.1 Fill Behavior Control

Chapter 7: *Basic SMIL Timing* introduced SMIL's facilities for controlling object persistence using the fill attribute. In that chapter, we considered the simple attribute settings of *freeze* and *remove*. In Chapter 10: *Transition Effects*, as part of the discussion on the need for existing content associated with a transition to extend beyond its normal rendering lifetime, we discussed the *transition* attribute setting for fill. In addition to these three values, fill also accepts three other values: *hold, auto* and *default*. The discussion below unifies our presentation on fill behavior and discusses how all of these attribute values relate to each other. We start with a review of fill behavior, then discuss the attributes and attribute values for fill and fillDefault, and then look at several examples of using fill behavior.

14.1.1 Understanding the Fill Behavior

Timed objects in a SMIL presentation have several types of durations: their intrinsic, simple, active duration and rendered durations. The intrinsic duration is determined by the media object. The simple duration is determined by taking the intrinsic duration and adding explicit object timing (most often using the dur attribute). The active duration is determined by applying repeat behavior to the simple duration. When all of these times have been determined, the setting of the fill attribute determines the rendered duration: it defines how long a media object remains visible after its active duration has ended. The rendered duration depends on many things in a SMIL presentation, of which the most important is usually the temporal context of the parent element. This section reviews the important aspects of rendering duration and object persistence.

The Temporal Scope of Objects

The fact that fill behavior is an issue in a SMIL presentation is a direct result of the timed-based nature of SMIL documents. For languages and formats for which time is not central — like HTML or PDF — an object typically remains on the screen until the viewer performs some explicit action: scrolling past the object, following a link to another page or closing the browser. In a SMIL presentation, the temporal scope of an object usually determines its visibility. To understand the rules and issues in determining rendering duration we consider the three temporal topics: the temporal scope of continuous media object, the temporal scope of discrete media objects and the temporal scope of time containers.

The temporal scope of continuous media. In many ways, the temporal scope of a continuous media object provides the easiest and most obvious starting point for defining fill behavior. As illustrated in Figure 14-1, a continuous media object normally will be visible for the period defined by that object's intrinsic duration. Once the intrinsic durations ends, the object is usually removed from the display, although the actual fill behavior will be determined by several factors. If the simple duration is extended by applying an explicit duration which is longer than the intrinsic duration, the final frame of a visual media object will be extended. If the active duration repeats the simple duration, any extended visibility after the simple duration will also be repeated.

Once the active duration ends, the rendered visibility will be determined by a combination of the temporal scope of the parent element and the effective setting of the `fill` attribute. The effective fill behavior can be determined on the element itself or by one of its ancestors. There are, of course, default rules for determining how long an element remains visible.

It is important to realize that the fill behavior only determines the behavior of an object after the active duration: the fact that the last frame of a media object is extended by the simple duration is *not* due to the fill behavior but due to the definition of the `dur` attribute.

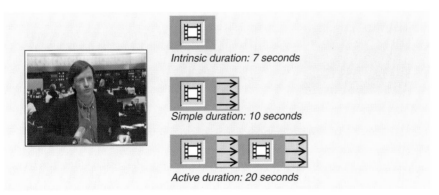

Intrinsic duration: 7 seconds

Simple duration: 10 seconds

Active duration: 20 seconds

Figure 14-1. Temporal scope of a continuous media object.

The temporal scope of discrete media. The rendering of discrete media — images and text — presents a radically different set of persistence needs than the rendering of continuous media. Many newcomers to SMIL are surprised that the default duration of a discrete media object is 0 seconds.[2] Considering that the default duration of text and images on an HTML page is effectively infinite, they wonder why anyone would bother defining an image as part of a presentation when it will only be active for 0 seconds!

Although there are many justifications that have been offered for the default duration of 0, the real reason it is used is this: if you don't use 0, what *should* you use? The RealNetworks G2 player for SMIL 1.0 assigned a default duration of five seconds to each discrete media object. While five is a nice number, it is not really any more appropriate for discrete media than, say, three, six or ten seconds. The only consistently useful alternative to 0 seconds is to set the default at the other end of the temporal spectrum: an infinite duration. This is the approach used in applications that support a painter's canvas model: discrete media remains part of the visible portion of the presentation until it is explicitly covered by some other object.

The advantage of an infinite default duration is that you get to see the image. The disadvantage is that a presentation author needs to keep track of all of the objects displayed in the past to make sure that the screen is cleaned up during the presentation. The advantage of a 0 second default duration is that it makes the timing model simple and consistent. The disadvantage of a 0 second default is that it makes discrete content difficult to view unless each object explicitly overrides the intrinsic duration using the dur attribute. While specifying an explicit duration is possible, it presents a new problem: you often don't know in advance exactly how long you want some discrete content to stay active — the duration will often be determined by other objects on the screen. This is illustrated in Figure 14-2. Here, we want the image containing the headline text and logo to stay on the screen as long as the continuous media

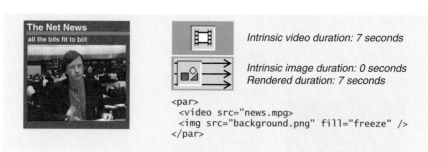

```
<par>
  <video src="news.mpg>
  <img src="background.png" fill="freeze" />
</par>
```

Figure 14-2. Temporal scope of a discrete media object.

---

2 Actually, the default duration is really ε (epsilon) seconds: the smallest time increment available in the player in which an object can be rendered and then removed. The — largely philosophical — distinction between ε and 0 seconds allows an object in the presentation to be differentiated from an object that is not included in the presentation.

object is active. We could potentially find out the intrinsic duration of the video, but what we really want to specify is that the image should remain visible as long as the continuous object is active.

SMIL's fill behavior provides an elegant solution to this duration problem. It lets an author say: put a media object on the screen and keep it around until the presentation context changes. Of course, if you want to specify more exact control, SMIL provides the core timing attributes of begin, dur and end.

The temporal scope of a time container. The presentation context used to determine the rendering duration of the image in Figure 14-2 is not determined directly by the duration of the companion video object, but by the duration of the parent time container: the active duration of the parent will determine the visibility of the image. In this example, the active duration of the <par> is the duration of the video media object, but the active duration could also have been determined by other timing attributes. In Figure 14-3, we see a parent container with a dur attribute: this will determine the fill behavior of the <par> but not directly of the video, since the <par> fill behavior will start after 20 seconds, while the fill behavior of the video (*freeze*) starts when it ends.

SMIL's fill behavior lets you define the rendering duration of objects that are tied to the duration of the time container in which they are presented — and perhaps also to an entire timing hierarchy. This provides simple but powerful control over how media objects are managed for display.

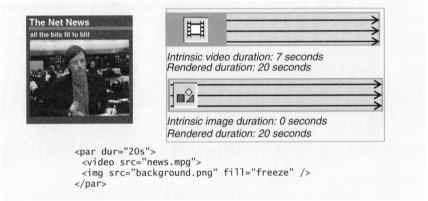

```
<par dur="20s">
  <video src="news.mpg">
  <img src="background.png" fill="freeze" />
</par>
```

Figure 14-3. Temporal scope of a parent time container.

Linking, Interaction and Fill Behavior

The definition of a rendered behavior is an important concept for SMIL. It determines the composition of objects on the screen, but it also determines how long an object that has some form of linking anchor or interactive behavior associated with it will remain active. In general, elements remain 'clickable' as long as they are visible: the active duration may have ended seconds, minutes or hours ago, but the element remains selectable as long as it is in its fill period.

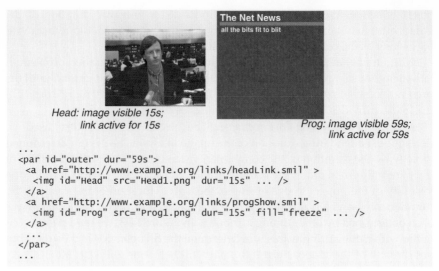

Head: image visible 15s;
link active for 15s

Prog: image visible 59s;
link active for 59s

```
...
<par id="outer" dur="59s">
  <a href="http://www.example.org/links/headLink.smil" >
    <img id="Head" src="Head1.png" dur="15s" ... />
  </a>
  <a href="http://www.example.org/links/progShow.smil" >
    <img id="Prog" src="Prog1.png" dur="15s" fill="freeze" ... />
  </a>
  ...
</par>
...
```

Figure 14-4. Link anchor sensitivity after the active duration.

Figure 14-4 shows an example of how linking behavior extends beyond an object's active duration. In this simple presentation, two images are defined: *Head* and *Prog*. Both are given explicit durations of 15 seconds. Image *Prog* is given fill="freeze" behavior, image *Head* is given no explicit fill attribute, which means that it has an effective behavior of fill="remove". *Head* and *Prog* are placed in a <par> container with an explicit active duration of 59 seconds.

The active durations of *Head* and *Prog* end after 15 seconds. During their active durations, both have active link anchors. After the active duration expires, *Prog*'s anchor remains active for an additional 44 seconds (until the end of the parent <par>); *Head*'s anchor is inactive because it has been removed from the display.

This method of specifying the active period of a link anchor it is an exceptionally useful way of providing behavior while reducing authoring effort.

Special Cases of Fill Behavior

The most often used value for the fill attribute is *freeze*. This keeps the final (or only) frame of a media object rendered until the end of its temporal context. While this is a useful tool, it is not always powerful enough to cover all situations. For example, when working with a transition, you often want to keep content around until after a transition completes, even if this is beyond the temporal scope of the original media. This is the motivation behind the fill="transition" behavior. In other situations — especially in a <seq> — you occasionally want to keep an object displayed until the end of that sequence. The fill="hold" value accomplishes this. As we will see, you should use it sparingly: most often, SMIL's structured timing elements provided a cleaner way of keeping media visible in the context of other media.

14.1.2 Fill Behavior Attributes

This section describes the behavior of two fill-related attributes: `fill` and `fillDefault`. The structure of these attributes, their legal values and the elements and profiles in which they are used is summarized in Table 14-2.

attribute	value			elements		Profiles
`fill`	`"remove"`, `"freeze"`, `"hold"`, `"transition"`,	`"default"`	*media object,*	*animation,* `<par>, <seq>, <excl>, <body>`	M B 1 L
`fillDefault`	`"auto"`,	`"inherit"`	`<brush>`	`<prefetch>`	

Table 14-2. Structure of fill behavior attributes

Fill Behavior Elements

The specification of fill behavior does not require any special SMIL 2.0 elements. In general, fill behavior is applied to media object elements (such as `<video>`, `<img>`, `<animation>` and `<ref>`) or to SMIL time containers (`<par>`, `<seq>`, `<excl>` and — for SMIL host languages — `<body>`). A fill behavior applied to a time container defines the behavior for all children of that parent unless explicitly overridden by the child.

Attribute: `fill`

The `fill` attribute controls object persistence after its active duration has ended. It is also used to describe the rendering duration of an object when it has a simple duration that is shorter than the duration specified by the `min` timing attribute, but it *does not* define the rendering behavior of an object when the intrinsic duration is shorter than the simple duration.

The legal values for this attribute are:

- *remove*: remove the element from the display at the end of its active duration. Under some circumstances (described below), this is the effective default behavior.

- *freeze*: do not remove the element from the screen when its active duration ends. The object will remain displayed until the end of the fill period of its parent time container. For continuous media items, the frame that is displayed is the last frame in the last instance of the object's simple duration: if the object was only partially displayed — in terms of duration — then the last displayed frame would be frozen. Under some circumstances (described below), this is the effective default behavior.

- *transition*: keep the object visible until the end of the next transition that uses the same display area. The object is removed when the transition ends.

- *hold*: keep the element visible until the parent element ends. For `<par>` parents, this is equivalent to a behavior of *freeze,* since the ending of the `<par>` triggers the ending of its children. When used with a `<seq>` or `<body>` time container, it keeps the object visible throughout the entire duration of the `<seq>` container.

- *auto*: keep the element visible or remove the element, depending on other attributes on the element. If the element contains a `dur`, `end`, `repeatCount` or `repeatDur` attribute (regardless of the value), then use `fill="remove"` behavior. If the element does not contain a `dur`, `end`, `repeatCount` or `repeatDur` attribute, use `fill="freeze"` behavior. Note that the effective fill behavior based on the presence or absence of the listed attributes occurs only when the `fill="auto"` value has been explicitly defined.

- *default*: determine the fill behavior based on the (effective) value of the `fillDefault` attribute. This is the default behavior when no `fill` attribute is explicitly defined. (As discussed in the next section, the default behavior for `fillDefault` is *auto.*)

In cases where an element is frozen or extended, the actual visibility of the object will depend on other objects rendered during or after the element's definition. In particular, if a frozen object is partially covered by another object that is subsequently removed, the entire frozen object must be re-rendered (refreshed) by the player.

Attribute: fillDefault

The `fillDefault` attribute sets the default fill behavior of that element and its descendants. It accepts the *remove, freeze, transition, hold* and *auto* values of the `fill` attribute, but not the *default* value. It also defines an additional value:

- *inherit*: the associated element inherits the value for `fillDefault` from the parent of this element. If the parent does not exist, use *auto*. The *inherit* value is the default.

Only the SMIL Language profiles uses this attribute.

14.1.3 Examples of Fill Behavior

This section considers various aspects of defining a fill behavior in a SMIL 2.0 document. We organize the examples by the setting of the attribute value. Before we start, a word of caution for readers who use these examples as a basis for their presentations: some SMIL players (such as RealOne) freeze the final state of an entire presentation on the display when the presentation ends, while other players (such as GRiNS and Ambulant) clear the screen at the end. Neither of these approaches are described using SMIL fill semantics, but instead are choices of the various player developers. Both represent legal SMIL behavior, but both choices can influence the apparent fill behavior of the final state of the presentation.

The fill="remove" *Value*

The *remove* value for `fill` is used when you want to explicitly remove element content from view. The most obvious form is illustrated in Figure 14-5. Here we see a 10 second `<par>` that contains a 5 second teaser video and a background image. When the `<par>` starts, the background image is placed on the screen and the movie starts. At the end of the video, a message of interest to viewers is shown "under" the video.

What if we had not placed the explicit fill behavior on the video element? The element would then be defined as follows:

```
<video src="fiveSecTeaser.mpg" ... />
```

The correct behavior in this case is that a fill value of *default* is assumed. The `fill="default"` value tells the SMIL player to look at the setting for the `fillDefault` attribute on the parent `<par>`. (Note that it is the `fillDefault` value that is important, not the default fill value: a subtle but important distinction.) In our example, there is no `fillDefault` defined for the element, so we look to see if a `fillDefault` is defined for the parent. The `<par>` also has no `fillDefault` defined, so we bubble up the tree. Since the tree is fairly short, we can easily determine that the root of the tree (the `<body>` element) also has no `fillDefault` defined. In this case, the value of *auto* is used for `fillDefault`. The consequence is that the video object without a `fill` attribute and with no `fillDefault` in its ancestry, acts as if it had been defined as:

```
<video src="fiveSecTeaser.mpg" fill="auto" region="V" />
```

The *auto* behavior is defined as follows:

1) If the element explicitly defines a simple or active duration using the dur, end, `repeatCount` or `repeatDur` attribute(s), then the fill behavior will be identical to having stated a `fill="remove"` attribute value; or

```
0:05                    0:08                    0:08
video: playing          video: fill="remove"    video: fill="freeze"
```

```
<smil xmlns="http://www.w3.org/2001/TR/SMIL20" >
...
  <body>
    <par dur="10s">
      <video src="fiveSecTeaser.mpg" fill="remove" region="V" />
      <img src="background.png" fill="freeze" region="B" />
    </par>
  </body>
</smil>
```

Figure 14-5. Example of `fill="remove"` and `fill="freeze"` behavior.

2) If the element does not explicitly define a simple or active duration using the `dur`, `end`, `repeatCount` or `repeatDur` attribute(s), then the fill behavior will be identical to having stated a `fill="freeze"` attribute value.

Since in our example the video element does not explicitly define a simple duration, `fill="freeze"` behavior is provided.

Assume now that the video element had been specified with an explicit duration but no explicit fill behavior:

```
<video src="fiveSecTeaser.mpg" dur="5s" region="V" />
```

Here, an effective `fill="remove"` value would be used.

The `fill="freeze"` Value

In the example used in Figure 14-5, the image element that was played in parallel with the video object had a `fill="freeze"` attribute value declared. Note that the image had no explicit duration defined. In terms of its SMIL behavior, this means that it had a simple (and active) duration of 0 seconds and a fill period that lasts until the end of the parent time container. We could have gotten the same visual behavior by explicitly specifying a duration, but this only would have made presentation authoring more cumbersome. In cases where you don't know (or don't care about) the length of companion media object, the *freeze* value on the `fill` attribute is a good way of making objects persistent.

In the example in Figure 14-5, the image element with the `fill="freeze"` attribute was placed inside a `<par>` container. What would have happened in elements were placed in a `<seq>`? This is illustrated by Example 14-1. Here we see a sequence of *n* images that are displayed against a common background. Each of the images in the sequence has a slightly different combination of begin times, durations and fill values. (This was created by trained professionals who apparently had some extra time on their hands.) Luckily, each can be used to identify an important fill-related topic.

The first image (*Pict1.jpg*) begins at the start of the element *I1* in the sequence; it has no duration declared, so its active duration ends immediately. It has a fill behavior defined as *freeze*, which will keep it rendered until the start of the next element in the sequence. The question is: when does the next element in the sequence begin? Is it at the conclusion of the previous element

```
...
<par >
  <seq>
    <img id="I1" src="Pict1.jpg" fill="freeze" region="P" />
    <img id="I2" src="Pict2.jpg" begin="5s" dur="5s" region="P" />
    <img id="I3" src="Pict3.jpg" dur="3s" fill="freeze" region="P" />
    ...
    <img id="In" src="Pictn.jpg" dur="5s" fill="freeze" region="P" />
  </seq>
  <img src="background.png" fill="freeze" region="B" />
</par>
...
```

Example 14-1. Example of `fill="freeze"` behavior in a `<seq>`.

(which happens essentially immediately) or does it start when the rendering period of the following element begins? The answer is that the fill period of an object in a sequence ends when the content in the successor element begins its active duration. The active duration in our example begins at 3 seconds after the end of the previous image, thus the fill period is three seconds long.

As a quick aside, it may well be that the fill period of three seconds is exactly what the author wanted, but this is a dangerous way to author the presentation. For example, assume that we replace the initial sequence with the following fragment:

```
...
  <seq>
    <img id="I1" src="Pict1.jpg" fill="freeze" region="P" />
    <par>
      <img id="I2" src="Pict2.jpg" begin="5s" dur="5s" region="P" />
    </par>
    <img id="I3" src="Pict3.jpg" dur="3s" fill="freeze" region="P" />
    ...
    <img id="In" src="Pictn.jpg" dur="5s" fill="freeze" region="P" />
  </seq>
...
```

On the surface, wrapping the definition of *I2* in a <par> seems pretty harmless, except that the <par>'s active duration will now begin at the moment the active duration of I1 ends (which is about 0 seconds after it starts); thus the fill period is also 0 seconds, thus you will not see *Pict1.jpg* — or, if you do see it, it will only flash briefly on the screen. Understanding this example is important to understanding the nature of SMIL's fill behavior in a sequence.

Back to the example of Example 14-1. After playing element *I2*, which has an active duration of 5 seconds, a freeze behavior is again declared to tide us over until the start of element *I3*. In this case, the fill period is 0, since the active duration of the successor begins immediately after element *I2* ends. (The fill="freeze" is superfluous here.) In a sequence, declaring a fill="freeze" behavior only makes sense if the active duration of the successor does not begin immediately.

The final image in this sequence, contained in element *In*, has a duration of 5 seconds. It, too, declares a fill="freeze" behavior. Since *I2*'s fill period ends at the end of the <seq>, this freeze will have little impact. The only exception is for players such as RealOne that freeze the final state of the presentation on the screen. If this is the last time container in the presentation and if the default behavior would otherwise be fill="remove" (because of a fillDefault somewhere on an ancestor), having an explicit fill="freeze" will keep the image on the display at the end of the presentation. Note that this is only for RealOne. It has no effect for the GRiNS or the Ambulant players.

The fill="hold" *Value*

The previous section discussed using fill="freeze" within a SMIL <seq> container. This value has only limited utility — and only under particular circumstances. A more generally useful value for fill in a <seq> is *hold*. This value

| 0:03 | 0:08 | 0:13 |

```
...
<seq>
 <img src="background.png" fill="hold" region="B" />
 <seq fill="hold" >
  <img id="I1" src="Pict1.jpg" dur="5s" fill="hold" region="Captain" />
  <img id="I2" src="Pict2.jpg" dur="5s" fill="hold" region="Mate" />
  <img id="I3" src="Pict3.jpg" dur="5s" fill="hold" region="Flag" />
 </seq>
 ...
</seq>
...
```

Figure 14-6. Example of `fill="hold"` behavior.

allows content displayed in the sequence to remain active until the end of the entire <seq>, not simply until the beginning of a successor's active duration.

The primary advantage of using `fill="hold"` is that it brings a painter's canvas semantic to a sequence. This is illustrated in Figure 14-6. Here we see three images that are displayed in a <seq> against a background image. (In the example, all three images are displayed in separate regions, but we also could have used the sub-region positioning features of advanced layout to place them within one region.) The result of the display is shown after the active durations of each of the images have expired. At the end of the <seq>, all three images remain on the display. In addition, the <seq> also has a `fill="hold"` behavior, so that the contents will stay active until the end of its parent.

The behavior of the <seq> in Figure 14-6 could also have been created by placing all of the image elements in a <par> and assigning them explicit begin times. This is demonstrated in Example 14-2. In many ways, the <par> approach is preferable from a SMIL perspective (although it does require basic addition skills), but the `fill="hold"` functionality was considered useful as an

```
...
<par dur="15s">
 <img src="background.png" fill="freeze" region="B" />
 <img id="I1" src="Pict1.jpg" fill="freeze" region="X" />
 <img id="I2" src="Pict2.jpg" begin="5s" fill="freeze" region="Y" />
 <img id="I3" src="Pict3.jpg" begin="10s" fill="freeze" region="Z" />
</par>
...
```

Example 14-2. Example of effective `fill="hold"` behavior in a <par>.

```
...
<seq >
  <img src="background.png" fill="hold" region="B" />
  <img id="I1" src="Pict1.jpg" fill="hold" region="X" />
  <img id="I2" src="Pict2.jpg" begin="5s" fill="hold" region="Y" />
  <img id="I3" src="Pict3.jpg" begin="10s" dur="5s" fill="freeze"
       region="Z" />
</par>
...
```

Example 14-3. Example of fill="hold" behavior in a <seq>.

authoring metaphor in the early days of SMIL. (It was similar to the way that
RealPix managed image content.)

The code in Figure 14-6 uses dur timing to provide a sequencing of images.
We could also have used begin timing. If this was the case, then the final image
would still have needed an explicit duration; without one, it would never be
visible because the sequence ends as soon as the active duration of the final
object ends. The sequence using begin timing is shown in Figure 14-3.

The fill="transition" *Value*

Where fill="freeze" and fill="hold" allow content to remain active until the
end of the parent time containers, another method of rendering control was
required for transitions. With transition behavior, content often needs to stay
on the screen long enough to last through the transition itself, but not any
longer. (The duration of the parent will almost always be too long.) The
fill="transition" value was created to support this need.

The *transition* value of fill is useful in a <seq>. It allows a predecessor to
remain on the screen until a transition completes. The behavior presented is
very similar to fill="hold" except that the temporal scope of the fill period
ends at the end of the next transition rather than at the end of the parent.

An example of the specification of transition behavior is given in Example
14-4. The first two images have fill="transition" declared. This will extend
their rendering period through the following 1 second fade. The third image
does not need a fill because there is no follow-on transition defined.

The main difference between this and other forms of fill is that there are no
restrictions on the scope of the transition: it may come in a successor element in

```
...
<seq >
  <img id="I1" src="Pict1.jpg" dur="5s" fill="transition" region="X" />
  <img id="I2" src="Pict2.jpg" dur="5s" fill="transition" region="X"
    transIn="fade1s" />
  <img id="I3" src="Pict3.jpg" begin="10s" fill="freeze" region="Z"
        transIn="fade1s" />
</par>
...
```

Example 14-4. Example of fill="transition" behavior in a <seq>.

the same <seq>, but it may also occur much later in the presentation, in another time container. (This would be the case if the final image also had a fill="transition" defined.) This provides both a powerful means of providing transition effects and a potential pitfall for authors: if you add a fill="transition" to an element and then neglect to define a follow-on transition, the content might stay on the screen during the rest of the presentation.

The fill="auto" *Value*

The main use of the fill="auto" value is to serve as an internal default value for the fill attribute. It provides a fallback functionality that can be used when no other behavior is defined. The key to understanding the auto behavior is that in most cases when an explicit active duration is defined, it is assumed that this will result in a desire to limit the visibility of an object to that defined period. Thus, when dur, end, repeatCount or repeatDur is used to craft an explicit duration, the object is removed when this duration is complete.

If, on the other hand, an implicit duration is used to define timing for the object, the assumption is that the visual duration should also be implicitly extended to the end of the container. As a result, the object is frozen until the end of the parent container. For a detailed walk-though of fill="auto" behavior, see the example on page 335.

The fill="default" *Value*

The main use of fill="default" is to explicitly state that the value of the fillDefault attribute should be applied. Since this is the default when such an attribute has been defined, the value is almost never explicitly used in practice. It is intended to provide a consistent modelling of SMIL fill behavior. For a detailed walk-though of fill="default" behavior, see the example on page 335.

Examples *of* fillDefault

The fillDefault attribute can be used to assign an explicit default value for all fill behavior on an element and its descendants. Consider the code in Example 14-5. This example, which is a re-coding of Figure 14-6, shows how a single fillDefault value can be applied to all of the children. The fillDefault

```
...
<seq fillDefault="hold">
  <img src="background.png" region="B" />
  <seq >
    <img id="I1" src="Pict1.jpg" dur="5s" region="X" />
    <img id="I2" src="Pict2.jpg" dur="5s" region="Y" />
    <img id="I3" src="Pict3.jpg" dur="5s" region="Z" />
  </seq>
  ...
</seq>
...
```

Example 14-5. Example of fill="freeze" behavior in a <seq>.

attribute can simplify authoring and maintenance of presentations, although it does have the disadvantage that in large, highly nested presentations, the fill value that is applied to an interior node may not always be obvious. As an example, if you overlook the definition of the `fillDefault` attribute in the first `<seq>` of Example 14-5, the persistence of the images defined on the interior nodes will be very bewildering.

14.2 Restart Behavior

The SMIL timing and activation model provides attributes that control when an element starts and stops. It also provides attributes to control duration. With the advent of interactive begin and end times, the timing model was extended to include attributes to control element *restart behavior*. An element can restart if the same event that caused it to start in the first place happens again. Since this behavior can be very useful or very irritating, SMIL provides the `restart` attribute to help authors control when and how restarts should take place. It also provides a `restartDefault` attribute to define default functionality for the `restart` attribute.

Before discussing restart semantics, it is important to note the distinction between restart behavior and repeat behavior. An element can be repeated when it has a `repeatDur` or a `repeatCount` attribute. While a repeated element will restart, this is not the restart behavior addressed by the `restart` attribute. There are similarities in semantics, but for purposes of the discussion below, restart semantics will always be considered to be in response to SMIL 2.0's `begin` attribute behavior.

14.2.1 Understanding Restart Behavior

The basic model used for restart behavior in SMIL is illustrated in Figure 14-7. Here, a video element is started at the beginning of the presentation and is

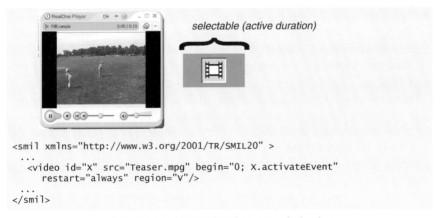

```
<smil xmlns="http://www.w3.org/2001/TR/SMIL20" >
...
  <video id="X" src="Teaser.mpg" begin="0; X.activateEvent"
     restart="always" region="V"/>
...
</smil>
```

Figure 14-7. Unrestricted `restart` behavior.

allowed to restart when a user clicks on the video object. The `restart` attribute is set to *always* to allow restarts, which is usually the default behavior.

The `restart` attribute allows bounds to be placed on restart behavior of an element. The general choices are to always allow restarts, to never allow restarts, and to allow restarts only when the object is not active. It is not possible to state that an object can be restarted only when it is active, although you can effectively get this behavior by using `fill="remove"` on the object.

There are many subtle aspects of restart behavior that need to be understood by SMIL player developers. Here is a summary:

- *What happens when an active element restarts?*: The first thing that happens when an active element restarts is that it ends it current iteration. While this seems obvious, it has a number of concrete consequences. These include that any other elements that are waiting on an end event of the running object get this event: the element first ends then begins a-new. Once it restarts, any objects that are waiting on a begin event for that element will receive the event. (This may in turn cause *them* to restart.)

- *Can an element be selected for restart during its fill period?*: Yes, assuming that the `restart` attribute allows restarting. Note that although an element is selectable during the fill period, it is outside its active duration.

- *Is there a notion of state in a presentation, so that a restarted object 'knows' that it has restarted?*: In general, no. The SMIL scheduler certainly maintains state information on the restart history of objects, but once an object restarts, it is considered to be the first (and only) instance of that object. Any fill behavior is reset and any objects that depend on the start of the element in question get restarted/ended.

- *Can an element restart after its parent time container has ended?*: No. Once a parent ends, none of its children are active or can be reactivated, unless the parent time container restarts. The only way that an element can restart after its parent time container has ended is if the parent (or direct ancestor) is restarted.

- *Can a parent time container restart during the active duration of a child object which is not restartable?*: Yes. The restart behavior of a parent container depends on its restart attribute setting. If the parent restarts, all of the children will begin their rendering lifetimes as if they were starting for the first time.

The restart behavior of elements must always be evaluated in the context of their operational environment. The combination of event behavior and restart behavior opens a host of possibilities for interesting media presentations, but the impact on the performance of player may be non-trivial. In general, the restarting of media items that are not stored locally can also have a substantial performance impact on a presentation — streaming servers will usually restart by re-sending a stream from the beginning rather than expecting the player to cache the object.

14.2.2 Restart Behavior Attributes

This section describes the behavior of two restart-related attributes: `restart` and `restartDefault`. The structure of these attributes, their legal values and the elements and profiles in which they are used is summarized in Table 14-3.

attribute	value		elements		Profiles
restart	*"always"*,	"default"	*media object,* <brush>	<par>, <seq>, <excl>, <body>	H L
restartDefault	"never", "whenNotActive"	"inherit"			

Table 14-3. Structure of restart behavior attributes.

Restart Behavior Elements

The specification of restart behavior does not require any special SMIL 2.0 elements. In general, restart behavior is applied to media object elements (such as <video>, <img>, <animation> and <ref>) or to SMIL time containers (<par>, <seq>, <excl> and — for SMIL host languages — <body>). A restart behavior applied to a time container does not enable individual child elements to also be restartable; local restart behavior is dependent on the setting of the `begin` attribute of each child.

Attribute: `restart`

The restart attribute allows an element to define how it should react to restart events. These events may come from SMIL event based timing (as part of one or more begin conditions for an element) or, when available, via a restart method in a profile's DOM. The legal values for the `restart` attribute are:

- *always*: The value *always* allows an element to restart from its beginning whenever a restart event or condition exists. The element is restarted even if it is already active.

- *whenNotActive*: The value *whenNotActive* restricts the period during which restarts requests are honored to be outside of the element's active duration. Usually this means the fill period, but it can be any period during which the element's parent is active but the element is not active.

- *never*: The value *never* states that an element may not be restarted during this iteration of the parent. It does not mean that the element will never restart: if the parent restarts, the child may begin again as part of the parent's behavior. SMIL does not have a way of enforcing a 'run only once' semantic (other than by appropriate authoring of a document).

- *default*: The value *default* states that the restart behavior is determined by the value of (the element's) `restartDefault` attribute. This is the default value for the `restart` attribute. Note that since the default behavior for the `restartDefault` attribute is *always,* the `restart="always"` assignment represents the effective default behavior of the `restart` attribute.

The `restart` attribute in supported by the SMIL 2.0 Language and the XHTML+SMIL profiles.

Attribute: restartDefault

The `restartDefault` attributes defines the default restart behavior for an element and its descendants. It accepts the *always, whenNotActive* and *never* values of the `restart` attribute, but not the *default* value. It also defines an additional value:

- *inherit*: the associated element inherits the value for `restartDefault` from the parent of this element. If the parent does exist or if no ancestor defined a `restartDefault` value, use *alwyas*. The *inherit* value is the default value for `restartDefault`.

Only the SMIL Language profile uses this attribute.

14.2.3 Examples of Restart Behavior

This section provides various examples of apply restart control behavior. The examples are organized by `restart` attribute value, although some descriptions illustrate the behavior of multiple values. For an overview of general event-based timing and start/end semantics, please see Chapter 13: *Advanced SMIL Timing Behavior and Control.*

Examples of restart="always" *Behavior*

The basic restart behavior used in SMIL 2.0 was illustrated in Figure 14-7 on page 341. The video object could be restarted at any point during its active

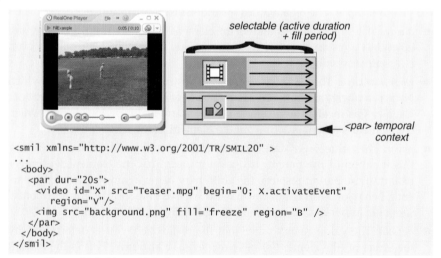

```
<smil xmlns="http://www.w3.org/2001/TR/SMIL20" >
...
  <body>
    <par dur="20s">
      <video id="X" src="Teaser.mpg" begin="0; X.activateEvent"
        region="V"/>
      <img src="background.png" fill="freeze" region="B" />
    </par>
  </body>
</smil>
```

Figure 14-8. Unrestricted `restart` behavior extended into the fill period.

duration. Figure 14-8 illustrates an extension of the period of selectivity to include the fill period. A presentation containing a background image and a video is shown in which the video starts at the beginning of the presentation (at 0s after the start of the parent <par>) and either runs to completion and freezes, or is cut off after 20 seconds. The lack of a restart attribute and the lack of a restartDefault attribute in the parent yields a default behavior of restart="always"; the video can be restarted at any point during the 20 second duration of the parent <par>.

Although it is permissible to restart an object during the fill period, the parent of the object to be restarted must be active in order for the child to restart. Figure 14-9 illustrates the (interesting) case where the video X is defined as being restartable. X has a fill="transition" defined, meaning that the rendering of the object will extend past the temporal context of its parent <par> P1. Based on the behavior shown in Figure 14-8, one would expect that the object remains selectable during its active duration and the fill interval — or does it? What should happen is that it remains selectable during the active duration only, which also defines the end of the parent <par>. Once the parent ends, the restart behavior ends. The last video frame remains visible during the transition, but it should not be selectable for restart.

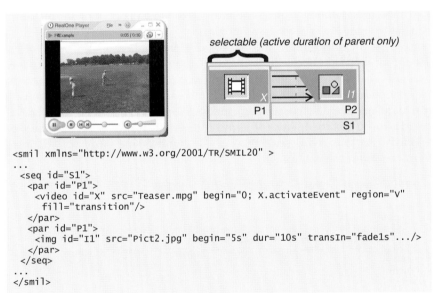

```
<smil xmlns="http://www.w3.org/2001/TR/SMIL20" >
...
 <seq id="S1">
  <par id="P1">
   <video id="X" src="Teaser.mpg" begin="0; X.activateEvent" region="V"
    fill="transition"/>
  </par>
  <par id="P1">
   <img id="I1" src="Pict2.jpg" begin="5s" dur="10s" transIn="fade1s".../>
  </par>
 </seq>
...
</smil>
```

Figure 14-9. The restart behavior only applies while the parent is active.

Examples of restart="whenNotActive" Behavior

In general, an object may be restarted either during its active duration or during its fill period (assuming it has an active parent). In Figure 14-10, the restart

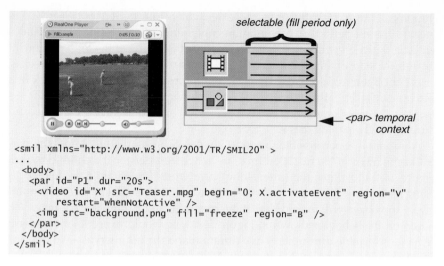

selectable (fill period only)

◄— *<par> temporal context*

```
<smil xmlns="http://www.w3.org/2001/TR/SMIL20" >
...
  <body>
    <par id="P1" dur="20s">
      <video id="X" src="Teaser.mpg" begin="0; X.activateEvent" region="V"
          restart="whenNotActive" />
      <img src="background.png" fill="freeze" region="B" />
    </par>
  </body>
</smil>
```

Figure 14-10. Restricting `restart` behavior to the fill period only.

condition has been set to `restart="whenNotActive"` and the default fill behavior is once again `fill="freeze"`. Under these circumstances, the video will be able to be restarted only during the fill period (which only occurs if the duration of the video is less than 20 seconds).

Note that in this example, the fill period is present because the video object default fill behavior. Recall from the discussion on default fill semantics (see page 335) that if the `dur="20s"` had been placed on the `<video>` as in Example 14-6, the video would not have its final frame used as fill behavior (that is, it would default to `fill="remove"` semantics). In this case, the video would never be able to be restarted, since it as no fill period during which it could be selected. As we will see, this is a cumbersome way of defining `restart="never"` semantics.

```
<smil xmlns="http://www.w3.org/2001/TR/SMIL20/Language" >
...
  <body>
    <par >
      <video id="X" src="Teaser.mpg" begin="0; Y.activateEvent" dur="20s"
          reepeat="whenNotActive" region="V"/>
      <img id="Y" src="background.png" fill="freeze" region="B" />
    </par>
  </body>
</smil>
```

Example 14-6. Restricting `restart` behavior to a non-existent fill period.

Examples of `restart="never"` Behavior

The `restart="never"` behavior explicitly states that an object should not be restarted during its active duration or its fill period. This is not a guarantee that the element will never restart, however. Consider Example 14-7. Here, an outer

```
<smil xmlns="http://www.w3.org/2001/TR/SMIL20/Language" >
...
  <body>
    <par begin="0s; X.activateEvent">
      ...
      <par>
        <video id="X" src="Teaser.mpg" begin="0"
          restart="never" region="V"/>
        <img id="Y" src="background.png" fill="freeze" region="B" />
      </par>
    </par>
  </body>
</smil>
```

Example 14-7. Restricted `restart="never"` behavior.

<par> element has an event-driven begin specified, based on the video object X. An inner <par> defines this video element with the `restart="never"` assignment to explicitly turns off a restart. During the activation of this presentation, the video will start. Since the activation of the outer <par> will have the behavior of restarting the inner <par> — but only indirectly the child video of that inner <par> — the video will restart. This is because the restart of a parent will reset any restart status for the descendants of that parent.

14.3 Synchronization Behavior Control

In a perfect world, all of the defined timing in a specification would be implemented perfectly by a SMIL 2.0 player. Unfortunately, the world is not only imperfect, it is also unpredictable. In order to provide some measure of control in the face of unpredictably, SMIL 2.0 provides three high-level synchronization control attributes: syncBehavior allows a presentation to define whether there can be slippage in implementing the composite timeline of the presentation; syncTolerance defines how much slip is allowed; and syncMaster allows a particular element to become the "master timebase against which all others are measured.

This section considers all three attributes plus two additional attributes that control the default behavior of an embedded time line or time container: syncBehaviorDefault and syncToleranceDefault.

We begin with a short overview of synchronization issues. We then consider the individual attributes and values that provide synchronization behavior control. We close this section with several examples of synchronization behavior use.

14.3.1 Understanding Synchronization Behavior Control

In networked media presentations, several components determine the availability of media samples for rendering:

- *Media Server*: the media server is often located on a different computer than that of the media player. If a given media server has many simultaneous requests pending for delivering media content, it may not be able to sustain a guaranteed delivery rate for data objects within any one stream. This may cause a presentation delay at the client-side player or browser.

- *Network Infrastructure*: the Internet usually provides non-guaranteed, best effort service when delivering data packets associated with a media stream. Individual packets may get lost or may be routed via delay-sensitive routes. Even when used with streaming protocols, packets may either never arrive or they may arrive later than required for optimal playback. This may cause a presentation delay at the client side player.

- *Player Architecture*: the local architecture available to the player will also determine the playback characteristics of a piece of media. If many time-sensitive streams need to be supported in parallel, or if the memory or processor resources available at local clients is insufficient, a presentation delay may result during playback.

While the capacity of the international Internet increases each year, the demands on that capacity also increase. For popular events, even the most powerful media servers can become taxed to the point where they can no longer offer reliable media serving services. And while the perception is that all client-side machines contain enough processing power to handle media presentation, the reality is that the diversity in clients — from desktops through PDA's to telephones — means that there will always be a shortage of resources somewhere in the transmission and delivery pipeline.

Delays in media presentations are usually unavoidable. From a SMIL perspective, since these delays are a fact of presentation life, a mechanism needs to be defined to help an author determine how these delays can best be managed in the content of an individual presentation. In early media players, the internal architecture of the player determined how delays were managed, but as presentations become more complex, a one-size-fits-all approach is not always appropriate.

Figure 14-11 illustrates three cases of synchronization delay problems. In Figure 14-11(a), we see a single video object whose delivery has encountered some sort of delay. A SMIL player will usually have few alternatives in this case: since it can't display frames that don't exist, it can either simply delay the video until the required frames arrive, or it can request that the server send only new frames so that the presentation skips over the unavailable data.

Figure 14-11(b) illustrates a more complex case. Here, two time-sensitive media objects are being delivered, one of which encounters a delay. The media player now needs to decide if the delayed video object needs to impose a similar delay on the (un-delayed) audio object, or whether the audio object can simply continue to be presented. Both of these cases illustrate that a SMIL presentation must manage several levels of time: the time relationships within a media object and the time relationships across media objects and within a presentation.

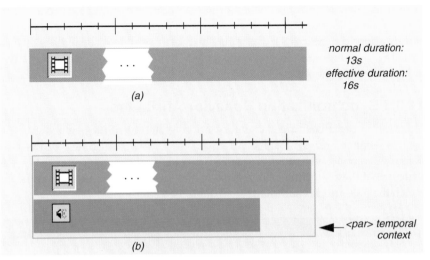

normal duration:
13s
effective duration:
16s

(a)

<par> temporal
context

(b)

Figure 14-11. Delay during object presentation.

SMIL provides a fine-grained synchronization control model that allows advanced authors to influence how media delivery delays are managed. The syncBehavior attribute is used to determine the behavior of an element relative to that of its siblings and parents. Either a hard synchronization relationship can be defined (using the *locked* value) or a soft synchronization relationship can be defined (using the *canSlip* value). While it may seem that a hard relationship is always required, this is often not the case. If there is a delay in presenting background music in a presentation, this is often less important than a delay in supporting synchronized audio and video. By explicitly relaxing synchronization relationships for unimportant objects, the player and the infrastructure can often provide more support for elements that have stricter synchronization needs.

Even when a hard synchronization relationship has been defined, there may be some degree of flexibility available in processing the relative skew among media elements. The syncTolerance attribute can be used to determine the amount of skew that is acceptable before the player needs to take action in re-aligning media clocks. An example of when skew may be allowed is when a voice-over is used on top of a video; less skew tolerance exists when lip synchronization is required.

SMIL provides these attributes because fine-grained synchronization is often associated with the semantics of the presentation rather than its SMIL structure. For most uses, a streaming media player will provide a set of defaults that allow it to process information efficiently in most cases. The extra SMIL attributes can be used when an author explicitly wants to direct player resources to maintaining critical relationships at the expense of less critical ones.

In using synchronization behavior support, keep in mind that SMIL deals with media at the inter-object level, not at the intra-object level. If detailed synchronization requirements exist, it may be more useful to resolve these by constructing a composite audio/video object than providing SMIL with two independent media objects.

14.3.2 Synchronization Behavior Attributes

This section describes three synchronization-related attributes: `syncBehavior`, `syncTolerance` and `syncMaster`. It also considers two attributes for defining default behavior: `syncBehaviorDefault` and `syncToleranceDefault`. The structure of these attributes, their legal values and the elements and profiles in which they are used is summarized in Table 14-4.

attribute	value		elements		Profiles
syncBehavior	"canSlip", "locked", "independent"	"default"			H
syncBehaviorDefault		"inherit"	media object, `<brush>`	`<par>`, `<seq>`, `<excl>`, `<body>`	L
syncTolerance	clock value	"default"			H
syncToleranceDefault		"inherit"			
syncMaster	"true", "false"				H

Table 14-4. Structure of synchronization behavior attributes.

Synchronization Behavior Elements

The specification of fine-grained synchronization behavior does not require any special SMIL 2.0 elements. The coarse-grained synchronization elements in SMIL are <seq>, <par> and <excl>; these define how the contents of a time container are to behave during a presentation without regard to implementation problems or constraints. The fine-grained control attributes allow a time container to react in a predictable manner to server, transmission or player rendering constraints. In general, synchronization behavior is applied to media object elements (such as <video>, <img>, <animation> and <ref>) or to SMIL time containers (<par>, <seq>, <excl> and — for SMIL host languages — <body>). A synchronization behavior applied to a time container defines the behavior for all children of that parent unless explicitly overridden by the child.

Attribute: syncBehavior

The `syncBehavior` attribute controls the runtime synchronization scheduling of an element with respect to its parent time container. Ordinarily, a parent time container (such as a `<par>`) defines a strict timeline upon which all of the child elements are scheduled. Sometimes, child elements will not be able to be scheduled precisely because of delays encountered at the media server, across the network work or at the player. In these cases, the `syncBehavior` attribute can specify whether the entire parent timeline should be artificially delayed to maintain global synchronization or whether the local element can vary within the parent timeline.

The legal values for this attribute are:

- *canSlip*: An element that has *canSlip* declared may slip in time relative to that of the parent time container. This means that the element may be rendered before or (more typically) after its exact scheduled time. This has the consequence that a *soft* synchronization relationship is maintained with the parent — and by extension, with all of its siblings. When soft synchronization is defined, the `syncTolerance` value is ignored. Any delay in this element will not impact the presentation of other elements.

- *locked*: An element that has *locked* declared will remain a strict synchronization relationship with other elements in the parent time container. This means that any delay in one of the children will impact the rendering of all elements. This has the consequence that a hard synchronization relation is defined. The 'hardness' of the relationship — that is, the degree to which transient errors are allowed — is defined by the `syncTolerance` attribute. Note that SMIL 2.0 does not proscribe a particular behavior to ensure that locked elements are kept temporally consistent: the approach used by the player architecture may include delaying all elements when one is delayed, or forcing delayed elements to jump ahead in time to remain consistent with other elements.

- *independent*: An element that has *independent* declared defines a local timeline that, while initially scheduled in the context of the parent time container, does not depend on the timing of other elements for its rendering. This has broad consequences, including the responses to pause and interactive behavior of the siblings. For example, it means that it ignores any hyperlink seek operations on it parent (and other ancestors).

- *default*: An element that has *default* declared obtains its behavior from the setting of the `syncBehaviorDefault` attribute. This is the default setting for the `syncBehavior` attribute.

Given the unpredictable nature of network media delivery, it is impossible to define that a given media object should be rendered without problems; the synchronization behavior attribute only defines how the player should respond to any delays associated with that element.

Attribute: syncBehaviorDefault

The `syncBehaviorDefault` attribute defines a default synchronization behavior for an element and its children. It accepts the *canSlip*, *locked* and *independent* values of the `syncBehavior` attribute, but not the *default* value. It also defines an additional value:

- *inherit*: the associated element inherits the value for `syncBehavior` from the parent of this element. If the parent does not exist or if no ancestor define a `syncBehaviorDefault` behavior, the synchronization behavior will be player dependent. The *inherit* value is the default value for `syncBehaviorDefault` attribute.

Only the SMIL Language profile uses this attribute.

Note that unlike other default attributes in this chapter, the actual default synchronization used by a media player is implementation dependent. This is a result of the complexity of media player architectures and media playback environment. A value of *locked* is used by the RealOne player as default. A value of *canSlip* is used by GRiNS, Ambulant and many mobile SMIL players.

Attribute: syncTolerance

The `syncTolerance` attribute defines tolerance to synchronization delays for time containers in which the synchronization behavior has been declared to be locked. This attribute define the amount of skew or delay that is acceptable before the player needs to enforce re-synchronization of all of the effected elements.

The legal values for this attribute are:

- *clock-value*: this attribute value consists of a SMIL clock value, measured in element simple time, that defines the amount of skew allowed within a hard synchronization relationship. Times are typically seconds or fractions of a second.
- *default*: this attribute value declares that the tolerance is determined by the `syncToleranceDefault` attribute. This is the default value for the `syncTolerance` attribute.

The shorter the synchronization tolerance, the more precise the synchronization relations among peer elements. This can be useful for maintaining lip synchronization, but it may impose a substantial (and unrealistic) performance requirement on the player architecture and the delivery infrastructure. Note that very tight synchronization relationships are often better migrated to the media definition than to the runtime synchronization among independent elements.

Attribute: syncToleranceDefault

The `syncToleranceDefault` attribute defines a default synchronization tolerance value for an element and its children. It accepts a clock-value but not the *default* value of the `syncTolerance` attribute. It also defines an additional value:

- *inherit*: the associated element inherits the value for `syncTolerance` from the parent of this element. If the parent does not exist or if no `syncTolelranceDefault` was defined, the synchronization tolerance will be player dependent. The *inherit* value is the default.

Only the SMIL Language profiles uses this attribute.

Attribute: syncMaster

The `syncMaster` attribute can be used to identify which element should be used to identify a master synchronization timing relationship. The `syncMaster` attribute can be used to inform a SMIL browser of a desired temporal hierarchy within a group of peer elements. The `syncMaster` only has effect if a hard synchronization relationship has been declared among elements.

The `syncMaster` attribute accepts the following Boolean values:

- *true*: the associated element is declared the synchronization master.
- *false*: the associated element is declared to be a synchronization slave.

If more than one peer element declares itself the synchronization master, only the first non-paused element encountered will be given master properties.

The `syncMaster` attribute is *not* used in the SMIL 2.0 Language profiles. At present, it is only supported by the XHTML+SMIL profile.

14.3.3 Examples of Synchronization Behavior Control

The following code fragment defines a <par> element that contains two media objects. Both media object define a hard synchronization relationship with their parent <par>:

```
...
<par>
   <video src="fiveSecTeaser.mpg" syncBehavior="locked" ... />
   <audio src="music.mp3" syncBehavior="locked" ... />
</par>
...
```

In both cases, the hard synchronization relationship is with the parent and not directly with the other children. If there is a delay in either child, the player will need to take action to keep the other object in sync.

Since audio continuity is often more important than video continuity, an author may want to give explicit priority to audio data by specifying the following fragment:

```
...
<par>
   <video src="fiveSecTeaser.mpg" syncBehavior="canSlip" ... />
   <audio src="music.mp3" syncBehavior="locked" ... />
</par>
...
```

It may also be useful to localize synchronization constraints to a portion of a presentation. In the following presentation, an audio object is presented in parallel with a video and an animation:

```
...
<audio src="music.mp3" ... />
...
<par syncBehavior="canSlip">
   <video src="fiveSecTeaser.mpg" syncBehavior="locked" ... />
   <animation src="logo.svg" syncBehavior="locked" ... />
</par>
...
```

The audio will play as a continuous source of background music. The <par> has been defined so that any slippage from its children will not impact (delay) the rendering of the audio. Within the <par> the video and the animation objects have been defined to remain in explicit synchronization with each other via the parent's timeline.

A SMIL player often needs to perform a substantial number of internal checks to make sure that all media elements remain synchronized. The task of the player can be eased — or, perhaps more correctly, this work can be focused — by declaring a portion of the presentation to be beyond the strict temporal scope of the fine-grained synchronization. This is illustrated in the following fragment:

```
...
<img src="backgroundImage.png" syncBehavior="canSlip"
    fill="freeze" ... />
...
<par>
    <video src="fiveSecTeaser.mpg" ... />
    <audio src="music.mp3" syncBehavior="locked" ... />
</par>
...
```

Here, the background image is independent of the detailed timing of the rest of the presentation. This allows the resources of the player to be focused on the inner media objects. Note that in this example, the synchronization behavior of the video will be determined by the implementation of the player. Most players will enforce either a best effort scheduling policy or an explicit hard synchronization policy. You should check the documentation for the SMIL player to determine the defaults.

In each of these cases, the syncBehavior attribute describes how the player should react to problem situations. If an author wants to guarantee that all media assets are rendered without server or network delays, then these objects will need to be pre-fetched and stored locally. (This may be done using a separate download agent or SMIL's content control facilities, when supported.) Note that the synchronization problem is often greatest on devices that have the least pre-fetching processing capabilities. In these cases, the complexity of the presentation should be reduced.

14.4 Time Manipulation

For most conventional media playback purposes, time is assumed to elapse at a constant pace. The media player does its best to gather all of the elements it needs for the presentation so that a smooth presentation can be created. For some types of media (and for some types of playback) it is useful to consider pace of time as a variable rather than a constant. If the pace of time is increased, the rate at which a media object is played also increases, and if the pace is slowed, the presentation also slows.

SMIL provides support for time manipulation by supplying four attributes: speed, accelerate, decelerate and autoReverse. Each of these attributes are discussed in this section.

The implementation support for time manipulation attributes is sparse in SMIL players. Most presentation-centric players provide no support at all: only XHTML+SMIL profile players accept these attributes. In media-centric SMIL (such as SVG), the attributes may be supported but most current SVG players do not provide time manipulation extensions. Only the internal SVG engine in the GRiNS player supports time manipulation. Since there are only a few implementations, we will provide a summary treatment of the various attributes in this section. Interested readers are directed to the SMIL 2.0 specification for more details.

14.4.1 Understanding Time Manipulations

When a parallel element plays, it defines a timeline for all of its children. This timeline defines a temporal framework for the <par>. When a child of a <par> plays, it often defines a local temporal framework. This framework can be based on the intrinsic duration of the media object and a known sampling rate. It is the responsibility of the SMIL player/browser to implement the conversion of the local temporal framework to that of the parent. Under normal rendering circumstances, the local and parent temporal frameworks use a common notion of time. This common notion is made explicit in the following fragment by providing a speed="1.0" factor to each element:

```
...
<par speed="1.0">
    <video src="fiveSecTeaser.mpg" speed="1.0" .../>
    <audio src="music.mp3" speed="1.0" ... />
</par>
...
```

Here, the relative speeds of each component's clock are set to be equal.

Such a common notion of the pace of time is not required, however, as long as the player can translate from the local notion of time to that of the parent. Consider the following hypothetical presentation fragment:

```
<par speed="2.0">
    ...
</par>
```

The speed="2.0" tells the player to play the element (and all of its content) at twice the speed it would otherwise have used. If an attribute value of speed="0.5" had been used, the container would have played at half its speed.

The manipulation of time in the previous example involves the *active duration* of an object. All times that are used to define the active duration are manipulated: this includes the intrinsic duration and any duration that is the result of applying the dur attribute. A specification of an active duration via a repeatDur attribute will also be temporally scaled:

```
<par speed="2.0">
  <video dur="10s" repeatDur="20s" src="ball.mpg" ... />
</par>
```

Here, the active duration will be 10 seconds. In this time, a video that would normally consume 10 seconds of play time will now show in 5 seconds. This means that the video will be repeated two times. (A `repeatCount` is not scaled.)

SMIL extends the behavioral possibilities on media rendering by also defining an `autoReverse` attribute. If set to *true*, an element will run backwards after first completing a forward temporal path. The speed with which an object appears to start and stop — its acceleration/deceleration times — can also be manipulated.

There are several aspects of time manipulation to consider when integrating objects in a presentation. Often, time manipulation works very nicely with media types such as animations: having the animation run faster or slower is not a difficult concept, and having an animation auto-reverse is also clear. For other media, the mappings are less clear either because of the way that the media is stored or the way that it is encoded. Consider a video server that provides streaming support for videos encoded in the MPEG-1 format. Such an external server often can not deliver frames in reverse order. Even if it could supply reverse frames, the decoding of MPEG-1 relies on a forward progression though the video file. Playing a video backwards is conceptually simple but often practically impossible.

The SMIL time manipulations model allows certain media to ignore the manipulation function if it cannot be supported. This itself has consequences for a presentation. In the following fragment, an animation is played in parallel with a video. Both have a `speed="2.0"` set, but the video renderer will ignore this attribute. Unfortunately, since both have been declared to share a hard synchronization relationship with the parent, the player will spend a great deal of effort in re-synchronizing media that is inherently out of sync.

```
...
<par speed="1.0" syncTolerance="0.25s">
  <video src="fiveTeaser.mpg" speed="2.0" syncBehavior="locked".../>
  <audio src="music.mp3" speed="2.0" syncBehavior="locked" ... />
</par>
...
```

In cases such as this, it is best to always use *canSlip* behavior for object synchronization.

Although the time manipulation applies to the active duration of element and its children, it does not impact the timing of the parent. Any `begin` or `end` conditions measured in an ancestor's or peer's timeline will not be affected.

14.4.2 Time Manipulation Attributes

This section describes four attributes for manipulating time: `speed`, `accelerate`, `decelerate` and `autoReverse`. The structure of these attributes, their legal values and the elements and profiles in which they are used is summarized in Table 14-5.

attribute	value			elements			Profiles
autoReverse	"true", "false"			media object, \<brush\>	animate, \<par\>, \<seq\>, \<excl\>,	\<transition-Filter\>	H
speed	decimal number ...	≠ "0.0"	"1.0"				
accelerate, decelerate		"0.0" to "1.0"	"0.0"				

Table 14-5. Structure of the time manipulation attributes.

Time Manipulation Elements

The specification of fine-grained time manipulation does not require any special SMIL 2.0 elements. The time containers, media objects, transition filters and animation elements may all potentially use the time manipulation facilities of SMIL although, as noted, support is not widespread. A time manipulation behavior applied to a time container defines the behavior for all children of that parent unless explicitly overridden by the child. The total affect can accumulate is multiple levels of time manipulation are defined.

Attribute: autoReverse

The `autoReverse` attribute specifies whether an attribute should reverse the logical direction of rendering at the end of its simple duration. This only takes effect if the simple duration is shorter than the active duration and will only have meaning if the element can support reverse rendering.

The `autoReverse` attribute allows the following values:

- *true*: The assignment `autoReverse="true"`causes an element's media to play once forward, and then once backwards. As a result, it's simple duration is doubled. If the active duration has not expired and if a repeat attribute has been specified, the forward/reverse rendering behavior will continue.

- *false*: The assignment `autoReverse="false"` causes and element to not reverse at the end of its simple duration. This is the default behavior.

The simple duration of the object must be resolved before the reverse motion can take place.

Attribute: speed

The `speed` attribute defines the local playback speed of an element relative to that of its parent time container. The value may be fractional, indicating a relative decrease in speed. Negative values are also allowed; they will cause an element to play in the reverse direction.

The speed attribute accepts the following value:

- *number*: this number defines the playback speed in element time. It is a relative value (since the speed of the parent may also have been modified.) A value of 0 is valid — it *does not* mean that the clock is frozen; it will be ignored. The default value is 1.0, meaning the same rate as the parent.

The simple duration of the object must be resolved before a negative speed manipulation can take place.

Attribute: accelerate

The acccelerate attribute specifies a perceptual acceleration factor that is applied to the beginning of a temporal pass though an object. If a decelerate factor is also used, the sum of the acceleration and deceleration must be less than or equal to 1.0.

The accelerate attribute accepts the following value:

- *number*: this value defines a real number in the range 0.0-1.0 that is interpreted as a time bound during which an acceleration function will apply to a media object. The smaller the number, the quicker the acceleration. The default value is 0, meaning no acceleration.

If the sum of the acceleration and deceleration factors is greater than 1, both will be ignored. If a repeat is specified on the element, the accelerate will be applied on each iteration.

Attribute: decelerate

The decelerate attribute specifies a perceptual deceleration factor that is applied to the end of a temporal pass though an object. If an accelerate factor is also used, the sum of the acceleration and deceleration must be less than or equal to 1.0.

The decelerate attribute accepts the following value:

- *number*: this value defines a real number in the range 0.0-1.0 that is interpreted as a time bound during which an deceleration function will apply to a media object. The smaller the number, the quicker the deceleration. The default value is 0, meaning no deceleration.

If the sum of the acceleration and deceleration factors is greater than 1, both will be ignored. If a repeat is specified on the element, the decelerate will be applied on each iteration.

14.4.3 Examples of Time Manipulation

This section provides several examples of the use of time manipulation attributes. Please note that while the format of elements and attributes is that of the SMIL Language profile, significant support for time manipulation is only provided in the XHTML+SMIL profile.

Specifying the Speed Factor

The following fragment illustrates several properties of using the speed attribute on elements in a time container:

```
...
<par speed="2.0">
    <video src="fiveSecTeaser.mpg" speed="-0.5" .../>
    <audio src="music.mp3" speed="0.5" ... />
</par>
...
```

The speed on the <par> element is defined to be twice its nominal speed. The video defines a speed of a negative 50%, meaning that it will play backward at an effective normal playback speed: 50% of 2.0. The audio element will play at normal speed in the forward direction: 50% of 2.0.

Specifying an Acceleration and Deceleration Factor

The element in the following fragment will have an acceleration and deceleration effect over 40% of their simple duration. The effect will be repeated for each of the four iterations of the object.

```
...
<img src="flag.jpg" ... >
    <animateMotion dur="10s" accelerate="0.2" decelerate="0.2"
    by="10,0" repeatCount="4" .../>
</img>
...
```

The motion animation will provide an acceleration during the first 2 seconds, then move at a slightly faster than normal rate for 6 seconds and then slow-down during the final 2 seconds.

Specifying an Auto-Reverse

In the previous example, if 20 second video is moved, the motion can also be repeated in a pendulum-like motion by specifying an auto-reverse function:

```
...
<video dur="20s" src="flags.mpg" ... >
    <animateMotion dur="20s" accelerate="0.2" decelerate="0.2"
    by="10,0" repeatCount="4" autoReverse="true" .../>
</img>
...
```

Each time the movement reverses, the acceleration and deceleration takes place.

14.5 Summary and Conclusion

This chapter provides an overview of several advanced timing control attributes for controlling fill behavior, restart behavior, synchronization behavior and time manipulation.

The fill behavior attributes allow the visual persistence of objects to be extended past the active duration. They can also be extended past the duration of their parent time container. Of all of the attributes discussed in this chapter, a fill="freeze" setting will probably be the most used advanced timing effect in SMIL.

The restart behavior attributes allow the integration of event-based timing in a presentation to be controlled in a coordinated fashion. Once events are allowed, a mechanism is required to stop multiple events from (re)starting an attribute. The model for event behavior was developed in Chapter 13: *Advanced SMIL Timing Behavior and Control*.

The synchronization behavior attributes in SMIL allows a presentation author to define critical sections of a presentation directly rather than relying on default behavior from the player. The main use of these attributes will be to control which sections of a presentation are *not* sensitive to exact synchronization requirements so that the players resources can be focused on key code sections.

We concluded this chapter with a discussion of advanced timing attributes for controlling the interpretation of the system clocks in a hierarchical manner. This facility, which is especially useful for animation, is currently only broadly supported by Microsoft's IE-6 renderer for XHTML+SMIL. Future support can be expected in SVG implementations.

15
SMIL Animation

For many people, the word *animation* conjures up memories of television cartoons: drawings in which part of the image is moved from one place on the
screen to another over the duration of the scene. Animation in the cartoon
sense is actually a combination of two factors: support for object drawing and
support for object motion — or, more correctly, support for object alteration as a
function of time.

SMIL is not a content format. SMIL does not have support for creating media
items and it does not have a generalized method for altering media object content. Instead, SMIL is a scheduling and orchestration format: it allows media
objects to be selected and then rendered under a variety of timing and spatial
constraints. This means that, unlike animation creation languages like SVG or
Flash, SMIL can't be used to make cartoons, but (unlike SVG and Flash), SMIL
can be used to display cartoon objects in the context of a general presentation
— and to change the timing and rendering properties of the cartoon object as a
whole while it is displayed.

SMIL's animation primitives allow the values of attributes to be changed
during the active duration of their associated elements. These attributes can be
visual or aural (such as the sound level, background color or opacity level) or
geometric (such as placement within a rendering region). Some profiles allow
arbitrary attribute value changes.

This chapter considers the support for animation found in the SMIL Basic
Animation and Spline Animation modules. SMIL Basic Animation is supported
in the full SMIL 2.0 Language profile and in XHTML+SMIL. It is also supported
in a separate specification called SMIL Animation; this allows animation support — the ability to change a document's attributes as a function of time — to
be integrated in other XML languages such as SVG. Since SMIL animation can
be computationally intensive, it is generally not supported in light-weight
SMIL profiles.

We begin this chapter with a general discussion of the SMIL animation
model. We then consider animation elements and attributes and conclude with
several animation examples. Note that while the facilities provided by the SMIL
Transitions Effects modules (see Chapter 10: *Transition Effects*) are closely
related to SMIL animation, they are not the same as the animation primitives
described in this chapter.

15.1 Overview of SMIL Animation

The purpose of SMIL Animation is to provide a mechanism for altering the values of attributes on elements. While the SMIL animation model is very general, there are several restrictions on the use of attribute animation defined by various SMIL profiles. These restrictions have more to do with implementation efficiency than philosophical constraints on the animation model.

In this section, we review the functional characteristics of the SMIL animation model and we summarize the application of animation in the various SMIL profiles. We also contrast the animation elements with the <animation> media reference synonym.

15.1.1 The SMIL Animation Model

In order to manage the complexity and behavior of animation implementations, SMIL provides a detailed animation model. A complete understanding of the SMIL animation implementation model is not necessary to use SMIL animations in a document. If you are simply interested in using the four SMIL animation elements, you can go directly to *Basic Animation Elements and Attributes* on page 367. However, the more you know about the background animation assumptions made by SMIL, the better able you will be to control — and debug! — animation effects.

This section provides an overview of the SMIL animation model and a discussion of various aspects of SMIL animation, including the specification of the target element and attributes, the computation of intermediate results and animation repeat behavior. A complete discussion of all of SMIL animation would require a separate book. Our discussion will be focused primarily on the use of animation in the SMIL 2.0 Language and XHTML+SMIL profiles.

Overview of the Model

The SMIL animation model is illustrated in Figure 15-1. The animation model defines an animation filter, which takes as input a target element and an attribute within that element, as well as a set of attribute values and an animation duration. A presentation value for the target attribute is computed during the animation and is applied to the rendered version of the attribute.

The initial state of the animation is determined by either the from attribute or by the first value (or value pair) in the value list. The animation engine will compute the number of steps required to bring the animation to the final (to) state based on the calculation control parameters supplied. Nearly all parameters except for duration have reasonable defaults; the default for the duration is indefinite, which for animation purposes is essentially useless.[1] You should always explicitly specify an animation duration unless the duration is inherited from the parent element.

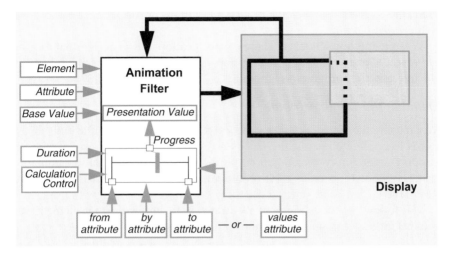

Figure 15-1. SMIL animation model.

Defining the Target Element

The animation supported by SMIL is based on the notion of a target attribute within a target element. For most forms of animation control, these target elements will be explicitly specified. They can also be implicitly specified, however, by making the animation a child of the implied target object.

In the following code fragment, the animation target element is defined explicitly:

```
...
<region id="M" top="7" left="10" height="216" width="280"/>
...
<animate targetElement="M" attributeName="top"
         from="50" to="100" dur="5s" />
<animate targetElement="M" attributeName="left"
         from="290" to="10" dur="5s" />
...
```

This form of statement can appear anywhere in a SMIL presentation.

The target element can also be defined implicitly, by placing the animation as the child of a parent container:

```
...
<region id="M" top="7" left="10" height="216" width="280"/>
...
<video id="F" src="snarf.mpg" region="b">
 <animate attributeName="top" from="50" to="100" dur="5s" />
 <animate attributeName="left" from="290" to="10" dur="5s" />
</video>
...
```

---

1 Animation is inherently time based, so that an animation duration is always required. Since animation is modelled as a continuous media object, it probably would have been better to have the animation duration default to 0 seconds — this is also not so useful, but at least it would have been consistent with other media.

Here, the element to which the motion animations are applied is implicitly set to the video parent.

When using implicit target element specification, it is expected that the parent object is of a type that is appropriate for the animation specified. If this is not the case, the animation is ignored.

Defining the Target Attribute

When using the SMIL `<animate>` and `<set>` elements, a target attribute always needs to be defined explicitly. This is because these elements are intended to support general purpose animation specification. For some common animation cases, SMIL also provides a set of animation short-hand elements. These are `<animateMotion>` and `<animateColor>`.

The following code fragment illustrates both implicit target element and implicit target attribute specification:

```
...
<region id="M" top="7" left="10" height="216" width="280"/>
...
<video id="F" src="snarf.mpg" region="M">
  <animateMotion values="(50,290); (100,10)" dur="5s" />
</video>
...
```

The `<animationMotion>` element always targets the `top` and `left` attributes of the rendering region of the associated element, so there is no need to specify the attributes directly.

It is assumed that the target element (whether implicitly or explicitly supplied) will support the `top` and `left` attributes. If not, the animation is ignored.

Computing and Restoring Attribute Values

When an animation starts, the original value of the attribute being animated is saved as the *base attribute value*. This base value can be used in the animation if no `from` attribute or `values` list is present, or it can be overridden by the animation's `from` (or `values`) specification. During the course of the animation, a *presentation attribute value* is created by the animation engine and used by the SMIL player. At the end of the active duration of the animation element, the base value will be restored unless a `fill="freeze"` is defined in the animation specification; in this case, the last state of the animation will be frozen on the display until the end of the parent time container of the animation element.

Computing Intermediate Points

SMIL animation allows various types of computations to be supported on intermediate points. For profiles supporting basic animation, animation is considered to take place over an ordered set of points, each of which is visited in sequence.

Figure 15-2 illustrates the types of functions that can be used to calculate intermediate points.

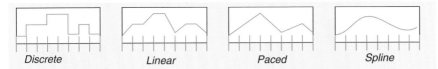

| Discrete | Linear | Paced | Spline |

Figure 15-2. Animation calculation function examples.

The intermediate points can be calculated using three methods:

- *Discrete animation*: each point defined for the animation is considered as a discrete value, with no intermediate points computed. They give a step function behavior, where the animation jumps from one value to the next.

- *Linear animation*: each point is seen as a set of temporal way-points. The animation engine computes the differences between these way-points and then computes a series of intermediate steps so that each way-point gets an equal percentage of the animation's duration. This is the default mode.

- *Paced animation*: each point is an intermediate value and the animation effect is spread evenly across the duration with a constant change rate.

SMIL Spline animation also supports the definition of a complex *spline path*.

Repeating Animations

Animations define SMIL time containers and, as such, they have the benefits and privileges that other time containers enjoy. This includes repeat behavior.

As we saw in Chapter 14: *Advanced SMIL Timing Attributes*, SMIL elements can have repeat behavior specified in two ways: in terms of a repeat duration or a repeat count. Both are illustrated in the following code fragment:

```
<video id="F" src="snarf.mpg" dur="10s" region="b">
  <animate attributeName="top" from="50" to="100"
           dur="5s" repeatCount="2"/>
  <animate attributeName="left" from="290" to="10"
           dur="5s" repeatDur="10s"/>
</video>
```

The video object *F* plays for a duration of 10 seconds. During this time, two animations are applied: in the first animation, the value of top goes from 50 to 100; it then gets reset to the original (base) value and the animation is applied again. (It has a repeat count of 2.) The second animation is defined to have a repeat duration of 10 seconds; this means that the original animation is also applied two times.

Unusual repeat behavior. While most of the repeat behavior of SMIL animation is obvious, there is one case in which the behavior — while predictable — can seem somewhat strange.Consider the following fragment:

```
...
<video id="F" src="snarf.mpg" dur="10s" region="b">
  <animate attributeName="left" from="290" to="10" dur="10s"
           repeatDur="5s" fill="freeze"/>
</video>
...
```

In this modified version of our earlier examples, the left attribute is animated from *290* to *10* over a period of 10 seconds. If we look at the results on a second-by-second basis, we see the following progression for left:

```
 0: 290;
 1: 262;
 2: 234;
 3: 206;
 4: 178;
 5: 150;
 6: 122;
 7: 94;
 8: 66;
 9: 38;
10: 10
```

The SMIL animation engine will compute a set of intermediate values for the target attribute based on the simple duration of the animation (before the repeat count or duration is applied). If, as in our example, the active duration (that is, the duration after the repeat count/duration is applied) is *shorter* than the simple duration defined by the dur attribute, the animation is cut-off. In our example, this happens after 5 seconds; the then-active frame is frozen until the end of the parent time container because of the fill="freeze" attribute.

Accumulating Animation Results

Usually, when an animation repeats, the presentation value of the attribute is reset to the initial value (either the base value or the effective from value) and the animation path is repeated. For some types of animations, it is also possible to specify that the results of a previous iteration get accumulated and passed on to the next repeat cycle. This form of animation accumulation only applies to presentation values that are derived by additive behavior.

Figure 15-3 illustrates this process for an SVG animation of a square. At the start of the first iteration, the square has a width of 5 pixels. After the first repeat cycle the square has become a rectangle with width of 10 pixels. At the end of the repeat cycle, it has grown to 35 pixels.

```
          0:00          0:05                                    0:30
      (width=5px)   (width=10px)                            (width=35px)
 1 <svg ... >
 2  ...
11    <rect width="5px" height="10px" color="red">
12      <animate attributeName="width" dur="5s" repeatCount="6"
            values="0;5" additive="sum" accumulate="sum"/>
13    </rect>
14  ...
15 </svg>
```

Figure 15-3. Animating region motion using the values attribute.

15.1.2 SMIL Animation and the `<animation>` Element

The SMIL animation modules define the `<animate>`, `<animateMotion>`, `<animateColor>` and `<set>` elements. The SMIL media object modules define the `<animation>` element as a convenience notation for referencing media objects that contain animated content (such as SVG or Flash files). The `<animation>` element has nothing to do with the SMIL animation facilities. It is, of course, possible to animate various spatial attributes of an `<animation>` object, but there is no way to influence the contents of the `<animation>` object with SMIL's animation facilities.

The following fragment illustrates how an animation object can be animated:

```
...
<animation id="S" src="Earth.svg" dur="20s" region="b">
  <animateColor attributeName="backgroundColor"
          values="(#000000;#0000FF)" dur="20s" />
</animation>
...
```

15.2 Basic Animation Elements and Attributes

The SMIL Basic Animation Module defines four animation elements and a set of attributes that can be used to define simple animations on object placement, size and color. SMIL basic animation restricts target attributes and value ranges, but it provides the foundation for animation behavior in new SMIL releases. This section considers the elements and attributes available in basic animation, and gives examples of how these elements and attributes are used.

15.2.1 Basic Animation Elements

The animation elements of SMIL are `<animate>`, `<animateMotion>`, `<animateColor>` and `<set>`. Of these, the `<animate>` element provides the most general animation control; it can perform all of the functions supported by the three other animation elements and also several functions that the others do not support. The RealOne SMIL player says it will optimize the performance of the `<animate>` element at the expense of the others.

The structure of the basic SMIL animation elements is given in Table 15-1. All of the animation elements can be a peer-level object in the SMIL timing hierarchy, or as children of a timed element. If specified as a child, the animation elements are assumed to relate to their parent, although this is not strictly required. Child animations always inherit the temporal scope of their parents, even if the animations are applied to other elements.

	<animateColor>	<animateMotion>	<animate>	<set>	Profiles
attributes	for animation attributes, see Table 15-2				L H S
	general timing, skip-content, test, core				
parents	<body>, <par>, <seq>, <excl>, media object, <brush>, <a>, <switch>, <priorityClass>				L H S
			<area>		

Table 15-1. Structure of the basic SMIL animation elements

Element: <animate>

The <animate> element allows a target element and a target attribute to be defined and it allows a set of values and a calculation mode to be defined to control the interpretation and interpolation of animation results. The <animate> element accepts all of the animation attributes discussed in the next section except the origin attribute.

Element: <animateMotion>

The <animateMotion> element is a short-hand element that can animate the top and left attributes of the target element. It accepts all of the attributes available in Basic Animation except attributeName and attributeType, since these are implied by the animate motion function. Depending on the layout model used, the motion animation will apply to the region or sub-region defined for the object specified as the target element. Some players, such as the RealNetworks RealOne player, give preference to the <animate> element instead of using <animateMotion> except for diagonal motion paths.

Element: <animateColor>

The <animateColor> element is a short-hand element that can animate the color attribute of a region or a <brush> media object. When not applied to a <brush> element, <animateColor> will target the backgroundColor attribute. When applied to a <brush>, it animates the color of the brush element. It accepts all attributes except the origin attribute.

Element: <set>

The <set> element is used to set a target attribute on a target element to a specific single value for the duration of the animation. It only accepts the targetElement, attributeName, attributeType and to attributes.

15.2.2 Basic Animation Attributes

SMIL Basic Animation provides three sets of attributes to control the animation function:

- *Target specification attributes*. These attributes allow a target element and a target attribute to be identified. It also allows attributes of different types to be disambiguated.

- *Animation value attributes*. These four attributes allow the begin and end state of the animation to be specified, as well as one or more intermediate values. It is syntactically possible to specify all four attributes on the same animation, but the provision of an explicit values list always has precedence over the specification of start and end values.

- *Animation function attributes*. These attributes control how the animation takes place. It allows a particular visual effect to be supported by allowing intermediate results to accumulate or reset.

Table 15-2 outlines the basic animation attributes introduced in this chapter.

attribute		value	elements	Profiles
target	attributeName	name of an attribute	‹set›	L H S
	attributeType	"auto", "XML", "css"		
	targetElement	IDREF		
values	from, to	legal value of target attribute	‹animate› ‹animateColor› ‹animateMotion›	L H S
	by	offset of value		
	values	';'-split list of attribute values		
function	additive	"replace", "sum"		L S H
	accumulate	"none", "sum"		
	calcMode	"linear","discrete","paced"		
	origin	"element", "parent", ("default")		

Table 15-2. Basic animation attributes

15.2.3 Attributes for Specifying the Animation Target

The target of the animation consists of an attribute on a single target element. In most cases, the target element and attribute are specified explicitly using the attributes defined in this section. If no target element is defined, the parent element that contains the animation as a child is assumed to be the target. If the resolved target element cannot accept the animation, then the animation is ignored. In most SMIL 2.0 Language profile cases, the type of the resolved target attribute will be unambiguous. In other profiles, there may be an ambiguity of attribute type. In order to resolve this ambiguity, a means is provided of specifying the desired attribute type.

This section considers the four attributes: `targetElement`, `attributeName`, `attributeType` and `href`. Both `targetElement` and `href` can be used to specify the target of the animation, although most languages will support only one of the two means. In general, `targetElement` will be more terse and `href` will be more flexible.

The structure of the target specification attributes is shown in Table 15-3.

		attribute	value	elements	Profiles
basic animation	target	attributeName	name of an attribute	`<animate>` `<animateColor>` `<animateMotion>` `<set>`	L H S
		attributeType	"auto", "XML", "CSS"		
		targetElement	IDREF		

Table 15-3. Basic animation target-related attributes

Attribute: targetElement

The `targetElement` attribute is used to identify the target element of the animation. It is an XML IDREF.

Attribute: attributeName

The attributeName attribute identifies which attribute within the target element is to be animated. Each profile restricts the attributes which may be animated using SMIL animation. (See *Animation Support in SMIL Profiles and SVG* on page 381 for details.) Some implementations provide support for additional attributes; these attribute names need to be qualified with an XML namespace identifier.

The following fragment illustrates the specification of an attribute name that includes an XML namespace identifier:

```
<smil xmlns="http://www.w3.org/2001/SMIL20/Language"
      xmlns:rn="http://features.real.com/2001/SMIL20/Extensions" >
...
<video id="x" src="snarf.mpg" region="M" />
 <animate attributeName="rn:mediaOpacity" values="80%" />
</video>
...
</smil>
```

In this example, the target element is specified implicitly to be the parent object. The duration of the animation is that of the parent. During the display of the video, the opacity of the media is set to 80%; this allows it to be blended in with its background. The "rn" qualifier indicates that this is an extension supported by the RealNetworks RealOne player.

Attribute: attributeType

In general XML implementations of SMIL animation, an `attributeName` can refer to either a CSS property or an XML attribute. In cases of conflict, the `attributeType` attribute clarifies which form applies to the animation. A value of XML states that the animated construct is the XML attribute of the element whose name matches `attributeType`'s value. If the value has any namespace prefixes, then these apply to the default namespace of the target element. A value of CSS makes the named CSS property the animated construct. The default value of `attributeType` is `auto`. This allows the animated construct to be either the XML attribute or the CSS property matching the given name. With this value, the browser checks the CSS properties first, applying the animation to the matching property if there is one. If not, the browser then checks the attributes of the target element. The `attributeType` attribute is typically not supported in SMIL 2.0 Language profile implementations.

15.2.4 Attributes for Providing Animation Values

Once a target element and attribute have been identified, it is necessary to provide a set of values for the animation. SMIL provides two mechanisms to provide these values: a set of three attributes that specify the initial and final state of the animation and an increment factor, and an explicit list of values. If the value list is present, it overrides any other value specification attribute. In all cases, if legal values for the attribute to be animated are *not* supplied, the entire animation is ignored. SMIL will compute intermediate values based on the calculation mode of the animation function. See page 373 for details.

The structure of the value-related attributes is shown in Table 15-4.

attribute			value	elements			Profiles			
basic animation	values	from, to	legal value of target attribute	`<animate>`	`<animateColor>`	`<animateMotion>`				
		by	offset of value				L		H	S
		values	';'-split list of attribute values							

Table 15-4. Basic animation value-related attributes

Attribute: from

The `from` attribute specifies the begin value for the animation using a value that is legal for the target attribute. The use of the `from` attribute is optional; if it is not present (and if the `values` attribute is not used), then the base value of the attribute (the initial value in the SMIL source) is used as the begin point for the animation.

Attribute: to

The to attribute specifies the end value for the animation using a value that is legal for the target attribute. The use of the to attribute is optional; if it is not present (and if the values attribute is not used), then the base value of the attribute is used as the end point for the animation.

Attribute: by

The by attribute specifies the increment value for the animation using a value that is legal for the target attribute. The use of the by attribute is optional; if it is not present (and if the values attribute is not used), then an increment is computed based on the begin and end values and the animation duration.

Combining from, to *and* by.

A common use case for SMIL animation is to define a simple animation function using a combination of the from, to and by attributes. We consider the useful cases:

- from *animation*: If only a from value is given, the animation is defined to run from the from value to the base attribute value. The duration will determine the number of intermediate steps.
- from/to *animation*: If both from value and to values are given, the animation is defined to run from the from value to the to value. The duration will determine the number of intermediate steps.
- from/by *animation*: If both from value and by values are given, the animation is defined to run from the from value to the base attribute value. The value of the by attribute will determine the intermediate values.
- from/to/by *animation*: If all three of the from, to and by values are given, the animation is defined to run from the from value to the to value. The value of the by attribute will determine the intermediate values.
- to *animation*: If only a to value is given, the animation is defined to run from the base attribute value to the to value. The duration will determine the number of intermediate steps.
- to/by *animation*: If both to and by values are given, the animation is defined to run from the base attribute value to the from value. The value of the by attribute will determine the intermediate values.
- by *animation*: If only a by value is given, the animation is defined to run from the base attribute value. The end state will be determined by applying the by value over the duration of the animation.

Legal values for each of the from, to and by attributes are determined by the profile specification. For the SMIL Language and XHTML+SMIL profiles, these are typically coordinate values or color names.

Attribute: values

The values attribute allows addition control to be given over the intermediate values of the animation. It consists of a semicolon-separated list of attribute value (or sometimes value pairs) that are legal for the attribute specified for the animation. White space in the list is ignored.

The following code fragment provides two examples of the values attribute:

```
<region id="M" top="7" left="10" height="216" width="280"
        backgroundColor="red"/>
...
<animate targetElement="M" attributeName="backgroundColor"
   values="#000000; #000088; #0000AA" dur="10s" />
...
<video id="F" src="snarf.mpg" region="M">
  <animateMotion values="(50,290); (100,10)" dur="5s" />
</video>
...
```

The first <animate> element specifies three color values (black, dark blue and a lighter blue) that get applied to the background color of region M. The second <animate> element illustrates the use of value-pairs in the values list: each pair is a comma-separated set of coordinates; each set of coordinates is wrapped in parentheses and separated by semicolons.

15.2.5 Attributes for Defining the Animation Function

Once the target element and attribute have been defined and the begin/end values have been specified, an *animation function* can be computed. The animation function can be controlled using four attributes: calcMode, additive, accumulate and origin. Of these, only the <animateMotion> element supports the origin attribute.

The structure of the various animation function attributes is shown in Table 15-5.

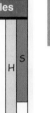

attribute		value	elements			Profiles			
	additive	"replace", "sum"							
basic animation function	accumulate	"none", "sum"	<animate>	<animateColor>	<animateMotion>	L	H	S	
	calcMode	"linear", "discrete", "paced"							
	origin	"element", "parent", ("default")							

Table 15-5. Basic animation function-related attributes

Attribute: additive

The additive attribute states how to treat the base attribute.

- *replace*: The *replace* value specifies that the starting position of the animation is not determined by the base value of the animated constructs. That it, the initial value of the animation *replaces* the original value. If the animation's starting value is different from the original value, then a "jump" occurs in the animated construct when the animation begins.

- *sum*: The *sum* value states that the progressive values defined by the animation are added to the original base value for each rendering of the animation. The *sum* value is also used by the `accumulate` attribute.

The `additive` attribute's default value is *replace*.

Attribute: accumulate

The `accumulate` attribute allows a repeating animation to retain and use the value defined by a previous iteration of an animation with each repetition. It is only used with repeating animations. The attribute's default value is *none*, which states that the animation does not accumulate. In this case, the initial value of each iteration is reset to the base value. A value of *sum* causes the incremental values of the animation to be added to the final value of the previous loop. This is similar to `additive="sum"`, except here the progressive value is added to the value at the end of the previous iteration rather than to the value just before the first loop of the animation began.

Attribute: calcMode

The `calcMode` (calculation mode) attribute is used to determine how and when intermediate values are applied to the animation result. Three values are defined for use with Basic Animation:

- *discrete*: Assigning a calculation mode of *discrete* makes the animation jump immediately from one value to the next, without any interpolation.
- *linear*: The *linear* value states that the animation should produce a linear interpolation between values. The animation bases the number of interpolated results on the simple duration of the animation: if four points are specified, 25% of the simple duration is used to determine interpolated results between each set of points. This can result in varying speeds of the animation effect if the points are not evenly spaced. The default value for `calcMode` is *linear*.
- *paced*: The value *paced* is similar to *linear* except that the animation pace is kept constant over all of the points. The simple duration is used to determine the spacing between intermedia results. Note that the smoothness provided by this fixed linear pace is broken by abrupt changes in direction at reversing value points.

A fourth value of `calcMode` is defined for Spline Animation (see page 376).

Attribute: origin

The `origin` attribute allows a position context to be defined for the animation target. It is used for motion animations in profiles in which the positioning context is determined indirectly. The values are:

- *element*: The *element* value makes the target element animate in terms of its original position. That is, the animating position values are relative to the CSS-determined position of the element itself. This is the default value of the `origin` attribute in XHTML+SMIL.

- *parent*: The *parent* value allows the animation target element animate in the CSS-defined space of its parent element. In this case, the element's original position within this space has no impact on its animation.

Only XHTML+SMIL supports this attribute.

15.3 Support for SMIL Spline Animation

For complex motion paths or smooth color transitions, it is often useful to specify a complete motion path as a spline instead of a set of (interpolated) points. The SMIL *SplineAnimation* module provides this support.

15.3.1 Spline Animation Elements

The SMIL Spline Animation module does not introduce any new elements. Spline animation support can be used with the `<animate>`, `<animateColor>` and `<animateMotion>` attributes defined in Basic Animation. Spline animation cannot be used with the `<set>` animation element.

15.3.2 Spline Animation Attributes

Three new attributes are defined for supporting spline animation and one existing attribute (`calcMode`) is extended to support the spline value. Table 15-6 summarizes the values available for spline animation. Note that spline animation support is only available as part of the XHTML+SMIL and the SVG profiles; it is not provided in the SMIL 2.0 Language profile.

	attribute	value	elements	Profiles
spline animation	path	SVG path	`<animate>` `<animateColor>` `<animateMotion>`	H S
	keyTimes	';'-split list of "0.0" to "1.0"		
	keySplines	';'-split list of space-split 4-tuples of "0.0" to "1.0"		
	calcMode	'"spline"		

Table 15-6. Spline animation attributes

15.3.3 Attributes for Spline Specification

A spline is a smooth, non-linear animation path. The characteristic of the spline are determined by a set of control points and spline values.

Attribute: calcMode

The Spline Animation module extends the list of calculation types with the *spline* value. This value states that the interpolation between values in the values list is determined according to a time function defined by a cubic Bezier spline algorithm. The values and keyTimes attributes determine the temporal moments and associated values for the spline, and the keySplines attribute determines the set of Bezier control points.

Attribute: keyTimes

The keyTimes attribute allows a set of time values in the range 0.0-1.0 to be specified. (These are treated as percentage values based on the simple duration.) Each successive value in the time list must be greater than its predecessor. The values correspond to the temporal moments at which the values in the associated values list (see page 373) are evaluated. The number of time values in the keyTimes list must match the number of values in the values list. If no keyTimes list is provided, the simple duration is used to determine the evaluation point of the values list.

Attribute: keySplines

The keySplines attribute provides a semicolon-separated list of Bezier control points. Each control point consists of four floating point numbers separated by commas or white space. Each of the values must be in the range 0.0-1.0. If there are errors in the attribute list, the animation is ignored.

Attribute: path

The path attribute applies to the <animateMotion> element only. It provides a means of specifying a motion path using SVG path syntax. The path syntax consists of a set of tuples containing:

- *Motion command*: A path component may contain commands to move to a specified point, to draw a line to a specified point, to close an existing path to a specified point, or to draw a curve to a specified point.

- *Point commands*: the "specified point" is defined as a set of coordinates.

A complete discussion of spline animation is beyond the scope of this book. Interested readers are referred to books on computer graphics or the SMIL 2.0 specification.

15.4 Examples of SMIL Attribute Animation

This section give examples of SMIL's four animation elements: <animate>, <animateColor>, <animateMotion> and <set>. Together, they can be used to change the color, position or settings of a host of SMIL attributes. Of these, the <animate> element is the most general. This section shows how each of these elements can be applied in typical use cases to manipulate SMIL elements.

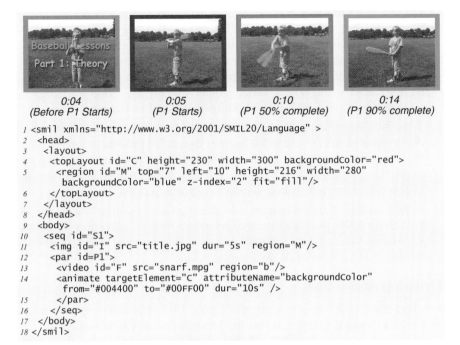

| 0:04 | 0:05 | 0:10 | 0:14 |
| (Before P1 Starts) | (P1 Starts) | (P1 50% complete) | (P1 90% complete) |

```
1  <smil xmlns="http://www.w3.org/2001/SMIL20/Language" >
2  <head>
3   <layout>
4    <topLayout id="C" height="230" width="300" backgroundColor="red">
5     <region id="M" top="7" left="10" height="216" width="280"
        backgroundColor="blue" z-index="2" fit="fill"/>
6    </topLayout>
7   </layout>
8  </head>
9  <body>
10  <seq id="S1">
11   <img id="I" src="title.jpg" dur="5s" region="M"/>
12   <par id=P1>
13    <video id="F" src="snarf.mpg" region="b"/>
14    <animate targetElement="C" attributeName="backgroundColor"
        from="#004400" to="#00FF00" dur="10s" />
15   </par>
16  </seq>
17 </body>
18 </smil>
```

Figure 15-4. Animating background color.

Changing the Background Color of a Region

Figure 15-4 illustrates the use of <animate> to change the background color of a region. The presentation defines a general canvas as the top layout, with the ID of *C* and a background color of *red*. It defines an interior region *M* (the main media region) with a background color of blue. The presentation body contains a sequence of a title image and a video object. The title image plays for 5 seconds, after which the 10-second video starts in a parallel component named *P1*.

At 4 seconds into the presentation (just before *P1* starts), the title image is shown against the red background of the top layout. When P1 starts, the video object *snarf.mpg* begins. At the same time, a 10 second animation starts. The animation directs the player to:

- Search for an element named *C*. (This is the top layout canvas.)
- Search for an attribute within *C* named backgroundColor.
- Change the color attribute over an interval of 10 seconds from the color values #004400 (dark green) to the color value #00FF00 (full green).

Three images show the progress of the video and the changing background color of the background canvas.

The are several issues that need to be resolved in order to support this animation. First, an update rate needs to be defined to determine how often the background color changes. Second, a set of intermediate color steps need to be defined in the progression from #004400 to #00FF00. These changes also need to be managed for smoothness: either the changes will be gradual or they will be sharp and discrete. We will consider all of these topics later in the chapter.

In the example of Figure 15-4, our animation interval lasted exactly as long as the associated video object. What happens when the video is shorter or longer than the animation? Figure 15-5 illustrates these two cases.

1) If the duration of the animation is shorter than the associated media object, the original state of the object is reset at the end of the animation. This is a very important aspect of SMIL animation: once the animation ends, the original values are restored. In Figure 15-5(a) the animation duration is set to 5 seconds; the background is reset to red after it ends.

2) If the duration of the animation is longer than the associated media object, the media object is either frozen or removed, but the animation continues. Like other SMIL objects, animations are timed elements that have a SMIL duration. They observe all SMIL timing rules.

Animating Region Size

A second animation example is given in Figure 15-6. Here, we want to animate the size of a rendering region during the presentation of a media object.

At the start of the video, the size of the rendering region is set to 10% of its base size. As the video is displayed, it grows in size until, at the end of the video, it reaches 100%. (Note that because the layout's fit attribute is set to *fill*, the entire region is filled with the video content, even if it were to be deformed.) Unlike a zoom transition, the size manipulation can be staggered.

In this example, we see two animations operating in parallel with a video object. The durations of both animations (and the size ranges) have been set to identical values, but this is not necessary. We could have removed one of the animations: if only a width animation was present, then the height would have stayed at 100%.

In both animations, the begin time is implicitly set to the start of the video object. This, too, can be changed. The SMIL begin, dur and end attributes can be fully applied to all animation objects.

Both the duration of the animations and that of the associated video object are the same. If the duration of the animation(s) was shorter, then at the end of

0:06	*0:14*
(a) The animation duration is shorter than the media.	(b) The animation duration is longer than the media.

Figure 15-5. Animation timing cases.

the animation the original values are restored. If the duration of the animation(s) are longer, then the final state of the video is (by default) frozen.

Animating Region Motion

Another type of animation supported by SMIL is *motion*: changing the position of a rendered object while it is active. As with color and size, we can't change the position of a part of a media object, but by layering one object on top of another, we can create some interesting motion results.

There are several aspects of motion animation that need to be considered. In the simplest form of motion animation, we specify start and end positions plus a duration; SMIL animation will define a straight-line path between the two points by default. (More complex paths can be defined if required.) This approach is illustrated in Figure 15-7. At 3 seconds into the video, a ball appears at the top right corner of the display. During the 5 second duration of the ball, it travels to the bottom left part of the screen, following the path shown in blue. Since the duration of the animation is equal to the duration of the ball image — and because the ball image has an explicit fill="remove" — the ball disappears at the end of the animation. Otherwise, if the duration of the image was longer than that of the ball and the ball had fill="freeze" behavior, the ball would have jumped back to the top-right initial position after the anima-

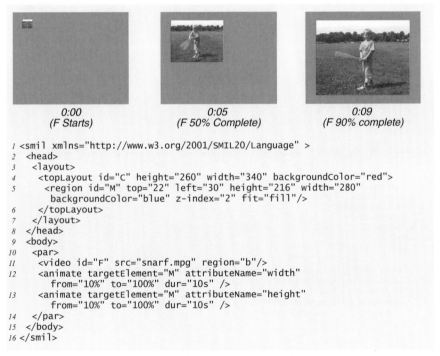

0:00 *(F Starts)*	*0:05* *(F 50% Complete)*	*0:09* *(F 90% complete)*

```
 1  <smil xmlns="http://www.w3.org/2001/SMIL20/Language" >
 2    <head>
 3      <layout>
 4        <topLayout id="C" height="260" width="340" backgroundColor="red">
 5          <region id="M" top="22" left="30" height="216" width="280"
              backgroundColor="blue" z-index="2" fit="fill"/>
 6        </topLayout>
 7      </layout>
 8    </head>
 9    <body>
10      <par>
11        <video id="F" src="snarf.mpg" region="b"/>
12        <animate targetElement="M" attributeName="width"
              from="10%" to="100%" dur="10s" />
13        <animate targetElement="M" attributeName="height"
              from="10%" to="100%" dur="10s" />
14      </par>
15    </body>
16  </smil>
```

Figure 15-6. Animating region size.

tion. The ball could be frozen at the final point of the animation by putting a fill="freeze" on both of the animation elements on lines 14 and 15.

In Figure 15-7, it is handy that the young baseball player misses the ball, since this makes the animation easy to describe. But what happens if he gets lucky and hits the ball? In this case, we would want to provide a motion *path* instead of two motion points.

The path and the path specification syntax is shown in Figure 15-8. Here, the from and to attributes are replaced by a list of values that represent the path. While only three values are shown, the path can be made arbitrarily complex. For some SMIL profiles, such as XHTML+SMIL and SVG, a spline-based path can be defined — this is handy if the pitcher had thrown a curve ball!

SMIL animation supports several ways of specifying the bounds and the paths of animation components. These are considered in sections *Basic Animation Elements and Attributes* on page 367 and *Support for SMIL Spline Animation* on page 375.

Combining Animations

The examples in the previous sections each illustrate one type of animation. SMIL allows multiple animations to be combined. For example, to provide a three-dimensional effect in the previous example, we could have scaled the size

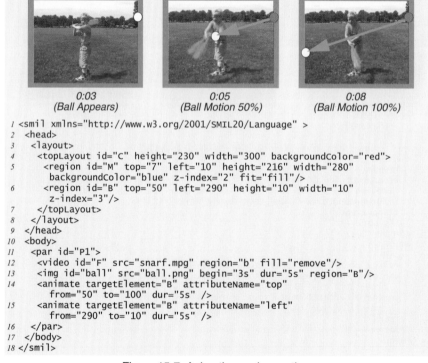

| *0:03* | *0:05* | *0:08* |
| (Ball Appears) | (Ball Motion 50%) | (Ball Motion 100%) |

```
1  <smil xmlns="http://www.w3.org/2001/SMIL20/Language" >
2  <head>
3    <layout>
4      <topLayout id="C" height="230" width="300" backgroundColor="red">
5        <region id="M" top="7" left="10" height="216" width="280"
           backgroundColor="blue" z-index="2" fit="fill"/>
6        <region id="B" top="50" left="290" height="10" width="10"
           z-index="3"/>
7      </topLayout>
8    </layout>
9  </head>
10 <body>
11   <par id="P1">
12     <video id="F" src="snarf.mpg" region="b" fill="remove"/>
13     <img id="ball" src="ball.png" begin="3s" dur="5s" region="B"/>
14     <animate targetElement="B" attributeName="top"
         from="50" to="100" dur="5s" />
15     <animate targetElement="B" attributeName="left"
         from="290" to="10" dur="5s" />
16   </par>
17 </body>
18 </smil>
```

Figure 15-7. Animating region motion.

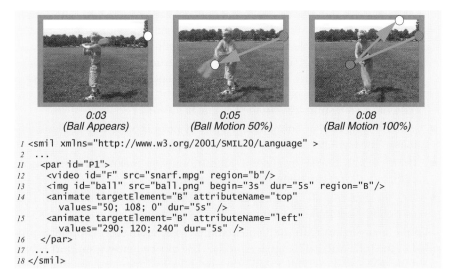

0:03	0:05	0:08
(Ball Appears)	*(Ball Motion 50%)*	*(Ball Motion 100%)*

```
 1 <smil xmlns="http://www.w3.org/2001/SMIL20/Language" >
 2 ...
11   <par id="P1">
12     <video id="F" src="snarf.mpg" region="b"/>
13     <img id="ball" src="ball.png" begin="3s" dur="5s" region="B"/>
14     <animate targetElement="B" attributeName="top"
          values="50; 108; 0" dur="5s" />
15     <animate targetElement="B" attributeName="left"
          values="290; 120; 240" dur="5s" />
16   </par>
17 ...
18 </smil>
```

Figure 15-8. Animating region motion using the `values` attribute.

of the ball image so that it got smaller as it travelled across the screen (or that it deformed slightly at the moment the ball was hit). We could have also changed the background color at the moment the ball passed the batter.

SMIL defines a fairly complex model (called the *animation sandwich model*) to describe how each of the animations are structured and layered, and how priorities are assigned to individual animation elements. (The name comes from an analogy with a layered submarine sandwich.) For purposes of this section, it is sufficient to note that combining animations is possible.

15.5 Animation Support in SMIL Profiles and SVG

The SMIL animation model is a general purpose mechanism for describing changes to the values of attributes over time. While it is conceptually possible to animate all element attributes, each SMIL profile limits the attributes it supports for a variety of reasons: error checking is very difficult, attribute value specification can be very complex, and preserving a predictable state throughout the presentation was considered to be essential. More comprehensive support for attribute animation was beyond the needs of the SMIL 2.0 release.

While each SMIL 2.0 profile makes an attribute selection, designers of other XML language can apply attribute animation to any elements and attributes they choose. This is also true for designers of new SMIL profiles. This has been done to a large extent in the SVG profile, but other languages could go considerably further in terms of the animation scope.

For the various SMIL profiles, here are the main attribute selections:

- *SMIL 2.0 Language Profile.* In general, only attributes associated with a layout region (such as top, left, bottom, right, height, width, `backgroundColor, z-index` and `regionName`) can be animated. The animation can occur directly on the region, or indirectly by animating the placement of the media object and the `color` attribute on the `<brush>` element. It is also possible to animate the spatial properties of a link anchor via the `coords` attribute of the `<area>` element. It is not possible to animate XML ID's, source media object names, durations or begin/end times. Spline animations are not supported in the Language Profile.

- *SMIL 2.0 Basic Profile.* Animation is typically not supported by implementations at the low-end of the SMIL Language spectrum.
- *XHTML+SMIL Profile.* In general, all attributes on major elements can be animated. (For restrictions, see Table 15-8 on page 383.)
- *SVG.* In general, all drawing element attributes can be animated. (For restrictions, see Table 15-9 on page 383 and Table 15-10 on page 384.)

Of the mainstream SMIL implementations, basic animation support is provided in the full SMIL 2.0 Language profile. The most extensive support is provided by SVG and XHTML+SMIL (in the HTML+Time implementation in Microsoft's Internet Explorer).

The exact set of elements and attributes supported by each of the profiles is listed in the following sections.

15.5.1 Animation and the SMIL 2.0 Language Profile

Table 15-7 summarizes the target elements and attributes that may be animated using the indicated animation element.

Target Element	Animation Element	Target Attributes
region	animate, set	soundLevel, left, right, top, bottom, width, height, z-index, backgroundColor, regionName
	animateMotion	top, left
	animateColor	backgroundColor
media objects	animate, set	soundLevel, left, right, top, bottom, width, height, z-index, backgroundColor
	animateMotion	top, left
	animateColor	ackgroundColor
area	animate, set	coords
brush	animate, set	left, right, top, bottom, width, height, z-index, color
	animateColor	color

Table 15-7. Permissible target elements and attributes for the Language profile.

15.5.2 Animation and the XHTML+SMIL Profile

XHTML+SMIL allows animation to be specified on all elements except the following:

- `<head>`, `<title>`, `<style>`, `<meta>`, `<base>`, `<link>`
- `<script>`
- `<par>`, `<seq>`, `<excl>`
- `<switch>`
- `<animate>`, `<animateMotion>`, `<animateColor>`, `<set>`
- `<frameset>`, `<frame>`, `<noframes>`

Not all of the elements available for animation may be specified implicitly. All elements that support animation may be identified explicitly with the targetElement attribute.

Table 15-8 summarizes the attributes within the allowed target elements that may be animated using the indicated animation element.

Animation Element	Target Attributes
animate, set	align, bgcolor, border, cellhalign, cellpadding, cellspacing, cellvalign, checked, class, clear, color, cols, dir, disabled, face, frame, frameborder, height, href, marginwidth, marginheight, rows, rules, selected, noshade, size, style, title, valign, value, width
animateMotion	posX, posY
animateColor	only CSS color properties

Table 15-8. Permissible target elements and attributes for XHTML+SMIL.

15.5.3 Animation and SVG

SVG supports the animation elements defined in SMIL Basic Animation module. These are extended with the `<animateTransform>` element.

Table 15-9 summarizes the SVG data types that may be animated using the indicated animation element

Animation Element	SVG Datatypes
animate, set	angle, color, coordinate, integer, length, lists, number, paint, percentage, uri. Also all other data types used in animatable attributes.
animateColor	color, paint
animateTransform	transform-list

Table 15-9. Permissible target data types for SVG.

Table 15-10 summarizes the SVG elements that can be animated with the `<animateMotion>` element:

Animation Element	SVG Datatypes
animateMotion	g, defs, use, image, switch, path, rect, circle, ellipse, line, polyline, ploygon, text, clipPath, mask, a, foreignObject.

Table 15-10. Permissible target elements and attributes for SVG.

15.6 Summary and Conclusion

The SMIL Animation modules provide a flexible means of introducing time-based alteration of attribute values. The Basic Animation module defines four animation attributes, three of which are short-hand elements. The SMIL Spline Animation modules allows a cubic Bezier path to be defined in a SMIL document or a host language integrating SMIL Animation functionality.

In addition to the SMIL 2.0 Language and the XHTML+SMIL profiles, SMIL Animation forms a core part of SVG functionality.

15.7 Further Resources

SVG

Scalable Vector Graphics (SVG) 1.0 Specification, Jon Ferraiolo (ed.), W3C Recommendation, 4 September 2001, `http://www.w3.org/TR/SVG`.

16

Extended Content Control

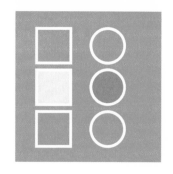

The SMIL *BasicContentControl* module defines a set of elements and attributes that allow the presentation of parts of the document to be determined based on the setting of one or more system test attributes. The facilities provided by the basic content control primitives are essentially the same as those supported in SMIL 1.0, with some minor naming differences and the extension that test attributes can also be placed on SMIL elements without being wrapped in a `<switch>`.

The SMIL 2.0 content control mechanisms also provide a number of advanced features. These include the ability to load media objects before they are actually needed, so that presentation can occur as smoothly as possible, and the ability to extend the set of test attributes to include special-purpose test variables that are defined by the document author. SMIL 2.0 also supports the `skip-content` attribute from SMIL 1.0.

This chapter looks at the three general areas of advanced content control. We begin with a discussion of the `skip-content` attribute, since this attribute is supported by all SMIL 2.0 Language and Basic profile players. We then look at support for pre-fetching media and close with a discussion of the custom test attribute facilities in SMIL 2.0.

The nature of the material in this chapter is such that we segment each topic area into separate sections, each with their own examples. We build on the material presented in Chapter 9: *Content Selection and Control*; readers are encouraged to read that chapter before continuing with the discussions below.

16.1 Skip Content Control

If a prize were to be given for the worst attribute description in the SMIL 2.0 standard, `skip-content` would stand an excellent chance of winning. While nothing in the description is incorrect, there is very little text to help language users and language designers understand the intent and use of skip-content control. In order to understand the operational aspects of skip-content, it is handy to consult the SMIL 1.0 specification. The section *Extending* SMIL *1.0* provides a useful summary of skip-content behavior. (The section below also provides all the information you need to know to effectively use the skip-content attribute.)

16.1.1 Motivation: Future-Proofing SMIL

SMIL has strict rules that govern how a SMIL parser must react to errors in a document. In general, if an error is found, the entire document should be rejected. While the reason for this is clear — the temporal structure of the document depends on the total evaluation of the SMIL file, which means that a syntax error in one part can radically impact the timing of other parts — it has the unhandy side-effect that if older parsers attempt to process a newer version of SMIL (in which new element structures have been defined), then the entire document must be rejected when this is not really necessary.

In order to future-proof SMIL, an attribute was defined that can control the parsing and evaluation of elements and element content. The `skip-content` attribute covers two cases:

- If a new element is introduced in some future version of the SMIL language, the `skip-content` attribute can be used to instruct older parsers either to ignore the new element but to still process the children of that element as normal SMIL statements, or to ignore the element and its contents.

- If an existing empty element — that is, it is defined not to have any child content — is changed in a future version of the language to include child content, the `skip-content` attribute can instruct the older parser either to ignore the contents of that element (but to still process the element) or to generate a syntax error.

The content addressed by the `skip-content` directive has nothing to do with any object pointed at by a `src` attribute: `skip-content` only considers the element and the children of that element. This is a key concept in understanding how `skip-content` works.

16.1.2 Skip Content Control Attributes

The *SkipContentControl* module defines one attribute: `skip-content`. Note that since this attribute is a hold-over from SMIL 1.0, it uses old-style hyphenated naming instead of camel cased naming.

Attribute: skip-content

The `skip-content` attribute is a Boolean variable that accepts two values:

- *true*: This value covers two cases.
  (1) If the element containing this attribute is not recognized, ignore the element and ignore its contents.
  (2) If the element containting this attribute is recognized but if its content model changes from empty to non-empty, then process the element but ignore the child content.

- *false*: This value covers two cases.
  (1) If the element containing this attribute is not recognized, skip the elment but process the content (its child elements) as if the unknown element did not exist.

(2) If the element containting this attribute is recognized but if its content model — that is, the fact that it has child elements — is not recognized, generate a syntax error.

The values of the `skip-content` attribute determine the actions of the document parser on unknown elements and content. If the elements and content are recognized by the parser, then the `skip-content` attribute has no effect (it is ignored). The `skip-content` attribute is only evaluated at the point that a parser would otherwise generate an error when processing the document.

The default value for `skip-content` is *true*; this means that for all elements that accept the attribute, any unknown content should be skipped by the parser and not generate syntax errors. Unknown elements are ignored and processed as if `skip-content` is set to *true* (unless `skip-content` is explicitly declared *false*).

16.1.3 Using the `skip-content` Attribute

We will use the code fragment in Example 16-1 to illustrate the use of the `skip-content` attribute.

Assume that a SMIL 2.0 parser were to process Example 16-1. The following steps will be taken when the document is parsed:

1) This example carries no XML namespace definition. The SMIL 2.0 parser will continue processing the document and will treat it as SMIL 1.0.

2) When SMIL 1.0 was designed, the <region> element on line 4 was not allowed to accept content (in this case, the specification of a hierarchical region as a child on line 5). Since `skip-content` is set to *true* on the parent, the region *F* is processed and the hierarchical region *C* is ignored.

3) When SMIL 1.0 was designed, the <a> element was not part of the language. As a result, the definition on line 11 would ordinarily cause a syntax error during parse. However, since the `skip-content` attribute is defined and is set to *false*, the parser will ignore the <a> element but its contents (in

```
 1 <smil >
 2   <head>
 3     ...
 4     <region id="F" height="240" width="280" skip-content="true" >
 5       <region id="C" top="220" height="20" width="280" />
 6     </region>
 7   </head>
 8   <body>
 9     ...
10     <par>
11       <a id="anchor1" href="http://www.example.org/doc.smil"
             target="destination" skip-content="false">
12         <video id="F" src="snarf.mpg" region="b"/>
13       </a>
14       <img id="caption" src="caption.txt" dur="15s" region="C" />
15     </par>
16     ...
17   </body>
18 </smil>
```

Example 16-1. Using the `skip-content` attribute in a SMIL 1.0 file.

this case, the video object) will be processed as if the <a> element wrapper did not exist. If `skip-content` has been set to *true*, both the <a> element and the <video> element would be ignored. If there had been no `skip-content` attribute, the statement on line 11 would be processed as if `skip-content` was declared and set to *true*.

4) The <img> element on line 14 now references a region that does not exist — the definition of the *C* region was ignored. As a result, the content of the media object will be rendered using SMIL default layout semantics, but it will be rendered.

Now, let's see what happens if a SMIL 2.0 parser processes the same file, but this time with a SMIL 2.0 namespace declaration. (This is illustrated in Example 16-2.) The following aspects will occur during parsing:

1) The SMIL 2.0 parser will recognize the SMIL 2.0 namespace definition. It will process this file as SMIL 2.0 content.

2) The region definition on line 4 contains content that is understood by the parser. As a result, the `skip-content` attribute is ignored.

3) In SMIL 2.0, the <a> element is defined and allowed to have <video> object content. Thus, the parser will again ignore the `skip-content` attribute and process the statements normally.

4) The <img> element will render to the requested sub-region.

If a future SMIL 3.0 parser were to process this file, it should recognize the SMIL 2.0 namespace and process the file as described above.

The discussion up to this point represents the theory of how SMIL 2.0 (and SMIL 1.0) parsers should work. In practice, the ability to skip document content is of marginal utility. It is really only useful if the namespace declaration is changed to a recognized but unsupported type. In this case, unknown elements will be ignored, but it is doubtful that the result will be meaningful.

```
1 <smil xmlns="http://www.w3.org/2001/SMIL20/Language">
2   <head>
3     . . .
4     <region id="F" height="240" width="280" skip-content="true" >
5       <region id="C" top="220" height="20" width="280" />
6     </region>
7   </head>
8   <body>
9     . . .
10    <par>
11      <a id="anchor1" href="http://www.example.org/doc.smil"
           target="destination" skip-content="false">
12        <video id="F" src="snarf.mpg" region="b"/>
13      </a>
14      <img id="caption" src="caption.txt" dur="15s" region="C" />
15    </par>
16    . . .
17  </body>
18 </smil>
```

Example 16-2. Using the `skip-content` attribute in a SMIL 2.0 file.

16.2 Custom Test Attributes

One of the important contributions of SMIL 1.0 was the introduction of system test attributes which, together with the `<switch>` element, allowed a choice to be made among various content paths in a presentation. The SMIL specification defines a set of system test attributes that cover many of the basic selection needs with SMIL documents. These attributes and the `<switch>` statement are discussed in Chapter 9: *Content Selection and Control*.

The disadvantage of the system test attribute architecture is that all test variables need to be defined as part of the language specification. There is no mechanism to extend the choices available to users on a per-presentation basis. Although it is possible to define custom namespaces with new sets of test attributes, the author would have no control over the recognition of these extensions by a particular SMIL player.

The SMIL *CustomTestAttributes* module defines an architecture for extending the set of test variable available for use in `<switch>` statements (or as stand-alone test variables). It allows authors to create new test variables for adaptivity that still work on existing SMIL 2.0 players. The module defines two elements and four attributes: the `<customAttributes>` and `<customTest>` elements and the `customTest`, `uid`, `defaultState` and `override` attributes.

16.2.1 Understanding Custom Test Attributes

The custom test attribute architecture is similar in scope and intent to the system test attribute architecture defined in Chapter 9: *Content Selection and Control*: a test variable is defined that can be used to select an element for inclusion in a presentation. The (custom) test variable is defined as an attribute that may be attached to any element: if the attribute evaluates to *true*, the element is included in the presentation; if it evaluates to *false*, it is ignored.

Unlike the system test attribute architecture, there is no pre-defined set of custom test variables. As a result, a mechanism is required to define custom test variables within the SMIL source document.

Custom test variables are defined as part of the `<head>` section of a presentation by using the `<customTest>` element. All of the `<customTest>` elements are defined as children of the `<customAttributes>` element. At the time of definition, each custom test variable can be given a default value (*true* or *false*). This value may be overridden by either the user (via the user interface of the player) or by consulting an external settings file that is provided via the `uid` attribute.

Within the user interface community, the issue of providing overrides to system-defined values has always been a hot topic. There are many who feel that, philosophically, the user should always have the final say over the content that is presented. Document authors often feel that they are in the best position to decide which content is appropriate for which set of users. SMIL takes a neutral position in this debate. The override attribute is made available to define author intentions: the author can state whether the value in the custom test may be overridden by the user (or user agent). User agents are free to enforce or ignore this setting. It is expected that some higher-level protocol will ultimately manage the access to the custom test variable definitions.

We give an example of using custom test variables on page 393 after a more precise definition of the available elements and attributes.

16.2.2 Custom Test Elements

SMIL defines two elements to manage the definition and processing of custom test variables. All of these are considered in this section.

Element: <customAttributes>

Table 16-1 defines the structure of the <customAttributes> element. This element delineates a section in the SMIL <head> that is used to define a set of custom test variables. It contains specifications for all the custom tests used in a presentation.

<customAttributes>		Profiles				
attributes	system test	L				
	skip-content					
	core					
parent	<head>	L				
child	<customTest>	L				

Table 16-1. Structure of the <customAttributes> element.

Element: <customTest>

The <customTest> element defines a custom test variable for use in the presentation. The element's id attribute lets the test be referred to from elements in the <body> section that are to be tested. Its structure is laid out in Table 16-2.

A <customTest> element's initial value may be overridden by values found at a location defined by the uid attribute or by user interaction though the player interface. The author may specify a preference for the persistence of a test variable value via the override attribute.

<customTest>		Profiles				
attributes	defaultState	L				
	override					
	uid					
	skip-content					
	core					
parent	<customAttributes>	L				

Table 16-2. Structure of the <customTest> element

16.2.3 Custom Test Attributes

SMIL defines four attributes to manage the definition and processing of custom test variables. Each of these are considered in this section.

Attribute: customTest

The `customTest` attribute takes a list of custom test names defined in the `<head>` section as an argument. If all of the names refer to custom test variables that resolve to *true*, the associated element is included in the presentation. If any of the custom test attributes listed resolve to *false*, the element is not included in the presentation.

All of the rules pertaining to the evaluation of system test variables apply to custom test variables.

Attribute: defaultState

The `defaultState` attribute defines an initial value for the custom test variable. It is used in the `<customTest>` element only. Permissible values are:

- *true:* the associated test variable is true and should allow rendering.
- *false:* the associated test is false and should block rendering.

The default value is *false*.

Attribute: override

The `override` attribute states whether or not the custom test's state should be readily changeable by the user. It accepts the following values:

- *visible*: this value lets the user alter the test's state through the browser's interface for changing custom test states.
- *hidden*: do not list this variable as alterable in this interface.

The default value is *hidden*.

Note that the browser may still provide the user with other, less obvious means to change a *hidden* test state.

Attribute: uid

The `uid` attribute provides a URI to a resource determining the test's state. The URI may simply be a registration of a fixed state for the test. On the other hand, it could be a process that communicates with the browser to set the test's state. This attribute takes priority over the `defaultState` attribute in assigning the state. In turn, the user has highest priority, being able to change the state given by the `uid` attribute.

16.2.4 Examples Using Custom Test Attributes

Use of the custom test attribute facility is illustrated in Figure 16-1. This application illustrates part of a medical dossier. The dossier (of which this fragment is a small part) contains information on a problem with a patient's right back leg. It also contains media objects that describe the operation on the right leg.

The application of custom test attributes is partitioned across two sections of the document. The `<head>` section contains the definitions of two custom test attributes (*Annotations* and *medicalStaff*), and the `<body>` section contains references to the state of the attribute values.

In the `<head>` section, the `<customAttributes>` element on line 3 contains the definition of the two custom test attributes. Each test variable is defined in a separate `<customTest>` element. The first definition, of *Annotations* on line 4, creates a test variable with a default state of *true* and with an override value of *visible*. This means that the UI of the player may provide an obvious means of selectively changing the attribute value from *true* to *false* (or vice versa). The second definition, of *medicalStaff* on line 5, creates a test variable with a default state of *false* and with an override value of *hidden*. The intention is that, as part of the user's profile, there is some indication on the capabilities of this viewer. If he or she is a member of the medical staff, they will get access to more detailed information in the presentation.

The `<body>` section contains several examples of the application of the custom test variables, as well as the use of other content control mechanisms. Line 11 contains a `<switch>` element. The `<switch>` evaluates its children in document order, activating the first child that has a test variable (*system* or *custom*) that resolves to true.

If the bandwidth of the network link has been determined by the player to be 56Kb or greater, the `<par>` element (and its contents) on line 12 is played. If the bandwidth is determined to be lower, then the `<seq>` on line 20 is selected. Both the `<par>` on line 12 and the `<seq>` on line 20 contain a collection of media objects. One of the two elements in the collection is a video object or an image (depending on the bitrate) and the other is a conditional piece of content that is only displayed if the *Annotations* variable resolves to `true`. At the top of Figure 16-1, we see three images. The left two images represent the output of this section of the presentation: if the *Annotations* custom test variable resolves to *true*, the base media object is displayed with an (animated) annotation overlay. If it resolves to *false*, only the base media object is presented.

On line 29, we see another use of the custom test variable. Here, the 29 second `<par>` is only played is the *medicalStaff* attribute value is *true*. This segment — which illustrates how a scalpel breaks during the operation — consists of a base media object and a separate annotation object; this latter object is only shown if the *Annotations* custom test variable resolves to true. The top-right portion of Figure 16-1 shows the video of the operation with the annotation overlay.

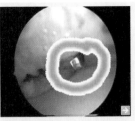

Annotations="true"   *Annotations="false"*   *medicalStaff="true"*

```
1  <smil xmlns="http://www.w3.org/2001/SMIL20/Language">
2  <head>
3    <customAttributes>
4      <customTest id="Annotations" title="View Annotations"
          defaultState="true" override="visible"/>
5      <customTest id="medicalStaff" title="Medical Staff Use"
          uid="http://www.example.org/Doctors/list.txt"
          defaultState="false" override="hidden"/>
6    </customAttributes>
7    ...
8  </head>
9  <body>
10   ...
11   <switch>
12     <par systemBitrate="56000">
13       <video region="Image" dur="11s" src="Video/Symptoms.mpg"/>
14       <img id="Annotation1" region="Overlay" begin="1.55" dur="8.7s"
            src="Images/Overlay.gif" customTest="Annotations">
15         <animateMotion ... />
16         <animate attributeName="width" ... />
17         <animate attributeName="height" ... />
18       </img>
19     </par>
20     <seq>
21       <par dur="5s">
22         <img region="Image" fill="freeze" src="Images/Symp-F20.jpg"/>
23         <img region="Overlay" begin="1" dur="3s" src="Images/Overlay.gif"
            customTest="Annotations"/>
24       </par>
25       ...
26     </seq>
27   </switch>
28   ...
29   <par dur="29s" customTest="medicalStaff">
30     <video region="Image" dur="29s" src="Video/ScalpelBreaks.mpg"/>
31     <img region="Overlay" begin="15" dur="4s" src="Images/Overlay.gif"
          customTest="Annotations"/>
32   </par>
33   ...
34 </body>
35 </smil>
```

Figure 16-1. Using custom test attributes.

The custom test facility provides an interesting basis for experimentation with user-centered presentation design. Unfortunately, the attributes — although they are part of the SMIL 2.0 Language profile — are not universally implemented. Only the *GRiNS* and Ambulant players provide full support for custom test attribute implementation and integration.

16.3 Prefetch Control

The *PrefetchControl* module allows an author to give hints to the player on when various media items should be fetched from the media server in advance of that media's use. This can allow a presentation to execute more efficiently, since media objects that are needed later in a presentation can be fetched during times when not much transfer activity takes place in the player. This can help spread any peaks in network transfer use across the duration of an entire presentation

16.3.1 Understanding Pre-Fetching of Media

Media objects tend to be relatively large items that require substantial time to transfer across a network infrastructure. Often, a player can optimize presentation performance by pre-loading parts of currently active media items or pre-fetching the next media element in its display queue. Such pre-load and pre-fetch behavior is nearly always local in scope.

In contrast to the player, a presentation author has a global view of which objects will play an important role in the presentation. For this reason, the author is sometimes in a better position to decide which elements should be fetched early. Unfortunately, most authors have little information available about the characteristics of the network connection state during the presentation or the amount of buffer space available to the player. As a result, author pre-fetch directives are taken as informed hints by the player, but the player remains in final control over which objects get fetched when.

In the SMIL pre-fetch model, the loading of future media is not a transparent activity that occurs in the background: an explicit request for a pre-fetch will result in the creation of a pseudo-media reference with a simple duration that gets factored into the timing of the document. (We give an example of this on page 396.)

Pre-fetching media works best when the media object is static — that is, it is an image or video that is not expected to change during the presentation. If you were to pre-fetch stock ticker information, the data that you pre-fetch may actually be stale by the time you present it: since the SMIL player has no means to reliably detecting that the stored information has changed other than information in the original transport header, it cannot invalidate the version in its buffer. Authors should be aware of this problem. For example, if the *http* protocol header indicates that a media object is valid but if the media object changes at the server, this will not be detected.

Another problem of which authors should be aware is the potential for incurring media charges in a pay-per-view (PpV) environment. If a media item is pre-fetched from a PpV server but never rendered because of early termination of the presentation (or because of the settings on a SMIL <switch>), users may be presented with charges that they may not realize they had made. SMIL has no mechanisms for guarding against the (mis)use of this situation.

16.3.2 Pre-Fetch Elements

The SMIL *PrefetchControl* module defines <prefetch> to selectively pre-load media objects. Table 16-3 shows the structure of the <prefetch> element.

Element: <prefetch>

The <prefetch> element is used to identify a media object that is to be pre-loaded into the the player. The element contains the name of the media object and zero or more control attributes. The intrinsic duration of the element is the duration of the media fetching activity. This duration can be qualified as a simple duration by providing a dur attribute.

The player may decide not to process the pre-fetch hint. If no pre-fetch takes place, the player must still respect any explicit simple duration on the <prefetch> element. If a pre-fetch is repeated, a fresh copy of the media object must be loaded each iteration.

The author of a presentation may only supply the pre-fetch command as a hint to the player; no control over actual pre-fetch behavior is provided. SMIL 2.0 players should support parsing of the <prefetch>

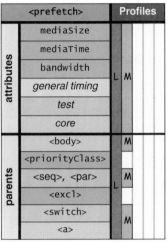

<prefetch>	Profiles	
attributes		
mediaSize		
mediaTime		
bandwidth	L	M
general timing		
test		
core		
parents		
<body>		M
<priorityClass>		
<seq>, <par>	L	M
<excl>		
<switch>		M
<a>		

Table 16-3. Structure of the <prefetch> element

element and attributes, even if no implementation support for pre-fetching media is provided.

The amount of data that is pre-fetched is determined by the settings of the pre-fetch control attributes. It is also determined by any control information in the protocols used to transfer the media data: if, for example, media caching is prohibited by the transfer protocol, a pre-fetch may occur but the information will not be saved for reuse.

16.3.3 Pre-Fetch Attributes

The SMIL *PrefetchControl* module defines three attributes to specify pre-fetch control behavior: mediaSize, mediaTime and bandwidth.

Attribute: mediaSize

The mediaSize attribute defines how much of the media object will be pre-loaded in terms of size (number of bytes). It accepts either a byte count or a percentage value. A value of 100% is equal to a request to load the entire object. The default is 100%. A value of 0% is ignored, meaning that the default value of 100% will be applied. If specified together with the mediaTime attribute, the value of the mediaTime attribute will be ignored.

Attribute: mediaTime

The `mediaTime` attribute defines how much of the media object will be pre-loaded in terms of its duration. It accepts either a clock value or a percentage value. A value of 100% is equal to a request to load the entire object. The default is 100%. A value of 0% is ignored, meaning that the default value of 100% will be applied. Discrete media is always completely downloaded. If specified together with the `mediaSize` attribute, the value of the `mediaTime` attribute will be ignored.

Attribute: bandwidth

The `bandwidth` attribute defines how much network bandwidth is allocated to the pre-load activity. It accepts either a bitrate value or a percentage value. A value of 100% implies that all of the bandwidth should be used. An implementation is free to use less bandwidth than requested.

16.3.4 Using Pre-Fetch Control

Example 16-3 illustrates the use of the `<prefetch>` element. An opening logo is shown at the start of the presentation. The logo has an intrinsic duration of 0 seconds, but the `fill="freeze"` behavior will keep it displayed until the end of the parent `<par>` element.

During the display of the logo, two pre-fetch operations are started. The first is a request to pre-load the closing logo: it is an image, 100% of which will be fetched and stored (if possible). The simple duration is set to 10 seconds; this forms the minimum activation time for the `<par>` element. A pre-fetch request is also made for a video object. A fetch of the total media object is requested, using 80% of the available bandwidth (if possible). Since there is no simple duration defined for this pre-fetch, the operation will last as long as it takes to transfer the (large) object. This can consume a considerable amount of time. (This is clearly an unwise strategy, but it is allowed by the SMIL architecture. A better strategy is to limit the amount of information that will be transferred by specifying a `mediaSize` or `mediaTime` attribute) Note that if a simple duration

```
 1 <smil xmlns="http://www.w3.org/2001/SMIL20/Language">
 2  ...
 3  <par>
 4   <img id="intro" src="openingLogo.png" fill="freeze" region="M"/>
 5   <prefetch id="case1" src="closingLogo.png" mediaSize="100%" dur="10s"/>
 6   <prefetch id="case2" src="bigVideo.mpg" bandwidth="80%" />
 7  </par>
 8  ...
 9  <seq>
10   <video id="Feature" src="bigVideo.mpg" region="M" end="activateEvent"/>
11   <img id="theEnd" src="closingLogo.png" region="M" dur="5s" />
12  </seq>
13  ...
14 </smil>
```

Example 16-3. Using the `<prefetch>` element and attributes.

was defined (for example, dur="10s"), this would bound the delay within this directive. If the entire video could not be fetched in this period, the implementation is free to cancel the pre-fetch activity.

At some later point in the presentation, the video is shown. The video will run until completion unless the user initiates a mouse click on the rendering region M. If so, the video ends and the closing logo is displayed. If the pre-fetch on the closing logo was successful, the image would pop up very quickly.

Note that even if only a few seconds of the video were viewed, it is possible that the entire object was pre-fetched. This can have pay-per-view consequences.

16.4 Summary and Conclusion

The purpose of the extended content control attributes is to provide additional document processing control for advanced users. Of the various features presented, all are supported only in the full SMIL 2.0 Language profile. The skip-content attribute is often recognized and parsed, but it is not always correctly supported by SMIL players. The pre-fetch control attributes are generally supported, but they represent only a high level of presentation performance control. The custom test attributes, although very useful in designing custom-tailored presentations, do not enjoy wide player support.

One would think that there is little reason to use all three sets of attributes. Still, gaining experience with advanced content control features that remain declarative rather than scripted exposes powerful features that will probably only be expanded upon in future versions of the SMIL language.

16.5 Further Resources

SMIL 1.0 Specification.

Synchronized Multimedia Integration Language (SMIL) 1.0 Specification.
W3C Recommendation, 15 June 1998. http://www.w3.org/TR/REC-smil .
See the appendix on *Extending SMIL 1.0* for the motivation for the skip-content attribute.

17

Meta-Information, Media Description and XML Accessibility

This chapter is about the various types of meta-information supported by the SMIL 2.0 standard. Meta-information does not contain content that is used or displayed during a presentation. Instead, it contains information *about* content that is used or displayed. Very often, meta-information can be used to help locate (parts of) a document, but meta-information can also be used to control which parts of a document are loaded by a presentation processor.

This chapter considers four aspects of meta-information use in SMIL: the <meta> and <metadata> elements and attributes found in the SMIL *Metainformation* module, the set of media description attributes defined as part of the SMIL *MediaDescription* module, the media accessibility attributes found in the *MediaAccessibility* module and the set of XML language attributes that support high-level media selection. Note that SMIL's native selection mechanisms for content control are discussed in Chapter 9: *Content Selection and Control* and Chapter 16: *Extended Content Control*.

It is difficult to present abstract summaries of meta-information architecture or structure: most meta-information supported by SMIL is either too simple or, in the case of RDF, way too complex. So, unlike our other chapters, we'll simply dive into the various element and attribute descriptions.

17.1 Meta-Information

The SMIL *Metainformation* module defines two elements and two attributes that can be used to annotate SMIL files with meta-information. The <meta> element was defined as part of SMIL 1.0 and allowed meta-information to be described that was compatible with the architecture of the Dublin Core. The <meta> element contains two meta-information attributes: name and content.

The <metadata> element is new to SMIL 2.0. It is used as a wrapper to include RDF specifications.

17.1.1 Elements for Meta-Information

The <metadata> element can be used for structured meta-information. An alternative is the <meta> element; it provides a simple mechanism for including meta-information name/value pairs. Both constructs are placed in the <head> section of a SMIL 2.0 Language profile file.

Element: <metadata>

The <metadata> element is a wrapper element for RDF meta-information. The structure of the <metadata> element is shown in Table 17-1.

The <metadata> element does not define any new attributes. The name and content attributes of the <meta> element may not be used on the <metadata> element. The parent container for the <metadata> element is the <head> element. The children of the <metadata> element are an RDF tree.

The <metadata> element is optional. Not all SMIL Basic implementations will be able to process the contents of the <metadata> element.

If the <metadata> element is used, it must be placed before the <layout> and <transition> definitions and after the definition of any <customTest> attributes (if used).

<metadata>	Profiles
attributes id	
parents <head>	L M B
children RDF Tree	

Table 17-1. Structure of the <metadata> element

Element: <meta>

The structure of the <meta> element is shown in Table 17-2. The element allows the id attribute and defines the name and contents attributes. The <meta> element is empty (it has no children). The parent element for <meta> is the <head> element.

The <meta> element is optional. While it is usually good practice to include a standard set of meta-information components such as copyright date and owner, author, title, etc., some profiles discourage use of meta-information components because of the overhead associated with presentation download, parsing and processing. This is principally true for the various SMIL Basic profiles for mobile handsets.

The <meta> element may be placed anywhere in the <head> section.

<meta>	Profiles
attributes name	
content	L M B 1
id	
parents <head>	L M B 1
children -none-	L M B 1

Table 17-2. Structure of the <meta> element

17.1.2 Attributes for Meta-Information

Two primary attributes are provided for meta-information: name and content.

Attribute: name

The name attribute is a CDATA character string.

There is an open-ended collection of values for the name attribute, but the W3C defines the following values that are used in processing the document:

- *base*: when present, the value of the content attribute is the base URI for all relative URI's in the document. This value is kept for compatibility with SMIL 1.0. For new SMIL2.0 presentations, use of the XML base URL mechanism is recommended.
- *pics-label*: when present, it is assumed that the content attribute contains a valid PICS content rating for the presentation.
- *PICS-label*: a synonym for *pics-label*.
- *title*: when present, the content attribute contains the title of the presentation. This can be used by User Agents to identify the presentation in the player/browser display.

There may be many instances of the <meta> element in the <head> section, but each instance may have at most one (required) name attribute.

Attribute: content

The content attribute is a CDATA string that specifies a value to be associated with the name attribute within a <meta> element. Other than the values associated with the name attribute just discussed, the contents of the content attribute is not interpreted.

There may be many instances of the <meta> element in the <head> section, but each instance may have only one content attribute. The content attribute is required.

17.1.3 Examples Using Meta-Information

This section gives overview examples of <meta> and <metadata>.

Using the <meta> *Element*

The following code fragments illustrates the use of the <meta> element:

```
<smil xmlns="http://www.w3.org/2001/SMIL20/Language" >
  <head>
  ...
    <meta name="title" content="SMIL2 Slideshow"/>
    <meta name="generator" content="GRiNS Pro for Mobile SMIL, v2.2 win32" />
    <meta name="project_html_page" content="external_player.html"/>
    <meta name="copyright" content="2003 D. Bulterman" />
    <meta name="base" content="http://www.example.org/here/" />
    <meta name="pics-label" content="..." />
  </head>
  ...
</smil>
```

The <meta> elements may be placed anywhere in the <head> section.

Using the `<metadata>` *Element*

While a full treatment of the Resource Description Framework (RDF) language is beyond the scope of this book, the following example shows how a RDF tree can be anchored in a document using the `<metadata>` element:

```
<smil xmlns="http://www.w3.org/2001/SMIL20/Language" >
  <head>
    <meta name="title" content="SMIL2 Slideshow"/>
    <meta name="generator" content="GRiNS Pro for Mobile SMIL, v2.2 win32" />
    <meta name="project_html_page" content="external_player.html"/>
    <meta name="copyright" content="2003 D. Bulterman" />
    <customAttributes>
      ...
    </customAttributes>
    <metadata id="shortExampleRDF" >
      <rdf:RDF xmlns:rdf="http://www.w3.org/1999/02/22-rdf-syntax-ns#"
        dc:="http://purl.org/metadata/dublin_core#"/>
        <rdf:Description >
          ...
        </rdf:Description>
      </rdf:RDF>
    <layout>
      ...
    </layout>
    <transition ... />
  </head>
...
</smil>
```

The `<metadata>` element must be placed in the `<head>` section between the elements shown. This is a SMIL DTD restriction.

17.2 Media Description

The SMIL `<meta>` and `<metadata>` elements provide facilities to give meta-information descriptions about an entire SMIL presentation. The SMIL *MediaDescription* module provides a collection of attributes that allow meta-information to be provided on individual media objects.

The structure of the media description attributes is given in Table 17-3. All of these attributes are optional, although the use of the `title` attribute is pedagogically encouraged. No SMIL processing is performed on the attributes listed, although some SMIL players or browsers may use the media description meta-data to provide information on the media object being rendered.

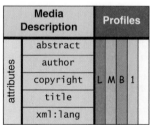

	Media Description	Profiles			
attributes	abstract				
	author				
	copyright	L	M	B	1
	title				
	xml:lang				

Table 17-3. Structure of the media description attributes.

17.2.1 Media Description Attributes

The media description attributes are: abstract, author, copyright, title and xml:lang.

Attribute: abstract

The abstract attribute was used in SMIL 1.0 to provide a summary of both the media object referenced by the element containing the abstract attribute and a description of that media object's use in the context of the SMIL presentation. The description is *not* intended as alternative content if the media object cannot be displayed.

The attribute is still available in SMIL 2.0 Language and Basic profile implementations, although authors are now encouraged to provide media object descriptions using the <metadata> tag in the <head> section.

Attribute: author

The author attribute is a CDATA string that may be used to identify the author, composer, or artist that created the media object.

Attribute: copyright

The copyright attribute is a CDATA string that may be used to identify the copyright date and holder of the associated media object. Note that no processing or control operations are associated with this attribute.

Attribute: title

The title attribute, which is defined as part of the SMIL Structure module, is a CDATA string that is intended to contain a brief, meaningful description of the associated media object. The title may be used for various purposes by the user agent, including providing a description that could be rendered by screen readers or other UI devices. The W3C strongly recommends that all authoring tools enforce the definition of a title on each media object but to date, most tools do not require that a title be generated as a precondition for document publishing.

Attribute: xml:lang

The lang attribute is an xml-namespaced attribute defining the language (natural or formal) used in the media object. The lang attribute is used to provide an extra description of the object's contents for use in searching, indexing or content analysis. The xml:lang attribute should not be confused with the systemLanguage attribute defined by SMIL content control (see Chapter 9: *Content Selection and Control*): the purpose of the systemLanguage attribute is to aid in the selection of content based on user preferences at runtime, while the xml:lang attribute is intended for archival processing.

17.2.2 Example Using Media Object Descriptions

The following code fragment illustrates the use of the media object description attributes. Note that the abstract attribute is shown even though it has been depreciated in favor of an RDF description.

```
<smil xmlns="http://www.w3.org/2001/SMIL20/Language" >
  <head>
  ...

  </head>
  <body>
    ...
    <video id="F" title="Baseball Lessons: Theory" abstract="A young
      talent illustrates the proper technique for hitting a baseball
      thrown by his sister." copyright="2001, New Amsterdam MTT"
      author="The father of the talent." xml:lang="nl" src="snarf.mpg" region="|
    ...
  </body>
</smil>
```

17.3 XML Accessibility

The meta-information considered to this point has provided (sometimes abstract) descriptions about media objects or entire presentations. The Media Accessibility attributes, defined as part of the SMIL *MediaAccessibility* module, are intended to provide alternative content in case the base content cannot be rendered by the system or perceived by the user.

The structure of the media accessibility attributes is shown in Table 17-4.

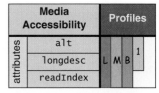

	Media Accessibility	Profiles			
attributes	alt				1
	longdesc	L	M	B	
	readIndex				

Table 17-4. Structure of the media description attributes.

17.3.1 Media Accessibility Attributes

The alt, longdesc and readIndex attributes can be applied to either media objects or to SMIL structure elements and time containers. The use of these attributes is optional, although, as with title, the support for alt and longdesc is strongly encouraged.

Attribute: alt

The alt attribute is a CDATA text string that contains a (short) description of a media item that can be rendered if the base media object is not available. This attribute is included for compatibility with HTML, where no selection mechanism such as SMIL's test attributes are provided. In the context of a SMIL presentation, the alt attribute can be used in instances where no content alternatives are provided via the SMIL <switch> element, or in cases where short descriptions in user agent tool tips are required.

As with the `title` attribute, authoring tools are encouraged to enforce the definition of `alt` attribute content.

Attribute: longdesc

The `longdesc` attribute is a URI that points to a long description of the contents of the media object or structure container. The long description can also describe the contents of a link target if an anchor is associated with the media object. The `longdesc` attribute is intended to supplement information in the `abstract` and `alt` attributes.

Attribute: readIndex

This attribute is an integer value that represents a presentation order for rendering meta-information on a (collection of) media objects. When two or more objects are presented in parallel, the readIndex can be used to determine which object's description is presented first by a screen reader or other accessibility assistive device.

17.3.2 Using Media Accessibility Attributes

The following code fragment provides a set of examples on the use of the media accessibility description attributes.

```
<smil xmlns="http://www.w3.org/2001/SMIL20/Language" >
  <head>
  ...

  </head>
  <body>
    ...
    <par alt="A baseball lesson."
        longdesc="http://www.example.org/intros/general/baseball.html">
        readIndex="1" >
      <video id="F" alt="A movie showing a boy and a baseball bat."
        longdesc="http://www.example.org/video/boy/baseball.html"
        readIndex="3" src="snarf.mpg" region="M" />
      <audio id="L" alt="A musical recording of three accordions playing
        Take Me Out to the Ballgame."
        longdesc="http://www.example.org/audio/accordions/baseball.html"
        readIndex="2" src="takeMe.mp3" region="A" />
    </par
    ...
  </body>
</smil>
```

This fragment contains two media objects and a parallel structure container. Each of these objects have `alt`, `longdesc` and `readIndex` attributes defined. The alt attribute may be used to highlight the content being displayed or, in the case of the media objects, to provide replacement content if the objects cannot be rendered. The readIndex attributes define an ordering among object so that, if processed by a screen reader, first the <par> description will be read, then the audio object description and finally the video description.

SMIL provides an extensive set of facilities for including alternative content in presentations; these allow audio or visual captions to be inserted at arbitrary parts of a media object or as entire replacement content sets for the visually or hearing impaired. The attributes provided here are primarily intended to supplement these facilities.

17.4 Summary and Conclusion

One of the standard jokes in the structured language community is that future documents will have more meta-information than media content. (Who says engineers have no sense of humor!) New meta-information standards, such as RDF, are doing their best to turn this quip into reality. The advantages of providing sufficient meaningful meta-information is that machines will be able to process Web document such as SMIL presentations, providing support for indexing and accessibility. While current SMIL implementations make only marginal use of the SMIL's meta-information facilities, they do provide a foundation upon which future systems — which hopefully will make meta-information collection and encoding convenient — can build.

The use of meta-information for content description should not be confused with attributes and elements that can be used for runtime document processing. These latter elements are described in Chapter 9: *Content Selection and Control* and Chapter 16: *Extended Content Control*.

17.5 Further Resources

XML

Extensible Markup Language (XML) 1.0 (Second Edition), Tim Bray, Jean Paoli, C.M. Sperberg-McQueen and Eve Maler (eds), W3C Recommendation, 10 February 1998, `http://www.w3.org/TR/REC-xml`.

XML Base

XML Base, Jonathan Marsh (ed.), W3C Recommendation, 27 June 2001. `http://www.w3.org/TR/xmlbase/`.

Language Tags

Tags for the Identification of Languages, Harald T. Alvestrand, RFC 1766, UNINETT, March 1995.
`ftp://ftp.isi.edu/in-notes/rfc1766.txt`.

Primary Language Tags

ISO CD 639/2:1991. Code for the Representation of Names of Languages: alpha-3 Code, International Organization for Standardization (ISO), 1991.
`http://lcweb.loc.gov/standards/iso639-2/langhome.html`.

Language Sub-tags

ISO 3166:1999. Codes for the representation of names of countries and their subdivisions, International Organization for Standardization (ISO), 1999.
`http://www.iso.ch/iso/en/prods-services/iso3166ma/index.html`.

Web Accessibility Guidelines

Web Content Accessibility Guidelines 1.0,
`http://www.w3.org/TR/WAI-WEBCONTENT`.

Resource Description Framework (RDF)

Resource Description Framework (RDF): Concepts and Abstract Syntax,
`http://www.w3.org/TR/2004/REC-rdf-concepts-20040210/`.

SMIL Family Reference

Part Four provides a collections of appendices, each with a description of the module and module dependencies for each of the major profiles of SMIL 2.0 We also provide a table defining which elements can be found in which modules.

There are no players for SMIL 2.0 itself. Instead, there are players for each profile of SMIL 2.0, making the profiles equivalent to what most people consider "languages" or "formats". Each profile serves as the basis for a set of inter-operable SMIL player implementations. All players that conform to a particular profile are required to support all of the standard modules defined for that profile; extensions may be provided using the XML namespace mechanism.

Profiles Covered

Appendix A describes the modules and module dependencies supported by the SMIL 2.0 Language profile, as defined by W3C.

Appendix B describes the modules and module dependencies supported by the SMIL Mobile profile, as defined by the 3GPP consortium as release 5 of the packet switched services (PSS).

Appendix C describes the modules and module dependencies supported by the SMIL 2.0 Basic profile, as defined by W3C.

Appendix D describes the modules and module dependencies supported by the XHTML+SMIL candidate profile, as defined by W3C.

Appendix E describes the SMIL modules, module dependencies and major constructs supported by the SVG specification, as defined by W3C.

Appendix F provides a complete element and attribute summary for each module of SMIL 2.0, as defined by W3C.

Goals

Part Four is intended to serve as a pure reference section for accomplished SMIL authors and system implementers.

Prerequisites

In order to understand the tables in these appendices, a comprehensive understanding of SMIL is recommended. This understanding can be gained by reading Parts One, Two and Three of this book!

A
SMIL 2.0 Language Profile Module Reference

The SMIL 2.0 Language profile is SMIL's "flagship" profile because of its size and purity in terms of SMIL — it uses (almost) all SMIL 2.0 constructs and (almost) only SMIL 2.0 constructs. The SMIL Language profile uses the vast majority of SMIL features, more than any other profile. A distinguishing characteristic of the SMIL Language profile is that all multimedia content is placed in separate files; a SMIL Language profile document contains SMIL directives and a set of pointers to media objects.

Modules Architecture

The SMIL Language profile uses all SMIL modules except: *TimeContainerAttributes*, *SplineAnimation*, *SyncMaster* and *TimeManipulations*. The TimeContainerAttributes module is not supported because the SMIL Language profile explicitly defines time containers and time container attributes in the language. As for *Spline Animation*, *SyncMaster* and *TimeManipulations*, there is no clear conceptual reason for excluding these modules, other than that they are unusually demanding on implementations and that they serve specialized user communities.

SMIL Player/Browser Implementations

The dominant player for the SMIL Language profile is the RealNetworks Real One player, which is installed on hundreds of thousands of desktops and devices. Another popular SMIL 2.0 player is Oratix's GR*i*NS-2.0. A third complete SMIL 2.0 Language profile player is the Ambulant player, which is available on the book's Web site.

The core of the RealNetworks SMIL player is now available under a RealNetworks source code distribution license through the Helix project. The Ambulant player is available under a GNU open source license.

Modules and Module Dependencies

Table A-1 lists the modules and module dependencies for the SMIL 2.0 Language profile.

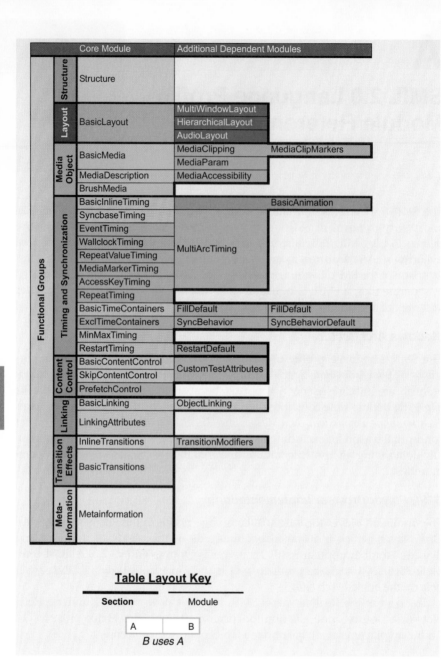

Core Module		Additional Dependent Modules	
Structure	Structure		
Layout	BasicLayout	MultiWindowLayout	
		HierarchicalLayout	
		AudioLayout	
Media Object	BasicMedia	MediaClipping	MediaClipMarkers
		MediaParam	
	MediaDescription	MediaAccessibility	
	BrushMedia		
Timing and Synchronization	BasicInlineTiming		BasicAnimation
	SyncbaseTiming		
	EventTiming		
	WallclockTiming	MultiArcTiming	
	RepeatValueTiming		
	MediaMarkerTiming		
	AccessKeyTiming		
	RepeatTiming		
	BasicTimeContainers	FillDefault	FillDefault
	ExclTimeContainers	SyncBehavior	SyncBehaviorDefault
	MinMaxTiming		
	RestartTiming	RestartDefault	
Content Control	BasicContentControl	CustomTestAttributes	
	SkipContentControl		
	PrefetchControl		
Linking	BasicLinking	ObjectLinking	
	LinkingAttributes		
Transition Effects	InlineTransitions	TransitionModifiers	
	BasicTransitions		
Meta-Information	Metainformation		

Table Layout Key

Section	Module

A	B

B uses A

Table A-1. SMIL 2.0 Language profile module dependency table.

B

3GPP SMIL Module Reference

The 3GPP (Third Generation Partnership Project) consortium has adopted SMIL as the standard for the emerging third-generation mobile telephony player infrastructure. We expect that the wide-spread implementation of 3GPP will greatly proliferate the distribution of industrial grade SMIL players.

As a host language profile, 3GPP SMIL consists of a `<smil>` element containing a `<head>` and a `<body>`, all in a single namespace. It has the minimum required media support, plus facilities for integrating clips of audio and video. 3GPP media support also includes describing the media and improving its accessibility. Transitions can also occur in the format. Furthermore, it extends foundational timing support with event timing, adding primarily synchronization between elements and with user interaction. Finally, 3GPP extends minimal content control with the ability to schedule pre-fetching of media, helping to maintain a smooth presentation under the constrained bandwidth of mobile devices.

3GPP SMIL Player/Browser Implementations

Several mobile device manufacturers, such as Nokia and Ericsson, and many wireless operators have announced SMIL-based players on their mobile devices. We refer you to the book's Web site for current information.

Modules and Module Dependencies

Table B-1 lists the SMIL modules 3GPP adopts in release 5 of the 3GPP/PSS specification. This table shows that 3GPP is mostly SMIL Basic with select modules added.

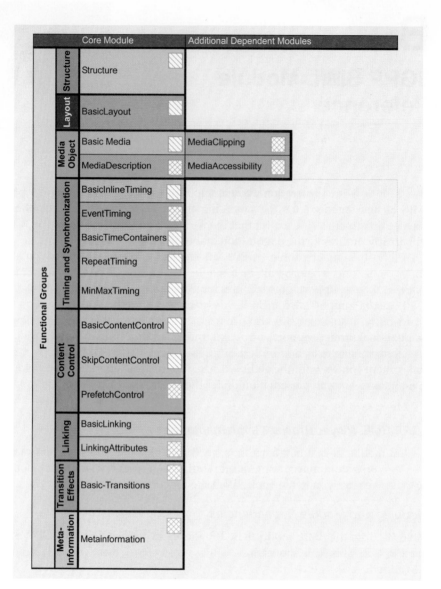

		Core Module		Additional Dependent Modules	
Functional Groups	**Structure**	Structure	▨		
	Layout	BasicLayout	▨		
	Media Object	Basic Media	▨	MediaClipping	▩
		MediaDescription	▩	MediaAccessibility	▩
	Timing and Synchronization	BasicInlineTiming	▨		
		EventTiming	▩		
		BasicTimeContainers	▨		
		RepeatTiming	▨		
		MinMaxTiming	▨		
	Content Control	BasicContentControl	▨		
		SkipContentControl	▨		
		PrefetchControl	▩		
	Linking	BasicLinking	▨		
		LinkingAttributes	▩		
	Transition Effects	Basic-Transitions	▩		
	Meta-Information	Metainformation	▩		

▨ from Basic ▩ 3GPP beyond Basic

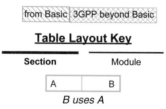

Table Layout Key

Section	Module
A	B

B uses A

Table B-1. 3GPP SMIL profile module and construct table.

C

SMIL 2.0 Basic Profile Module Reference

While the SMIL 2.0 Language profile embodies the full power of SMIL 2.0, the SMIL 2.0 Basic profile is a minimized subset of SMIL features that is suitable for low-power devices such as cell phones and PDAs.

Modules Architecture

The Basic profile does not have a fixed module architecture. Instead, it is defined as a *scalability framework* that makes it a starting point for mobile multimedia formats. Conforming formats must have at least SMIL Basic's features, but further SMIL modules may be added, allowing competition between mobile vendors in a technological arena whose capability to support the more demanding SMIL features will increase rapidly. (See Appendix B for an example.)

Like the Language profile, the Basic profile uses the *Structure* module; this allows it to play SMIL host language documents. Further, it supports the baseline functionality of the timing and synchronization, layout, media object, content control and linking modules.

The most restrictive versions of the SMIL 2.0 Basic profile do not support transitions, animation or meta-information.

SMIL Basic Player/Browser Implementations

SMIL Basic enjoys a large number of small-scale implementations, mostly by research groups. Keep in mind that all SMIL Language players are SMIL Basic players. This is also true for reduced functionality SMIL players that go beyond the module set supported in the Basic profile. An example of this is 3GPP SMIL, discussed in Appendix B.

Modules and Module Dependencies

Table C-1 lists the modules of the Basic profile. Note that none of the modules are dependent on functionality in any of the others.

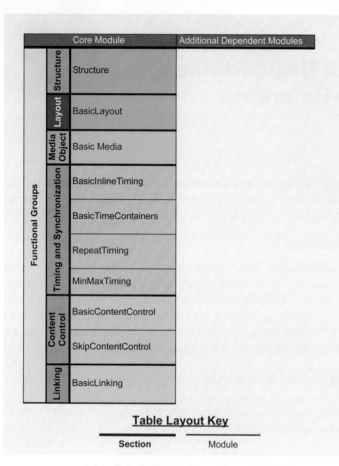

Core Module	Additional Dependent Modules

Functional Groups

Structure	Structure	
Layout	BasicLayout	
Media Object	Basic Media	
Timing and Synchronization	BasicInlineTiming	
	BasicTimeContainers	
	RepeatTiming	
	MinMaxTiming	
Content Control	BasicContentControl	
	SkipContentControl	
Linking	BasicLinking	

Table Layout Key

Section	Module

Table C-1. SMIL Basic profile module table.

D
XHTML+SMIL Module Reference

XHTML+SMIL adds SMIL timing and adaptivity to HTML. It is media-based SMIL, with text and other media mixed in with the extended SMIL directives.

Module and Implementation Information

XHTML+SMIL provides HTML's constructs for text with SMIL 2.0 constructs for media objects and timing. Like all media-based SMIL formats, XHTML+SMIL does not use SMIL's *Structure* module and puts SMIL constructs in a separate namespace. However, SMIL 2.0 still has a strong presence in XHTML+SMIL.

Non-SMIL functionality is implemented as follows:

- *Media*: XHTML+SMIL provides a means of putting all displayed text and SMIL integration directives together in one file. XHTML+SMIL uses HTML and CSS to format the text that it contains as PCDATA element content: all text content, format and SMIL code in one file. Non-text(-encoded) media is external.

- *Layout*: All layout in XHTML+SMIL comes from HTML and CSS, not from SMIL. This results in a sequential and hierarchical structure with two separate behavioral semantics. From SMIL timing, the sequence and hierarchy in XHTML+SMIL results in temporal composition, determining much of the presentation's timing, as it does for all SMIL. From HTML and CSS, the sequence determines text flow, which in turn defines much spatial layout. Hierarchy in HTML also determines CSS containing boxes and inherited layout properties. Having the general element structure affect space and time simultaneously results in some conceptual complications in working with this profile.

- *Timing*: XHTML+SMIL lacks SMIL timings min/max facilities and some of its default specification attributes. Some types of timing attribute value substrings are absent as well: specifically, synchronizing with repeat and marker events, and with key clicks. XHTML+SMIL includes time container attributes, as these apply specifically to media-based SMIL profiles: they enable non-SMIL elements to have SMIL temporal composition properties.

Unique to this profile is support of assigning synchronization masters. XHTML+SMIL also goes beyond the SMIL Language profile with support of spline animation, which it shares with SVG. The most powerful facility that remains, as of this writing, unique to XHTML+SMIL is time manipulations. This allows author-specified speeding up and slowing down of temporal media incorporated into the presentation.

One particularly handy result of combining SMIL timing with CSS layout is animating CSS classes. By assigning `class` attribute values to the end states of SMIL animations on document presentation properties, we allow the specification of how these properties change to be separated from the document itself into any number of cooperative or alternative associated CSS style sheets. However, while this provides useful encapsulation of desired change, it results in abrupt switches from original to destination values of the specified properties. Thus, this technique does not apply to properties whose values should animate gradually.

- *Linking*: All linking in XHTML+SMIL comes from HTML. No SMIL linking constructs are used. Furthermore, all interaction with linking constructs results in no change to the temporal status of the presentation.

- *Content Control*: XHTML+SMIL has minimal content control. This consists of the <switch> element and the system test attributes.

Player/Browser Support

Currently, XHTML+SMIL's only implementation is in the HTML+TIME extensions to Microsoft's Internet Explorer. Through this implementation, the majority of Web users have access to XHTML+SMIL functionality. Other than Microsoft's implementation, there is currently no public or announced private development for XHTML+SMIL. Although it was developed by the W3C, XHTML+SMIL has not achieved Recommendation status, and its future as a standard is unclear. The X-Smiles project holds some promise for future development of text in SMIL.

Modules and Module Dependencies

Table D-1 lists the SMIL modules XHTML+SMIL includes. XHTML+SMIL has fewer SMIL constructs than the SMIL Language profile, but also enjoys the full wealth of HTML constructs.

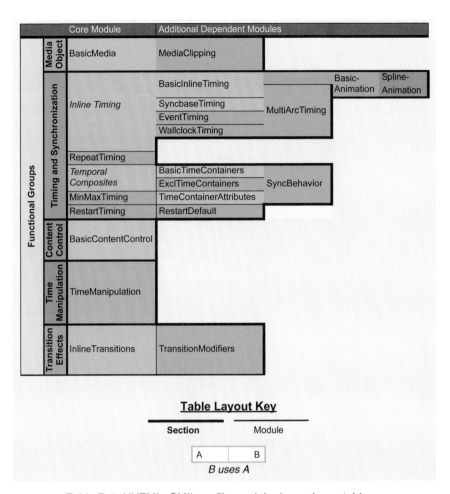

		Core Module	Additional Dependent Modules		
Functional Groups	**Media Object**	BasicMedia	MediaClipping		
	Timing and Synchronization	*Inline Timing*	BasicInlineTiming		Basic-Animation	Spline-Animation
			SyncbaseTiming	MultiArcTiming	
			EventTiming		
			WallclockTiming		
		RepeatTiming			
		Temporal Composites	BasicTimeContainers	SyncBehavior	
			ExclTimeContainers		
		MinMaxTiming	TimeContainerAttributes		
		RestartTiming	RestartDefault		
	Content Control	BasicContentControl			
	Time Manipulation	TimeManipulation			
	Transition Effects	InlineTransitions	TransitionModifiers		

Table Layout Key

Section	Module

A	B

B uses A

Table D-1. XHTML+SMIL profile module dependency table.

E

SMIL in SVG

SVG (Scalable Vector Graphics) is the W3C Recommendation for graphics on the Web. SVG is perhaps the most widely used of SMIL formats. This may be surprising, since many do not know that SVG uses SMIL at all. But SMIL constructs do indeed appear in SVG to apply timing to the graphic objects that SVG's constructs define. Anytime you see SVG graphics move, SMIL is at work animating them. SVG does not use as many SMIL constructs as XHTML+SMIL — it primarily has SMIL's animation constructs, with a few general timing and content control constructs added.

Module Use and Implementation Information

SVG's structure is in terms of SMIL is similar to that of XHTML+SMIL. Without the *Structure* module, it uses its own root element: <svg>. The elements underneath are predominantly SVG in typical files, with some SMIL constructs used as necessary. These SMIL constructs have namespace prefixes.

Support for other functionality is considered in the following list:

- *Media*: SVG defines natively extensive graphics displays. It also has a small subset of HTML constructs for defining text displays. By including SMIL's *BasicMedia* module, SVG can also incorporate external media resources into graphics presentations. This is necessary for including media other than graphics and text. Currently, SVG only supports the inclusion of images, but incorporation of other media types in SVG graphic presentations may be on the way.

- *Layout*: Like XHTML+SMIL, SVG makes no use of SMIL layout. Unlike XHTML+SMIL, its layout is not based on text flow as defined by CSS. SVG has its own layout model based on its inherent media type: that of the spatial mathematics developed to define the vector graphics primitives.

- *Timing*: SVG's support of SMIL timing is very rudimentary, even less than that of the SMIL Basic profile. SMIL Animation, on the other hand, enjoys full adoption and implementation in SVG, exceeding that of even the SMIL Language profile. It is animation that characterizes SMIL's main contribution to SVG.

- *Linking*: SVG uses no SMIL linking functions. However, it defines its own linking with familiar constructs, such as the <a> element and the xlink:href attribute. There is no connection between link traversal and timing in SVG.

- *Content Control*: SVG does not formally use SMIL content control. However, it has its own <switch> element and systemLanguage attribute, which define the same abilities to adapt to the user's language as SMIL.

Implementations

By far the dominant player for SVG is Adobe SVG Viewer, which is available free-of-charge from the Adobe Web site. It's editor companion, Adobe Illustrator, does not support the authoring of animation constructs. Several other graphics editors have SVG export functions, but none with SMIL animation.

Modules and Module Dependencies

Table E-1 shows the SMIL features that SVG uses.

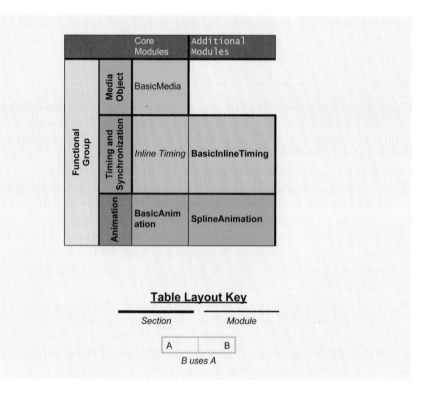

Table E-1. SVG SMIL module and construct table.

F

SMIL 2.0 Module and Construct Chart

This section gives a graphical summary of the various SMIL modules and the constructs contained within each module.

SMIL 2.0 Modules

Table F-1 gives a listing of all of SMIL's modules. Note that no module dependency information is given by this table. The tables on the next two pages detail all of the elements and attributes available for these modules.

Functional Groups		Module	
Structure	Structure	
Layout	BasicLayout	MultiWindowLayout
	AudioLayout	HierarchicalLayout
Media Object	BasicMedia	MediaClipping
	MediaClipMarkers	MediaParam
	MediaDescription	MediaAccessibility
	BrushMedia	
Timing and Synchronization	BasicInlineTiming	TimeContainerAttributes
	SyncbaseTiming	BasicAnimation
	EventTiming	SplineAnimation
	WallclockTiming	MultiArcTiming
	RepeatValueTiming	RepeatTiming
	MediaMarkerTiming	FillBehaviorDefault
	AccessKeyTiming	SyncBehavior
	BasicTimeContainers	SyncBehaviorDefault
	ExclTimeContainers	MinMaxTiming
	RestartTiming	RestartDefault
Content Control	BasicContentControl	CustomTestAttributes
	SkipContentControl	PrefetchControl
Linking	BasicLinking	ObjectLinking
	LinkingAttributes	
Transition Effects	InlineTransitions	TransitionModifiers
	BasicTransitions	
Meta-Information	Metainformation	
Time Manipulation	TimeManipulation	

Table F-1. SMIL 2.0 module table.

A

Appendix F: SMIL 2.0 Module and Construct Chart

Structure

Structure^S
`<smil>` `<head>^H` `<body>^H` xml:lang=^H
id=^{H,G} title=^{H,G} class=^{H,G} xmlns=^{H,G}

Layout

Basic-Layout^S
`<layout>` `<region>` `<root-layout>` type= backgroundColor=^D
top= left= height= width= bottom= right= z-index= fit=
region= regionName=showBackground=

MultiWindowLayout `<topLayout>` open= close=
HierarchicalLayout `<regPoint>` regPoint= regAlign=
AudioLayout soundLevel=

Media Object

Basic-Media^S
`<ref>` `<text>` `<img>` `<audio>` `<video>`
`<animation>` `<textstream>` src= type=

MediaDescription abstract= author= copyright=

BrushMedia `<brush>` color=

MediaClipping clipBegin=^D clipEnd=^D
MediaParam `<param>` name= value= valuetype= erase= mediaRepeat= sensitivity=
MediaClipMarkers "marker= ... "
MediaAccessibility alt=^H longdesc=^H readIndex=

Timing and Synchronization

Inline Timing
fill= end= dur= begin= endsync=

BasicInlineTiming^S =" nbr s " ="indefinite"
SyncbaseTiming^S =" idref . (begin | end) ... "^D
EventTiming =" idref . event "
WallclockTiming ="wallclock(wallclock value)"
RepeatValueTiming =" idref .repeat(nbr)"
MediaMarkerTiming =" idref .marker(...)"
AccessKeyTiming ="accesskey(char)"
MultiArcTiming — "or" of multiple ';'-separated values

RepeatTiming repeatDur=^D repeatCount=^D

BasicTimeContainers^S `<par>` `<seq>`
ExclTimeContainers `<excl>` `<priorityClass>` peers= lower= higher= pauseDisplay=
TimeContainerAttributes timeContainer= timeAction=

MinMaxTiming min= max=
RestartTiming restart=

Animation
Basic-Animation `<animate>` `<set>` `<animateColor>` `<animateMotion>` href= values= attributeName= attributeType= targetElement= calcMode= accumulate= additive= from= to= by= origin=
Spline-Animation path= keyTimes= keySplines= ="spline"

Sync-Behavior
syncBehavior= syncTolerance=
SyncBehaviorDefault syncBehaviorDefault= syncToleranceDefault=
SyncMaster syncMaster=

FillDefault fillDefault=
RestartDefault restartDefault=

Content Control

Basic-Content-Controls `<switch>`^G systemLanguage=^{D,G}
systemOverdubOrSubtitle=^D systemCaptions=^D systemAudioDesc=
systemBitrate=^D systemScreenDepth=^D systemScreenSize=^D systemRequired=^D
systemOperatingSystem= systemComponent= systemCPU=

SkipContentControl^S skip-content=

PrefetchControl `<prefetch>` mediaSize= mediaTime= bandwidth=

CustomTestAttributes `<customAttributes>` uid= `<customTest>` customTest= defaultState= override=

SMIL 2.0 Sub-Format, Module and Construct Dependency Graph

Linking

BasicLinking	`<a>`[H,G] `href=`[H,L]	ObjectLinking	`fragment=`
LinkingAttributes	`<area>`[D,H] `coords=`[H] `shape=`[H] `nohref=`[H]		
	`accesskey=`[H] `tabindex=`[H] `target=`[H]		
	`show=`[L] `sourceLevel=` `destinationLevel=` `sourcePlaystate=` `destinationPlaystate=` `external=` `actuate=`[L]		

Transition Effects

Inline-Transitions	`<transitionFilter>` `mode=` `targetElement=`	Transition-Modifiers	`horzRepeat=` `vertRepeat=` `borderColor=` `borderWidth=`
Basic-Transitions	`<transition>` `type=` `subtype=` `dur=` `transIn=` `transOut=`		
	`startProgress=` `endProgress=` `direction=` `fadeColor=`		

Time Manipulations

| TimeManipulations | `accelerate=` `decelerate=` `autoReverse=` `speed=` |

Meta-Information

| Metainformation | `<meta>` `<metadata>`[G] `content=` `name=` |

S These modules scattered throughout the chart are also **required by the Structure Module**.
D These SMIL 2.0 constructs are **new forms of deprecated SMIL 1.0** constructs with the same behavior. In most cases, they have camel-cased names in SMIL 2.0 that replace dashed names in SMIL 1.0.
H These SMIL constructs are also in XHTML+SMIL and have the same behavior. Officially, however, they are **defined for XHTML+SMIL by HTML** 4.01, not by SMIL 2.0.
G These SMIL constructs are also in SVG and have the same behavior. Officially, however, they are **defined for SVG by SVG** itself, not by SMIL 2.0.
L These SMIL constructs are also in SVG with the same behavior, but appear there with an "xlink:" namespace prefix. **SVG uses XLink** to define these constructs, not SMIL 2.0.

Table Layout Key

Section separation	Module separation

A
B

B uses A

A
B — C

C uses A or B

Font-to-Syntax Key

Section
Module
Construct Group
`<element>`
`attribute=`
`="attribute value"`
`=" value substring type "`
`from SMIL 1.0`

Color-to-Format Key

Basic & Profile	Profile only
all but SVG	XHTML+SMIL & Profile
all but Basic	XHTML+SMIL only
SVG & XHTML+SMIL	

Profile

Basic

SVG

XHTML+SMIL

Index

aspect ratio 116
attributeName attribute **370**, 369–371, 424
attributes 369–371
attributeType attribute **371**, 369–370, 424
audio 123, 282
audio descriptions 16
<audio> element **88**, 424
AudioLayout module 412, 423–424
author attribute **403**, 424
authoring 10, 15–16, 18, 80, 92
"auto" attribute value **113**, 109, 112, 333–334, 369–371
autoReverse attribute **357**, 327, 357, 425

B

background color 110, 116
backgroundColor attribute **110**, 107–109, 113, 118, 272, 277, 282, 424
background-color attribute **108**
background-color property of CSS 282
bandwidth 189
bandwidth attribute **396**, 395, 424
"barnDoorWipe" attribute value **231**
"barnVeeWipe" attribute value **231**
"barnZigZagWipe" attribute value **231**
"barWipe" attribute value **230–231**
base URIs 64, 80
basic inline timing 154
basic linking attributes 242
basic time containers 154, 136–137
BasicAnimation elements 79
BasicAnimation module 419, 423–424
BasicContentControl module 412, 414, 416, 419, 423–424
BasicInlineTiming module 412, 414, 416, 419, 423–424
BasicLayout module, 412, 414, 416, 423–424
BasicLinking module 412, 414, 416, 419, 423, 425
BasicMedia module 85, 98, 412, 414, 416, 419, 422–424
BasicTimeContainers module **137**, 412, 414, 416, 419, 423–424

BasicTransitions module 412, 414, 423, 425
begin attribute **142**, 39–40, 154–155, 162–163, 285, 335–336, 338–339, 344, 346–347, 419, 424
"begin" attribute value substring, 424
begin event 39–40
begin time 22, 34, 90, 117, 138, 140, 150, 154, 278–279, 285
begin/end values 141, 155
"beos" attribute value **192**
binary encoding 18
body 98, 282, 390
<body> element **79**, x, 23–25, 77, 88–89, 121–122, 137, 162–163, 184, 302, 368, 395, 424
borderColor attribute **221**, 96, 425
borderWidth attribute **221**, 425
bottom attribute **113**, 33, 108, 111–112, 118, 263, 268, 272, 282, 424
"bottom" attribute value **233**
bottom property of CSS 281–282
"bottomCenter" attribute value **231**
"bottomLeft" attribute value 231, 262
"bottomLeftClockwise" attribute value **234**
"bottomLeftCounterClockwise" attribute value **234**
"bottomLeftDiagonal" attribute value **234**
"bottomMid" attribute value, 262
"bottomRight" attribute value, 231, 262
"bottomRightClockwise" attribute value **234**
"bottomRightCounterClockwise" attribute value **234**
"bottomRightDiagonal" attribute value **234**
"bowTieWipe" attribute value **231**
"boxSnakesWipe" attribute value **234**
"boxWipe" attribute value **231**
browsers 193, 391
<brush> element **89–90**, xi, 79, 85, 88, 95, 98, 141, 147, 149–151, 155, 162, 242, 252, 327, 333, 343, 350, 357, 368, 424
BrushMedia module 98, 412, 423–424
"bsdi" attribute value **192**

override attribute **391**, 390, 424

P

"paced" attribute value **374**, 369, 373
"palmos" attribute value **192**
<par> element **137**, x–xi, 39–40, 79,
    88–89, 121, 137, 141, 147, 149–151,
    154–155, 302–303, 327, 333, 335, 338,
    340–341, 344–347, 368, 395, 424
parallel playback 154
"parallelDiagonal" attribute value
    233
"parallelDiagonalBottomLeft"
    attribute value **233**
"parallelDiagonalTopLeft"
    attribute value **233**
"parallelSnakesWipe" attribute
    value **234**
"parallelVertical" attribute value
    233
<param> element **252**, 88–89, 252, 424
"parent" attribute value **375**, 369, 373
parent elements 33, 375
parentheses 412, 419, 423–424
path attribute **376**, 375, 424
path, of URI **63**, 62–64
pathnames 63
paths, from SVG 375
"pause" attribute value **171**, 166, 303–
    304
pauseDisplay attribute **304**, 303, 424
peers attribute **303–304**, 303, 424
"pentagonWipe" attribute value **232**
percentage as spatial measure 282
percentages as attribute values 112,
    166, 263, 282
Perl 16
Perly SMIL 16
"pinWheelWipe" attribute value **233**
pixel units 110, 112–113, 281–282
pixels 105, 190, 263
"play" attribute value **171**, 166
points as spatial measure 282
"ppc" attribute value **192**
pre-defined registration points 262–
    263
<prefetch> element **395**, xi, 79, 141,
    149, 155, 162, 182, 327, 333, 395, 424

PrefetchControl module 412, 414, 423–
    424
"preserve" attribute value **253**
primary language tags 186–187, 200,
    406
<priorityClass> element **302–303**,
    x, 88–89, 137, 162, 302–304, 368, 395,
    424
privacy 192
profiles 7, 11, 18, 35, 98, 103–105
properties of CSS 282–283, 371
proprietary formats 17–18
"pushWipe" attribute value **234**
"px" attribute value substring **112**,
    110, 112

Q

"qnx" attribute value **192**
QuickTime 9

R

readIndex attribute **405**, 88, 424
RealNetworks 9, 16
RealOne 18
RealPlayer 9
Recommendation, W3C 6, 14, 53–54,
    82–83, 98, 123, 176, 257, 283, 326,
    384, 406
"rectangle" attribute value **230**, 232
"ref" attribute value **253**
<ref> element **88**, 31, 88, 424
regAlign attribute **263**, 88, 261, 263,
    424
region attribute **117**, x, 24–25, 88, 90,
    117, 120–121, 137, 268, 281–282, 302,
    424
<region> element **108**, 272, 24–25,
    105–108, 112, 118–119, 121–123, 263,
    267–268, 272, 276–277, 279, 282, 424
region positioning 33, 112–113, 268
region positioning attributes **111**, 112
regionName attribute **111**, 108–109,
    118, 272, 282, 424
regions 33, 80, 102, 105, 123, 267
registration points 260
regPoint attribute **263**, 88, 261, 424
<regPoint> element **262**, 261, 263,
    424

transitions 6, 10, 78, 90, 333
transOut attribute **214**, 88, 90, 425
transparency 116
"transparent" attribute value **110**, **254**, 113
tree, of elements **23**, 22–23, 98
"triangleWipe" attribute value **232**
"true" attribute value **166**, 350, 357
"twoBladeHorizontal" attribute value **233**
"twoBladeVertical" attribute value **233**
"twoBoxBottom" attribute value **234**
"twoBoxLeft" attribute value **234**
"twoBoxRight" attribute value **234**
"twoBoxTop" attribute value **234**
type attribute
  in <layout> elements, 107, 276, 281, 424
  in media object elements **92–94**, 85, 88, 90, 98, 424
  in <param> elements **253**, 252, 210
  in <transition> elements, 230–235, 425
types of media 17, 90, 103, 249, 92

U

uid attribute **391**, 390, 424
UNINETT 200, 406
unique identifier references 24
unique identifiers 24, 80, 249
"unixware" attribute value **192**
"unknown" attribute value **192**
"up" attribute value **231–233**
URIs (Uniform Resource Identifiers) **62**, 54, 62–63, 80, 83, 98, 166, 192–193, 257
URL(Uniform Resource Locator) 81
user preferences 8, 187–188, 192
users 92, 391

V

value attribute **253**, 252, 424
values attribute **373**, 219, 369, 371, 424
values, of attributes 369, 371

valuetype attribute **253**, 252–253, 424
"vax" attribute value **192**
"veeWipe" attribute value **231**
"vertical" attribute value **231–233**
"verticalBottomLeftOpposite" attribute value **234**
"verticalBottomSame" attribute value **234**
"verticalLeft" attribute value **234**
"verticalRight" attribute value **234**
"verticalTopLeftOpposite" attribute value **234**
"verticalTopSame" attribute value **234**
vertRepeat attribute **221**, 425
<video> element **88**, 424
viewport 282
"visible" attribute value **391**
visible value of CSS 282
volume property of CSS 282

W

W3C (World Wide Web Consortium) 3, 6, 10, 14, 53–54, 81–83, 98, 123, 176, 257, 283, 326, 384, 406–407
wallclock value 424
"wallclock()" attribute value substring 424
WallclockTiming module 412, 419, 423–424
"waterfallWipe" attribute value **234**
"whenActive" attribute value **278**, 109
"whenDone" attribute value **254**
"whenNotActive" attribute value **278–279**, 343
white space characters 193, 192
width attribute **112–113**, 33, 107–108, 110–113, 118–119, 121–122, 268, 272, 277, 282, 424
width property of CSS 282
"win16" attribute value **192**
"win32" attribute value **192**
"win9x" attribute value **192**
"wince" attribute value **192**
windows 278 6, 33–112, 123, 281–282
"windshieldWipe" attribute value **233**
"winnt" attribute value **192**

X

'x' attribute value character 190

"x86" attribute value **192**

XHTML 10

XHTML+SMIL 13, 16, 76, 105, 140, 375, 424–425

XLink (XML Linking Language) 425

XML viii–ix, xxviii, 1, 3, 9–11, 13–18, 21–26, 28, 31, 34, 45, 47, 53–54, 64, 73, 75–78, 80–83, 88, 98, 111, 121–122, 125, 136, 153, 162–164, 171, 176, 208, 210, 220, 248–250, 257, 281, 285, 318–319, 326, 361, 369–371, 381–382, 387, 399, 401, 404, 406, 409

"XML" attribute value **371**, 369–370

"xml:" namespace prefix **81**, 424

xml:base attribute **80**, 64, 80–81

xml:lang attribute **403**, 80–81, 424

xmlns attribute **81**, 28, 75, 77–78, 81–82, 121–122, 424

XMT (eXtensible MPEG-4 Textual Format) 11, 14, 18

XPointer **250**, 10, 176, 257

XSLT (XSL Transforms) 10

Z

"zigzagwipe" attribute value **231**

z-index attribute **116**, 105, 108–109, 118–119, 121–122, 272, 282, 424

z-index property of CSS 282